A Longman Cultural Edition

JOHN KEATS

Edited by

Susan J. Wolfson
Princeton University

D1479045

PEARSON
Longman

New York Boston San Francisco
London Toronto Sydney Tokyo Singapore Madrid
Mexico City Munich Paris Cape Town Hong Kong Montreal

Editor-in-Chief: Joseph P. Terry
Development Editor: Christine Halsey
Executive Marketing Manager: Ann Stypuloski
Production Coordinator: Scarlett Lindsay
Project Coordination, Text Design, and Electronic Page Makeup:
    Grapevine Publishing Services, Inc.
Cover Designer/Manager: John Callahan
Manufacturing Buyer: Roy L. Pickering, Jr.
Printer and Binder: R.R. Donnelley and Sons Company / Harrisonburg
Cover Printer: Coral Graphic Services, Inc.

Cover Image: *La Belle Dame sans Merci*, Exh.1902 (oil on canvas) by Dicksee, Sir
Frank (1853–1928) © Bristol City Museum and Art Gallery, UK/ The Bridgeman
Art Library.

Library of Congress Cataloging-in-Publication Data

Keats, John, 1795-1821.
    [Selections. 2006]
    John Keats / edited by Susan J. Wolfson.
        p. cm. — (Longman cultural edition)
    Selected poems and letters of John Keats.
    Includes bibliographical references and indexes.
    I. Wolfson, Susan J., 1948– II. Title. III. Series.

PR4832.W66 2006
821'.7—dc22
                                                                2006032300

Please visit our Web site at www.ablongman.com

ISBN: 0-321-23616-5

1 2 3 4 5 6 7 8 9 10—DOH—09 08 07 06

Charles Brown's charcoal sketch, 1819.

This image, not printed until the twentieth century, presents Keats in Regency style:
handsome, contemplative, a modern "young poet."

Contents

List of Illustrations

About Longman Cultural Editions

Reading always seems to vibrate with the transformation of the day—now, yesterday, and centuries ago, when the presses first put printed language into wide circulation. Correspondingly, literary culture has always been a matter of change: of new practices confronting established traditions; of texts transforming under the pressure of new techniques of reading and new perspectives of understanding; of canons shifting and expanding; of informing traditions getting reviewed and renewed, recast and reformed by emerging cultural interests and concerns; of culture, too, as a variable "text"—a reading. Inspired by the innovative *Longman Anthology of British Literature*, Longman Cultural Editions respond creatively to the changes, past and recent, by presenting key texts in contexts that illuminate the lively intersections of literature, tradition, and culture. A principal work is made more interesting by materials that place it in relation to its past, present, and future, enabling us to see how it may be reworking traditional debates and practices, how it appears amid the conversations and controversies of its own historical moment, how it gains new significances in subsequent eras of reading and reaction. Readers new to the work will discover attractive paths for exploration, while those more experienced will encounter fresh perspectives and provocative juxtapositions.

Longman Cultural Editions serve not only several kinds of readers but also (appropriately) their several contexts, from various courses of study to independent adventure. Handsomely produced and affordably priced, our volumes offer appealing companions to *The Longman Anthology of British Literature*, in some cases enriching and expanding units originally developed for the *Anthology*, and in other cases presenting this wealth for the first time. The logic and composition of the contexts vary across the series. The constants are the complete text of an important literary work, reliably edited, headed by an inviting introduction, and supplemented by helpful annotation; a table of dates to track its composition, publication, and public reception in relation to biographical, cultural, and historical events; and a guide for further inquiry and study. With these common measures and uncommon assets, Longman Cultural Editions encourage your literary pleasures with resources for lively reflection and adventurous inquiry.

SUSAN J. WOLFSON
General Editor
Professor of English
Princeton University

About This Edition

Arrangement

Keats was nothing if not an experimenter in form. With so many editions available, I thought to distinguish this one by an experiment in editorial form, chiefly to give a sense of Keats's thinking from letters to poems to publications. Whereas the most common (almost only) practice has been to arrange poems in sequence of composition, with the letters as a separate unit, usually after the poems, I thought it would be illuminating to intersperse these texts in their order of composition or publication.

Since it was not possible in the constraints of this Longman Cultural Edition to present texts in multiple forms (with the singular exception of the two poems with *La Belle Dame* in their titles), I have had to make choices between or among texts. So, for instance, sonnets published in the newspapers in 1816 and then republished in the *Poems* of 1817 are not given twice, though important "substantive" variants (wording) are footnoted.

§ Contexts

From time to time, this edition presents contextual items to frame Keats's work: a sample of Chapman's translation of Homer, along with one by the chief "Homer" of Keats's day, Alexander Pope's translation; sonnets written by other poets in the contests that produced Keats's; the poems by J. H. Reynolds with which Keats's are in dialogue, the reviews of his publications that Keats read, the canceled stanza of *Ode on Melancholy*. These items are signaled by § in the text and the table of contents.

Texts and Editorial Principles

Obvious printers' errata (especially in the newspapers, where, for example, *u* often got set as *n* or vice versa) are corrected without comment. I also modernize some punctuation in printed sources, reflecting standard house style then but no necessary authorial preference, for example, opening quotation marks (") in successive lines of poetry by the same speaker, and semicolons and colons placed within closing quotation marks (;" / :"). I set the letters based on Keats's originals in cursive, to distinguish these from letters based on print sources.

Poems: titles and annotation

Keats left some poems untitled, or sometimes, as in the case of the "Sonnets" in the 1817 *Poems*, he just applied a roman numeral. When I follow the editorial tradition of giving titles from the first words, I set these in quotations marks: "I stood tip-toe"; "When I have fears." Keats's own titles appear in italics.

Line numbers and side glosses are my additions, as are headnotes and footnotes, unless otherwise credited.

Poems: texts

For poems published during Keats's lifetime, I have made various decisions about the textual bases, especially for the early poetry. I present some poems not only in their earliest published texts, in the newspapers, but also in the immediate context of these sites. Thus Keats's very first publication, *To Solitude*, has a somewhat different look from its situation in the *Poems* of 1817; in *The Examiner* it appears at the bottom of a column below a grim report of one of the casualties of war. "After dark vapours," ending in an imagination of a poet's death, gains a darker shade from being followed by an article on military torture. *On First Looking into Chapman's Homer* has an important framing in an essay about three compelling "Young Poets." While I am not proposing that these contexts are exclusively determinative, I do want to give a sense of how their contingencies inflect the way Keats's first publications were encountered by their first readers. When Keats supervised a later, often revised publication, I indicate the most important variants, as well as placement in that publication.

Many of the poems familiar to us were unknown to Keats's contemporaries, and published after his death—among the most notable, the sonnet on rereading *King Lear*, *Ode on Indolence*, and *The Fall of Hyperion*. In some cases, I present these texts from manuscript sources; in others, from their first, or most influential print source. In one case I do give two texts: *La Belle Dame sans Merci* from Keats's letter, and from its first publication in 1848 until the 1990s, the canonical text; and *La Belle Dame sans Mercy*, in the context of Leigh Hunt's magazine, *The Indicator*—the text published in Keats's lifetime, but after 1848, forgotten or suppressed. My implied argument is that this is a poem in at least two distinct versions, with two distinct titles and contexts.

Poems published posthumously derive from various sources, among the key ones: Keats's letters and manuscripts; copies made by others; newspapers and annuals; and Richard Monckton Milnes's landmark *Life, Letters, and Literary Remains, of John Keats* (1848), a crucial force in presenting a Keats not dominated by, successively, "Cockney" identifications, obscurity, the fable of fatal fragility in Shelley's elegy, *Adonais*. My textual bases are eclectic. I like the letter-texts for the contexts of Keats's thinking and correspondence. On another front, it is intriguing to see Thomas Hood (married to the sister of one of Keats's closest friends) putting some of Keats's poems in the anthology he edited in the 1820s, *The Comic Annual*, or the essays at the beginning of the twentieth century that presented Keats's earliest poetry.

Letters

These are a selection, both from the full canon of letters, and often of passages within a particular letter. Full texts are available in the editions listed in Further Reading.

Unless otherwise indicated, the texts are freshly edited from Keats's originals. With very few exceptions (the chief one being the typesetting for this volume), I have not interfered with the text, wanting to give a sense of Keats's letter-writing in all its verbal playfulness and the immediacies of casual punctuation; idiosyncratic, often punning spellings; pepperings of capital letters (more common then than now) and dropped or compressed letters. I depart from editorial tradition in one matter. Keats is often said to drop letters as he writes, but my study of his manuscripts convinces me that he likes to use a strong downstroke as a shorthand for two letters at once. Thus, I don't think he misspells words, or doesn't write letters such as *s*, *i*, *l*, or most famously *r* (so that *harm* looks like *ham*), but in one bold stroke implies two letters. Since it's not possible to reproduce Keats's shorthand, I give him the two letters that I believe he has implied, without the usual editorial brackets around the supposedly dropped letter.

In the few instances where editorial notation is advisable, these symbols appear:

> [ ] enclose my interpolation for letters in Keats's hand
> { } enclose a transcriber's interpolation; or for letters from published sources, an editor's mark

For published, letter-press sources, I convert italics back to original underlining and remove any editorial interference. With a faith in Keats's eventual fame, Richard Woodhouse assiduously transcribed a wealth of correspondence. I have noticed, in comparing his copies with Keats's originals, that Woodhouse tends to normalize capitalization and lower-casing, to correct spelling, and not to transcribe Keats's cross-outs (he edits as he transcribes). In cases where Woodhouse's transcription is the only text, I have deleted the cross-outs as probable scribal errors (his or his clerk's) and not Keats's first thoughts.

In order to give my transcriptions of Keats's autograph letters and manuscripts a different look from the published texts, I present these in a cursive font; my editorial interventions are distinguishable by regular font in square brackets. Strike-throughs and underlinings are Keats's. When my ellipses separate widely disparate texts (not, say, within the same paragraph or page), I begin a new page-line.

As my ellipses indicate, as with the poetry, I've had to be unhappily selective, not only from the whole inventory, but also within individual letters. For reference and advice, I have been grateful for the superb editions of Henry Buxton Forman, Maurice Buxton Forman, Hyder E. Rollins, and recent editions from Robert Gittings and Jon Mee, and Grant Scott. My selections feature not only passages that have become canonical in Keats studies, but also ones that show Keats's acute eye for social comedy and his generous candor about the vexations of living in the world with a fervid dedication to becoming as good a poet as he can.

What I have not elided is Keats's amazing, amusing invention of language: my notes report new usages, new grammars, and new words (with reference to the latest online *OED*).

Supplements

In addition to the contextual items marked §, this Longman edition includes the following:

- A brief introduction to Keats
- A table of dates, to put his life and publications in context
- Notes on unfamiliar words or idioms, references, and allusions
- A glossary of mythological and literary figures and places (for handy reference and to spare repetition in the footnotes)
- A glossary of key recurring contemporary names: Keats's family, friends, correspondents; the chief reviews and reviewers of the day; others on the literary or historical scene
- An index of poem-titles and first lines, as well as some of the key topics in the letters (for example, Negative Capability, "camelion Poet")

Abbreviations

Textual sources

Publications

1817   *Poems* (London: C. & J. Ollier).

1820   *Lamia, Isabella, The Eve of St. Agnes, and Other Poems* (London: Taylor & Hessey).

1848   Richard Mockton Milnes, *Life, Letters, and Literary Remains, of John Keats*, 2 vols. (London: Edward Moxon). This was the first consolidated publication of uncollected publications (lifetime and posthumous) and the first-time publication of most of the letters.

KC   *The Keats Circle*, ed. Hyder E. Rollins. 2d edition; 2 vols. (Cambridge: Harvard University Press, 1965).

HBF   Harry Buxton Forman, ed. *The Poetical Works and Other Writings of John Keats*, 4 vols. (London, Reeves & Turner, 1883). The first rigorous collection and annotation of the poems, letters, essays, and marginalia.

Manuscripts

ALS   Autograph letter, signed
WLB   Richard Woodhouse's Letter-Book (Houghton Library, Harvard)

The Keats family

K   John Keats
GK   George Keats
G&GK George and Georgiana Keats
TK   Tom Keats

Other abbreviations

FQ   *The Faerie Queene* (Edmund Spenser), by book, canto, stanza
MBF   Maurice Buxton Forman, ed., *The Letters of John Keats*, 2d edition (London, Oxford University Press, 1935)
ms / mss manuscript(s)
OED   *Oxford English Dictionary* (online)
PL   *Paradise Lost* (John Milton), by book, line

Shakespeare's plays are given by title only, assumed his, by act, scene, and sometimes lines. For other abbreviated names and titles, see Further Reading.

Acknowledgments

My first thanks go to Joseph Terry, who said, "Do it!" and has been a steady, patient inspiration. I am also fortunate to have the extraordinarily able assistance of Christine Halsey, Chrysta Meadowbrooke, and Dianne Hall in all phases of production. And for conversation on matters Keatsian, I am grateful to fellow editors Christopher Ricks, Jack Stillinger, Grant Scott, and Beth Lau, as well as attentive conversations with William Keach and Peter Manning.

My work on this edition would not have been possible without the archives at the Houghton Library at Harvard University and the generosity of Leslie Morris in giving me permission to use my transcriptions of its manuscripts. The Berg and Pforzheimer collections at New York Public Library; the British Library; the Bodlean Library;

and the Keats House have also been generous with resources and permission. Firestone Library at Princeton University has been a valuable resource for almost everything else, including print sources, the rare books and manuscripts in its archives, and the generous assistance of Meg Rich. All the illustrations are from this trove and appear with the generous permission of Princeton University Libraries. From beginning to end, I have been singularly fortunate in the research assistance and sharp conversation of Jasper Cragwall at Princeton University.

Those "who live together have a silent moulding, and influencing power over each other. They interassimulate" (Keats always sums up matters in the most sovereign manner). With habitual gratitude for my unequal benefit from such company, for advice, conversation, consolation and support, and decades of happy living together, I dedicate this project to Ron Levao—as Keats (again) would put it, my most sincere and affectionate friend.

SUSAN J. WOLFSON
Princeton University

Introduction

John Keats
1795–1821

Keats's poetry is so familiar that it seems to have a life of its own, honored on the walls of the world's most prestigious libraries and reading rooms, endowing book titles and popular songs: "A thing of beauty is a joy for ever"; "tender is the night"; "Beauty is truth; truth Beauty." This cultural presence is all the more remarkable given Keats's short career as a poet, and his decidedly local, though enthusiastic praise during his lifetime. He wrote his first poem, as a medical student, in 1814; his last effort may have been his revision of his sonnet "Bright star" in September 1820 while sailing to Italy, where he would die early the next year. "Oh, for ten years, that I may overwhelm / Myself in poesy," he hoped in 1816 (*Sleep and Poetry*).

Not even claiming a decade, Keats had stopped writing, except for a few painful letters, by his twenty-fifth birthday. At the same age, Geoffrey Chaucer and Edmund Spenser had yet to write anything, and if William Shakespeare had died at twenty-four, he would be known only (if at all) by a few early works. Victorian sage Thomas Carlyle was born the same year as Keats. What if Keats had been given the same span, of tens and tens of years, not dying until 1881? The fascination of Keats still vibrates to this poignancy of genius nipped in the bud, of unknown potential. Would he have continued with poetry, having hit his stride with the 1820 volume—*Lamia, Isabella, The Eve of St. Agnes, Ode to a Nightingale, Ode on a Grecian Urn, Ode on Melancholy, To Autumn*, and the spectacular fragment of *Hyperion*? Would he have followed his dream to write modern drama? Might he, as his lively letters suggest, have developed a talent for journalism (one thought he had), the personal essay (the genre of his friends Leigh Hunt, Charles Lamb, and William Hazlitt), or even, with his sharp and wry sense of character and social behavior, the novel? Would he have become a political journalist "on the liberal side of the question" (also a possibility he entertained)?

Keats's origins were fairly modest. He was the eldest of four children, their father an ostler (one who takes care of horses) who married the daughter of the owner of the suburban livery stable where he worked, and then inherited this business. Keats's parents enrolled the boys in the progressive Enfield Academy, and they thrived in the environment. But then their father died in a riding accident, and their mother quickly remarried. Her affection for her children was as erratic as it was doting, and Keats was devastated when, apparently miserable in her second hasty marriage, she disappeared, abandoning the children to their grandmother. When she returned four years later, sick and consumptive, Keats devoted himself to her care; he watched her die when he was fourteen. The shocks of this bewildering flux of events would emerge in the series of adored and adoring but inconstant women in his later poetry. At the time, Keats found solace and escape in the excitements of his education. At Enfield he was tutored and befriended by Charles Cowden Clarke, the headmaster's son, who introduced him to literature, music, the theater—and eventually to the London and suburban literary culture in which Keats's aspirations as a poet took root and flourished.

After Keats's mother died, the children were remanded to the guardianship of a practical businessman whose chief concern was to apprentice the boys to some viable trade and to keep their young sister from their influence. He apprenticed Keats to a surgeon in the grim days before anesthesia. Keats was soon enrolled as a student at one of the progressive London hospitals and stayed with his medical training long enough to earn his license as an apothecary and surgeon's assistant (a kind of general practitioner), but he was frequently drawn from his medical studies by the lure of reading and poetry-writing. The poets who mattered most to him were Spenser (his first poem, written in 1814, is a deft *Imitation of Spenser* in Spenserian stanzas), Chaucer, Shakespeare,

Milton, Chatterton, and, among his contemporaries, Hunt, Wordsworth, and Byron. Soon after he came of age in October 1816, encouraged by Hunt's praises, he gave up medicine to try a career as a poet. By this point, Keats was already enjoying the society of Clarke and his circle of politically progressive thinkers, artists, poets, journalists, and publishers, many of whom became his close friends. One of the hubs of this culture was radical journalist and poet Hunt, who launched Keats's career, publishing his first sonnets in his weekly paper, *The Examiner*, and advertising him in a critical essay as one of the age's rising "Young Poets." It was through him that Keats met some of the chief non-establishment writers of the day—Hazlitt, Lamb, Percy Shelley—and the controversial painter Benjamin Robert Haydon, who introduced him to Wordsworth, who was emerging as England's national poet.

In the spring of 1817 Keats's first volume, *Poems*, was published. Its themes—great poets and poetic greatness; political liberty; ideals of imagination; an enthusiasm for classical mythology—were advanced in a performance of poetic skill and versatility. In addition to twenty sonnets (some previewed in *The Examiner*), there were Spenserian stanzas, odes, verse epistles, romance fragments, and meditative long poems—in other words, a poet-aspirant's performance of his skills. Keats warmly dedicated the volume to Hunt, and in its long concluding piece, a poetic essay titled *Sleep and Poetry*, he boldly took to task "the foppery and barbarism," "musty laws," and "wretched rule" of a still prestigious eighteenth-century neoclassical poetry. Byron privately despised Keats for this tirade, and it magnetized Keats as a target for the conservative literary critics of the Tory journals, only too eager to jab at their enemy Hunt through his protégé. Appearing in a year when civil rights were weakened and radical publisher William Hone was brought to trial, *Poems* was ridiculed in terms marked by social snobbery and political prejudice: Keats was one of Hunt's tribe of "Cockney Poets"—vulgar suburban upstarts, enemies of Church and State. Though Keats had anticipated this reception, he was stung by the intensity of the venom and ridicule.

He was determined to persevere, and immediately took on a major challenge, its genesis a contest with Hunt and Shelley to see who could finish a 4,000-line poem by the end of 1817. Keats was the only one to succeed, with *Endymion: A Poetic Romance*, which he regarded as "a test" or "trial" of his talents, his chance to advance his career with a strong credential. "A thing of beauty is a joy for ever" begins this tale of a shepherd-prince who dreams of a goddess, and on waking is profoundly alienated from ordinary life in the world. In the 4,050 lines of this romance epic—the longest poem Keats ever wrote—the hero, after several ordeals, finally gets the girl, and they seem destined to live happily ever after. Yet by the time Keats was preparing *Endymion* for press in winter 1818 he had lost confidence in its fable, and said so in his Preface, describing the poem as a work of "inexperience, immaturity," indeed a "failure" that made him "regret" its publication. Whether an honest confession or a tactic to forestall another round of ridicule scarcely mattered. The same reviewers who had hooted at Keats's debut were waiting to savage *Endymion*. But Keats had already dosed himself with what he called "my own domestic criticism." He thought the poem "slipshod," and had decided that the most powerful poets did not write escapist, "golden-tongued Romance" but embraced the "fierce dispute" of life in the world—terms he used as he was rereading Shakespeare's *King Lear*. His self-assigned syllabus in 1818 included not only this tragedy but also Hazlitt's lectures on English poetry, *Paradise Lost*, *Hamlet* (Keats once said he thought he had read this play forty times), and Dante's *Divine Comedy* in Henry Cary's recent translation. Although, like Hazlitt, he was irritated by Wordsworth's didacticism and egotism, he also recognized that Wordsworth was working out a profoundly modern sense of the "dark Passages" of life—the pains, heartbreaks, and oppression that no simple romance such as *Endymion* nor any simplistic moral philosophy (so Keats regarded *Paradise Lost*) could argue away.

It was in this temper that he began a second epic, a deliberate revision of Milton. The intended hero of *Hyperion* was Apollo, the god of knowledge, poetry, and medicine—a linkage dear to Keats. The most powerful and most deeply felt poetry he wrote, however (in the two books he completed), described, with heartfelt sympathy, the painful bewilderment of the fallen Titan clan and Hyperion's incipient anxiety about his impending fate as he realizes that his brothers have died into mortality. When Keats started to write of Hyperion's designated successor, Apollo, he lost inspiration. Could the "Knowledge enormous" that the god of poetry claimed to gain "all at once" be reconciled with the poet's own acute sympathy with the very mortal pain of his beloved brother Tom, dying of tuberculosis, the disease that had killed their mother? Tom died at the end of 1818, and Keats, almost instinctively by now, sought relief in his poetry, but not the too-burdensome *Hyperion*. In a burst of inspiration that lasted well into the fall of 1819 (when he returned to *Hyperion*), he produced his most admired work: *The Eve of St. Agnes*, *La Belle Dame*, *Lamia*, all the Great Odes, and a clutch of brilliant sonnets including "Bright star."

Unlike most of his contemporaries, Keats wrote no theoretical prefaces, no defenses, no self-promoting polemics, no critical essays. But he did write letters, ones that reflect a critical intelligence as brilliant as the poetic talent. A number of Keats's formulations therein—among them, "Negative Capability," "the egotistical sublime," truth "proved upon our pulses"—have entered the syntax of literary criticism and theory. From their first publication (several in 1848), Keats's letters have been admired for their wit and playfulness, their generosity and candor, and their insight and critical penetration.

Keats had been suffering from a chronically sore throat since the summer of 1818. Just as his talents were generating this incredible body of work—the poetry that would secure his immortality—his health weakened, and he suffered a major pulmonary hemorrhage early in 1820. With the force of his medical training, he read his "death warrant" and was devastated about lost prospects. Despite the shaky reception of his first two volumes, he was optimistic about the forthcoming volume (as well he might be) and full of enthusiasm for new writing (journalism or plays). He was also in love with the girl next door, Fanny Brawne, whom he met in the summer of 1818 and hoped to marry once he was financially capable. But he and everyone knew that he could not survive another English winter, and so in September 1820 he sailed for Italy. He died in Rome, at the end of the next February, four months after his twenty-fifth birthday—far from Fanny Brawne, far from his friends, and in such despair of what he had accomplished that he asked his tombstone to read "Here lies one whose name was writ in water." He did live long enough to see some favorable reviews of his 1820 volume. The mythology Shelley sympathetically advanced in *Adonais*, of a young sensitive poet slain by hostile reviews, though it would often be retold throughout the nineteenth century as if it were the documentary truth, could not have been further from it. "This is a mere matter of the moment," Keats assured his brother George about his first reviews, adding, "I think I shall be among the English Poets after my death."

Table of Dates

K: John Keats
GK: George Keats
TK: Tom Keats
FK: Fanny Keats

1795   John Keats born, 31 October, to Frances Jennings Keats and Thomas Keats, chief ostler at the Swan and Hoop inn, owned by Frances's father.

Famine in England (high prices, scarcity); Napoleon's army moves into Italy.

1796   Matthew Lewis, *The Monk*; Mary Robinson, *Sappho and Phaon*. Death of Robert Burns.

1797   George Keats born. H. F. Cary, *Ode to General Kosciusko*.

1798   Battle of the Nile; Irish Rebellion; *Lyrical Ballads* (Wordsworth and Coleridge).

1799   Tom Keats born. Napoleon returns to France and in a coup d'état becomes first consul; Religious Tract Society formed; Six Acts against political societies, Combination Acts against labor unions.

1800   *Lyrical Ballads*, second edition (with Preface); first collected edition of Robert Burns. Union of England and Ireland; Alessandro Volta produces electricity from a cell.

1801   Edward Keats born, dies before age 4. First census; Pitt resigns after George III refuses Catholic Emancipation. Thomas Moore, *The Wreath and the Chain*.

1802   Founded: Cobbett's *Weekly Political Register*; *Edinburgh Review*; the Society for the Suppression of Vice. Peace of Amiens between England and France; France reoccupies Switzerland; Napoleon made First Consul for life.

Walter Scott, *Minstrelsy of the Scottish Border*.

1803   Fanny Keats born; K and GK enroll at John Clarke's Enfield Academy.

England declares war on France; British capture Delhi, India. Lord Elgin brings sculptural fragments from the Athenian Parthenon to England.

1804   April: K's father dies. June: mother remarries, and the children go to live with her parents.

Pitt becomes Prime Minister; Napoleon crowned Emperor and prepares to invade England; Britain declares war on Spain. First Corn Laws (taxation of imported grain).

1805   K's grandfather Jennings dies.

Scott, *Lay of the Last Minstrel*; Hazlitt, *Essay on the Principles of Human Action*. Nelson dies in the naval battle with France at Trafalgar; French victory over Austria and Russia.

1806   Scott, *Ballads and Lyrical Pieces*; revised Bowles's edition of Pope with a controversial Preface detractive to his character. End of the Holy Roman Empire; Napoleon closes Continental ports to British ships and defeats Prussia at Jena.

1807   Wordsworth, *Poems, in Two Volumes*; Byron, *Hours of Idleness*. France invades Spain and Portugal. British fight against French in Spain and Portugal. Abolition of slave trade in England.

1808   *Edinburgh Review* ridicules *Hours of Idleness*. Leigh Hunt becomes editor of *The Examiner*. Charles Lamb, *Specimens of English Dramatic Poets*. Spanish uprising against Napoleon (May); Convention of Cintra (August).

1809   Byron, *English Bards and Scotch Reviewers*. William Gifford becomes editor of *The Quarterly Review*.

British war in Spain. Napoleon beaten by the Austrians. K's future biographer and editor, R. M. Milnes, born in London.

1810   K's mother dies from tuberculosis; grandmother Jennings appoints John Sandall and Richard Abbey as the children's guardians.

1811   K leaves Enfield and begins apprenticeship to Edmonton surgeon and apothecary Thomas Hammond; GK becomes a clerk at Abbey's counting-house.

Prince of Wales becomes Regent, after George III deemed incompetent. Worker riots against the weaving frames. National Society for the Education of the Poor founded. Lord Elgin offers to sell the British government his Greek Marbles, and public debate ensues about their acquisition, their value, and the costly purchase. Percy Shelley's pamphlet, *The Necessity of Atheism*, gets him expelled from Oxford. Mary Tighe, *Psyche; or the Legend of Love* (privately printed, 1805); Leigh Hunt, *The Feast of the Poets*.

1812   Byron's "maiden" speech in the House of Lords opposes the Frame-Breaking Bill, which prescribed the death penalty; *Childe Harold's Pilgrimage* is an overnight sensation (Canto II opens with a diatribe against Elgin as a thief and pirate). Britain declares war on U.S.; Napoleon invades Russia in June and retreats from Moscow at the end of the year, with catastrophic losses.

1813   Byron becomes a celebrity in London society, with further success from his poetic romances *The Giaour* and *The Bride of Abydos*. Coleridge's play *Remorse* is a success in London. Southey publishes *Life of Nelson*, becomes Poet Laureate; Wordsworth gets a government patronage position; Hunt publishes *The Prince of Wales v. The Examiner* (defending *The Examiner*'s attacks on the policies of the Prince Regent) and is imprisoned for libel. Shelley, *Queen Mab*.

Austria joins the Alliance against France; Napoleon defeated at Leipzig.

1814   K writes his first poems. After grandmother Jennings dies in December, FK goes to live with the Abbeys.

Byron's *The Corsair* sells 10,000 copies on the day of publication. H. F. Cary's translation of *The Divine Comedy*; Wordsworth, *The Excursion* (criticized by Hazlitt in *The Examiner* for "egotism"); J. H. Reynolds, *Safie, An Eastern Tale*, and *The Eden of Imagination*; Hunt, new version of *The Feast of the Poets*; Shelley, *A Refutation of Deism*. Edmund Kean's debut at Covent Garden; Charles Brown's *Narensky* a success at Drury Lane theater.

The Allies invade France; Napoleon abdicates and is exiled; Bourbon monarchy is restored. Shelley elopes to the Continent with Mary Wollstonecraft Godwin.

1815   2 February: Hunt finishes his sentence, and via C. C. Clarke, K sends Hunt *Written on the Day that Mr. Leigh Hunt left Prison*. October: begins medical studies at Guy's Hospital and becomes a surgeon's assistant.

Byron's poems in 4 vols.; Wordsworth's collected poems, including the fully titled version of *Ode, Intimations of Immortality from Recollections of Early Childhood*; Hunt, *The descent of Liberty, a Mask*.

Napoleon escapes from Elba; battle of Waterloo; Napoleon exiled; restoration of the French monarchy. Corn Bill, with enormous benefits to landlords. New agitation for Parliamentary reform. Parliamentary debates on the Elgin Marbles.

1816   K meets Haydon and Reynolds. June: "To one who has been long in city pent." July: K passes medical qualifying exams. July–August: with TK at Margate. September: K, TK, and GK living together in Hampstead. October: K meets Leigh Hunt, who puts *O Solitude* (written in late 1815) in *The Examiner* (K's first publication); writes *On First Looking into Chapman's Homer*. November: visits Haydon's studio and writes "Great Spirits." October–December: *Sleep and Poetry*. December: "I stood tip-toe"; K is featured with Shelley and Reynolds in Hunt's "Young Poets" article in *Examiner*, which includes the sonnet on Chapman's Homer. Abbey becomes the children's sole guardian.

In *The Examiner*: Haydon's defense of the Elgin Marbles (March); Hazlitt, *On Gusto* (May) and defense of the Marbles (June); Wordsworth's *To B. R. Haydon* (also in *The Champion*). Hunt, *The Story of Rimini*; Shelley, *Alastor & c*; Reynolds, *The Naiad*; Coleridge, *Christabel, Kubla Khan*. Byron leaves England amid the scandal of his separation from Lady Byron. At a sales dinner at the end of the year, Byron's publisher sells 7,000 each of *The Prisoner of Chillon & c* and *Childe Harold's Pilgrimage III*. Elgin Marbles purchased by the government and displayed in the British Museum; prosecution of William Hone; Spa Field Riots.

1817   K meets Charles Brown and Richard Woodhouse. February: Hunt shows K's poetry to Shelley, Hazlitt, and Godwin, and publishes more sonnets in *The Examiner*. March: K and TK move to Hampstead, north of London; Haydon takes K to see the Elgin Marbles; K's two sonnets on the occasion appear in *The Champion* and *The Examiner*. *Poems* praised by Reynolds in *The Champion*. April–November: writing *Endymion*. April: at Isle of Wight, reads Shakespeare, writes *On the Sea* (in *The Champion*, August). June–July: sees Kean in *Riches*; Hunt's review of *Poems* in *The Examiner*. August: finishes *Endymion II*. September (TK and GK in Paris): with Bailey at Oxford, writing *Endymion III*, reading Katherine Phillips's poetry and Hazlitt's essays. October: visits Stratford-on-Avon with Bailey. November: reads Coleridge's *Sibylline Leaves* (1817), finishes *Endymion*. December: for the *Champion*, reviews Kean in Shakespeare's *Richard III*; sees Benjamin West's paintings at the Royal Academy; discusses "Negative Capability"; at Haydon's "immortal dinner" with Lamb gives a jesting toast to "Newton's health, and the confusion of mathematics." Meets Wordsworth.

Byron, *Manfred*; Hazlitt, *Characters of Shakespear's Plays*. October: Z writes first "Cockney School" paper in the new *Blackwood's Edinburgh Magazine*, attacking Hunt and targeting K.

Habeas corpus suspended; Hone tried for blasphemous libel for parodies of the liturgy. Princess Charlotte dies from the delivery of a stillborn child; death of Polish patriot Kosciusko, who also fought in U.S. Revolutionary War.

1818   January: K visits Wordsworth and recites the "Hymn to Pan" from *Endymion*; attends theater and dines often with Haydon; rereads *King Lear*; attends Hazlitt's lectures on English Poetry; prepares *Endymion* for press; begins *Isabella*; reads Voltaire and Gibbon. March: drafts preface to *Endymion*. March–April: takes a very ill TK to Teignmouth (resort). April: redrafts the preface; the sonnets on the Elgin Marbles reprinted in *Annals of the Fine Arts*; *Endymion* published; finishes *Isabella*. May: *Hymn to Pan* in *The Yellow Dwarf*; dines with Hazlitt at Haydon's; GK marries Georgiana Wylie and leaves for America; *Blackwood's* sharpens its aim on K. June: nasty review of *Poems* in *The British Critic*. June–August: walking tour of the Lake District and Scotland with Brown; visits Wordsworth's home and Burns's tomb, climbs Ben Nevis; reads Cary's translation of *The Divine Comedy*; sore throat and chills force a return to London, where K finds TK very ill; meets Fanny Brawne. September: K ridiculed by Z in *Blackwood's* and in *Quarterly Review*; writes *Hyperion* while nursing TK and smitten with Fanny Brawne. October: Reynolds's praise of *Endymion* in a minor journal is reprinted in *The Examiner*. To K's embarrassment, Hunt prints two sonnets in *Literary Pocket-Book*, an annual Hunt edited. December: TK dies; K accepts Brown's invitation to live with him at Wentworth Place, Hampstead, where the Brawnes live.

Byron, *Childe Harold IV*; Hunt, *Foliage, or Poems Original and Translated*. Hazlitt, *Lectures on the English Poets*, and in *The Examiner* a scathing *Letter to William Gifford, Esq.* Radical publisher Richard Carlile imprisoned. Habeas corpus restored.

1819 Throughout the year, K is beset with money problems; Haydon pesters him for loans. January: writes *The Eve of St. Agnes*. March: visits the British Museum with Joseph Severn, whose miniature of K is exhibited at the Royal Academy. April: the Brawnes become next-door neighbors at Wentworth place; K meets Coleridge and talks of nightingales; writes *La Belle Dame*, *Ode to Psyche*, "If by dull rhymes." May: *Ode to a Nightingale*, *Ode on a Grecian Urn*, *Ode on Melancholy*, *Ode on Indolence*; sets aside *Hyperion*, describes the world as "a vale of Soul-making"; burns old letters and returns all borrowed books. July: *Ode to a Nightingale* in *Annals of the Fine Arts*. July–August: at Isle of Wight, works with Brown on *Otho the Great*; writes *Lamia* and *The Fall of Hyperion*. September: at Winchester, writes *To Autumn*, and gives up on *Hyperion*. November: reading Holinshed's *Chronicles*, decides not to publish anything for a while, but returns to *Hyperion*. December: *Otho* accepted by Drury Lane for the next season; worsening sore throat; engagement to Fanny Brawne.

  Hazlitt, *Lectures on the English Comic Writers*; Cary's translation of *Divine Comedy* republished by Taylor and Hessey; Byron, *Don Juan I–II*; *Childe Harold's Pilgrimage I–IV*; Reynolds's satire, *Peter Bell, A Lyrical Ballad*, appears in advance of Wordsworth's *Peter Bell* and is reviewed by K. Hunt edits *The Indicator*. Scathing review of Shelley's poetry and character in the *Quarterly*; Shelley's drama *The Cenci* (not staged) meets outraged reviews.

  August: "Peterloo Massacre"—a militia charge on a peaceful worker's demonstration for Parliamentary representation, at which reform champion "Orator" Hunt is arrested; the controversy plays for weeks in the London papers. September: K witnesses Hunt's triumphant entry into London. December: the Six Acts (abridging freedom of assembly, speech, and print). William Parry's Arctic expedition.

1820 January: GK, in London to raise funds from TK's estate, depletes K's share; this is the last time K sees GK, and doesn't write to him again; *Ode on a Grecian Urn* in *Annals of the Fine Arts*; *Otho* offered to Covent Garden. February: a bad hemorrhage that K takes as his "death warrant," housebound for weeks. March: revises *Lamia*; Haydon exhibits *Christ's Entry into Jerusalem*, a painting with K in the crowd. April: *London Magazine* praises *Endymion*. May: when Brown rents his apartment, K has to move; *La Belle Dame sans Mercy* in *The Indicator*. June: K has an attack of blood-coughing and moves into Hunt's home; Hunt publishes *On a Dream* in *Indicator*.

July: *Lamia, Isabella, The Eve of St. Agnes, and Other Poems*. *Ode to a Nightingale*, *To Autumn*, and other poems published in *Literary Gazette*; *To Autumn* also in *London Chronicle*; Lamb's praise of *Lamia & c* in *New Times* is reprinted in *The Examiner*. August: Hunt praises *Lamia & c* in *The Indicator*; K moves in with the Brawnes. His friends raise money for him to spend the winter in Italy; K hopes Brown will go with him, but Brown can't be located. K writes his will and assigns his copyright to Taylor and Hessey for £200.

September: *Monthly Magazine* and *The British Critic* praise *Lamia & c*; with Severn, K sails for Italy; the horrible voyage terminates in Naples in late October, where they are quarantined in the harbor for 10 days; on K's twenty-fifth birthday, they leave for Rome. November: lodgings at the foot of the Spanish Steps, in the English district of Rome; writes his last known letter, to Brown. December: serious relapse.

Murray's 8-vol. edition of Byron's poems. *London Magazine* founded. Shelley, *Prometheus Unbound*; Clare, *Poems Descriptive of Rural Life*.

1821   23 February: K dies in Severn's arms; 26 February: buried in the Protestant Cemetery at Rome. 17 March: the news reaches London. In Pisa, Shelley publishes *Adonais*, an elegy for K with a preface that sets the fable of the sensitive poet fatally wounded by hostile reviewers. Though not published in England, it is generously quoted in several journals that reviewed it, and is ridiculed in *Blackwood's*.

Byron writes two public letters defending Pope and attacking his detractors among the Lake poets and the Cockneys, with nasty remarks about K, which he asks publisher Murray to strike when he learns from Shelley of K's death. Taylor and Hessey buy *London Magazine*.

1822   Death of P. B. Shelley.

1823   Byron's *Don Juan* Canto XI with the soon to be famous line about K "snuff'd out by an article."

1824   Death of Byron in Greece.

1826   FK marries novelist Valentin Llanos, born just weeks after K.

1828   *Adonais* published in England, sponsored by R. M. Milnes and Alfred Tennyson. Leigh Hunt, *Lord Byron and Some of His Contemporaries*, chapter on K.

1829   *The Poetical Works of Coleridge, Shelley and Keats* published by A. and W. Galignani in Paris; all the lifetime volumes plus unpublished or uncollected poetry, along with a memoir based on Hunt's.

1833   Fanny Brawne marries Louis Lindo (later Lindon).

1834   Afflicted from 1829, Woodhouse dies from tuberculosis.

1835   Hunt writes about K in *Leigh Hunt's London Journal*.

1836   Brown gives a public lecture on K.

1841   Brown gives all his K materials to R. M. Milnes; GK dies on Christmas Eve.

1842   Brown dies in New Zealand.

1843   Georgiana Keats marries John Jeffrey.

1844   Hunt's *Imagination and Fancy*, its first chapter on K.

1845   Taylor sells his rights to K's poems and letters to Edward Moxon, R. M. Milnes's publisher. Jeffrey transcribes K's poems and letters for Milnes.

1846   Haydon kills himself.

1848   Milnes, *Life, Letters, and Literary Remains, of John Keats* includes the first publication of many of K's letters and many poems.

1854   Milnes, *The Poetical Works of John Keats* (London: Edward Moxon), with a memoir and handsomely illustrated: a harbinger of K's re-emergence in Victorian literary culture.

1856   Milnes publishes *The Fall of Hyperion*—assumed to be the first draft.

1863   Severn's "The Vicissitudes of Keats's Fame" in *Atlantic Monthly*.

1865   Fanny Brawne dies.

1867   New edition of Milnes's *Life, Letters, and Literary Remains*.

1874   Charles Cowden Clarke's "Recollections of John Keats," *Gentleman's Magazine*.

1876   Milnes (now Lord Houghton), a new edition of *The Poetical Works of John Keats*.

1878   Fanny Brawne's identity exposed in H. B. Forman's *Letters of John Keats to Fanny Brawne*. K's love letters disgusted many, including Arnold and Swinburne.

1883   H. B. Forman's 4-vol. *The Poetical Works and Other Writings of John Keats*, the sign of K's canonical status.

1885   Death of Milnes in Vichy, France.

1887   *Keats*, by Sidney Colvin, added to "The English Men of Letters" series.

1889   Death of FK.

John Keats

Poems, Letters,
§ Contextual Supplements

To Solitude

Keats composed this poem during fall 1815, just after he began his work at Guy's Hospital in a grim, dingy, oppressive district of south London. This is his first publication, appearing in The Examiner, *5 May 1816 (then in 1817: Sonnet VII). The weekly newspaper's editor, Leigh Hunt, had not yet met Keats and accepted the poem over the transom. In* The Examiner, *the sonnet sits at the bottom of p. 582, col. 2, just below this news:*

A letter has been forwarded to us respecting the death of a soldier named *Hegg*, belonging to the 3d regiment of Guards. The Writer asserts, that the sister of the deceased, on visiting him in the hospital, was told by him, that he had received an injury in his arm, and that he should not see her any more. He died soon after. Previous to this, he had complained of severe pain in his arm, which he attributed to the extent of the incision made when he was bled, which is described in the letter as being large enough to admit to the first joint of the little finger. The Writer says, it has been given out that hard drinking occasioned Hegg's death; but this he strongly denies; and he adds, that the Sister of the deceased was refused admittance to see the remains, till the body was so changed that she with difficulty recognized it to be her bother's, and the blood was then oozing through the shroud.

3

TO SOLITUDE.[1]

O SOLITUDE! if I must with thee dwell,
  Let it not be among the jumbled heap
  Of murky buildings;—climb with me the steep,
Nature's Observatory——whence the dell,
Its flowery slopes—its river's crystal swell,
  May seem a span: let me thy vigils keep
  'Mongst boughs pavilioned; where the Deer's swift leap
Startles the wild Bee from the Fox-glove bell.
Ah! fain would I frequent scenes with thee;[2]
  But the sweet converse of an innocent mind,
  Whose words are images of thoughts refin'd,
Is my soul's pleasure; and it sure must be
  Almost the highest bliss of human-kind,
When to thy haunts two kindred spirits flee.

J.K.

Letters to Benjamin Robert Haydon, November 1816[3]

Keats met Haydon in October 1816 and visited his studio for the first time on 3 November. He had spent the evening of 19 November with Haydon, and messengered this note the following day, with the first version of Sonnet XIV *in* Poems *(see "Great Spirits"; p. 30). Haydon was delighted, saying he wanted to send it to his friend, William Wordsworth, arguably the most important poet in England.*

Nov 20th

My dear Sir—
        Last Evening wrought me up, and I cannot forbear sending you the following—Your's unfeignedly John Keats—

---

[1]*1817*] Sonnet VII, untitled, with some variants.
[2]*1817*] But though I'll gladly trace these scenes
[3]ALS, Houghton Library, Harvard.

Thursday Af^{rn} [21 November]
My dear Sir,
    Your letter has filld me with a proud pleasure and shall be kept by me as a stimulus to exertion – I begin to fix my eye upon one horizon — . My feelings fall in with yours' in regard to the Elipsis and I glory in it⁴ – The Idea of your sending it to Wordsworth put me out of breath⁵ – you know with what Reverence – I would send my Wellwishes to him—

Your's sincerely
John Keats

On First Looking into Chapman's Homer

> *Leigh Hunt's article, "Young Poets," appearing in the 1 December 1816* Examiner *(a few months before Keats's* Poems*), greeted a new generation, heralded by Lord Byron, with younger members Shelley, J. H. Reynolds, and Keats. Keats met Reynolds soon after, and Shelley the next January. Hunt's public notice convinced Keats to give up surgery and attempt a career as a poet. "Young Poets" featured a poem that was only his second publication, written after an all-nighter with his friend Charles Cowden Clarke reading George Chapman's vibrant, early seventeenth-century translation of Homer. At daybreak, Keats walked two miles home from Clarke's but, too excited to sleep, wrote a sonnet, then walked it back to Clarke later the same morning.*

YOUNG POETS

In sitting down to this subject, we happen to be restricted by time to a much shorter notice than we could wish: but we mean to take it up again shortly. Many of our readers however have perhaps observed for themselves, that there has been a new school of poetry rising of late, which promises to extinguish the French one that has

---

⁴See *Sonnet XIV*, line 13, note (p. 30).

⁵K enclosed a clean copy (with the "Elipsis") on a separate sheet for Wordsworth. Haydon kept this ms, showed it to Reynolds, and sent a copy to Wordsworth on 31 Dec. Wordsworth replied with praise but also irony about not being an "impartial" judge: "it is assuredly vigorously conceived and well expressed; Hunt's compliment is well deserved, and the sonnet is very agreeably concluded" (20 Jan. 1817); he had read Hunt's "Young Poets" in *The Examiner*.

prevailed among us since the time of Charles the 2d.[1] It began with something excessive, like most revolutions, but this gradually wore away; and an evident aspiration after real nature and original fancy remained, which called to mind the finer times of the English Muse. In fact it is wrong to call it a new school, and still more so to represent it as one of innovation, it's only object being to restore the same love of Nature, and of *thinking* instead of mere *talking*, which formerly rendered us real poets, and not merely versifying wits, and bead-rollers of couplets.

We were delighted to see the departure of the old school acknowledged in the number of the *Edinburgh Review* just published,—a candour more generous and spirited, inasmuch as that work has hitherto been the greatest surviving ornament of the same school in prose and criticism, as it is now destined, we trust, to be still the leader in the new.[2]

We also felt the same delight at the third canto of Lord Byron's *Child Harolde*, in which, to our conceptions at least, he has fairly renounced a certain leaven of the French style, and taken his place where we always said he would be found,—among the poets who have a real feeling for numbers, and who go directly to Nature for inspiration. [. . .]

The object of the present article is merely to notice three young writers, who appear to us to promise a considerable addition of strength to the new school. Of the first who came before us, we have, it is true, yet seen only one or two specimens, and these were no sooner sent us than we unfortunately mislaid them; but we shall procure what he has published, and if the rest answer to what we have seen, we shall have no hesitation in announcing him for a very striking and original thinker. His name is PERCY BYSSHE SHELLEY, and he is the author of a poetical work entitled *Alastor, or the Spirit of Solitude*.[3]

The next with whose name we became acquainted, was JOHN HENRY REYNOLDS, author of a tale called *Safie*, written, we believe in imitation of Lord Byron, and more lately of a small set of poems

---

[1]For K's diatribe against French-school neoclassicism, see *Sleep and Poetry* 181–206.

[2]A long essay on Swift's *Works* in the Sept. 1816 issue declared that "the writers who adorned the beginning of the last century have been eclipsed by those of our own time . . . a revolution in our literature."

[3]Published March 1816, this 720-line poem in heroic blank verse is a tale of visionary quest fulfilled in death.

published by Taylor and Hessey,[4] the principal of which is called the *Naiad*.

[quotes 1–27; . . .]

The author's style is too artificial, though he is evidently an admirer of Mr. Wordsworth. Like all young poets too, properly so called, his love of detail is too over-wrought and indiscriminate; but still he is a young poet, and only wants a still closer attention to things as opposed to the seduction of words, to realize all that he promises. His nature seems very true and amiable.

The last of these young aspirants, whom we have met with, and who promises to help the new school to revive Nature and

"To put a spirit of youth in every thing,"—[5]

is, we believe, the youngest of them all, and just of age. His name is JOHN KEATS. He has not yet published any thing except in a newspaper;[6] but a set of his manuscripts was handed us the other day, and fairly surprised us with the truth of their ambition, and ardent grappling with Nature. In the following Sonnet there is one incorrect rhyme, which might be easily altered, but which shall serve in the mean time as a peace-offering to the rhyming critics. The rest of the composition, with the exception of a little vagueness in calling the regions of poetry "the realms of gold," we do not hesitate to pronounce excellent, especially the first six lines. The word *swims* is complete; and the conclusion is equally powerful and quiet:—

ON FIRST LOOKING INTO CHAPMAN'S HOMER.

Much have I travel'd in the realms of Gold,[7]
　　And many goodly states and Kingdoms seen;
　　Round many western Islands have I been,
　　Which Bards in fealty to Apollo hold.[8]

---

[4]After the publishers of *1817* ditched him, Taylor and Hessey took on K, publishing *Endymion* and *1820*. The poet's middle name is Hamilton, not Henry.

[5]Shakespeare, Sonnet 98, describing "April."

[6]*To Solitude*

[7]In *A Defence of Poesie* (1595), Sir Philip Sidney argued that poets "deliver a golden" world from the "brazen" nature; K's metaphor also involves early modern gold-searchers such as Cortez, conquistador of Mexico.

[8]*fealty*: feudal oath of fidelity.

> But of one wide expanse had I been told
> That deep-brow'd Homer ruled as his demesne;[9]
> Yet could I never judge what men could mean,[10]
> Till I heard CHAPMAN speak out loud and bold,
> Then felt I like some watcher of the skies,
> When a new planet swims into his ken;[11]
> Or like stout CORTEZ, when with eagle eyes
> He stared at the Pacific,—and all his men
> Looked at each other with a wild surmise,—
> Silent, upon a peak in Darien.[12]
>
> *Oct.* 1816   JOHN KEATS.

We have spoken with the less scruple of these poetical promises, because we really are not in the habit of lavishing praises and announcements, and because we have no fear of any pettier vanity on the part of young men, who promise to understand human nature so well.

§ Pope's Homer / Chapman's Homer

Alexander Pope's "Homer" was the standard in Keats's day. His acclaimed translation of the Iliad *(1715–16) launched the first poetic career in English letters capable of independence from aristocratic or court patronage. Pope renders neoclassical couplets of carefully paced meter, balanced syntax, and tight rhyme. Chapman's* Iliad *uses the epic*

[9]Medieval diction: domain, region.

[10]*1817*] Yet did I never breathe its pure serene;
serene: expanse of clear sky. K told Clarke that he thought the first version of this line "bald and too simply wondering." K may be remembering "deep serene" in Coleridge's *Hymn before Sunrise, in the Vale of Chamouni* (1802), 72; or part of a simile in Pope's *Iliad*: "When not a Breath disturbs the deep Serene; / And not a Cloud o'ercasts the solemn Scene" (8: 689–90).

[11]*ken*: range of apprehension; Uranus was discovered by William Herschel in 1781. William Robertson's *History of America* (K read it in school) reports on Cortez in Panama; and John Bonnycastle's *Introduction to Astronomy*, which K received as a school prize, has an account of Herschel's discovery.

[12]Panama. There is no reason to agree with Tennyson's often repeated comment (1861) that K confused Cortez with Balboa (the first European to see the Pacific). As K is first looking into Chapman's Homer (not unknown to others), so Cortez is first looking at an ocean (of which he had been told).

"*fourteener*" *(seven iambic feet). Here are two passages Keats read with Clarke in both versions.*

from *The Iliad*, Book V: the armor of Diomedes, a Greek warrior

Pope

High on his helm celestial lightnings play,
His beamy shield emits a living ray;
Th' unwearied blaze incessant streams supplies,
Like the red star that fires th' autumnal skies,
When fresh he rears his radiant orb to sight,
And bath'd in Ocean, shoots a keener light.   10
Such glories Pallas on the chief bestow'd,
Such, from his arms, the fierce effulgence flow'd:
Onward she drives him, furious to engage,
Where the fight burns, and where the thickest rage.

Chapman

From his bright helme and shield did burne a most unwearied fire,
Like rich Autumnus' golden lampe, whose brightnesse men admire
Past all the other host of starres when, with his chearefull face
Fresh washt in loftie Ocean waves he doth the skies enchase.
    To let whose glory lose no sight, still Pallas made him turne
Where tumult most expresst his powre, and where the fight did
      burne.   10

from *The Odyssey*, Book V: having prayed to a river-god for relief, a shipwrecked, tempest-tossed Ulysses staggers ashore at Phæacia

Pope

He pray'd, and straight the gentle stream subsides,
Detains the rushing current of his tides,
Before the wand'rer smooths the wat'ry way,
And soft receives him from the rolling sea.
That moment, fainting as he touch'd the shore,   580
He dropp'd his sinewy arms; his knees no more
Perform'd their office, or his weight upheld;

His swoln heart heav'd; his bloated body swell'd;
From mouth and nose the briny torrent ran;
And lost in lassitude lay all the man,
Deprived of voice, of motion, and of breath,
The soul scarce waking in the arms of death.

Chapman

This (though but spoke in thought) the Godhead heard,
Her Current strait staid, and her thicke waves cleard
Before him, smooth'd her waters, and just where
He praied, halfe downd, entirely sav'd him there.
Then forth he came, his both knees faltring, both
His strong hands hanging downe, and all with froth
His cheeks and nosthrils flowing, voice and breath   610
Spent to all use; and downe he sunke to Death.
The sea had soakt his heart through: all his vaines
His toiles had rackt t'a labouring woman's paines.
Dead wearie was he.

from *The Examiner*, Sunday, 23 February 1817: Sonnet ("After dark vapours")

Keats was now a frequent guest at the Hunts' and enjoying the literary society there. This sonnet is set in the middle of the second column of p. 124, just above the start of an article on military torture. It was not republished until 1848, in a section of twenty sonnets as III (2.289, there dated "Jan. 1817").

ORIGINAL POETRY

SONNET

AFTER dark vapors have oppress'd our plains
    For a long dreary season, comes a day
    Born of the gentle SOUTH, and clears away
From the sick heavens all unseemly stains,
The anxious Month, relieved of its pains,

Takes as a long lost right the feel of MAY:
The eyelids with the passing coolness play
Like Rose leaves with the drip of Summer rains.
The calmest thoughts come round us; as of leaves
    Budding—fruit ripening in stillness—Autumn Suns
Smiling at Eve upon the quiet sheaves—
Sweet SAPPHO'S Cheek——a smiling infant's breath—
The gradual Sand that through an hour-glass runs—
A woodland rivulet—a Poet's death.

                              J.K.

MILITARY TORTURE

The following letter from Calcutta contains the genuine effusion of a mind highly gifted with the best sentiments of man. It is from an Officer of the Staff, who is conversant in military matters. As the annual Mutiny Bill is shortly to be submitted to the consideration of Parliament, those contents cannot be unworthy the notice and reflection of every honest Member. Let it not be said, that those whom we call *Barbarians* are more alive to the dignity of our nature than the civilized inhabitants of Europe, and most especially the natives of Britain and Ireland. It has been urged, as a palliative for flogging that the service abroad cannot be carried on without it. We deny the position: for armies, equally as brave, and perhaps better disciplined, have been managed without that disgraceful and degrading severity. But suppose it to be so, where is the necessity of exercising the cat-o'-nine-tails at home? If report says true, the peaceful precincts of the Tilt-yard have very lately been invaded by the horrid vice of tortured soldiers!* We hope the rumour is not well founded; but whether it be so or not, it is high time, that a clause should be introduced in the Mutiny Act to prevent the recurrence of this brutal and inefficient practice.

> *The report is, that a private of the 1st Guards, named *R. Griffiths*, has received TWO HUNDRED AND FIFTY LASHES, merely for saying words to the effect in a public house: *that he saw no reason why the people should not meet in Spafields to obtain a redress of grievances* . . . This matter will of course not rest here, if true.

Poems,

BY

JOHN KEATS.

" What more felicity can fall to creature,
" Than to enjoy delight with liberty."
Fate of the Butterfly.—SPENSER.

LONDON:

PRINTED FOR

C. & J. OLLIER, 3, WELBECK STREET,

CAVENDISH SQUARE.

1817.

Title page of *Poems*, 1817.

from *Poems*

Keats's debut volume was published 3 March 1817 (London: C. & J. Ollier), priced at 6 shillings. Reynolds reviewed it immediately in The Champion (9 March). Its title page features a laurel-wreathed profile head of Spenser (regarded as the first Poet Laureate) with an epigraph from his Fate of the Butterfly: "What more felicity can fall to creature, / Than to enjoy delight with liberty?" (209–10). The question seems rhetorical, but it's also serious, for this is an imperiled felicity; at the end of the stanza, the butterfly falls prey to a spider. In Keats's day, "liberty" carried political meaning: opposition to monarchal tyranny. Hunt was affectionately dubbed Libertas (Latin: Liberty) for his principled critiques of the British monarchy. Keats is also playing against Wordsworth's assignment of "delight and liberty" to "the simple creed of Childhood," a creed replaced by the mature "philosophic mind" ("Intimations" Ode, 1815; lines 137–38) that focuses hope on eternity rather than historical events.

DEDICATION.[1]
TO LEIGH HUNT, ESQ.

GLORY and loveliness have passed away;[2]
    For if we wander out in early morn,
    No wreathed incense do we see upborne
Into the east, to meet the smiling day:
No crowd of nymphs soft voic'd and young, and gay,
    In woven baskets bringing ears of corn,
    Roses, and pinks, and violets, to adorn

---

[1]One of the last compositions for *Poems*, written after K received proof sheets from the printer.

[2]K is echoing Wordsworth: "there hath past away a glory from the earth" ("Intimations" *Ode* 18).

The shrine of Flora in her early May.
But there are left delights as high as these,
   And I shall ever bless my destiny,   10
That in a time, when under pleasant trees
   Pan is no longer sought, I feel a free
A leafy luxury, seeing I could please
   With these poor offerings, a man like thee.[3]

"I stood tip-toe"

In the volume's opening poem, completed December 1816, Keats releases the signature form of eighteenth-century public poetry, the heroic couplet (rhymed iambic pentameter), from the protocols of strict meter and a coordination of syntax with "masculine" stressed-syllable rhymes. He plays a jauntier rhythm on the pulse of enthusiasm and passion, with rhyming extravagances and enjambments. Leaving the poem untitled, he seems to have let the epigraph serve this function.

"Places of nestling green for Poets made."
STORY OF RIMINI.[1]

I STOOD tip-toe upon a little hill,
The air was cooling, and so very still,
That the sweet buds which with a modest pride
Pull droopingly, in slanting curve aside,
Their scantly leaved, and finely tapering stems,
Had not yet lost those starry diadems
Caught from the early sobbing of the morn.
The clouds were pure and white as flocks new shorn,
And fresh from the clear brook; sweetly they slept
On the blue fields of heaven, and then there crept   10
A little noiseless noise among the leaves,

---

[3]The *free/thee* rhyme picks up, in homage, *Leigh* as part of the extended rhyme field.

---

[1]From Hunt's *Story of Rimini* (pub. Feb. 1816): III.430, about Francesca's favorite bower, where she and Paolo, reading of (adulterous) Sir Lancelot and Queen Guinevere, were so overcome with sympathy for them that, famously, they "read no more" and gave in to their own passion. K's gesture is riskier than its debt of poetic form (modern couplets). Hunt's own sympathy for the lovers (as victims of parental tyranny) would draw Z's fire in *The Cockney School of Poetry*, Oct. 1817—a series of abuses that would include K.

Born of the very sigh that silence heaves:
For not the faintest motion could be seen
Of all the shades that slanted o'er the green.
There was wide wand'ring for the greediest eye,
To peer about upon variety;
Far round the horizon's crystal air to skim,
And trace the dwindled edgings of its brim;
To picture out the quaint, and curious bending
Of a fresh woodland alley, never ending;   20
Or by the bowery clefts, and leafy shelves,
Guess w[h]ere the jaunty streams refresh themselves.
I gazed awhile, and felt as light, and free
As though the fanning wings of Mercury
Had played upon my heels: I was light-hearted,
And many pleasures to my vision started;
So I straightway began to pluck a posey
Of luxuries bright, milky, soft and rosy.[2]

A bush of May flowers with the bees about them;
Ah, sure no tasteful nook would be without them;   30
And let a lush laburnum oversweep them,
And let long grass grow round the roots to keep them
Moist, cool and green; and shade the violets,
That they may bind the moss in leafy nets.

A filbert hedge with wild briar overtwined,
And clumps of woodbine taking the soft wind
Upon their summer thrones; there too should be
The frequent chequer of a youngling tree,
That with a score of light green breth[r]en shoots
From the quaint mossiness of aged roots: 40
Round which is heard a spring-head of clear waters
Babbling so wildly of its lovely daughters
The spreading blue bells: it may haply mourn
That such fair clusters should be rudely torn
From their fresh beds, and scattered thoughtlessly
By infant hands, left on the path to die.

[2]A meta-poetic punning: the first stanza, 28 lines, is a piece of poesy, two sonnets.

Open afresh your round of starry folds,
Ye ardent marigolds!
Dry up the moisture from your golden lids,
For great Apollo bids   50
That in these days your praises should be sung
On many harps, which he has lately strung;
And when again your dewiness he kisses,
Tell him, I have you in my world of blisses:
So haply when I rove in some far vale,
His mighty voice may come upon the gale.

Here are sweet peas, on tip-toe for a flight:
With wings of gentle flush o'er delicate white,
And taper fingers catching at all things,
To bind them all about with tiny rings.   60

Linger awhile upon some bending planks
That lean against a streamlet's rushy banks,
And watch intently Nature's gentle doings:
They will be found softer than ring-dove's cooings.
How silent comes the water round that bend;
Not the minutest whisper does it send
To the o'erhanging sallows:° blades of grass   *willows*
Slowly across the chequer'd shadows pass.
Why, you might read two sonnets, ere they reach
To where the hurrying freshnesses aye° preach   *ever* 70
A natural sermon o'er their pebbly beds;
Where swarms of minnows show their little heads,
Staying their wavy bodies 'gainst the streams,
To taste the luxury of sunny beams
Temper'd with coolness. How they ever wrestle
With their own sweet delight, and ever nestle
Their silver bellies on the pebbly sand.
If you but scantily hold out the hand,
That very instant not one will remain;
But turn your eye, and they are there again.   80
The ripples seem right glad to reach those cresses,
And cool themselves among the em'rald tresses;
The while they cool themselves, they freshness give,

And moisture, that the bowery green may live:
So keeping up an interchange of favours,
Like good men in the truth of their behaviours
Sometimes goldfinches one by one will drop
From low hung branches; little space they stop;
But sip, and twitter, and their feathers sleek;°   *(verb)*
Then off at once, as in a wanton freak: 90
Or perhaps, to show their black, and golden wings,
Pausing upon their yellow flutterings.
Were I in such a place, I sure should pray
That nought less sweet, might call my thoughts away,
Than the soft rustle of a maiden's gown
Fanning away the dandelion's down;
Than the light music of her nimble toes
Patting against the sorrel as she goes.
How she would start, and blush, thus to be caught
Playing in all her innocence of thought.   100
O let me lead her gently o'er the brook,
Watch her half-smiling lips, and downward look;
O let me for one moment touch her wrist;
Let me one moment to her breathing list;
And as she leaves me may she often turn
Her fair eyes looking through her locks aubùrne.
What next? A tuft of evening primroses,
O'er which the mind may hover till it dozes;
O'er which it well might take a pleasant sleep,
But that 'tis ever startled by the leap   110
Of buds into ripe flowers; or by the flitting
Of diverse moths, that aye their rest are quitting;
Or by the moon lifting her silver rim
Above a cloud, and with a gradual swim
Coming into the blue with all her light.
O Maker of sweet poets, dear delight
Of this fair world, and all its gentle livers;
Spangler of clouds, halo of crystal rivers,
Mingler with leaves, and dew and tumbling streams,
Closer of lovely eyes to lovely dreams,   120
Lover of loneliness, and wandering,
Of upcast eye, and tender pondering!

Thee must I praise above all other glories
That smile us on to tell delightful stories.
For what has made the sage or poet write
But the fair paradise of Nature's light?
In the calm grandeur of a sober line,
We see the waving of the mountain pine;
And when a tale is beautifully staid,
We feel the safety of a hawthorn glade: 130
When it is moving on luxurious wings,
The soul is lost in pleasant smotherings:
Fair dewy roses brush against our faces,
And flowering laurels spring from diamond vases;
O'er head we see the jasmine and sweet briar,
And bloomy grapes laughing from green attire;
While at our feet, the voice of crystal bubbles
Charms us at once away from all our troubles:
So that we feel uplifted from the world,
Walking upon the white clouds wreath'd and curl'd.   140
So felt he, who first told, how Psyche went
On the smooth wind to realms of wonderment;
What Psyche felt, and Love, when their full lips
First touch'd; what amorous, and fondling nips
They gave each other's cheeks; with all their sighs,
And how they kist each other's tremulous eyes:
The silver lamp,—the ravishment,—the wonder—
The darkness,—loneliness, —the fearful thunder;
Their woes gone by, and both to heaven upflown,
To bow for gratitude before Jove's throne.³   150
So did he feel, who pull'd the boughs aside,
That we might look into a forest wide,
To catch a glimpse of Fawns, and Dryades
Coming with softest rustle through the trees;
And garlands woven of flowers wild, and sweet,
Upheld on ivory wrists, or sporting feet:
Telling us how fair, trembling Syrinx fled

---

³See also *Ode to Psyche* (in *1820*). It was by her silver lamp that Psyche took a forbidden peek at her mysterious nocturnal lover, rumored to be a snake. This was
against their bargain, and Cupid fled.

Arcadian Pan, with such a fearful dread.
Poor nymph,—poor Pan,—how he did weep to find,
Nought but a lovely sighing of the wind   160
Along the reedy stream; a half heard strain,
Full of sweet desolation—balmy pain.[4]

What first inspired a bard of old to sing
Narcissus pining o'er the untainted spring?[5]
In some delicious ramble, he had found
A little space, with boughs all woven round;
And in the midst of all, a clearer pool
Than e'er reflected in its pleasant cool,
The blue sky here, and there, serenely peeping
Through tendril wreaths fantastically creeping.   170
And on the bank a lonely flower he spied,
A meek and forlorn flower, with naught of pride,
Drooping its beauty o'er the watery clearness,
To woo its own sad image into nearness:
Deaf to light Zephyrus it would not move;
But still would seem to droop, to pine, to love.
So while the Poet stood in this sweet spot,
Some fainter gleamings o'er his fancy shot;
Nor was it long ere he had told the tale
Of young Narcissus, and sad Echo's bale.°   *woe* 180

Where had he been, from whose warm head out-flew
That sweetest of all songs, that ever new,
That aye refreshing, pure deliciousness,
Coming ever to bless
The wanderer by moonlight? to him bringing
Shapes from the invisible world, unearthly singing
From out the middle air, from flowery nests,
And from the pillowy silkiness that rests
Full in the speculation of the stars.
Ah! surely he had burst our mortal bars;   190

[4]This rendition of the myth is sympathetic to the pain of frustrated nymph-ravisher Pan.
[5]This version of the legend is sympathetic to "young Narcissus."

Into some wond'rous region he had gone,
To search for thee, divine Endymion!⁶

He was a Poet, sure a lover too,
Who stood on Latmus' top, what time there blew
Soft breezes from the myrtle vale below;
And brought in faintness solemn, sweet, and slow
A hymn from Dian's temple; while upswelling,
The incense went to her own starry dwelling.
But though her face was clear as infant's eyes,
Though she stood smiling o'er the sacrifice,   200
The Poet wept at her so piteous fate,
Wept that such beauty should be desolate:
So in fine wrath some golden sounds he won,
And gave meek Cynthia her Endymion.

Queen of the wide air; thou most lovely queen
Of all the brightness that mine eyes have seen!
As thou exceedest all things in thy shine,
So every tale, does this sweet tale of thine.
O for three words of honey, that I might
Tell but one wonder of thy bridal night!   210

Where distant ships do seem to show their keels,
Phoebus awhile delayed his mighty wheels,⁷
And turned to smile upon thy bashful eyes,
Ere he his unseen pomp would solemnize.
The evening weather was so bright, and clear,
That men of health were of unusual cheer;
Stepping like Homer at the trumpet's call,
Or young Apollo on the pedestal:⁸
And lovely women were as fair and warm,
As Venus looking sideways in alarm.   220
The breezes were ethereal, and pure,
And crept through half closed lattices to cure
The languid sick; it cool'd their fever'd sleep,

⁶This is K's first attempt at the love legend of the shepherd Endymion and Moon-goddess Cynthia. K originally titled this (untitled) poem *Endymion*.
⁷Phoebus Apollo, who carries the sun in a chariot across the sky.
⁸The famous statue of the Apollo Belvedere.

And soothed them into slumbers full and deep.
Soon they awoke clear eyed: nor burnt with thirsting,
Nor with hot fingers, nor with temples bursting:
And springing up, they met the wond'ring sight
Of their dear friends, nigh° foolish with delight;   *nearly*
Who feel their arms, and breasts, and kiss and stare,
And on their placid foreheads part the hair.   230
Young men, and maidens at each other gaz'd
With hands held back, and motionless, amaz'd
To see the brightness in each others' eyes;
And so they stood, fill'd with a sweet surprise,
Until their tongues were loos'd in poesy.
Therefore no lover did of anguish die:
But the soft numbers, in that moment spoken,
Made silken ties, that never may be broken.
Cynthia! I cannot tell the greater blisses,
That follow'd thine, and thy dear shepherd's kisses: 240
Was there a Poet born?⁹——but now no more,
My wand'ring spirit must no further soar.——

§ William Wordsworth on the origin of mythology, from *The Excursion*, Book IV (1814)

Keats sent Poems *to Wordsworth, inscribed "with the Author's sincere Reverence." One of the "things to rejoice at in this Age," he told Haydon (10 January 1818), was* The Excursion. *Keats was quite taken with its passages of mytho-genesis, especially (as reported by both Bailey and Haydon) the one presented here. Wordsworth recited Book IV to Haydon while sitting for his portrait in 1815, and Haydon may have encouraged Keats's attention to it, later identifying the passage below as one Keats admired.*

Once more to distant Ages of the world
Let us revert, and place before our thoughts
The face which rural Solitude might wear

⁹A packed question: Was there a poet born from the union of Endymion and Cynthia? Was there a poet born from imagining this tale? And in this first poem of *Poems*, is Keats being born to the reader as a poet?

To the unenlightened Swains of pagan[1] Greece.
In that fair Clime, the lonely Herdsman, stretched
On the soft grass through half a summer's day,
With music lulled his indolent repose: 870
And, in some fit of weariness, if he,
When his own breath was silent, chanced to hear
A distant strain, far sweeter than the sounds
Which his poor skill could make, his Fancy fetched,
Even from the blazing Chariot of the Sun,
A beardless Youth, who touched a golden lute,
And filled the illumined groves with ravishment.
The nightly Hunter, lifting up his eyes
Towards the crescent Moon, with grateful heart
Called on the lovely wanderer who bestowed   880
That timely light, to share his joyous sport:
And hence, a beaming Goddess with her Nymphs,
Across the lawn and through the darksome grove,
(Not unaccompanied with tuneful notes
By echo multiplied from rock or cave)
Swept in the storm of chase; as Moon and Stars
Glance rapidly along the clouded heavens,
When winds are blowing strong. The Traveller slaked
His thirst from Rill or gushing Fount, and thanked
The Naiad.—Sunbeams, upon distant Hills   890
Gliding apace, with Shadows in their train,
Might, with small help from fancy, be transformed
Into fleet Oreads sporting visibly.
The Zephyrs, fanning as they passed, their wings,
Lacked not, for love, fair Objects whom they wooed
With gentle whisper. Withered Boughs grotesque,
Stripped of their leaves and twigs by hoary age,
From depth of shaggy covert peeping forth
In the low vale, or on steep mountain side;
And, sometimes, intermixed with stirring horns   900
Of the live Deer, or Goat's depending beard,—
These were the lurking Satyrs, a wild brood
Of gamesome Deities! or Pan himself,
The simple Shepherd's awe-inspiring God!

[1]pre-Christian

Imitation of Spenser

At age eighteen, in early 1814 while he was a surgeon's apprentice, Keats wrote his first poem, in homage to The Faerie Queene. *The Spenserian stanza (iambic pentameter of* ababbcbc, *with the last line a six-foot alexandrine) is an intricate verse-form, refreshed in imitative eighteenth-century Spenserian romances (by James Beattie and James Thomson), Mary Tighe's* Psyche *(1811), and Byron's overnight success, the retro-modern romance,* Childe Harold's Pilgrimage *(1812). The rows of seven asterisks that appear at the start and end of Keats's* Imitation *(the only verse so framed in* Poems*) imply a fragment that might be extended in either direction.*

* * * * * * *

Now Morning from her orient chamber came,
And her first footsteps touch'd a verdant hill;
Crowning its lawny crest with amber flame,
Silv'ring the untainted gushes of its rill;
Which, pure from mossy beds, did down distill,
And after parting beds of simple flowers,
By many streams a little lake did fill,
Which round its marge reflected woven bowers,
And, in its middle space, a sky that never lowers.[1]

There the king-fisher saw his plumage bright   10
Vieing with fish of brilliant dye below;
Whose silken fins, and golden scales' light
Cast upward, through the waves, a ruby glow:
There saw the swan his neck of arched snow,
And oar'd himself along with majesty;
Sparkled his jetty eyes; his feet did show
Beneath the waves like Afric's ebony,
And on his back a fay° reclined voluptuously.   *sprite*

Ah! could I tell the wonders of an isle
That in that fairest lake had placed been,   20
I could e'en Dido of her grief beguile;
Or rob from aged Lear his bitter teen:[2]

[1]threatens a storm

[2]Dido killed herself in grief. Shakespeare's King Lear was cruelly treated by two of his three daughters and went mad from rage. *teen:* grief, woe.

For sure so fair a place was never seen,
Of all that ever charm'd romantic eye:
It seem'd an emerald in the silver sheen
Of the bright waters; or as when on high,
Through clouds of fleecy white, laughs the cœrulean sky.

And all around it dipp'd luxuriously
Slopings of verdure through the glossy tide,
Which, as it were in gentle amity,   30
Rippled delighted up the flowery side;
As if to glean the ruddy tears, it tried,
Which fell profusely from the rose-tree stem!
Haply it was the workings of its pride,
In strife to throw upon the shore a gem
Outvieing all the buds in Flora's diadem.

* * * * * * *

SONNETS

This subsection in Poems *is a sequence of seventeen roman-numbered sonnets, some with titles. Across his career, Keats wrote scads of sonnets, joining a tradition made famous by Petrarch, Shakespeare, Milton, and Wordsworth. Fifteenth-century Italian poet Petrarch shaped a two-step affair: an octave (usually* abbaabba) *presenting a situation, then a turn (*volta*) at the* sestet *(variously rhymed, often* cde cde)*, giving a reaction, consequence, or elaboration. Shakespeare tightened the drama: three quatrains (the first two sometimes linked, as if a Petrarchan octave) and a pithy summation, turn, or reversal in a closing couplet. Keats's sonnetry plays experimentally with and against tradition.*

I.

TO MY BROTHER GEORGE

MANY the wonders I this day have seen:[1]
The sun, when first he kist away the tears

[1]Having taken his apothecary and surgeon's exams in July but not licensed to begin practice until 31 Oct. 1816 (at age 21), K vacationed at Margate, a coastal resort town about 70 miles SE of London, using the interlude to write poetry; he composed this sonnet in August.

That fill'd the eyes of morn;—the laurel'd peers
Who from the feathery gold of evening lean;—
The ocean with its vastness, its blue green,
 Its ships, its rocks, its caves, its hopes, its fears,—
 Its voice mysterious, which whoso hears
Must think on what will be, and what has been.
E'en now, dear George, while this for you I write,
 Cynthia is from her silken curtains peeping   10
So scantly, that it seems her bridal night,
 And she her half-discover'd revels keeping.
But what, without the social thought of thee,
Would be the wonders of the sky and sea?

II.

TO * * * * * *

HAD I a man's fair form,[2] then might my sighs
 Be echoed swiftly through that ivory shell
 Thine ear, and find thy gentle heart; so well
Would passion arm me for the enterprize:
But ah! I am no knight whose foeman dies;
 No cuirass° glistens on my bosom's swell;   *leather armor*
 I am no happy shepherd of the dell
Whose lips have trembled with a maiden's eyes.
Yet must I dote upon thee,—call thee sweet,
 Sweeter by far than Hybla's honied roses   10
  When steep'd in dew rich to intoxication.
Ah! I will taste that dew, for me 'tis meet,
 And when the moon her pallid face discloses,
  I'll gather some by spells, and incantation.

III.

Written on the day that Mr. Leigh Hunt left Prison

On 2 February 1815, Hunt (and his brother John) completed a two-year sentence for "libeling" the Prince Regent in an article in The Examiner *(22 March 1812) that castigated his "libertine" profligacy during widespread social misery. Each was fined £500, a considerable*

---

[2]A little under 5′1″, Keats was self-conscious about his appearance to "womankind" (see his letter to Bailey, 22 July 1818).

sum. Clarke went to greet Hunt on his release, and Keats walked part of the way with him, giving him this sonnet before they parted. It was Clarke's first awareness that Keats was writing poetry during his surgeon's apprenticeship. Long an admirer of Hunt, Keats finally met him in October 1816.

WHAT though, for showing truth to flatter'd state,
    Kind Hunt was shut in prison, yet has he,
      In his immortal spirit, been as free
As the sky-searching lark, and as elate.
Minion of grandeur! think you he did wait?
    Think you he nought but prison walls did see,
      Till, so unwilling, thou unturn'dst the key?
Ah, no! far happier, nobler was his fate!
In Spenser's halls he strayed, and bowers fair,
    Culling enchanted flowers; and he flew   10
      With daring Milton through the fields of air:
To regions of his own his genius true
Took happy flights.[3] Who shall his fame impair
When thou art dead, and all thy wretched crew?

IV.

HOW many bards gild the lapses of time![4]
    A few of them have ever been the food
    Of my delighted fancy,—I could brood
Over their beauties, earthly, or sublime:
And often, when I sit me down to rhyme,
    These will in throngs before my mind intrude:
    But no confusion, no disturbance rude
Do they occasion; 'tis a pleasing chime.
So the unnumber'd[5] sounds that evening store;

---

[3]Hunt transformed his cell into a salon, with wallpaper, a sky-painted ceiling, carpets, busts, a library, a piano, a small garden outside, the company of his wife, and visits from everyone, including Lord Byron. He wrote much of *The Story of Rimini* during his imprisonment.

[4]Written early Oct. 1816. The first line echoes Coleridge's *To the Nightingale* (1796): "Sister of love-lorn Poets, Philomel! / How many Bards in city garret pent, / . . . address *thy* name" (1–7). When Clarke showed Hunt the ms of this sonnet, Hunt urged him to bring K along on his next visit.

[5]A poet's pun: infinite, but also not yet rendered in poetic meters (numbers).

The songs of birds—the whisp'ring of the leaves—   10
The voice of waters—the great bell that heaves
   With solemn sound,—and thousand others more,
That distance of recognizance bereaves,
   Make pleasing music, and not wild uproar.[6]

V.

To a Friend who sent me some Roses.[7]

As late I rambled in the happy fields,
   What time the sky-lark shakes the tremulous dew
   From his lush clover covert;——when anew
Adventurous knights take up their dinted shields:
I saw the sweetest flower wild nature yields,
   A fresh-blown musk-rose; 'twas the first that threw
   Its sweets upon the summer: graceful it grew
As is the wand that queen Titania[8] wields.
And, as I feasted on its fragrancy,
   I thought the garden-rose it far excell'd: 10
But when, O Wells! thy roses came to me
   My sense with their deliciousness was spell'd:
Soft voices had they, that with tender plea
   Whisper'd of peace, and truth, and friendliness unquell'd.[9]

VIII.

TO MY BROTHERS.

SMALL, busy flames play through the fresh laid coals,
   And their faint cracklings o'er our silence creep
   Like whispers of the household gods that keep
A gentle empire o'er fraternal souls.

---

[6] "Confusion heard his voice, and wild Uproar / Stood ruled," recalls archangel Uriel of God's Creation (*PL* 3.710–11), lines marked by K.

[7] Written June 1816. Charles Wells (b. 1800), schoolfellow of Tom Keats, friend of Hunt and Hazlitt, would become a publishing author. The roses (the musk-rose is a white-rose rambler) may have been a genuine gesture, or a campy role-playing.

[8] The Fairy Queen in *A Midsummer Night's Dream.*

[9] This alexandrine may be an homage to the *FQ* stanza.

And while, for rhymes, I search around the poles,
    Your eyes are fix'd, as in poetic sleep,
    Upon the lore so voluble and deep,
That aye at fall of night our care condoles.
This is your birth-day Tom,[10] and I rejoice
    That thus it passes smoothly, quietly.   10
Many such eves of gently whisp'ring noise
    May we together pass, and calmly try
What are this world's true joys,—ere the great voice,
    From its fair face, shall bid our spirits fly.
November 18, 1816.

IX.[11]

KEEN, fitful gusts are whisp'ring here and there
    Among the bushes half leafless, and dry;
    The stars look very cold about the sky,
And I have many miles on foot to fare.
Yet feel I little of the cool bleak air,
    Or of the dead leaves rustling drearily,
    Or of those silver lamps that burn on high,
Or of the distance from home's pleasant lair:
For I am brimfull of the friendliness
    That in a little cottage I have found;   10
Of fair-hair'd Milton's eloquent distress,
    And all his love for gentle Lycid drown'd;
Of lovely Laura in her light green dress,
    And faithful Petrarch gloriously crown'd.[12]

---

[10]The brothers had just begun to live together in a small apartment in Cheapside, London's commercial district. Tom, 17 years old (b. 1799), was no longer able to work because of his health—hence the relief that his birthday passes comfortably.

[11]Composed Oct.–early Nov. 1816, after visiting Hunt's home on Hampstead Heath (over 5 miles north of London). K had just met Hunt.

[12]Poetry K discussed with Hunt: Milton's *Lycidas*, a pastoral elegy for drowned Edward King; Italian poet Petrarch's 14th-c. sonnets and songs about beloved Laura (who dies). Hunt had a picture of the pair in his study. Petrarch was honored with a laurel-wreath crown. K owned Petrarch's sonnets and odes in John Nott's translation (London, 1808).

X

To one who has been long in city pent,[13]
 'Tis very sweet to look into the fair
 And open face of heaven,—to breathe a prayer
Full in the smile of the blue firmament.
Who is more happy, when, with hearts content,
 Fatigued he sinks into some pleasant lair
 Of wavy grass, and reads a debonair[14]
And gentle tale of love and languishment?
Returning home at evening, with an ear
 Catching the notes of Philomel,[15]—an eye   10
Watching the sailing cloudlet's bright career,
 He mourns that day so soon has glided by:
E'en like the passage of an angel's tear
 That falls through the clear ether silently.

XIII
ADDRESSED TO HAYDON.[16]

HIGHMINDEDNESS, a jealousy for good,
 A loving-kindness for the great man's fame,
 Dwells here and there with people of no name,
In noisome alley, and in pathless wood:
And where we think the truth least understood,

---

[13]Composed June 1816, a few weeks after *To Solitude*, in the countryside beyond London (K was studying medicine in south London). The first line is a conscious echo of Milton's epic simile for Satan, escaped from the city of Pandemonium in Hell to Eden: "As one who long in populous city pent, / Where houses thick and sewers annoy the air, / Forth issuing on a summer's morn to breathe / Among the pleasant villages and farms . . ." (*PL* 9.445ff; K underlined 447–51). Coleridge refers to "city pent" in *Frost at Midnight* (1798) about his loneliness as a boy in London (52); in *This Lime-tree Bower my Prison* (1800), imagining Charles Lamb "hunger[ing] after Nature, many a year, / In the great City pent" (28–30); and in *To the Nightingale* (1796; see "How many bards," p. 26, n. 4).

[14]graceful and elegant; literally punning "of good air" (the air outside the city).

[15]literally, "lover of music" (*melody* has the same root)—a poet's term for nightingale, informed by the (considerably darker) tale in Ovid's *Metamorphoses*.

[16]Written between March and Nov. 1816 (when K first visited Haydon's studio). Haydon was painting *Christ's Entry into Jerusalem*, in which K, Lamb, Wordsworth, Hazlitt, and others Haydon admired appear in the crowd.

Oft may be found a "singleness of aim,"[17]
That ought to frighten into hooded shame
A money mong'ring, pitiable brood.
How glorious this affection for the cause
   Of stedfast genius, toiling gallantly!   10
What when a stout unbending champion awes
   Envy, and Malice to their native sty?
Unnumber'd souls breathe out a still applause,
   Proud to behold him in his country's eye.[18]

XIV
ADDRESSED TO THE SAME.

GREAT spirits now on earth are sojourning;
   He of the cloud, the cataract, the lake,
   Who on Helvellyn's summit, wide awake,
Catches his freshness from Archangel's wing:[19]
He of the rose, the violet, the spring,
   The social smile, the chain for Freedom's sake:[20]
   And lo!—whose stedfastness would never take
A meaner sound than Raphael's whispering.[21]
And other spirits there are standing apart
   Upon the forehead of the age to come;   10
These, these will give the world another heart,
   And other pulses. Hear ye not the hum
Of mighty workings?————[22]
   Listen awhile ye nations, and be dumb.

[17]Wordsworth's *Character of the Happy Warrior* (1807; 1815): "Keeps faithful with a singleness of aim" (40), a tribute to Adm. Nelson, who died at the Battle of Trafalgar in 1805. Not only does K put Haydon in this warrior company, he also signals his poetic alliance with Wordsworth, whose praising sonnet *To B. R. Haydon* appeared in *The Examiner*, 31 March 1816.

[18]Haydon passionately defended the authenticity and aesthetic value of the Elgin Marbles in *The Examiner*, 17 March 1816; the government approved their purchase for the British Museum.

[19]Wordsworth often climbed Helvellyn, the highest peak in his native Lake District.

[20]Hunt, with a reference to his going to prison on principle.

[21]K may be comparing Haydon to Italian Renaissance painter Raphael, as had Hunt in his sonnet *To Benjamin Robert Haydon* (Oct. 1816); K may also mean the affable Archangel Raphael of *PL*, who visits Eden to converse with Adam. *meaner*: humbler, less worthy.

[22]letter] "Of mighty Workings in a distant Mart?" K accepted Haydon's suggestion to halt the line at "workings." See p. 5, n. 5.

XV

On the Grasshopper and Cricket

On 30 December Hunt set a contest to write a sonnet in fifteen min-
utes on the title's subject; Keats finished first.

THE poetry of earth is never dead:
  When all the birds are faint with the hot sun,
  And hide in cooling trees, a voice will run
From hedge to hedge[23] about the new-mown mead;
That is the Grasshopper's—he takes the lead
  In summer luxury,——he has never done
  With his delights; for when tired out with fun
He rests at ease beneath some pleasant weed.
The poetry of earth is ceasing never:
  On a lone winter evening, when the frost   10
    Has wrought a silence, from the stove there shrills
The Cricket's song, in warmth increasing ever,
  And seems to one in drowsiness half lost,
    The Grasshopper's among some grassy hills.

December 30, 1816

§ The Sonnet-Contest

Of Keats's opening line, Hunt exclaimed, "Such a prosperous open-
ing" and of lines 10–11 (to "silence"), "Ah! that's perfect! Bravo
Keats!" He published his own sonnet underneath Keats's in The Examiner *(21 September 1817, p. 599), both headed with the main title,*
TWO SONNETS ON THE GRASSHOPPER AND CRICKET. *Titling Keats's son-*
net FROM THE POEMS BY JOHN KEATS, *he also meant to advertise the*
1817 volume.

BY LEIGH HUNT;—NEVER BEFORE PUBLISHED.

GREEN little vaulter in the sunny grass,
  Catching your heart up at the feel of June,
  Sole voice left stirring midst the lazy noon,

---

[23]A poet's pun on poetic form: the syntax enacts its *enjambment* ("striding across"),
running over the line-boundary.

When ev'n the bees lag at the summoning brass;—
And you, warm little housekeeper, who class
   With those who think the candles come too soon,
   Loving the fire, and with your tricksome tune
Nick the glad silent moments as they pass;—
O sweet and tiny cousins, that belong,
   One to the fields, the other to the hearth,   10
Both have your sunshine; both though small are strong
   At your clear hearts; and both were sent on earth
To ring in thoughtful ears this natural song,
   —In doors and out,—summer and winter,—Mirth.

December 30, 1816.

XVII

HAPPY is England! I could be content
   To see no other verdure than its own;
   To feel no other breezes than are blown
Through its tall woods with high romances blent:
Yet do I sometimes feel a languishment
   For skies Italian, and an inward groan
   To sit upon an Alp as on a throne,
And half forget what world or worldling meant.
Happy is England, sweet her artless daughters;
   Enough their simple loveliness for me,   10
      Enough their whitest arms in silence clinging:
Yet do I often warmly burn to see
      Beauties of deeper glance, and hear their singing,
And float with them about the summer waters.

SLEEP AND POETRY

*Keats composed this poem, the volume's longest, in late 1816 and,
though he completed it earlier than "I stood tip-toe," he made it the
closing piece, a summary declaration of aims and aspirations. Heralded by a separate page for the title and epigraph, with the title
reprised at the top of the poem, it opens with unabashed "romance"
couplets, flaunting "feminine" rhymes and rejecting regular iambic*

meter, as in "I stood tip-toe." The bold refusal of neoclassical poetics and poets (162ff) won praise from Hunt and Haydon, the contempt of conservative reviews, and the disdain of Byron, an admirer of Pope.

> "As I lay in my bed slepe full unmete
> Was unto me, but why that I ne might
> Rest I ne wist, for there n'as erthly wight
> [As I suppose] had more of hertis ese
> Than I, for I n'ad sicknesse nor disese."
>   CHAUCER.[1]

WHAT is more gentle than a wind in summer?
What is more soothing than the pretty hummer
That stays one moment in an open flower,
And buzzes cheerily from bower to bower?
What is more tranquil than a musk-rose blowing°   *blooming*
In a green island, far from all men's knowing?
More healthful than the leafiness of dales?
More secret than a nest of nightingales?
More serene than Cordelia's countenance?[2]
More full of visions than a high romance?   10
What, but thee Sleep? Soft closer of our eyes!
Low murmurer of tender lullabies!
Light hoverer around our happy pillows!
Wreather of poppy buds, and weeping willows!
Silent entangler of a beauty's tresses![3]
Most happy listener! when the morning blesses
Thee for enlivening all the cheerful eyes
That glance so brightly at the new sun-rise.

But what is higher beyond thought than thee?
Fresher than berries of a mountain tree?   20

---

[1] *The Floure and the Leafe*, a 600-line allegorical romance thought at the time to be by Chaucer (K owned a multi-volume 1782 edition). K's sonnet, *Written on a Blank Space at the End of Chaucer's Tale of "The Floure and the Lefe,"* was published by Hunt in *The Examiner*, March 1817, the same month that *Poems* appeared.

[2] King Lear's faithful daughter

[3] More poetic wit: the phrase "beauty's tresses" also entangles the letters of "beauty stresses"—the sway of beauty over strict metrics; this eleven-syllable line has only four stresses.

More strange, more beautiful, more smooth, more regal,
Than wings of swans, than doves, than dim-seen eagle?
What is it? And to what shall I compare it?
It has a glory, and nought else can share it:
The thought thereof is awful,° sweet, and holy,   *full of awe*
Chacing away all worldliness and folly;
Coming sometimes like fearful claps of thunder,
Or the low rumblings earth's regions under;
And sometimes like a gentle whispering
Of all the secrets of some wond'rous thing   30
That breathes about us in the vacant air;
So that we look around with prying stare,
Perhaps to see shapes of light, aerial lymning,°   *drawing*
And catch soft floatings from a faint-heard hymning;
To see the laurel wreath, on high suspended,
That is to crown our name when life is ended.
Sometimes it gives a glory to the voice,
And from the heart up-springs, rejoice! rejoice!
Sounds which will reach the Framer of all things,
And die away in ardent mutterings.   40

No one who once the glorious sun has seen,
And all the clouds, and felt his bosom clean
For his great Maker's presence, but must know
What 'tis I mean, and feel his being glow:
Therefore no insult will I give his spirit,
By telling what he sees from native merit.

O Poesy! for thee I hold my pen
That am not yet a glorious denizen⁴
Of thy wide heaven——Should I rather kneel
Upon some mountain-top until I feel   50
A glowing splendour round about me hung,
And echo back the voice of thine own tongue?
O Poesy! for thee I grasp my pen
That am not yet a glorious denizen
Of thy wide heaven; yet, to my ardent prayer,

⁴naturalized citizen

Yield from thy sanctuary some clear air,
Smoothed for intoxication by the breath
Of flowering bays, that I may die a death
Of luxury, and my young spirit follow
The morning sun-beams to the great Apollo   60
Like a fresh sacrifice; or, if I can bear
The o'erwhelming sweets, 'twill bring to me the fair
Visions of all places: a bowery nook
Will be Elysium—an eternal book
Whence I may copy many a lovely saying
About the leaves, and flowers—about the playing
Of nymphs in woods, and fountains; and the shade
Keeping a silence round a sleeping maid;
And many a verse from so strange influence
That we must ever wonder how, and whence   70
It came.[5] Also imaginings will hover[6]
Round my fire-side, and haply there discover
Vistas of solemn beauty, where I'd wander
In happy silence, like the clear meander[7]
Through its lone vales; and where I found a spot
Of awfuller shade, or an enchanted grot,°   *grotto*
Or a green hill o'erspread with chequered dress
Of flowers, and fearful from its loveliness,
Write on my tablets all that was permitted,
All that was for our human senses fitted.   80
Then the events of this wide world I'd seize
Like a strong giant, and my spirit teaze
Till at its shoulders it should proudly see
Wings to find out an immortality.

Stop and consider! life is but a day;
A fragile dew-drop on its perilous way
From a tree's summit; a poor Indian's sleep
While his boat hastens to the monstrous steep

[5]The musing on strange influence is influenced by Wordsworth's lines on his love of nature: "An instinct call it, a blind sense; / A happy, genial influence, / Coming one knows not how, nor whence, / Nor whither going" (*To the Daisy* 69–72).

[6]K sets *hover* to hover at the end of the line.

[7]A famously winding river in Asia Minor, the eponym of the verb.

Of Montmorenci.[8] Why so sad a moan?
Life is the rose's hope while yet unblown;   90
The reading of an ever-changing tale;
The light uplifting of a maiden's veil;
A pigeon tumbling in clear summer air;
A laughing school-boy, without grief or care,
Riding the springy branches of an elm.

O for ten years, that I may overwhelm[9]
Myself in poesy; so I may do the deed
That my own soul has to itself decreed.
Then will I pass the countries that I see
In long perspective, and continually   100
Taste their pure fountains. First the realm I'll pass
Of Flora, and old Pan:[10] sleep in the grass,
Feed upon apples red, and strawberries,
And choose each pleasure that my fancy[11] sees;
Catch the white-handed nymphs in shady places,
To woo sweet kisses from averted faces,—
Play with their fingers, touch their shoulders white
Into a pretty shrinking with a bite
As hard as lips can make it: till agreed,
A lovely tale of human life we'll read.   110
And one will teach a tame dove how it best
May fan the cool air gently o'er my rest;
Another, bending o'er her nimble tread,
Will set a green robe floating round her head,
And still will dance with ever varied ease,
Smiling upon the flowers and the trees:
Another will entice me on, and on
Through almond blossoms and rich cinnamon;
Till in the bosom of a leafy world
We rest in silence, like two gems upcurl'd   120
In the recesses of a pearly shell.

[8]This river in Quebec descends into a spectacular, lucid 275-ft. waterfall.
[9]Not only enjambed syntax but a daring, dramatic split of the couplet as well.
[10]pastoral poetry and light romance
[11]"Fancy" is regarded as a lesser, more juvenile mental exertion than "imagination"; see *Fancy* in the *Lamia* vol.

And can I ever bid these joys farewell?[12]
Yes, I must pass them for a nobler life,
Where I may find the agonies, the strife
Of human hearts: for lo! I see afar,
O'er sailing the blue cragginess, a car
And steeds with streamy manes—the charioteer
Looks out upon the winds with glorious fear:[13]
And now the numerous tramplings quiver lightly
Along a huge cloud's ridge; and now with sprightly   130
Wheel downward come they into fresher skies,
Tipt round with silver from the sun's bright eyes.
Still downward with capacious whirl they glide;
And now I see them on a green-hill's side
In breezy rest among the nodding stalks.
The charioteer with wond'rous gesture talks
To the trees and mountains; and there soon appear
Shapes of delight, of mystery, and fear,
Passing along before a dusky space
Made by some mighty oaks: as they would chase   140
Some ever-fleeting music on they sweep.
Lo! how they murmur, laugh, and smile, and weep:
Some with upholden hand and mouth severe;
Some with their faces muffled to the ear
Between their arms; some, clear in youthful bloom,
Go glad and smilingly athwart the gloom;
Some looking back, and some with upward gaze;
Yes, thousands in a thousand different ways
Flit onward—now a lovely wreath of girls
Dancing their sleek hair into tangled curls;   150
And now broad wings. Most awfully intent
The driver of those steeds is forward bent,
And seems to listen: O that I might know
All that he writes with such a hurrying glow.

---

[12]Another dramatically split couplet (this is a new stanza). The pattern of a poetic career, from classical times through the 18th c., matures from pastoral subjects and short poetic forms (sonnets, songs) to the "masculine" endeavors of epic poetry or tragic drama.

[13]Personification of the Epic poet when the enthusiasm of inspiration is upon him. [Woodhouse, in his annotated copy of Keats's *Poems*]

The visions all are fled—the car is fled
Into the light of heaven, and in their stead
A sense of real things comes doubly strong,
And, like a muddy stream, would bear along
My soul to nothingness: but I will strive
Against all doubtings, and will keep alive   160
The thought of that same chariot, and the strange
Journey it went.

       Is there so small a range[14]
In the present strength of manhood, that the high
Imagination cannot freely fly
As she was wont° of old? prepare her steeds,   *used to*
Paw up against the light, and do strange deeds
Upon the clouds? Has she not shewn us all?
From the clear space of ether, to the small
Breath of new buds unfolding? From the meaning
Of Jove's large eye-brow, to the tender greening   170
Of April meadows? Here her altar shone,
E'en in this isle; and who could paragon
The fervid choir that lifted up a noise
Of harmony, to where it aye° will poise   *forever*
Its mighty self of convoluting sound,
Huge as a planet, and like that roll round,
Eternally around a dizzy void?[15]
Ay, in those days the Muses were nigh cloy'd
With honors; nor had any other care
Than to sing out and sooth their wavy hair.   180

Could all this be forgotten? Yes, a scism°   *schism*
Nurtured by foppery and barbarism,
Made great Apollo blush for this his land.
Men were thought wise who could not understand
His glories: with a puling infant's force
They sway'd about upon a rocking horse,

[14]A dramatically split metrical line. K criticizes the present state of poetry, still dominated by 18th-c. principles; the imagery alludes to the winged horse Pegasus, dear to the Muses.
[15]English poetry before the neoclassical era, imaged as a heavenly planet that contributes to the music of the spheres (cosmic harmony).

And thought it Pegasus.[16] Ah dismal soul'd!
The winds of heaven blew, the ocean roll'd
Its gathering waves—ye felt it not. The blue
Bared its eternal bosom,[17] and the dew   190
Of summer nights collected still to make
The morning precious: beauty was awake!
Why were ye not awake? But ye were dead
To things ye knew not of,—were closely wed
To musty laws lined out with wretched rule
And compass vile: so that ye taught a school
Of dolts to smooth, inlay, and clip, and fit,
Till, like the certain wands of Jacob's wit,
Their verses tallied.[18] Easy was the task:
A thousand handicraftsmen wore the mask   200
Of Poesy. Ill-fated, impious race!
That blasphemed the bright Lyrist° to his face,   *Apollo*
And did not know it,—no, they went about,
Holding a poor, decrepid standard out
Mark'd with most flimsy mottos, and in large
The name of one Boileau![19]

               O ye whose charge
It is to hover round our pleasant hills!
Whose congregated majesty so fills
My boundly[20] reverence, that I cannot trace
Your hallowed names, in this unholy place,   210
So near those common folk; did not their shames
Affright you? Did our old lamenting Thames
Delight you? Did ye never cluster round

[16]A nod to Hazlitt's remark that neoclassical poets "Dr. Johnson and Pope, would have converted [Milton's] vaulting Pegasus into a rocking horse" (*Examiner*, 20 Aug. 1815, 542).

[17]Echoing Wordsworth's sonnet "The world is too much with us," a lament for modern life as "out of tune" with such natural beauty as "The Sea that bares her bosom to the moon" (5).

[18]*tallied*: got the desired number (of metrical feet). With a trickery of wands, Jacob got Laban's herds to conceive speckled issue, which by agreement would become his (Genesis 30.27–43); "certain wands" is from Shylock's reference to this stratagem in *The Merchant of Venice* (1.3.81).

[19]Nicolas Boileau-Despréaux, French poet and literary critic whose verse treatise *L'Art poétique* (1674) was a neoclassic primer.

[20]Keats's coinage

Delicious Avon, with a mournful sound,
And weep? Or did ye wholly bid adieu
To regions where no more the laurel grew?
Or did ye stay to give a welcoming
To some lone spirits who could proudly sing
Their youth away, and die?[21] 'Twas even so:
But let me think away those times of woe: 220
Now 'tis a fairer season; ye have breathed
Rich benedictions o'er us; ye have wreathed
Fresh garlands: for sweet music has been heard
In many places;—some has been upstirr'd
From out its crystal dwelling in a lake,
By a swan's ebon bill; from a thick brake,
Nested and quiet in a valley mild,
Bubbles a pipe; fine sounds are floating wild
About the earth: happy are ye and glad.[22]

These things are doubtless: yet in truth we've had   230
Strange thunders from the potency of song;
Mingled indeed with what is sweet and strong,
From majesty: but in clear truth the themes
Are ugly clubs, the Poets Polyphemes
Disturbing the grand sea.[23] A drainless shower
Of light is poesy; 'tis the supreme of power;
'Tis might half slumb'ring on its own right arm.
The very archings of her eye-lids charm
A thousand willing agents to obey,
And still she governs with the mildest sway: 240
But strength alone though of the Muses born
Is like a fallen angel: trees uptorn,
Darkness, and worms, and shrouds, and sepulchres
Delight it; for it feeds upon the burrs,

[21]All sad legends of poets who died young: Thomas Chatterton (1752–70), a suicide at age 17, and Henry Kirke White (1785–1806), dead of poverty and overwork at 21.

[22]Praising Hunt's poetry, in contrast to the dark turbulences of Coleridge and Byron.

[23]In his review for *The Examiner* (13 July 1817), Hunt glossed these lines as a reference to "the morbidity that taints the productions of the Lake Poets" (Wordsworth and Coleridge, who lived in the Lake District). In the *Odyssey*, giant Polyphemus, blinded with his own club by Ulysses, tries to sink Ulysses's ship by hurling a rock into the sea.

And thorns of life; forgetting the great end
Of poesy, that it should be a friend
To sooth[24] the cares, and lift the thoughts of man.

   Yet I rejoice: a myrtle fairer than
E'er grew in Paphos, from the bitter weeds
Lifts its sweet head into the air, and feeds   250
A silent space with ever sprouting green.
All tenderest birds there find a pleasant screen,
Creep through the shade with jaunty fluttering,
Nibble the little cupped flowers and sing.
Then let us clear away the choaking thorns
From round its gentle stem; let the young fawns,
Yeaned° in after times, when we are flown,   *birthed*
Find a fresh sward beneath it, overgrown
With simple flowers: let there nothing be
More boisterous than a lover's bended knee;   260
Nought more ungentle than the placid look
Of one who leans upon a closed book;
Nought more untranquil than the grassy slopes
Between two hills. All hail delightful hopes!
As she was wont, th' imagination
Into most lovely labyrinths will be gone,
And they shall be accounted poet kings
Who simply tell the most heart-easing things.

O may these joys be ripe before I die.

Will not some say that I presumptuously   270
Have spoken? that from hastening disgrace
'Twere better far to hide my foolish face?
That whining boyhood should with reverence bow
Ere the dread thunderbolt could reach? How!
If I do hide myself, it sure shall be
In the very fane,° the light of Poesy: *temple, altar*
If I do fall, at least I will be laid
Beneath the silence of a poplar shade;
And over me the grass shall be smooth shaven;
And there shall be a kind memorial graven.   280

[24]soothe, with a hint of the old word for "truth"

But off Despondence! miserable bane!
They should not know thee, who athirst to gain
A noble end, are thirsty every hour.
What though I am not wealthy in the dower
Of spanning wisdom; though I do not know
The shiftings of the mighty winds that blow
Hither and thither all the changing thoughts
Of man: though no great minist'ring reason sorts[25]
Out the dark mysteries of human souls
To clear conceiving: yet there ever rolls   290
A vast idea before me, and I glean
Therefrom my liberty; thence too I've seen
The end and aim of Poesy. 'Tis clear
As any thing most true; as that the year
Is made of the four seasons—manifest
As a large cross, some old cathedral's crest,
Lifted to the white clouds. Therefore should I
Be but the essence of deformity,[26]
A coward, did my very eye-lids wink
At speaking out what I have dared to think.   300
Ah! rather let me like a madman run
Over some precipice; let the hot sun
Melt my Dedalian wings, and drive me down
Convuls'd and headlong![27] Stay! an inward frown
Of conscience bids me be more calm awhile.
An ocean dim, sprinkled with many an isle,
Spreads awfully before me. How much toil!
How many days! what desperate turmoil!
Ere I can have explored its widenesses.
Ah, what a task! upon my bended knees,   310
I could unsay those—no, impossible!
Impossible!

　　　　For sweet relief I'll dwell
On humbler thoughts, and let this strange assay

[25]The sort of "Cockney rhyme" for which K would be mocked: K may have heard these
words as rhymes, or he may be indulging an *avant-garde* play against rhyme protocols.
[26]Though the rhyme is slant and half-stressed, it is arresting: this is the only instance
of a rhyme with "I" in this poem of self-declaration.
[27]Referring to artificer Daedalus and his reckless son Icarus.

Begun in gentleness die so away.
E'en now all tumult from my bosom fades:
I turn full hearted to the friendly aids
That smooth the path of honour; brotherhood,
And friendliness the nurse of mutual good.
The hearty grasp that sends a pleasant sonnet
Into the brain ere one can think upon it;   320
The silence when some rhymes are coming out;
And when they're come, the very pleasant rout:°   *crowd*
The message certain to be done to-morrow.
'Tis perhaps as well that it should be to borrow
Some precious book from out its snug retreat,
To cluster round it when we next shall meet.
Scarce can I scribble on; for lovely airs
Are fluttering round the room like doves in pairs;
Many delights of that glad day recalling,
When first my senses caught their tender falling.   330
And with these airs come forms of elegance
Stooping their shoulders o'er a horse's prance,
Careless, and grand—fingers soft and round
Parting luxuriant curls;—and the swift bound
Of Bacchus from his chariot, when his eye
Made Ariadne's cheek look blushingly.[28]
Thus I remember all the pleasant flow
Of words at opening a portfolio.

Things such as these are ever harbingers
To trains of peaceful images: the stirs   340
Of a swan's neck unseen among the rushes:
A linnet starting all about the bushes:
A butterfly, with golden wings broad parted,
Nestling a rose, convuls'd as though it smarted
With over pleasure—many, many more,
Might I indulge at large in all my store
Of luxuries: yet I must not forget
Sleep, quiet with his poppy[29] coronet:
For what there may be worthy in these rhymes

[28]K admired Titian's *Bacchus and Ariadne* when it was exhibited in London in 1816.
[29]the source of opium

I partly owe to him: and thus, the chimes   350
Of friendly voices had just given place
To as sweet a silence, when I 'gan retrace
The pleasant day, upon a couch at ease.
It was a poet's house who keeps the keys
Of pleasure's temple.[30] Round about were hung
The glorious features of the bards who sung
In other ages—cold and sacred busts
Smiled at each other. Happy he who trusts
To clear Futurity his darling fame!
Then there were fauns and satyrs taking aim   360
At swelling apples with a frisky leap
And reaching fingers, 'mid a luscious heap
Of vine leaves. Then there rose to view a fane
Of liny marble, and thereto a train
Of nymphs approaching fairly o'er the sward:
One, loveliest, holding her white hand toward
The dazzling sun-rise: two sisters sweet
Bending their graceful figures till they meet
Over the trippings of a little child:
And some are hearing, eagerly, the wild   370
Thrilling liquidity of dewy piping.
See, in another picture, nymphs are wiping
Cherishingly Diana's timorous limbs;—
A fold of lawny mantle dabbling swims
At the bath's edge, and keeps a gentle motion
With the subsiding crystal: as when ocean
Heaves calmly its broad swelling smoothiness o'er
Its rocky marge, and balances once more
The patient weeds; that now unshent° by foam   *unspoiled*
Feel all about their undulating home.   380

Sappho's meek head was there half smiling down
At nothing; just as though the earnest frown
Of over thinking had that moment gone
From off her brow, and left her all alone.[31]

---

[30]K spent the night on the sofa in Hunt's library.

[31]The celebrated poet of 7th c. BCE was often represented in an agony of love passion, most poignantly after being spurned by boatman Phaon.

Great Alfred's too, with anxious, pitying eyes,
As if he always listened to the sighs
Of the goaded world;[32] and Kosciusko's worn
By horrid suffrance[33]—mightily forlorn.

Petrarch, outstepping from the shady green,
Starts at the sight of Laura; nor can wean   390
His eyes from her sweet face.[34] Most happy they!
For over them was seen a free display
Of out-spread wings, and from between them shone
The face of Poesy: from off her throne
She overlook'd things that I scarce could tell.
The very sense of where I was might well
Keep Sleep aloof: but more than that there came
Thought after thought to nourish up the flame
Within my breast; so that the morning light
Surprised me even from a sleepless night;   400
And up I rose refresh'd, and glad, and gay,
Resolving to begin that very day
These lines; and howsoever they be done,
I leave them as a father does his son.[35]

𝔉𝔦𝔫𝔦𝔰

[32]Alfred the Great, 9th-c. Saxon king

[33]Polish patriot Tadeusz Kosciusko (1746–1817), hero of British liberalism, served in George Washington's army in 1776, led a vastly outnumbered Polish uprising against the Russian army in 1794, and in 1798 resisted Napoleon's designs on Poland. K's poem of praise, written Dec. 1816, appeared in *The Examiner*, 16 Feb. 1817 (Hunt promptly showed it to William Godwin, the Shelleys, and Hazlitt), and as Sonnet XVI in *Poems*.

[34]Petrarch wrote a famous series of sonnets and songs to his beloved Laura.

[35]A strangely double syntax, especially at the volume's close. The analogy proposes that the poet leaves his lines to his readers, as a father might leave a son to the world; but after the references to Icarus, who left his father, the syntax evokes a father who might abandon his son (K, whose own father was dead by now, abandoned by his poetic fathers).

To Haydon, with a sonnet written on seeing the Elgin Marbles

To Haydon *appeared in* The Examiner, *9 March 1817 (p. 155), and also in* The Champion *on the same date (with Reynolds's review of* Poems*). Later, it was published in Haydon's* Annals of the Fine Arts, *April 1818, and then 1848 (1: 27–28). Keats wrote the sonnets after visiting the British Museum with Haydon early in March, and he returned often to stare at the these sculptural fragments. Amid hot debates about their aesthetic value, authenticity, and the government's purchase, Keats shared Haydon's sense of the strange power of these marble remnants.*

ORIGINAL POETRY

TO HAYDON

WITH A SONNET WRITTEN ON SEEING THE ELGIN MARBLES.

HAYDON! forgive me that I cannot speak
    Definitively on these mighty things;
    Forgive me that I have not Eagle's wings—
That what I want I know not where to seek:
And think that I would not be overmeek
    In rolling out upfollow'd thunderings,
    Even to the steep[1] of Heliconian springs,
Were I of ample strength for such a freak[2]—
Think, too, that all those numbers[3] should be thine;
    Whose else? In this who touch thy vestur'd hem?
For when men star'd at what was most divine
    With browless idiotism—o'erwise phlegm[4]—
Thou hadst beheld the Hesperean shine
    Of their star in the East, and gone to worship them.

[1]*steep* is a misprint for sleep (K's ms, emended in *Champion* and *Annals*).

[2]misshapen fancy, extravagance, playful venture

[3]meters, verses

[4]shameless ignorance, too sophisticated contempt. Phlegm is one of the four humors of early physiology, its excess thought to produce coldness or indifference. K's praises of Haydon obliquely compare him to one of the magi seeking the infant Jesus.

ON SEEING THE ELGIN MARBLES.

My spirit is too weak—Mortality
  Weighs heavily on me like unwilling sleep,
  And each imagin'd pinnacle and steep
Of godlike hardship, tells me I must die
Like a sick Eagle looking at the sky.
  Yet 'tis a gentle luxury to weep
  That I have not the cloudy winds to keep,
Fresh for the opening of the morning's eye.
Such dim-conceived glories of the brain
  Bring round the heart an undescribable feud;
So do these wonders a most dizzy pain,
  That mingles Grecian grandeur with the rude
Wasting of old time—with a billowy main—
  A sun——a shadow of a magnitude.

                               J.K.

Letter to J. H. Reynolds, 17–18 April 1817[1]

Keats is on the Isle of Wight, reading Shakespeare and gearing up for the trail of Endymion.

My dear Reynolds,
Ever since I wrote to my Brothers from Southampton I have been in a taking, and at this moment I am about to become settled, for I have unpacked my books, put them into a snug corner - pinned up Haydon - Mary Queen Scotts, and Milton with his daughters in a row. In the passage I found a head of Shakspeare which I had not before seen. It is most likely the same that George spoke so well of, for I like it extremely. Well - this head I have hung over my Books, just above the three in a row, having first discarded a french Ambassador - now this alone is a good morning's work. - Yesterday I went to Shanklin, ~~which~~ *occasioned a great debate in my Mind whether I should live there or at Carisbrooke. Shanklin is a most beautiful place - sloping wood and*

[1]WLB 43–45

meadow ground reaches round the Chine, which is a cleft between the Cliffs of the depth of nearly 300 feet at least. This cleft is filled with trees & bushes in the narrow part; and as it widens becomes bare, if it were not for primroses on one side, which spread to the very verge of the Sea, and some fishermen's huts on the other, which perched midway in the Ballustrades of beautiful green Hedges along their steps down to the sands. – But the sea, Jack, the sea – the little waterfall – then the white cliff—then S[t] Catherine's Hill—"the sheep in the meadows, the cows in the corn."[2]– Then, why are you at Carisbrooke? say you – Because, in the first place, I sho[d] be at twice the Expense, and three times the inconvenience – next that from here I can see your continent— from a little hill close by, the whole north Angle of the Isle of Wight, with the water between us. In the 3[d] place, I see Carisbrooke Castle from my window, and have found several delightful wood-alleys, and copses, and quick freshes[3] – As for Primroses – the Island ought to be called Primrose Island: that is, if the nation of Cowslips agree thereto, of which there are diverse Clans just beginning to lift up their heads and if an how the Rain holds whereby that is Birds eyes abate – Another reason of my fixing is that I am more in reach of the places around me – I intend to walk over the Island east – West – North South – I have not seen many specimens of Ruins – I dont think however I shall ever see one to surpass Carisbrooke Castle. The trench is o'ergrown with the smoothest turf, and the Walls with ivy – The Keep within side is one Bower of ivy – a Colony of Jackdaws have been there many years. I dare say I have seen many a descendant of some old cawer who peeped through the Bars at Charles the first, when he was there in Confinement.[4] On the road from Cowes to Newport I saw some extensive Barracks which disgusted me extremely with Government for placing such a Nest of Debauchery in so beautiful a place – I asked a man on the coach about this – and he said that the people had been spoiled – In the room where I slept at Newport I found this on the Window "O Isle spoilt by the Mi<u>l</u>atary!" – I must in honesty however confess that I did not feel very sorry at the idea of the Women being a little profligate[5] – The wind is in a sulky fit, and I feel that it would be

[2]From the nursery rhyme, "Little Boy Blue, come blow your horn."

[3]fresh springs of water, about which the native Caliban knows (*Tempest* 3.2.71).

[4]During 1647–48; Charles I was executed in 1649, in the civil wars.

[5]Built during the Napoleonic wars, the barracks housed at least 3,000 troops. The women are the usual camp followers and prostitutes, and also teenagers, such as Kitty and Lydia in Austen's *Pride and Prejudice*, who like to flirt with soldiers.

no bad thing to be the favorite of some Fairy, who would give one the power of seeing how our Friends got on, at a Distance - I should like, of all Loves, a sketch of you and Tom and George in ink which Haydon will do if you tell him how I want them - From want of regular rest, I have been rather <u>narvus</u> - and the passage in Lear - "Do you not hear the sea?"[6] - has haunted me intensely.

[writes out a sonnet, *On the Sea*[7]]

April 18th [. . .]
I'll tell you what - on the 23rd was Shakespeare born - now If I should receive a Letter from you and another from my Brothers on that day 'twould be a parlous good thing - Whenever you write say a Word or two on some Passage in Shakespeare that may have come rather new to you; which must be continually happening, notwithstand[g] that we read the same Play forty times—for instance, the following, from the Tempest, never struck me so forcibly as at present,

> "Urchins
> <u>Shall, for that vast of Night that they may work,</u>
> All exercise on thee—"

How can I help bringing to your mind the Line—
<u>In the dark backward and abysm of time</u>[8]—
I find that I cannot exist without poetry - without eternal poetry - half the day will not do - the whole of it - I began with a little, but habit has made me a Leviathan - I had become all in a Tremble from not having written any thing of late - the Sonnet over leaf did me some good. I slept the better last night for it - this Morning, however, I am nearly as bad again—Just now I opened Spencer, and the first Lines I saw were these. -

> "The noble Heart that harbors virtuous thought,
> And is with Child of glorious great intent,
> Can never rest, until it forth have brought
> Th' eternal Brood of Glory excellent—"[9]

[6]"Hark! do you hear the sea?" Edgar prompts his blind father Gloucester, who wants to jump to his death from the cliffs of Dover; Edgar has brought them to the fields, away from the edge (*King Lear* 4.6.4).

[7]Published in *The Champion*, 17 August 1817 (see p. 58).

[8]Prospero's threatened punishment for Caliban (1.2.329–31); and his description of the distant past (1.2.50).

[9]*FQ* I.v.i, which continues: "Such restless passion did all night torment / The flaming corage of that Faery knight" eager to distinguish himself in tournament combat; the demonstration of virtue in action is relevant to K's poetic aspirations.

Let me know particularly about Haydon; ask him to write to me about Hunt, if it be only ten lines—I hope all is well – I shall forthwith begin my Endymion, which I hope I shall have got some way into by the time you come, when we will read our verses in a delightful place I have set my heart upon near the Castle [. . .]

Your sincere Friend
John Keats.

Letter to Leigh Hunt, 10 May 1817[1]

> *Keats is at Margate, with Tom, writing Book I of* Endymion. *Keats's friend G. F. Mathew had just published a review of* Poems *in* European Magazine. *Hunt is visiting Shelley, already known from* Queen Mab *and* Alastor *&c., and, as Keats is aware, likely to see this letter.*

My dear Hunt,

    The little Gentleman that sometimes lurks in a gossip's bowl ought to have come in very likeness of a <u>coasted</u> *crab[2] and choaked me outright for not having answered your Letter ere this – however you must not suppose that I was in Town to receive it; no, it followed me to the isle of Wight and I got it just as I was going to pack up for Margate [. . .] I went to the Isle of Wight – thought so much about Poetry so long together that I could not get to sleep at night [. . .] Another thing I was too much in Solitude, and consequently was obliged to be in continual burning of thought as an only resource. [. . .] I vow that I have been down in the Mouth lately at this Work. These last two day however I have felt more confident— I have asked myself so often why I should be a Poet more than other Men, - seeing how great a thing it is, - how great things are to be gained by it – What a thing to be in the Mouth of Fame — that at last the Idea— has grown so monstrously beyond my seeming Power of attainment that the other day I nearly consented with myself to drop into a*

---

[1]ALS, transcribed from a plate in T. J. Wise, *Ashley Library* 3 (1923), after p. 12. The first publication was in Hunt's *Lord Byron and some of his Contemporaries* (1828) 1.444–50.

[2]A riff on *A Midsummer Night's Dream*: "sometimes lurk I in a gossip's bowl, / In very likeness of a roasted crab," says Puck (2.1.47ff); Hunt thus reads "roasted," but it's clearly *coasted*, K's punning on his seaside situation.

Phæton[3] – yet 'tis a disgrace to fail even in a huge attempt, and at this moment I drive the thought from me. I began my Poem about a Fortnight since and have done some every day except travelling ones– – Perhaps I may have done a good deal for the time but it appears such a Pin's Point to me that I will not coppy any out. When I consider that somany of these Pin points go to form a Bod-kin point (God send I end not my Life with a bare Bodkin,[4] in its modern sense) and that it requires a thousand bodkins to make a Spear bright enough to throw any light to posterity – I see that nothing but continual uphill Journeying! Now is there any thing more unpleasant (it may come among the thousand and one) than to be so journeying and miss the Goal at last. But I intend to whistle all these cogitations into the Sea where I hope they will breed Storms violent enough to block up all exit from Russia. Does Shelley go on telling strange Stories of the Death of Kings?[5] Tell him there are strange Stories of the death of Poets – some have died before they were conceived "how do you make that out Master Vellum"[6] Does Mrs S. cut Bread and Butter as neatly as ever? Tell her to procure some fatal Scissars and cut the thread of Life of all to be disappointed Poets. Does Mrs Hunt tear linen in half as straight as ever? Tell her to tear from the book of Life all blank Leaves.[7] Remember me to them all—to Miss Kent and the little ones all.

Your sincere friend

John Keats alias Junkets[8]—

[3]A double reference: reckless charioteer Phaeton set the world on fire; a phaeton is a light, 4-wheeled, open carriage, drawn by a pair of horses, for recreational use.

[4]A play on Hamlet's suicidal thoughts; the imagined instrument, "bare bodkin," means "mere stiletto" (*Hamlet* 3.1.76); the modern sense may pun on "bare body."

[5]Richard II, in a melancholy, self-dramatizing mood (*Richard II* 3.2.155ff). In *Lord Byron* Hunt noted that Shelley was fond of quoting these lines and applying them "in the most unexpected manner"; once they were both in a coach with an old lady, who was so startled by Shelley's outburst that she expected them both promptly to sit on the coach floor.

[6]The Butler to Sir George Vellum, amused by his wit, in Joseph Addison's comedy, *The Drummer, Or The Haunted House* (1716): "How charmingly he talks! I fancy, Master Vellum, you cou'd make a Riddle. The same Man Old and Young! How do you make that out, Master Vellum?" (IV.i) (MBF).

[7]The wives of Shelley and Hunt are imagined as the Fates determining the span of a man's life. Miss Kent, Mrs. Hunt's sister, would be a publishing poet in the 1820s, with affection for Keats.

[8]Hunt's punning nickname, from *Amoretti* 7: "A goodly table of pure yvory, / All spred with juncats fit to entertayne / The greatest prince" (*junket*: rich dessert; more generally, a banquet); and Milton's *L'Allegro*: "stories told of many a feat, / How fairy Mab the junkets eat" (102). Queen Mab is the subject of Mercutio's famously extravagant speech in *Romeo and Juliet* (1.4), and the title of Shelley's controversial visionary epic.

Letter to Benjamin Robert Haydon, 10–11 May 1817[1]

Fame, money troubles, mood swings, Shakespeare—all in the mix as Keats, in Margate, begins Endymion.

My dear Haydon,

> *Let Fame, which all hunt after in their lives,*
> *Live register'd upon our brazen tombs,*
> *And so grace us in the disgrace of death:*
> *When spite of cormorant devouring time*
> *The endeavour of this present breath may buy*
> *That Honor which shall bate his Scythe's keen edge*
> *And make us heirs of all eternity.*[2]

To think that I have no right to couple myself with you in this speech would be death to me so I have e'en written it - and I pray God that our brazen Tombs be nigh neighbors. It cannot be long first the endeavor of this present breath will soon be over—and yet it is as well to breathe freely during our sojourn - it is as well if you have not been teased with that Money affair - that bill-pestilence. However I must think that difficulties nerve the Spirit of a Man - they make our Prime Objects a Refuge as well as a Passion. The Trumpet of Fame is as a tower of Strength the ambitious bloweth it and is safe - I suppose by your telling me not to give way to forebodings George has mentioned to you what I have lately said in my Letters to him - truth is I have been in such a state of Mind as to read over my Lines and hate them. I am "one that gathers Samphire dreadful trade"[3] the Cliff of Poesy Towers above me - yet when, Tom who meets with some of Pope's Homer in Plutarch's Lives reads some of those to me they seem like Mice to mine. I read and write about eight hours a day. There is an old saying well begun is half done" - 'tis a bad one. I would use instead - Not begun at all till half done" so according to that I have not begun my Poem and consequently (a priori) can say nothing about it. Thank God! I do begin arduously where I leave off, notwithstanding occasional depressions: and I hope for the support of a High Power while I clime this little eminence and especially in my Years of more momentous Labor. I remember your saying that you had notions of a

---

[1] ALS, Houghton Library, Harvard. K is still in Margate; Haydon is in London.

[2] See the opening of *Love's Labor's Lost*.

[3] *King Lear* 4.6.15—more of Edgar's stage-setting of the cliffs of Dover for his blind father.

good Genius presiding over you. I have of late had the same thought. for things which do half at Random are afterwards confirmed by my judgment in a dozen features of Propriety – Is it too daring to Fancy Shakspeare this Presider? When in the Isle of Whight I met with a Shakspeare in the Passage of the House at which I lodged – it comes nearer to my idea of him than any I have seen – I was but there a Week yet the old Woman made me take it with me though I went off in a hurry – Do you not think this is ominous of good? I am glad you say every Man of great Views is at times tormented as I am— <u>Sunday Aft</u>. This Morning I received a letter from George by which it appears that Money Troubles are to follow us up for some time to come perhaps for always – these vexations are a great hindrance to one – they are not like Envy and detraction stimulants to further exertion as being immediately relative and reflected on at the same time with the prime object – but rather like a nettle leaf or two in your bed. So now I revoke my Promise of finishing my Poem by the Autumn which I should have done had I gone on as I have done – but I cannot write while my spirit is fevered in a contrary direction and I am now sure of having plenty of it this Summer. At this moment I am in no enviable Situation – I feel that I am not in a Mood to write any to day; and it appears that the loss of it is the beginning of all sorts of irregularities. I am extremely glad that a time must come when every thing will leave not a wrack behind.[4] You tell me never to despair – I wish it was as easy for me to observe the saying – truth is I have a horrid Morbidity of Temperament which has shown itself at intervals – it is I have no doubt the greatest Enemy and stumbling block I have to fear – I may even say that it is likely to be the cause of my disappointment. However every ill has its share of good – this very bane would at any time enable me to look with an obstinate eye on the Devil Himself – ay to be as proud of being the lowest of the human race as Alfred could be in being of the highest. I feel confident I should have been a rebel Angel had the opportunity been mine.[5] I am very sure that you do love me as your own Brother – I have seen it in your continual anxiety for me – and I assure you that your wellfare and fame is and will be a chief pleasure to me all my Life. I know no one but

[4]Riffing on Prospero's farewell to his revels: "all we inherit, shall dissolve," and "Leave not a rack behind" (4.1.154–56), where *rack* means wisp of cloud. K's spelling puns the word into *wrack* (etymologically related): ruin or destruction.
[5]Referring to Alfred the Great (see *Sleep and Poetry* 385) and Satan's cohorts in PL.

you who can be fully sensible of the turmoil and anxiety, the sacrifice of all what is called comfort the readiness to Measure time by what is done and to die in 6 hours could plans be brought to conclusions – the looking upon the Sun the Moon the Stars, the Earth and its contents as materials to form greater things – that is to say ethereal things ———— but here I am talking like a Madman greater things that our Creator himself made!! I wrote to Hunt yesterday – scarcly know what I said in it. I could not talk about Poetry in the way I should have liked for I was not in humor with either his or mine. His self delusions are very lamentable they have inticed him into a Situation which I should be less eager after than that of a galley Slave – what you observe thereon is very true must be in time.

Perhaps it is a self delusion to say so – but I think I could not be be deceived in the Manner that Hunt is – may I die tomorrow if I am to be. There is no greater Sin after the 7 deadly than to flatter oneself into an idea of being a great Poet – or one of those beings who are privileged to wear out their Lives in the pursuit of Honor – how comfortable a feel it is that such a Crime must bring its heavy Penalty? That if one be a Selfdeluder accounts will be balanced? I am glad you are hard at Work – 't will now soon be done – I long to see Wordsworth's as well as to have mine in:[6] but I would rather not show my face in Town till the end of the Year – if that will be time enough – if not I shall be disappointed if you do not write for me even when you think best. I never quite despair and I read Shakspeare – indeed I shall I think never read any other Book much – Now this might lead me into a long Confab but I desist. I am very near Agreeing with Hazlit that Shakspeare is enough for us – [. . .] I was reading Anthony and Cleopatra [. . .] there are several Passages applicable to the events you commentate. You say that he arrived by degrees and not by any single struggle to the Hight of his ambition – and that his Life had been as common in particulars as other Mens. Shakspeare makes Enobarb say – Where's Antony Eros – He's walking in the garden —thus: <u>and spurns the rush that lies</u> before him; cries fool, Lepidus! In the same scene we find: "let determined things to destiny hold unbewailed their – way."[7] Dolabella says of Anthony's Messenger

[6]*Christ's Entry into Jerusalem*, in which he and Wordsworth are in the crowd.

[7]Eros and Enobarbus are friends of Antony, whose co-ruler Octavius Caesar has arrested third triumvir Lepidus and has murdered Antony's potential ally Pompey. In the next scene Octavius comforts his sister (Antony's neglected wife) with the advice about destiny (*Antony and Cleopatra* 3.5.16–18; 3.6.84–85).

"An argument that he is pluck'd when hither
  He sends so poor a pinion of his wing"[8] – Then again,
      Eno — "I see Men's Judgments are
    A parcel of their fortunes; and things outward
    Do draw the inward quality after them,
    To suffer all alike"[9] — The following applies well to Bertram

                    But how differently does Buonap
                    bear his fate from Antony!

   "Yet he that can endure
To follow with allegience a fallen Lord,
Does conquer him that did his Master conquer,
And earns a place i' the story"[10]

'T is good too that the Duke of Wellington has a good Word or so in the
Examiner.[11] A Man ought to have the Fame he deserves – and I begin
to think that detracting from him as well as from Wordsworth is the
same thing. I wish he had a little more taste – and did not in that
respect "deal in Lieutenantry"[12] You should have heard from me before
this – but in the first place I did not like to do so before I had got a little
way in the 1st Book and in the next as G. told me you were going to write
I delayed till I had heard from you. Give my Respects the next time you
write to the North and also to John Hunt[13]– Remember me to Reynolds
and tell him to write – Ay, and when you sent Westward tell your Sister
that I mentioned her in this – So now in the Name of Shakespeare
Raphael and all our Saints I commend you to the care of heaven!
                          Your everlasting friend
                             John Keats—

[8]When Antony sends a mere schoolmaster as messenger to Octavius, Octavius's
friend Dolabella comments that Antony's fortunes must be falling (his wings are
plucked of feathers).

[9]Enobarbus, lamenting the deterioration of Antony's famed military smarts
(3.13.31–34).

[10]Enobarbus, deciding against deserting Antony (3.13.43–46); Sidney Colvin identifies Bertram as General Count Bertrand, confidant of Napoleon.

[11]In a review of a recently published manuscript by Napoleon (*Examiner*, 27 April
and 4 May 1817), Haydon noted its failure to mention Wellington, Napoleon's vanquisher at Waterloo, June 1815.

[12]Antony's soldierly contempt of Octavius, who at Philippi "Dealt on lieutenantry,
and no practice had / In the brave squares of war" (3.1.35–40)—giving orders, but
not fighting.

[13]G is GK; the North is Wordsworth; John Hunt is Leigh's brother and publisher of
The Examiner.

Letter to John Taylor and James Augustus Hessey, 16 May 1817[1]

The firm had just agreed to publish Endymion. *Being witty and performative, Keats writes from Margate to thank them for an advance (one can live for several weeks on £20) against anticipated profits.*

My dear Sirs,
      I am extremely indebted to you for your liberality in the Shape of manufactured rag value £20 and shall immediately proceed to destroy some of the Minor Heads of that spring-headed Hydra the Dun[2] – To conquer which the Knight need have no Sword, Shield Cuirass Cuisses Herbadgeon Spear Casque, Greves, Pauldrons Spurs Chevron or any other scaly commodity, but he need only take the Bank Note of Faith and Cash of Salvation, and set out against the Monster invoking the aid of no Archimago or Urganda[3] – and finger me the Paper light as the Sybils Leaves in Virgil whereat the Fiend skulks off with his tail between his Legs.[4] Touch him with this enchanted Paper and he whips you his head away as fast as a Snail's Horn – but then the horrid Propensity he has to put it up again has discouraged many very valliant Knights – He is such a never ending still beginning sort of a Body[5]– like my Landlady of the Bell – I should conjecture that the very Spright that the "green sour ringlets makes hereof the Ewe not bites"[6] had manufactured it of the dew fallen on said sour ringlets – I think I could make a nice little Alegorical Poem called "the Dun" – Where we wold have the Castle of Carelessness – the Draw Bridge of Credit – Sir Novelty Fashion expedition against

[1]ALS, Houghton Library, Harvard.

[2]*dun*: creditor, bill-collector. Spenser's knight Guyon and the Palmer confront perils and such "dreadfull" creatures as "Spring-headed Hydraes, and sea-shouldring Whales" (*FQ* II.i.23). The hydra springs a new head if one is cut off. K adored the last line: "what an image that is—'*sea-shouldering whales!*'" (Charles and Mary Cowden Clarke, *Recollections of Writers*; London, 1878).

[3]Archimago is a magician, demonic poet, and Catholic in *FQ*; Urganda the Unknown is an enchantress in Vasco Lobeira's 15th-c. romance *Amadis of Gaul*, translated and abridged by Robert Southey (1803).

[4]The frenzied prophetess of Virgil's *Aeneid*, who writes her verses on leaves and then abandons them to the winds of her cave, often to the frustration of her expectant visitors (3.445–52). K knew this poem intimately, having won a prize at school for translating it.

[5]In Dryden's *Alexander's Feast* (1697), Alexander the Great's description of war (101).

[6]Prospero's adieu to his elves and fairies, who "By moonshine do the green sour ringlets make, / Whereof the ewe not bites" (*Tempest* 5.1.37–39).

the City of Taylors[7]- &c &c. —— — I went day by day at my
Poem for a Month at the end of which time the other day I found my
Brain so overwrought that I had neither Rhyme nor reason in it - so
was obliged to give up for a few days - I hope soon to be able to resume
my Work - I have endeavoured to do so once or twice but to no Purpose -
instead of Poetry I have a swimming in my head - And feel all the
effects of a Mental Debauch - lowness of Spirits - anxiety to go on
without the Power to do so which does not at all tend to my ultimate
Progression - However tomorrow I will begin my next Month. This
Evening I go to Canterbury - having got tired of Margate - I was not
right in my head when I came - At Cant[y]. I hope the Remembrance of
Chaucer will set me forward like a Billiard-Ball - [. . .] I have some
idea of seeing the Continent some time in the Summer—
       In repeating how sensible I am of your kindness I remain
                          Your Obedient Serv[t] and Friend

                          John Keats —

I shall be very happy to hear any little intelligence in the literrary or
friendly way when you have time to scribble -
       Mess[rs] Taylor and Hessey.—

On the Sea

On the Sea *appeared in* The Champion, *17 August 1817, p. 261. Keats
wrote it on 17 April, at the Isle of Wight (see the letter to Reynolds, p.
49). This was the last sonnet he wrote this year; he began* Endymion
the next day.

ORIGINAL POETRY

The following Sonnet is from the pen of Mr. Keats. It is quite sufficient, we think to justify all the praise we have given him,—and to
prove to our correspondent Pierre, his superiority over any poetical
writer in the *Champion.*—J.H.R. would be the first to acknowledge
this himself.[1]

---

[7]All characters in Colley Cibber's comedy, *Love's Last Shift; or The Fool in Fashion*
(1696), with a wink at John Taylor.

---

[1]"I have seen some lines in your paper, occasionally signed J. H. R. which have
pleased me much [. . .] better than your favourite Mr Keats, whom my perverseness of
taste, forbids me to admire" (letter from "Pierre" to *The Examiner*, 3 Aug., p. 245).

SONNET
ON THE SEA[2]

It keeps eternal whisperings around
Desolate shores, and with its mighty swell
Gluts twice ten thousand Caverns, till the spell
Of Hecate leaves them their old shadowy sound.
Often 'tis in such gentle temper found,
That scarcely will the very smallest shell
Be mov'd for days from where it sometime fell,
When last the winds of Heaven were unbound.
Oh ye! who have your eye-balls vex'd and tir'd,
Feast them upon the wideness of the Sea;
Oh ye! whose ears are dinn'd with uproar rude,
Or fed too much with cloying melody—
Sit ye near some old Cavern's Mouth, and brood
Until ye start, as if the sea-nymphs quir'd!

Letter to John Hamilton Reynolds, 21 September 1817[1]

*This is the day the "Grasshopper and Cricket" sonnet-contest appears
in* The Examiner. *Hunt's praise of* Poems *was published across three issues of* The Examiner *in June. Keats is with Bailey at Magdalen Hall,
Oxford University, writing* Endymion, *satirizing his money troubles,
and full of antipathy to literary women.*

My dear Reynolds,
*So you are determined to be my mortal foe – draw a Sword at
me, and I will forgive - Put a Bullet in my Brain, and I will shake it
out as a dew-drop from the Lion's Mane[2] - put me on a Gridiron, and*

[2]K's letter (17–18 April to Reynolds) indents lines 2–3, 6–7, 10, 12, and 14, to mark
the octave and sestet—an arrangement followed, except for 14, in its next publication, *1848* (2.291).

[1]WLB 46–48. Hunt's review of *Poems* noted a few faults but overall justified his esteem of the "young poet" he had introduced the previous December.

[2]Riffing on Patroclus's urging of Achilles to rise to action and quit his love-sick mop-
ing in his tent, to let it "like a dewdrop from the lion's mane, / Be shook to air"
(*Troilus and Cressida* 3.3.224–25).

I will fry with great complacency —but, oh horror! to come upon me in the shape of a Dun! Send me Bills! as I say to my Taylor send me Bills and I'll never employ you more³ [. . .]

For these last five or six days, we have had regularly a Boat on the Isis,⁴ and explored all the streams about, which are more in number than your eye lashes. We sometimes skim into a Bed of rushes, and there become naturalized riverfolks,—there is one particularly nice nest which we have christened "Reynolds's Cove" in which we have read Wordsworth and talked as may be. I think I see you and Hunt meeting [. . .] What Evenings we might pass with him, could we have him from Mʳˢ H—Failings I am always rather rejoiced to find in a Man than sorry for; they bring us to a Level—He has them,—but then his makes-up are very good. He agrees with the Northern Poet in this, "He is not one of those who much delight to season their fireside with personal talk"⁵- I must confess however having a little itch that way, and at this present I have a few neighbourly remarks to make - The world, and especially our England, has within the last thirty years been vexed and teazed by a set of Devils, whom I detest so much that I almost hunger after an acherontic promotion to a Torturer,⁶ purposely for their accomodation. These Devils are a set of Women, who having taken a snack or Luncheon of Literary Scraps, set themselves up for towers of Babel in Languages Sapphos in Poetry - Euclids in Geometry - and every thing in nothing. Among such the Name of Montague has been preeminent.⁷ The thing has made a very uncomfortable impression on me. - I had longed— for some real feminine Modesty in these things, and was therefore gladdened in the extreme on opening the other day one of Bayley's Books - a Book of Poetry written by one beautiful Mʳˢ Philips, a friend of Jeremy

³Tailors were sadly susceptible to being stiffed; at his death, K still owed £30–40 (Rollins).

⁴The name of the Thames in Oxfordshire.

⁵The opening of Wordsworth's sonnet-stanza poem, *Personal Talk* (1807; 1815).

⁶Acheron is a river in Hades.

⁷Elizabeth Montague is "The Queen of the Blues," a society of intellectual women (all, of course, barred from university education), celebrated in the 18th c., but mostly despised in K's day. While Hunt admired them (and proposed rebranding the color-code as violet), the general male antipathy, fed by women's power as purchasers, included Hazlitt and Byron. Taylor and Hessey published many popular female authors, including Jane Taylor and Ann Taylor.

Taylor's,[8] and called "the matchless Orinda" – You must have heard
of her, and most likely read her Poetry – I wish you have not, that I
may have the pleasure of treating you with a few stanzas – I do it at
a venture – You will not regret reading them once more. The following
to her friend Mrs M. A. at parting you will judge of.

[Keats copies out 10 stanzas (60 lines) of Katherine Philips's
intensely amatory poem, "To M. A. at Parting" (*Poems*; 1710)[9]]

[. . .] How is Hazlitt? We were reading his <u>Table</u>[10] last night – I know
he thinks himself not estimated by ten People in the world – I wish
he knew he is – I am getting on famous with my third Book – have
written 800 lines thereof, and hope to finish it next Week – Bailey
likes what I have done very much – Believe me, my dear Reynolds,
one of my chief layings-up is the pleasure I shall have in showing it
to you, I may now say, in a few days — [. . .]

Send us a few of your Stanzas to read in "Reynolds's cove" [. . .]
Yours faithfully

John Keats

Letter to Benjamin Bailey, 8 October 1817[1]

*Back in Hampstead with his brothers, Keats is trying to keep Hunt
from supervising* Endymion.

My dear Bailey, [. . .]
I went to Hunt's and Haydon's who live now neighbours. Shelley was
there. I know nothing about any thing in this part of the world –
every Body seems at Loggerheads. There's Hunt infatuated – there's
Haydon's Picture in statu quo. There's Hunt walks up and down his
painting room criticising every head most unmercifully – There's

---

[8] 17th-c. bishop and ecclesiastical writer, most famous for *Holy Living* and *Holy Dying* (1650–51).

[9] The "matchless Orinda" is Katharine Philips (b. 1631), married at age 17 to a 54-year-old man and dead at age 33 of smallpox. Mary Aubrey (wife of William Montague) was the most adored of her female friends: "To part with thee I needs must die / Could parting sep'rate thee and I" (stanza I). K's transcription of this 10-stanza poem appears in standard editions of his letters.

[10] *The Round Table* (1817), two volumes of essays in collaboration with Hunt.

---

[1] ALS, Houghton Library, Harvard.

Horace Smith[2] tired of Hunt. The web of our Life is of mingled Yarn"[3]
[. . .] I regret I cannot be transported to your Room to write to you. I
am quite disgusted with literary Men – and will never know another
except Wordsworth – no not even Byron – Here is an instance of the
friendships of such – Haydon and Hunt have known each other many
years – now they live pour ainsi dire[4] jealous Neighbours. Haydon
says to me Keats dont show your Lines to Hunt on any account or
he will have done half for you – so it appears Hunt wishes it to be
thought. When he met Reynolds in the Theatre John told him that I
was getting on to the completion of 4000 Lines. Ah! says Hunt had it
not been for me they would have been 7000! If he will say this to
Reynolds what would he to other People? Haydon received a Letter a
little while back on this subject from some Lady – which contains a
caution to me through him on this subject – Now is not all this a most
paultry thing to think about? You may see the whole of the case by
the following extract from a Letter I wrote to George in the Spring[5]

> "As to what you say about my being a Poet, I can return no
> answer but by saying that the high Idea I have of poetical fame
> makes me think I see it towering to high above me. At any rate I
> have no right to talk until Endymion is finished – it will be a test,
> a trial of my Powers of Imagination and chiefly of my invention
> which is a rare thing indeed – by which I must make 4000 Lines
> of one bare circumstance and fill them with Poetry; and when I
> consider that this is a great task, and that when done it will take
> me but a dozen paces towards the Temple of Fame – it makes me
> say – God forbid that I should be without such a task! I have
> heard Hunt say and may be asked – why endeavour after a long
> Poem? To which I should answer – Do not the Lovers of Poetry
> like to have a little Region to wander in where they may pick and
> choose, and in which the images are so numerous that many are
> forgotten and found new in a second Reading: which may be food
> for a Week's stroll in the Summer? Do not they like this better

[2]Satirist and close friend of Shelley and Hunt, famous for *Rejected Addresses*
(1812), a set of parodies of famous authors of the day (written with his brother
James).

[3]The comment from *All's Well That Ends Well* continues "good and ill together"
(4.3.68–69).

[4]French: so to speak.

[5]The letter is lost. Instead of K's quotation marks at the front of each page-line, I indicate the quoted text by indentation.

than what they can read through before Mrs *Williams comes
down stairs? a Morning work at most. Besides a long Poem is a
test of Invention which I take to be the Polar Star of Poetry, as
Fancy is the Sails, and Imagination the Rudder. Did our great
Poets ever write short Pieces? I mean in the shape of Tales – This
same invention seems indeed of late Years to have been forgotten
as a Poetical excellence – But enough of this, I put on no Laurels
till I shall have finished Endymion, and I hope Apollo is [not[6]]
angered at my having made a Mockery at him at Hunt's"*
You see Bailey how independant my writing has been – Hunts
dissuasion was of no avail – I refused to visit Shelley, that I might have
my own unfetterd Scope – and after all I shall have the Reputation of
Hunt's elevé.[7] His corrections and amputations will by the knowing
ones be trased in the Poem – This is to be sure the vexation of a day –
nor would I say so many Words about it to any but those whom I
know to have my wellfare and Reputation at Heart [. . .] My Brothers
kindest remembrances to you – we are going to dine at Brown's where
I have some hopes of meeting Reynolds. The little Mercury I have
taken has corrected the Poison and improved my Health -though I
feel from my employment that I shall never be again secure in
Robustness[8]—would that you were as well as
your sincere friend & brother[9]
John Keats

§ Leigh Hunt attacked in *Blackwood's Edinburgh Magazine* 2 (October 1817: 38–41)

This article was the first of a series on "The Cockney School of Poetry"—Z's mocking name for the politically liberal, Hunt-led revolt against eighteenth-century aesthetics. Z deploys "Cockney" (a term

[6]The page is torn; editors propose a missing "not." See *Ode to Apollo* (p. 82). On a spring evening in 1817, in the glow of after-dinner wine, K and Hunt crowned each other with laurel wreathes (an emblem of poetic fame).

[7]French: student.

[8]Mercury, a poison, was commonly prescribed for diseases, including tuberculosis; at the time, K did not believe he was infected. He wouldn't show any troubling symptoms for another half year or so.

[9]A striking intimacy.

*for an east-Londoner) to ridicule sham learning and vulgar pretension,
with hints of sexual license and effeminacy. Launched in 1817 as an
antidote to the liberal Edinburgh Review, Blackwood's was published
by William Blackwood, a business associate of John Murray, publisher
of London's conservative Quarterly Review. Z's caustic writing was
partly principle and partly a bid to attract readers to the new magazine. Though pleased with his influence, Z was widely despised.*

ON THE COCKNEY SCHOOL OF POETRY.
No. I.

Our talk shall be (a theme we never tire on)
Of Chaucer, Spenser, Shakespeare, Milton, Byron
(Our England's Dante)—Wordsworth—HUNT, and KEATS,
The Muses' son of promise and of what feats
He yet may do.

CORNELIUS WEBB.[1]

WHILE the whole critical world is occupied with balancing the merits, whether in theory or in execution, of what is commonly called
THE LAKE SCHOOL,[2] it is strange that no one seems to think it at all
necessary to say a single word about another new school of poetry
which has of late sprung up among us. This school has not, I believe, as yet received any name; but if I may be permitted to have the
honour of christening it, it may henceforth be referred to by the des-
ignation of THE COCKNEY SCHOOL. Its chief Doctor and Professor is
Mr Leigh Hunt, a man certainly of some talents, of extravagant pretensions both in wit, poetry, and politics, and withal of exquisitely
bad taste, and extremely vulgar modes of thinking and manners in
all respects. He is a man of little education. He knows absolutely
nothing of *Greek*, almost nothing of Latin, and his knowledge of
Italian literature is confined to a few of the most popular of Petrarch's sonnets, and an imperfect acquaintance with Ariosto [. . .]

With this stock of knowledge, Mr Hunt presumes to become
the founder of a new school of poetry, and throws away entirely the

[1]Z may have concocted the verse and mockingly attributed it to this minor magazine
poet (ca. 1790–ca. 1848). "The Muse's Son of Promise" would become a routine
ridicule of K.
[2]Wordsworth and Coleridge (also Southey, before his Tory phase and Poet Laure-
ateship), so called for their residence in the Lake District.

chance which he might have had of gaining some true poetical fame, had he been less lofty in his pretensions. [. . .] One feels the same disgust at the idea of opening Rimini,[3] that impresses itself on the mind of a man of fashion, when he is invited to enter, for a second time, the gilded drawingroom of a little mincing boarding-school mistress, who would fain have an *At Home*[4] in her house. Every thing is pretence, affectation, finery, and gaudiness. The beaux are attorneys' apprentices, with chapeau bras and Limerick gloves,[5] fiddlers, harp teachers, and clerks of genius: the belles are faded fan-twinkling spinsters, prurient vulgar misses from school, and enormous citizens' wives. The company are entertained with lukewarm negus,[6] and the sounds of a paltry piano forte.

All the great poets of our country have been men of some rank in society, and there is no vulgarity in any of their writings; but Mr Hunt cannot utter a dedication, or even a note, without betraying the *Shibboleth*[7] of low birth and low habits. He is the ideal of a Cockney Poet. He raves perpetually about "green fields," "jaunty streams," and "o'er-arching leafiness," exactly as a Cheapside shop-keeper does about the beauties of his box on the Camberwell road.[8] Mr Hunt is altogether unacquainted with the face of nature in her magnificent scenes; he has never seen any mountain higher than Highgate-hill,[9] nor reclined by any stream more pastoral than the Serpentine River.[10] But he is determined to be a poet eminently rural, and he rings the changes—till one is sick of him, on the beauties of the different "high views" which he has taken of God and nature, in the course of some Sunday dinner parties, at which he has assisted in the neighbourhood of London. His books are indeed not known in the country; his fame as a poet (and I might almost

[3]For *The Story of Rimini* (1816), see Paolo and Francesca (glossary); a 2d edn. appeared in 1817, and Keats honored it in *Poems*.

[4]social reception.

[5]inexpensive hats and gloves.

[6]a mixture of wine, hot water, sugar, and flavorings—inexpensive, and implicitly feminine, childish.

[7]identifying accent.

[8]Such diction marks K's poetry as well; Cheapside is a London commercial district, where the Keats brothers had lived; Camberwell Road is in the suburbs; a box is a) a small country house; b) a stand of boxwood trees.

[9]A suburb north of London, and residence of Coleridge, about 2 miles from Hampstead.

[10]In London's Regent Park.

say, as a politician too) is entirely confined to the young attorneys and embryo-barristers about town. In the opinion of these competent judges, London is the world—and Hunt is a Homer. [. . .]

The poetry of Mr Hunt is such as might be expected from the personal character and habits of its author. As a vulgar man is perpetually labouring to be genteel—in like manner, the poetry of this man is always on the stretch to be grand. He has been allowed to look for a moment from the antichamber into the saloon, and mistaken the waving of feathers and the painted floor for the *sine qua non's*[11] of elegant society. He would fain be always tripping and waltzing, and is sorry that he cannot be allowed to walk about in the morning with yellow breeches and flesh-coloured silk stockings. He sticks an artificial rosebud into his button hole in the midst of winter. He wears no neckcloth, and cuts his hair in imitation of the Prints of Petrarch.[12] In his verses he is always desirous of being airy, graceful, easy, courtly, and ITALIAN. If he had the smallest acquaintance with the great demi-gods of Italian poetry, he could never fancy that the style in which he writes, bears any, even the most remote resemblance to the severe and simple manner of Dante—the tender stillness of the lover of Laura—or the sprightly and good-natured unconscious elegance of the inimitable Ariosto. [. . .]

The extreme moral depravity of the Cockney School is another thing which is for ever thrusting itself upon the public attention, and convincing every man of sense who looks into their productions, that they who sport such sentiments can never be great poets. How could any man of high original genius ever stoop publicly, at the present day, to dip his fingers in the least of those glittering and rancid obscenities which float on the surface of Mr Hunt's Hippocrene? His poetry resembles that of a man who has kept company with kept-mistresses. His muse talks indelicately like a tea-sipping milliner girl.[13] Some excuse for her there might have been, had she been hurried away by imagination or passion; but with her, indecency seems a disease, she appears to speak unclean things from perfect inanition. Surely they who are connected with Mr Hunt by the tender relations of society, have good reason to complain that

[11]Latin: essentials ("without which nothing").

[12]All arty affectations of aristocratic style (hence "vulgar" in inferiors). Prints of Petrarch show him with longish, curly hair—a "poet" style.

[13]hat-maker; such girls were stereotyped as morally loose.

his muse should have been so prostituted. In Rimini a deadly wound is aimed at the dearest confidences of domestic bliss. The author has voluntarily chosen—a subject not of simple seduction alone—one in which his mind seems absolutely to gloat over all the details of adultery and incest.

The unhealthy and jaundiced medium through which the Founder of the Cockney School views every thing like moral truth, is apparent, not only from his obscenity, but also from his want of respect for all that numerous class of plain upright men, and unpretending women, in which the real worth and excellence of human society consists. Every man is, according to Mr Hunt, a dull potato-eating blockhead—of no greater value to God or man than any ox or drayhorse—who is not an admirer of Voltaire's *romans,* a worshipper of Lord Holland and Mr Haydon, and a quoter of John Buncle and Chaucer's Flower and Leaf.[14] Every woman is useful only as a breeding machine, unless she is fond of reading Launcelot of the Lake, in an antique summer-house.

How such an indelicate writer as Mr Hunt can pretend to be an admirer of Mr Wordsworth, is to us a thing altogether inexplicable. One great charm of Wordsworth's noble compositions consists in the dignified purity of thought, and the patriarchal simplicity of feeling, with which they are throughout penetrated and imbued. We can conceive a vicious man admiring with distant awe the spectacle of virtue and purity; but if he does so sincerely, he must also do so with the profoundest feeling of the error of his own ways, and the resolution to amend them. [. . .] The Founder of the Cockney School would fain claim poetical kindred with Lord Byron. [. . .] Lord Byron! How must the haughty spirit of Lara and Harold contemn the subaltern sneaking of our modern tuft-hunter.[15] The insult which he offered to Lord Byron in the dedication of Rimini,—in which he, a paltry cockney newspaper scribbler, had the

---

[14]See the epigraph to *Sleep and Poetry* (p. 33). French author and philosopher Voltaire had done jail-time for libeling a Regent (Hunt's alter ego): his *romans* are anonymous, anti-establishment novels. Lord Holland is a leading Whig (opposition party) politician; *The Life of John Buncle, Esq,* (1756–66), by Irish novelist Thomas Amory, recounts the successive marriages of its free-thinking, virtuous hero.

[15]social-climber. Hunt dedicated *The Story of Rimini* to Lord Byron, who by this time was celebrated for the romance *Lara* (1814) and *Childe Harold's Pilgrimage* (1812, 1816). Byron's public infidelities (one cause of the break-up of his short marriage, early in 1816) seem not to matter to Z; Hunt's marriage was famously happy and faithful.

assurance to address one of the most nobly-born of English Patricians, and one of the first geniuses whom the world ever produced, as "My dear Byron," although it may have been forgotten and despised by the illustrious person whom it most nearly concerned,— excited a feeling of utter loathing and disgust in the public mind, which will always be remembered whenever the name of Leigh Hunt is mentioned. We dare say Mr Hunt has some fine dreams about the true nobility being the nobility of talent, and flatters himself, that with those who acknowledge only that sort of rank, he himself passes for being the *peer* of Byron. He is sadly mistaken. He is as completely a Plebeian in his mind as he is in his rank and station in society. [. . .] Z.

Letter to Benjamin Bailey, 3 November 1817[1]

Keats reacts to the attack on Hunt.

My dear Bailey, [. . .]
There has been a flaming attack upon Hunt in the Endinburgh[2]
Magazine – I never read any thing so virulent – accusing him of the
greatest Crimes depeciating his Wife his Poetry – his Habits -his
company, his Conversation – These Philipics[3] are to come out in
Numbers – call'd 'the Cockney School of Poetry' There has been but
one Number published – that on Hunt to which they have prefixed a
Motto from one Cornelius Webb Poetaster – who unfortunately was of
our Party occasionally at Hampstead and took it into his head to write
the following – something about – "we'll talk on Wordsworth Byron –
a theme we never tire on and so forth till he comes to Hunt and
Keats. In the Motto they have put Hunt and Keats in large Letters –
I have no doubt that the second Number was intended for me: but
have hopes of its non appearance from the following advertisement in
last Sunday's Examiner. "To Z. The writer of the Article signed Z in

[1]ALS, Houghton Library, Harvard.
[2]A likely punning on the career-ending intent of the attack; see also p. 186.
[3]tirades; Cicero gave the title *Phillipics* (named for Demosthenes' invectives against Phillip II of Macedon) to his denunciations of the assassins of Julius Caesar and was sentenced to death for this.

Blackwood's Ednburgh magazine for October 1817 is invited to send his address to the printer of the Examiner, in order that Justice may be executed of the proper person"[4] *I dont mind the thing much – but if he should go to such lengths with me as he has done with Hunt I must infalibly call him to an account*[5] *– if he be a human being and appears in Squares and Theatres where we might possibly meet. I dont relish his abuse* [. . .]

your sincere and affectionate friend
John Keats

Letter to Benjamin Bailey, 22 November 1817[1]

> *Wondering at quarrels, especially among his friends, Keats ponders the difference between "Men of Genius" and "Men of Power," between "Imagination" and methodical reasoning, and the transience of happiness.*

My dear Bailey, [. . .]
To a Man of your nature such a Letter as Haydon's must have been extremely cutting – What occasions the greater part of the World's Quarrels? simply this, two Minds meet and do not understand each other time enough to prevent any shock or surprise at the conduct of either party – As soon as I had known Haydon three days I had got enough of his character not to have been surprised at such a Letter as he has hurt you with. Nor when I knew it was it a principle with me to drop his acquaintance although with you it would have been an imperious feeling. I wish you knew all that I think about Genius and the Heart — and yet I think you are thoroughly acquainted with my innermost breast in that respect or you could not have known me even thus long and still hold me worthy to be your dear friend. In passing

---

[4]2 Nov., p. 729 (continued 14 Dec., p. 788). Z was only further inspired, continuing his attack in January (*Blackwood's* 2: 414–17) and refusing to disclose his identity.

[5]challenge to a duel of honor, illegal though still done. On 16 Feb. 1821, Lockhart's (also Bailey's) friend J. H. Christie challenged John Scott, editor of *London Magazine*, for calling Lockhart "Emperor of the Mohocks" (18th-c. thugs, or New World warriors). Scott died of his wounds 11 days later; Christie was acquitted of murder.

---

[1]ALS, Houghton Library, Harvard.

however I must say of one thing that has pressed upon me lately and encreased my Humility and capability of submission – and that is this truth – Men of Genius are great as certain ethereal Chemicals operating on the Mass of neutral intellect – by they have not any individuality, any determined Character – I would call the top and head of those who have a proper self Men of Power –
– But I am running my head into a Subject which I am certain I could not do justice to under five years study and 3 vols octavo – and moreover long to be talking about the Imagination – so my dear Bailey do not think of this unpleasant affair if possible – do not – I defy any harm to come of it—I defy [. . .] so don't because you have suddenly discover'd a Coldness in Haydon suffer yourself to be teased. Do not my dear fellow. O I wish I was as certain of the end of all your troubles as that of your momentary start about the authenticity of the Imagination. I am certain of nothing but of the holiness of the Heart's affections and the truth of Imagination – What the imagination seizes as Beauty must be truth[2] – whether it existed before or not – for I have the same Idea of all our Passions as of Love they are all in their sublime, creative of essential Beauty – In a Word, you may know my favorite Speculation by my first Book and the little song I sent in my last[3] – which is a representation from the fancy of the probable mode of operating in these Matters – The Imagination may be compared to Adam's dream – he awoke and found it truth.[4] I am the more zealous in this affair, because I have never yet been able to perceive how any thing can be known for truth by consequitive[5] reasoning – and yet it must be – Can it be that even the greatest Philosopher ever ~~when~~ arrived at his goal without putting aside numerous objections – However it may be, O for a Life of Sensations[6] rather than of Thoughts! It is 'a Vision in the form of Youth' a Shadow of reality to come[7] – and this consideration has further convinced me for it has

---

[2] See, in a qualifying dramatic context, the last lines of *Ode on a Grecian Urn*.

[3] *Endymion* Book I, and a song in Book IV.

[4] Adam recounts how, dreaming of "the Garden of bliss," he "wak'd and found / Before mine Eyes all real, as the dream / Had lively shadow'd"; K marked these lines in *PL* (8.309ff).

[5] K's coinage, combining *consecutive* and *consequent*.

[6] Knowledge as an immediate sensation rather than abstract thought.

[7] "what if Earth / Be but the shadow of Heaven . . . ?" (K underlined this, but not the rest of Archangel Raphael's surmise, which suggests a wide gap between shadow and substance; *PL* 5.574–75).

come as auxiliary to another favorite Speculation of mine, that we
shall enjoy ourselves here after by having what we called happiness on
Earth repeated in a finer tone and so repeated – And yet such a fate
can only befall those who delight in Sensation rather than hunger as
you do after Truth – Adam's dream will do here and seems to be a
conviction that Imagination and its empyreal reflection is the same as
human Life and its Spiritual repetition .[8]

But as I was saying – the simple imaginative Mind
may have its rewards in the repetion of its own
silent Working coming continually on the Spirit with a fine Suddenness – to compare great
things with small – have you never by being
Surprised with an old Melody– in a delicious
place – by a delicious voice, felt over again your very Speculations
and Surmises at the time it first operated on your Soul – do you not
remember forming to yourself the singer's face more beautiful that it
was possible and yet with the elevation of the Moment you did not
think so – even then you were mounted on the Wings of Imagination
so high – that the Prototype must be here after – that delicious face
you will see – What a time! I am continually running away from the
subject – sure this cannot be exactly the case with a complex Mind –
one that is imaginative and at the same time careful of its fruits –
who would exist partly on Sensation partly on thought – to whom it is
necessary that years should bring the philosophic Mind[9]– such an one
I consider your's and therefore it is necessary to your eternal Happiness
that you not only ~~have~~ drink this old Wine of Heaven which I shall
call the redigestion of our most ethereal Musings on Earth; but also
increase in Knowledge and Know all things. [. . .] – but the world is
full of troubles and I have not much reason to think myself pesterd
with many – I think Jane or Marianne[10] has a better opinion of me
than I deserve – for really and truly I do not think my Brothers illness
connected with mine[11]– you know more of the real Cause than they do
nor have I any chance of being rack'd as you have been – You perhaps
at one time thought there was such a thing as Worldly Happiness to be

[8]K insets these seven lines flush left, almost as if he were drafting verse.

[9]Wordsworth would like to believe that the loss of childhood's "splendour in the
grass, glory in the flower," is compensated by "years that bring the philosophic
mind" ("Intimations" *Ode*, stanza 10).

[10]Reynolds's sisters.

[11]Tom was suffering from tuberculosis.

arrived at, at certain periods of time marked out – you have of necessity from your disposition been thus led away – I scarcely remember counting upon any Happiness – I look not for it if it be not in the present hour – nothing startles me beyond the Moment. The setting Sun will always set me to rights – or if a Sparrow come before my Window I take part in its existence and pick about the Gravel. The first thing that strikes me on hearing a Misfortune having befalled another is this. 'Well it cannot be helped. – he will have the pleasure of trying the resources of his spirit. and I beg now my dear Bailey that hereafter should you observe any thing cold in me not to but it to the account of heartlessness but abstraction – for I assure you I sometimes feel not the influence of a Passion or Affection during a whole week– and so long this sometimes continues I begin to suspect myself and the genuiness of my feelings at other times – thinking them a few barren Tragedy-tears – My Brother Tom is much improved – he is going to Devonshire[12]– whither I shall follow him – at present I am just arrived at Dorking to change the Scene, change the Air and give me a spur to wind up my Poem, of which there are wanting 500 Lines. [. . .]

> Your affectionate friend
> John Keats –

Letter to John Hamilton Reynolds, 22 November 1817[1]

Finishing Endymion, *Keats contemplates "heart-vexations" and the intensity of Shakespeare's poetic language.*

My Dear Reynolds, [. . .]
I cannot go with Tom into Devonshire—however I hope to do my duty to myself in a week or so; [. . .] I'll damn all Idleness – indeed, in superabundance of employment, I must not be content to run here and there on little two penny errands – but turn Rakehell, i e go a <u>making</u> [. . .] God knows, my Dear Reynolds, I should not talk any sorrow to you – you must have enough vexations – so I won't any more – If I ever start a rueful subject in a Letter to you – blow me! Why don't you – Now I was agoing to ask a very Silly Question neither you nor any body else could answer, under a folio, or at least a Pamphlet – you

---

[12]George had taken him there for his health.

---

[1]WLB 50–52. K is writing from the Surrey countryside southwest of London.

shall judge -Why don't you, as I do, look unconcerned at what may be called more particularly Heart-vexations? They never surprize me – lord! a man should have the fine point of his soul taken off to become fit for this world -I like this place very much – There is Hill & Dale and a little River – I went up Box hill[2] this Evening after the Moon – you a' seen the Moon – came down – and wrote some lines. Whenever I am separated from you, and not engaged in a continued Poem – every Letter shall bring you a lyric – but I am too anxious for you to enjoy the whole, to send you a particle. One of the three Books I have with me is Shakespear's Poems: I neer found so many beauties in the sonnets – they seem to be full of fine things said unintentionally -in the intensity of working out conceits – Is this to be borne? Hark ye!

When lofty trees I see barren of leaves
Which erst from heat did canopy the herd,
And Summer's green all girded   up in sheaves,
Borne on the bier with white and bristly beard.[3]

He has left nothing to say about nothing or any thing: for look at Snails, you know what he says about Snails, you know where he talks about "cockled snails"[4]– well, in one of these sonnets, he says –the chap slips into –no! I lie! this is in the Venus and Adonis: the Simile brought it to my Mind.

Audi[5] — As the snail, whose tender horns being hit,
Shrinks back into his shelly cave with pain
And there all smothered up in shade doth sit,
Long after fearing to put forth again:
So at his bloody view her eyes are fled,
Into the deep dark Cabins of her head.

He overwhelms a genuine Lover of Poesy with all manner of abuse, talking about—— "a poet's rage

And stretched metre of an antique song —"[6]

---

[2]A famous picturesque area and a key site in Austen's *Emma* (1816).

[3]Sonnet 12 (5–8); *erst*: formerly. K gets into the intensity with his preliminary *borne*.

[4]"Love's feeling is more soft and sensible / Than are the tender horns of cockled snails" (*Love's Labor's Lost* 4.3.338); *cockled*: shell-cased.

[5]Latin: hear. K writes out 1033–38, a simile for how Venus's eyes start back into her head when she comes upon her beloved Adonis, slain by the boar he was hunting.

[6]Sonnet 17 opens, "Who will believe my verse in time to come / If it were filled with your most high deserts?" and guesses that it will be regarded as this "stretched" (hyperbolic) praise (11). K puts this line on the title page of *Endymion*, punning on the English pronunciation *antic*.

Which by the by will be a capital Motto for my Poem – won't it? He speaks too of "Time's antique pen" – and "april's first born flowers" and "deaths eternal cold"[7] – By the Whim King! I'll give you a Stanza, because it is not material in connection and when I wrote it I wanted you to — give your vote, pro or con—

[writes out *Endymion* 4.581–90 . . .]

Now I hope I shall not fall off in the winding up, – as the Woman said to the [   ][8] – I mean up and down [. . .] remember me to each of our Card playing Club. when you die you will all be turned into Dice, and be put in pawn with the Devil –for Cards they crumple up like any King – I mean John in the stage play what pertains Prince Arthur — I rest

Your affectionate friend

John Keats

[. . .] Give my love to both houses – hinc atque illinc.[9]

from *The Champion*, 21 December 1817

Dramatic Review: MR. KEAN

Reynolds, the Champion's *drama critic, solicited Keats for this review. Dynamic actor Edmund Kean, waylaid by illness since November 24, returned on December 15 in* Richard III, *one of his acclaimed roles— especially the death scene, which, wrote William Hazlitt, "had a preter-natural and terrific grandeur." Keats saw this and another performance on 18 December at Drury Lane, where he ran into Godwin and Lamb.*

"In our unimaginative days,"—*Habeas Corpus'd*[1] as we are, out of all wonder, uncertainty and fear;—in these fire-side, delicate,

---

[7]Time's "antique pen" ages beauty (Sonnet 19); the other phrases are from Sonnets 21 and 13.

[8]K would finish *Endymion* the next week. Woodhouse's clerk decided not to tran-scribe this bawdy remark.

[9]On the quarrels among his friends, and riffing on Mercutio's dying words about the perpetual Capulet-Montague feuding that has claimed his life: "A plague a both your houses!" (*Romeo and Juliet* 3.1). The Latin means "here and there" (Virgil, *Georgics* 3.257).

---

[1]*OED* credits K with the first verbing of this phrase, referring to the writ to bring a body to court (as protection against prolonged, illegal imprisonment); this right had been suspended in March 1817 and would not be restored until January 1818. The quotation is from Wordsworth's *Excursion* (1814): 2.26.

gilded days,—these days of sickly safety and comfort, we feel very grateful to Mr Kean for giving us some excitement by his old passion in one of the old plays. He is a relict of romance;—a Posthumous ray of chivalry, and always seems just arrived from the camp of Charlemagne. In Richard he is his sword's dear cousin; in Hamlet his footing is germain to the platform. In Macbeth his eye laughs siege to scorn; in Othello he is welcome to Cyprus. In Timon he is of the palace—of Athens—of the woods, and is worthy to sleep in a grave "which once a day with its embossed froth, the turbulent surge doth cover."[2] For all these was he greeted with enthusiasm on his reappearance in Richard; for all these, his sickness will ever be a public misfortune. His return was full of power. He is not the man to "bate a jot." On Thursday evening, he acted *Luke* in *Riches*,[3] as far as the stage will admit, to perfection. In the hypocritical self-possession, in the caution, and afterwards the pride, cruelty and avarice, Luke appears to us a man incapable of imagining to the extreme heinousness of crimes. To him, they are mere magic-lantern horrors. He is at no trouble to deaden his conscience.

Mr. Kean's two characters of this week, comprising as they do, the utmost of quiet and turbulence, invite us to say a few words on his acting in general. We have done this before, but we do it again without remorse. Amid his numerous excellencies, the one which at this moment most weighs upon us, is the elegance, gracefulness and music of elocution. A melodious passage in poetry is full of pleasures both sensual and spiritual. The spiritual is felt when the very letters and points of charactered language show like the hieroglyphics of beauty:[4] the mysterious signs of an immortal freemasonry! "A thing to dream of, not to tell!"[5] The sensual life of verse springs warm from the lips of Kean, and to one

---

[2]From Timon's last speech, describing his seaside grave (*Timon of Athens* 5.1.218–19).

[3]Luke Traffic in James Bland Burges's comedy, *Riches: Or, the Wife and Brother* (1810), which K saw in June (Rollins).

[4]In a few weeks, K would hear Hazlitt at the Surrey Institution praise Shakespeare in similar terms: "His epithets and single phrases are like sparkles, thrown off from an imagination, fired by the whirling rapidity of its own motion. His language is hieroglyphical. It translates thoughts into visible images" (*Lectures on the English Poets* [Taylor & Hessey, 1818]; p. 107). Hazlitt may have read Keats's review.

[5]Riffing on Coleridge's *Christabel* 253 ("a sight to dream of, not to tell"), the tale-teller's horror at the grotesque revelation of enchantress Geraldine's unrobing. This poem was published in 1816.

learned in Shakespearean hieroglyphics,—learned in the spiritual portion of those lines to which Kean adds a sensual grandeur: his tongue must seem to have robbed "the hybla bees, and left them honeyless."[6] There is an indescribable gusto in his voice, by which we feel that the utterer is thinking of the past and future, while speaking of the instant. When he says in Othello, "put up your bright swords, for the dew will rust them,"[7] we feel that his throat had commanded where swords were as thick as reeds. From eternal risk, he speaks as though his body were unassailable. Again, his exclamation of "blood, blood, blood!" is direful and slaughterous to the deepest degree, the very words appear stained and gory. His nature hangs over them, making a prophetic repast. His voice is loosed on them, like the wild dog on the savage relics of an eastern conflict; and we can distinctly hear it "gorging, and growling o'er carcase and limb."[8] In Richard, "Be stirring with the lark to-morrow, gentle Norfolk!"[9] comes from him, as through the morning atmosphere, towards which he yearns. We could cite a volume of such immortal scraps, and dote upon them with our remarks; but as an end must come, we will content ourselves with a single syllable. It is in those lines of impatience to the night who "like a foul and ugly witch, doth limp so tediously away."[10] Surely this intense power of anatomizing the passion of every syllable—of taking to himself the wings of verse, is the mean by which he becomes a storm with such fiery decision; and by which, with a still deeper charm, he "does his spiriting gently."[11] Other actors are continually thinking of their sum-total effect throughout a play. Kean delivers himself up to the instant feeling, without the shadow of a thought about any thing else. He feels his being as deeply as Wordsworth, or any of our intellectual

[6]Cassius's praise of Antony's way with words (*Julius Caesar* 5.1.34–35); Hybla in Sicily is famed for its honeybees.

[7]Othello's contempt of those who have come to arrest him (*Othello* 1.2.59). Hazlitt's essay *On Gusto* (the aesthetics of intensity in visual arts and literature) had appeared in *The Examiner* in May 1816 and was collected in *The Round Table* (1817).

[8]Quoting Byron's *The Siege of Corinth* (411), the wild dogs feeding on the war-dead.

[9]Richard to his ally, the night before the battle in which he is slain (*Richard III* 5.3.56).

[10]The impatient French army's simile for waning night; they itch for daybreak, so they can vanquish the British (*Henry V* Act 4, Chorus 21–22).

[11]The sprite Ariel's pledge of obedience to Prospero (*The Tempest* 1.2.297).

monopolists. From all his comrades he stands alone, reminding us of him, whom Dante has so finely described in his Hell:

"And sole apart retir'd, the Soldan fierce!"[12]

Although so many times he has lost the Battle of Bosworth Field, we can easily conceive him really expectant of victory, and a different termination of the piece. Yet we are as moths about a candle, in speaking of this great man. "Great, let us call him, for he conquered us!"[13] We will say no more. Kean! Kean! have a carefulness of thy health, an in-nursed respect for thy own genius, a pity for us in these cold and enfeebling times! Cheer us a little in the failure of our days! for romance lives but in books. The goblin is driven from the heath, and the rainbow is robbed of its mystery![14]

Letter to George and Tom Keats, 21 and ?27 December 1817[1]

Keats writes about theater, politics, the intensity of art, "Negative Capability," and reactions to Shelley's visionary political poetry.

My dear Brothers,

I must crave your pardon for not having written ere this. . . . I saw Kean return to the public in "Richard III," and finely he did it, and, at the request of Reynolds, I went to criticize his Duke.[2] The critique is in to-day's "Champion," which I send you, with the "Examiner," in which you will find very proper lamentation on the obsoletion of Christmas gambols and pastimes: but it was mixed up with so much egotism of that driveling nature that pleasure is entirely lost.

---

[12]Henry Cary's translation of *Inferno* 4.129 (126 there), where Saladin (the great Muslim adversary of invading Crusaders Richard the Lion-Hearted of England and Phillip II of Spain), famed for his chivalry, fidelity, and generosity, is in Limbo.

[13]Riffing on the Moor Zanga's contempt of his Spanish captor at the opening of Edward Young's popular play *The Revenge. A Tragedy* (1.1.26), first produced in 1721. Zanga was one of Kean's celebrated roles, first performed in May 1815.

[14]Cf. *Lamia* 2.231–38 (p. 309), though the context there is complicated.

---

[1]*1848*, the first publication of this famous letter, based on John Jeffrey's transcription. I note some variants from the copy of Jeffrey's ms in WLB 9–10—now generally used for emendation.

[2]That is, *Luke* in *Riches*.

Hone, the publisher's trial, you must find very amusing, and, as Englishmen, very encouraging: his *Not Guilty* is a thing, which not to have been, would have dulled still more Liberty's emblazoning. Lord Ellenborough has been paid in his own coin. Wooler and Hone have done us an essential service.[3] I have had two very pleasant evenings with Dilke, yesterday and to-day, and am at this moment just come from him, and feel in the humour to go on with this, begun in the morning, and from which he came to fetch me. I spent Friday evening with Wells, and went next morning to see "Death on the Pale Horse."[4] It is a wonderful picture, when West's age is considered; but there is nothing to be intense upon; no women one feels mad to kiss, no face swelling into reality. The excellence of every art is its intensity, capable of making all disagreeables evaporate from their being in close relationship with Beauty and Truth. Examine "King Lear," and you will find this exemplified throughout:[5] but in this picture we have unpleasantness without any momentous depth of speculation excited, in which to bury its repulsiveness. The picture is larger than "Christ Rejected."[6]

I dined with Haydon the Sunday after you left, and had a very pleasant day. I dined too (for I have been out too much lately) with Horace Smith, and met his two Brothers, with Hill and Kingston, and one Du Bois. They only served to convince me how superior humor is to wit, in respect to enjoyment. These men say things which make one start, without making one feel; they are all

---

[3]Two notorious prosecutions. Radical journalist and bookseller William Hone had just been found *not guilty* on three counts of blasphemous libel for his parodies of the liturgy, of which nearly 100,000 copies had sold. Lord Chief Justice Ellenborough, who had earlier sent the Hunts to jail for libel, presided at two of Hone's trials and was humiliated by the loudly applauded verdict. Thomas Wooler, politician, journalist, and editor of the radical weekly *The Black Dwarf*, had been acquitted on similar charges in June. The trials were well attended and extremely amusing because the "offenses" had to be read into the record, gaining audience not only in the courtroom but also in reports in the "legitimate" press. K had been reading the accounts in the 21 Dec. *Examiner*.

[4]Wells is the friend who sent roses. *Death on a Pale Horse*, by American Benjamin West, is based on the image in Revelation of the fourth horseman of the Apocalypse. A subject of much buzz when it was exhibited at Pall Mall, it was criticized by Hazlitt in *Edinburgh Magazine* (Dec. 1817) for lacking "gusto" and "imagination." K. saw it at the Royal Academy with Dilke.

[5]West's painting of the storm scene; K's re-reading of *King Lear* the next month would provoke very different terms of description (see p. 92).

[6]Hundreds of thousands came to see *Christ Rejected* when it was exhibited in London in 1814.

alike; their manners are alike; they all know fashionables; they have a mannerism in their very eating and drinking, in their mere handling a decanter. They talked of Kean and his low company. "Would I were with that company instead of yours," said I to myself! I know such like acquaintance will never do for me, and yet I am going to Reynolds on Wednesday. Brown and Dilke walked with me and back from the Christmas pantomime. I had not a dispute, but a disquisition,[7] with Dilke on various subjects; several things dove-tailed in my mind, and at once it struck me what quality went to form a man of achievement, especially in literature, and which Shakespeare possessed so enormously—I mean *negative capability*, that is, when a man is capable of being in uncertainties, mysteries, doubts, without any irritable reaching after fact and reason. Coleridge, for instance, would let go by a fine isolated verisimilitude caught from the penetralium of Mystery, from being incapable of remaining content with half-knowledge.[8] This pursued through volumes would perhaps take us no further than this, that with a great Poet the sense of Beauty overcomes every other consideration, or rather obliterates all consideration. Shelley's poem is out, and there are words about its being objected to as much as "Queen Mab" was.[9] Poor Shelley, I think he has his quota of good qualities [in sooth la!![10]] Write soon to your most sincere friend and affectionate brother

John.

[7]legalese: formal inquiry.

[8]WLB] Negative Capability.
This famous formulation is a conscious oxymoron; cf. K's antipathy to egotistical assertions of "certain philosophy," "resting places and seeming sure points of Reasoning" (letters to Reynolds, 3 Feb. and 3 May 1818). In 1817 Coleridge published two works threaded with Christian theology, *Lay Sermons* and *Biographia Literaria*, as well as *The Rime of the Ancient Mariner* with a marginal gloss (K had been reading its host-volume, *Sibylline Leaves*). *Penetralium* is K's faux-Latin coinage, a retro-singular of *penetralia*, a temple's innermost chamber.

[9]Shelley's publishers, the Ollier brothers, no sooner issued his *Laon and Cythna*, a political epic idealizing brother-sister incest, than they withdrew it, fearing prosecution (a revision appeared the next January as *The Revolt of Islam*). Shelley's *Queen Mab* (1813), a visionary epic attacking "Kingcraft" and "Priestcraft," had been cited in the trial, earlier in 1817 (also presided over by Ellenborough), which refused him custody of his children by his first wife. The Olliers had been persuaded by Hunt and Shelley to publish K's *Poems*.

[10]WLB 10 (not in *1848*); "sooth la!" ("the truth!") is a campy echo of Cleopatra as she is trying, ineptly, to help Antony into his armor after a night of debauchery (*Antony and Cleopatra* 4.4.8).

Poems composed 1815–1817, published posthumously

(in order of publication, with dates of composition indicated)

"In a drear-nighted December"

Keats composed this poem in December 1817, just after finishing
Endymion. *It was first published in* The Literary Gazette: Journal of
Belles Lettres, Arts, Sciences, & c., *19 September 1829, p. 618, heading
a column of "Original Poetry"; then in* The Gem, A Literary Annual
(London 1830), *p. 80, there titled* Stanzas BY THE LATE JOHN KEATS—*the
surname correctly given, the verse with some variants. Other variants,
now commonly accepted, appear in Keats's ms.*

STANZAS
(Unpublished.)

In a drear-nighted[1] December,
  Too happy, happy Tree,
Thy branches ne'er remember
  Their green felicity:
The north cannot undo them,
With a sleety whistle through them;
Nor frozen thawings[2] glue them
  From budding at the prime.

In a drear-nighted December,
  Too happy, happy Brook,

10

---

[1] K ms] In drear-nighted
[2] The two-word compression enfolds a cruel sequence of thawing and refreezing.

Thy bubblings ne'er remember
  Apollo's summer look;
But with a sweet forgetting,
They stay their crystal fretting,[3]
Never, never petting°   *complaining*
  About the frozen time.

Ah! would 'twere so with many
  A gentle Girl and Boy!
But were there ever any
  Writhed[4] not of passed joy?   20
To know the change and feel it,[5]
When there is none to heal it,
Nor numbed sense to steel[6] it,
  Was never said in rhyme.

JOHN KEAT

"O Chatterton!" and "Byron!"

First published in 1848 (1.12–13), these sonnets are among Keats's earliest efforts, written during his surgeon's apprenticeship. Woodhouse's transcripts date "O Chatterton!" as early 1815 and "Byron!" as December 1814, and for both, he indents lines 2–3, 6–7, 10, 12, and 14, to mark out the Petrarchan form.

    The strange tragedy of the fate of Chatterton, "the marvellous Boy, the sleepless soul that perished in its pride,"[1] so disgraceful to

---

[3] agitation, but also with the sense of frozen ridges

[4] The verb shares an etymology with *write* (twist) and very obliquely implies it, especially with the reflex of *rime* (hoar-frost) in *rhyme* (as in Coleridge's *Rime of the Ancient Mariner*).

[5] K ms] The feel of not to feel it

[6] K ms] steal; editors tend to regard *steel* as K's misspelling, but the punning of one verbal sense into the other is apt, and K may have tested both.

---

[1] In 1770, Chatterton, destitute and despairing, committed suicide at age 17. The quoted phrase is from Wordsworth's *Resolution and Independence* 43–44 (1815 text). The first collection of Chatterton's poetry (1803) was assembled by Robert Southey and Joseph Cottle (publisher of *Lyrical Ballads*). K would inscribe *Endymion* to the memory of Chatterton.

the age in which it occurred and so awful a warning to all others of the cruel evils which the mere apathy and ignorance of the world can inflict on genius, is a frequent subject of allusion and interest in Keats's letters and poems, and some lines of the following invocation bear a mournful anticipatory analogy to the close of the beautiful elegy which Shelley hung over another early grave:[2]

> O Chatterton! how very sad thy fate!
> Dear child of sorrow—son of misery!
> How soon the film of death obscured that eye,
> Whence Genius mildly[3] flashed, and high debate.
> How soon that voice, majestic and elate,
> Melted in dying numbers![4] Oh! how nigh
> Was night to thy fair morning. Thou didst die
> A half-blown flow'ret which cold blasts amate.[5]
> But this is past: thou art among the stars
> Of highest Heaven: to the rolling spheres
> Thou sweetly singest: naught thy hymning mars,
> Above the ingrate world and human fears.
> On earth the good man base detraction bars
> From thy fair name, and waters it with tears.

Not long before this, Keats had become familiar with the works of Lord Byron, and indited a sonnet, of little merit, to him in December 1814:[6]

> Byron! how sweetly sad thy melody!
> Attuning still the soul to tenderness,
> As if soft Pity, with unusual stress,
> Had touched her plaintive lute, and thou, being by,
> Hadst caught the tones, nor suffer'd them to die.
> O'ershading sorrow doth not make thee less

---

[2]Shelley's *Adonais*, an elegy for Keats.

[3]Woodhouse ms] wildly

[4]Woodhouse ms] numbers (meters)

[5]Amate.—*Affright.* Chaucer [Milnes's note, *1848*]

[6]By 1814 Byron was the celebrated poet of *Childe Harold's Pilgrimage* (1812) and a train of sensational "Eastern tales": *The Giaour, The Bride of Abydos, The Corsair,* and *Lara.* K deploys the Petrarchan form to render an extended simile in the octave.

Delightful: thou thy griefs dost dress
With a bright halo, shining beamily,
As when a cloud the golden moon doth veil,
Its sides are tinged with a resplendent glow,
Through the dark robe oft amber rays prevail,
And like fair veins in sable marble flow;
Still warble, dying swan! still tell the tale,
The enchanting tale, the tale of pleasing woe.

Confused as are the imagery and diction of these lines, their feeling
suggests a painful contrast with the harsh judgment and late remorse of their object, the proud and successful poet, who never
heard of this imperfect utterance of boyish sympathy and respect.

ODE TO APOLLO

First published in 1848 *(2.252–54), there dated "Feb. 1815" under the
title.*

I

In thy western halls of gold
    When thou sittest in thy state,
Bards, that erst° sublimely told   *formerly*
    Heroic deeds, and sang of fate,
With fervour seize their adamantine° lyres,   *diamond*
Whose chords are solid rays, and twinkle radiant fires.

II

Here Homer with his nervous° arms   *sinewy*
    Strikes the twanging harp of war,
And even the western splendour warms,
    While the trumpets sound afar: 10
But, what creates the most intense surprise,
His soul looks out through renovated eyes.[1]

[1]Blind Homer regains his sight.

III

Then, through thy Temple wide, melodious swells
  The sweet majestic tone of Maro's lyre:
The soul delighted on each accent dwells,—
  Enraptur'd dwells,—not daring to respire,
The while he tells of grief around a funeral pyre.[2]

IV

'Tis awful° silence then again;   *awe-filled*
  Expectant stand the spheres;°   *planets*
  Breathless the laurell'd peers,°   *fellow poets* 20
Nor move, till ends the lofty strain,
  Nor move till Milton's tuneful thunders cease,
And leave once more the ravish'd heavens in peace.

V

Thou biddest Shakspeare wave his hand,
  And quickly forward spring
The Passions—a terrific band—
  And each vibrates the string
That with its tyrant temper best accords,
While from their Master's lips pour forth the inspiring words.

VI

A silver trumpet Spenser blows,   30
  And, as its martial notes to silence flee,
From a virgin chorus flows
  A hymn in praise of spotless Chastity.[3]
'Tis still! Wild warblings from the Æolian lyre
Enchantment softly breathe, and tremblingly expire.

VII

Next thy Tasso's[4] ardent numbers
  Float along the pleased air,

[2]Roman poet Virgil (Publius Verglius Maro) describes such scenes in his epic *The Aeneid*.

[3]*FQ* is dedicated to Elizabeth, the Virgin Queen; chastity is the theme of Book III.

[4]Italian Renaissance poet, 16th c.

Calling youth from idle slumbers,
   Rousing them from Pleasure's lair:—
Then o'er the strings his fingers gently move,   40
And melt the soul to pity and to love.

VIII

But when *Thou* joinest with the Nine,°   *the Muses*
And all the powers of song combine,
   We listen here on earth:
The dying tones that fill the air,
And charm the ear of evening fair,
From thee, great God of Bards, receive their heavenly birth.

Sonnet. *Written in disgust of Vulgar Superstition*

"Written in 15 minutes" (as Keats writes on the ms), 22 December 1816, this sonnet was first published in 1876, The Poetic Works of John Keats, *ed. Lord Houghton [Milnes]. The better text here is from H. B. Forman's* Poetic Works of John Keats, *1895. Vulgar Superstition is the Protestant view of Roman Catholicism, and in Keats's view, all religious institutions.*

The church bells toll a melancholy round,
   Calling the people to some other prayers,
   Some other gloominess, more dreadful cares,
More hearkening to the sermon's horrid sound.
Surely the mind of man is closely bound
   In some black spell; seeing that each one tears
   Himself from fireside joys, and Lydian airs,[1]
And converse high of those with glory crown'd.
Still, still they toll, and I should feel a damp,—
   A chill as from a tomb, did I not know   10

---

[1]An echo of Milton, "And ever against eating cares / Lap me in soft *Lydian* Aires" (*L'Allegro* 135–36), in tacit refusal of Plato's censure of Lydian music as morally corrupting (he favored the stately Dorian mode, more suited to military discipline). In Dryden's *Alexander's Feast*, Alexander the Great's heart is softened by music "Softly, sweet, in Lydian measures" (97).

That they are dying like an outburnt[2] lamp;
That 'tis their sighing, wailing ere they go
Into oblivion;—that fresh flowers will grow,
And many glories of immortal stamp.

"Fill for me a brimming bowl" and *On Peace*

These poems, from Keats's teenage apprentice years, were first published by Ernest de Sélincourt, "Recently Discovered Keats Mss," in Notes and Queries, *10th series, no. 58 (4 February 1905), 81–82.*

The earliest poem included in our manuscript bears the date August, 1814; it is therefore, so far as we know, only preceded among Keats's Juvenilia by the "Imitation of Spenser," which was written in 1813, and published among the "Poems" of 1817. Of as little intrinsic value as its predecessor, it is, I think, of equal interest in the light it throws upon the influences which affected his early work. It runs as follows:[1]—

Fill for me a brimming bowl
And let me in it drown my soul:
But put therein some drug, designed
To banish women from my mind:
For I want not the stream inspiring
That fills the mind with—fond desiring,
But I want as deep a draught
As e'er from Lethe's wave was quaff'd,[2]
From my despairing heart to charm
The Image of the fairest form   10
That e'er my reveling eyes beheld,

[2]OED credits K with the first use of this verb participle.

---

[1]epigraph in K ms] "What wondrous beauty! From this moment I efface from my mind all women." Terence's *Eunuch*, Act 2. Sc. 4. The octosyllabic couplets are modeled on Milton's *L'Allegro* and *Il Penseroso*.
[2]Echoing Thomas Moore's translation (1800) of a drinking song by Roman poet Anacreon: "Fill me, boy, as deep a draught, / As e'er was fill'd, as e'er was quaff'd" (Ode 62, opening lines).

That e'er my wandering fancy spell'd.
In vain! away I cannot chace
The melting softness of that face,
The beaminess of those bright Eyes,
That breast—earth's only Paradise.[3]
My sight will never more be blest;
For all I see has lost its zest:
Nor with delight can I explore
The classic page, or Muse's lore.   20
Had she but known how beat my heart,
And with one smile reliev'd its smart
I should have felt a sweet relief,
I should have felt "the joy of grief."[4]
Yet as the Tuscan mid the snow
Of Lapland thinks on sweet Arno,°   *river in Tuscany, Italy*
Even so for ever shall she be
The Halo of my Memory.

Aug. 1814.

[. . .] A sonnet "On Peace" is also found in the Woodhouse transcript.[5] It runs as follows:—

O Peace! and dost thou with thy presence bless
The dwellings of this war-surrounded Isle;
Soothing with placid brow our late distress,
Making the triple kingdom brightly smile?
Joyful I hail thy presence; and I hail
The sweet companions that await on thee;
Complete my joy—let not my first wish fail,
Let the sweet mountain nymph thy favourite be,

---

[3]Woodhouse notes the inspiration by the sight of a woman at Vauxhall pleasure
gardens.

[4]An epicurean pleasure; see Thomas Campbell's *The Pleasures of Hope* (1799):
"And teach impassioned souls the joy of grief" (1.182).

[5]Perhaps the second poem K ever wrote, c. April 1814, when Napoleon was exiled
to Elba, and Louis XVIII assumed the throne. With the exception of a brief peace in
1802–03, England had been at war with France since 1793, a conflict not concluded
until Waterloo in June 1815. Woodhouse's ms indents lines 2, 4, 6, 8, 11, and
13–14, to mark the Petrarchan structure (8/6), with the sestet ending in a Shakespearian couplet (with a hint of Spenser in the final alexandrine).

With England's happiness proclaim Europa's liberty.[6]
O Europe! let not sceptred tyrants see   10
That thou must shelter in thy former state;
Keep thy chains burst, and boldly say thou art free;
Give thy Kings law—leave not uncurbed the (great?)[7]
So with the horrors past thou'lt win thy happier fate!

The sonnet [. . .] was obviously inspired either by Napoleon's
retirement to Elba [1814] or by the peace which followed upon the
battle of Waterloo [1815]. The weakness of the sonnet would lead
us to favour the earlier date.

Lines on the Anniversary of Charles's Restoration

This text is from Amy Lowell, John Keats *(1925) 1.66, the first publi-*
cation. Some editors accept her dating of 1815; others propose 1814,
when Louis XVIII was restored to the throne of France. After Charles
I was executed in the civil wars of the 1640s, his son Charles II fled to
France. He was restored to the monarchy in 1660.

Hunt's liberation had aroused Keats to a fine fervour of patriotism,
the new patriotism which denounced "Minions of Grandeur," in
the words of the Leigh Hunt sonnet. The bells ringing the anniver-
sary of Charles II's restoration went against Keats's grain, and out
came this little burst of indignation:

LINES WRITTEN ON 29 MAY—THE ANNIVERSARY
OF CHARLES'S RESTORATION—ON HEARING THE BELLS RINGING.

Infatuate Britons, while[1] you still proclaim
His memory, your direst, foulest shame?
   Nor patriots revere?
Oh! while[2] I hear each traitorous lying bell,

---

[6]Milton allies mirth with the "Mountain Nymph, sweet Liberty" (L'Allegro 36).
[7]Editors now accept this word.

---

[1]Woodhouse's transcript (Morgan Library)] will
[2]Woodhouse's transcript (Morgan Library)] Ah! when

'Tis gallant Sydney's, Russel's, Vane's sad knell,[3]
   That pains my wounded ear.

The question marks seem oddly out of place, but I copy the transcript. The poem needs no comment. It is a boyish effusion, but all in line with Keats's attitude in these early years.

Letter to B. R. Haydon, 23 January 1818[1]

Taylor wants Haydon to do a portrait of Keats (a head) for a frontispiece in Endymion; *Keats is already thinking of his next endeavor, an epic that would be an antitype to the romance.*

My dear Haydon,
         I have a complete fellow-feeling with you in this business – so much so that it would be as well to wait for a choice out of Hyperion – when that Poem is done there will be a wide range for you – in Endymion I think you may have many bits of the deep and sentimental cast – the nature of Hyperion will lead me to treat it in a more naked and grecian Manner – and the march of passion and endeavour will be undeviating – and one great contrast between them will be – that the Hero of the written tale being mortal is led on, like Buonaparte, by circumstance; whereas the Apollo in Hyperion being a fore-seeing God will shape his actions like one. But I am counting &c. [. . .]
                                        Yours ever John Keats—

[3]All heroes to the liberals of K's day, executed for treason against Charles II: Algernon Sidney (1622–83), Lord William Russell (1639–83), and Sir Henry Vane (1613–62).

[1]ALS, British Library, 37538 f. 1.

Letter to Benjamin Bailey, 23 January 1818[1]

Bailey is at Oxford; Keats is preparing Endymion *for press, comparing speculation to philosophy.*

My dear Bailey,   Friday Jany 23rd
                    Twelve days have pass'd since your last reached me –
[. . .] One saying of yours I shall never forget – you may not recollect
it – it being perhaps said when you were looking on the surface and
seeming of Humanity alone, without a thought of the past or the
future – or the deeps of good and evil – you were at the moment
estranged from speculation and I think you have arguments ready
for the Man who would utter it to you – this is a formidable preface
for a simple thing – merely you said; "Why should Woman suffer?"
Aye. Why should she? 'By heavens I'd coin my very Soul and drop
my Blood for Drachmas"![2] These things are, and he who feels how
incompetent the most skyey Knight errantry its to heal this bruised
fairness is like a sensitive leaf on the hot hand of thought. Your tearing,
my dear friend, a spiritless and gloomy Letter up ~~and~~ to rewrite to me
is what I shall never forget – it was to me a real thing. Things have
happen'd lately of great Perplexity – You must have heard of them –
Reynolds and Haydon retorting and recriminating – and parting for
ever – the same thing has happened between Haydon and Hunt – It is
unfortunate – Men should bear with each other – there lives not the
Man who may not be cut up, aye hashed to pieces on his weakest side.
The best of Men have but a portion of good in them – a kind of spiritual
yeast in their frames which creates the ferment of existence – by which
a Man is propell'd to act and strive and buffet with Circumstance.
The sure way Bailey, is first to know a Man's faults, and then be
passive, if after that he insensibly draws you towards him then you have
no Power to break the link. Before I felt interested in either Reynolds
or Haydon – I was well read in their faults yet knowing them I have
been cementing gradually with both – I have an affection for them
both for reasons almost opposite – and to both must I of necessity
cling – supported always by the hope that when a little time – a few

[1]ALS, Houghton Library, Harvard.

[2]"By heaven, I had rather coin my heart / And drop my blood for drachmas than to
wring / From the hard hands of peasants their vile trash / By any indirection," cries
Brutus to an ally who has refused him gold to pay his troops (*Julius Caesar*
4.3.72–75).

years shall have tried me more fully in their esteem I may be able to bring them together - the time must come because they have both hearts - and they will recollect the best parts of each other when this gust is overblown. [. . .] I have sent my first book to the Press - and this afternoon shall begin preparing the second - my visit to you will be a great spur to quicken the Proceeding –[. . .] My Brother Tom is getting stronger but his Spitting of blood continues - I sat down to read King Lear yesterday, and felt the greatness of the thing up to the writing of a Sonnet preparatory thereto - in my next you shall have it There were some miserable reports of Rice's health - I went and lo! Master Jemmy had been to the play the night before and was out at the time - he always comes on his Legs like a Cat - I have seen a good deal of Wordsworth. Hazlitt is lecturing on Poetry at the Surry institution - I shall be there next Tuesday.

Your most affectionate Friend
John Keats—

Letter to George and Tom Keats, 23 and 24 January 1818[1]

Keats has just delivered Endymion *Book I to his publishers; this letter includes a sonnet on the occasion,* On sitting down to read King Lear *once again.*

MY DEAR BROTHERS,

I was thinking what hindered me from writing so long, for I have so many things to say to you and know not where to begin. It shall be upon a thing most interesting to you, my Poem. Well! I have given the first Book to Taylor; he seemed more than satisfied with it, and to my surprise proposed publishing it in quarto, if Haydon could make a drawing of some event therein, for a frontispiece.[2] I called on Haydon, he said he would do anything I liked, but said he would rather paint a finished picture, from it, which he

---

[1]The text here was first published in *1848*. This was the 4th letter of the day.

[2]*Endymion* was produced in a cheaper octavo printing (8 pages on each side of the sheet, instead of 4). Byron's *Childe Harold's Pilgrimage* was a handsome quarto (4 pages on each side). Although Haydon had sketched K's head for *Christ's Entry*, no portrait graced *Endymion*.

seems eager to do. This in a year or two will be a glorious thing for us; and it will be, for Haydon is struck with the first Book. I left Haydon, and the next day received a letter from him, proposing to make, as he says with all his might, a finished chalk sketch of my head, to be engraved in the first style, and put at the head of my Poem, saying, at the same time he had never done the thing for any human being, and that it must have considerable effect, as he will put the name to it. I begin to-day to copy my second Book——"thus far into the bowels of the Land"[3]—You shall hear whether it will be quarto or non-quarto, picture or non-picture. Leigh Hunt I showed my first Book to, he allows it not much merit as a whole; says it is unnatural, and made ten objections to it in the mere skimming over. He says the conversation is unnatural and too high-flown for Brother and Sister; says it should be simple,—forgetting, do ye mind, that they are both overshadowed by a supernatural Power, and of force could not speak like Francesca, in the "Rimini."[4] He must first prove that Caliban's poetry[5] is unnatural. This, with me, completely overturns his objections. The fact is, he and Shelley are hurt, and perhaps justly, at my not having showed them the affair officiously; and, from several hints I have had, they appear much disposed to dissect and anatomize any trip or slip I may have made.——But who's afraid? Ay! Tom! Demme if I am. I went last Tuesday, an hour too late, to Hazlitt's Lecture on Poetry, got there just as they were coming out, when all these pounced upon me:— Hazlitt, John Hunt and Son, Wells, Bewick, all the Landseers, Bob Harris, aye and more.[6]

   I think a little change has taken place in my intellect lately; I cannot bear to be uninterested or unemployed, I, who for so long a time have been addicted to passiveness. Nothing is finer for the purposes of great productions than a very gradual ripening of the intellectual powers. As an instance of this—observe—I sat down yesterday to read "King Lear" once again: the thing appeared to

[3]Richmond, leading his forces to vanquish Richard III (*Richard III* 5.2.3).

[4]See the footnote to "I stood tip-toe" (p. 14).

[5]Shakespeare wrote some wonderful poetry for the monster Caliban in *The Tempest*.

[6]Milnes elides some sentences about other news, reports of town life, and a visit to their sister Fanny, whose guardian made him feel very unwelcome. See Rollins's *Letters* 1.214. Keats missed this lecture on Jan. 20, but did attend the one on the 27th, "On Shakespeare and Milton."

demand the prologue of a sonnet. I wrote it and began to read. (I know you would like to see it.)[7]

> *On sitting down to read King Lear once again*
>
> *O golden-tongued Romance, with serene Lute!*
>   *Fair plumed Syren! Queen! of far-away!*
>   *Leave melodizing on this wintry day*
> *Shut up thine olden Pages, and be mute.*
> *Adieu! for once again, the fierce dispute,*
>   *Betwixt Damnation and impassion'd clay*[8]
>   *Must I burn through; once more humbly assay*[9]
> *The bitter-sweet of this Shakspearian fruit.*
> *Chief Poet! and ye Clouds of Albion,*[10]
>   *Begetters of ~~this~~ our deep eternal theme!*
> *When through the old oak forest*[11] *I am gone,*
>   *Let me not wander in a barren dream:*
> *But when I am consumed with the fire,*
> *Give me new Phœnix-wings to fly at my desire.*[12]

So you see I am getting at it, with a sort of determination and strength, though, verily, I do not feel it at this moment: this is my fourth letter this morning, and I feel rather tired, and my head rather swimming—so I will leave it open till to-morrow's post [. . .]

---

[7]Milnes follows Jeffrey's ms of a lost letter. I interpolate K's ms of the sonnet, written in his facsimile of Shakespeare's first folio, on a blank space opposite the opening of *King Lear*, there dated "Jany 22 – 1818–" (Keats House, Hampstead). Beginning with a Petrarchan pattern (*abba abba*), with a turn (*volta*) at 9, it adduces a Shakespearean sestet (*cdcdee*). The event of "reading" is critical, for K would not have been able to see the play as Shakespeare wrote it. The stage was held by Nahum Tate's "Romance" rewriting (1681), of which Dr. Johnson even approved. Tate's Lear doesn't die but regains the throne, then abdicates to newly married Edgar and Cordelia (she doesn't die either) and happily retires with Gloucester (ditto) and Kent. Shakespeare's original did not return to the stage until after K's death.

[8]flesh, the mortal body ("Adam" comes from the word for clay).

[9]analyze the content of—more specifically, the gold content.

[10]an old Celtic name for England (the era of *King Lear*), frequent in romance.

[11]the realm of English romance.

[12]A hypermetrical alexandrine, this meter is the last line of the Spenserian stanza, used for *FQ* and Byron's *Childe Harold's Pilgrimage. A Romaunt* (1812–). The phoenix bird is fabled to rejuvenate itself with cyclical self-immolation and rebirth from the ashes.

Hunt said he was nearly sure that the "Cockney School" was written by Scott;[13] so you are right, Tom! [. . .]
I remain,
My dear brothers, your affectionate brother,
JOHN.

Letter to John Taylor, 30 January 1818[1]

Preparing Endymion *Book II for press, Keats gives his publisher new verse for Book I on the ascent from sensual pleasure to divine fellowship and confesses his ambitions for drama.*

My dear Taylor,
These Lines, as they now stand, about Happiness have rung in my ears like a 'chime a mending'.[2] See here,

Behold
Wherein Lies happiness Pœona? fold—

This appears to me the very contrary of blessed. I hope this will appear to you more elegible.

Wherein lies Happiness? In that which becks
Our ready Minds to fellowship divine;
A fellowship with essence, till we shine
Full alchymized and free of space. Behold
The clear Religion of heaven - fold &c—[3]

You must indulge me by putting this in for setting aside the badness of the other, such a Preface is necessary to the Subject. The whole thing must I think have appeared to you, who are a consequitive

---

[13]Hunt was wrong about Z (the article is the first "Cockney School" paper). John Scott—who was writing for *The Champion*, often at odds with Hunt in 1816 about Byron's poetry and character (after the Byrons' separation)—was outraged by the abuse of K in the *Quarterly* and *Blackwood's*. When he reviewed *1820* for *London Magazine*, he would find much to praise.

---

[1]ALS, Pierpont Morgan Library.

[2]Ulysses tells general Agamemnon how alienated warrior Achilles mocks his voice (*Troilus and Cressida* 1.3.159). Taylor was reading *Endymion* carefully and offering K advice.

[3]These lines are for insertion in *Endymion* 1.777–81.

Man, as a thing almost of mere words – but I assure you that when I wrote it, it was a regular stepping of the Imagination towards a Truth. My having written that ~~Passage~~ Argument will perhaps be of the greatest Service to me of any thing I ever did. It set before me at once the gradations of Happiness even like a Kind of Pleasure Thermometer – and is my first Step towards the chief Attempt in the Drama – the playing of different Natures with Joy and Sorrow–

Do me this favor and believe Me, Your sincere friend

John Keats [. . .]

Letter to John Hamilton Reynolds, 31 January 1818[1]

Writing from Hampstead to fellow-poet Reynolds in London, Keats includes the songs "O blush not so," "Hence Burgundy," "God of the Meridian," *and the sonnet* "When I have fears."

My Dear Reynolds

I have parcell'd out this day for Letter Writing–more resolved thereon because your Letter will come as a refreshment and will have (sic parvis &c.[2]) the same effect as a Kiss in certain situations where people become over-generous. I have read this first sentence over, and think it savours rather; however an inward innocence is like a nested dove; or as the old song says.

1

O blush not so, O blush not so
or I shall think ye knowing;[3]
And if ye smile, the blushing while,
Then Maidenheads are going.

---

[1]WLB 53–55, which supplies the date.

[2]Virgil, *Eclogue I*, line 23: "sic parvis componere magna solebam" (I was thus used to compare great things and small). See also K's English echo to Bailey (p. 70).

[3]With the sense of sexually experienced. The song was considered unfit for print by such Victorian poets as Swinburne and D. G. Rossetti. Not in *1848*, it was first published by HBF in 1883. K marked relevant lines in *Troilus and Cressida*: Pandarus's chiding of a hesitant Cressida in 3.2: "Come, come, what need your blush?"; "What, blushing still?"

2

There's a blush for want, and a blush for shan't
    And a blush for having done it,
There's a blush for thought, and a blush for naught
    And a blush for just begun it.

3

O sigh not so, O sigh[4] not so
    For it sounds of Eve's sweet Pipin.[5]
By those loosen'd hips, you have tasted the pips
    And fought in an amorous nipping.

4

Will ye play once more, at nice cut core
    For it only will last our youth out,
And we have the prime, of the Kissing time
    We have not one sweet tooth out.

5

There's a sigh for yes, and a sigh for no,
    And a sigh for "I can't bear it"—
O what can be done, shall we stay or run
    O cut the sweet apple and share it?

==

Now I purposed to write to you a serious poetical Letter – but I find that a maxim I met with the other day is a just one "on cause mieux quand on ne dit pas <u>causons</u>" I was hindered however from my first intention by a mere muslin Handkerchief very neatly pinned—but "Hence vain deluding &c." Yet I cannot write in prose, It is a sun-shiny day and I cannot so here goes,[6]

---

[4]K may be punning on "say" (Cockney-sounding "sigh").

[5]All bawdy: an apple with red-flushed skin, a small fruit seed, a highly desired thing, something extraordinary; "hips" is human anatomy, as well as the false fruit of a rose; "pips" are seeds, but also acts of a chick breaking though a shell (and thus an image of sexual initiation).

[6]K is already rhyming (*prose/goes*). Milton opens *Il Penseroso*, "Hence, vain deluding joys. . . ." WLB presents these trimeter songs in two columns on p. 54, the first one ending after the first quatrain of "God of the Meridian." These poems were first published in *1848*.

Hence Burgundy, Claret& port,
    Away with old Hock and Madeira
Too couthly[7] ye are for my sport
    There's a beverage brighter and clearer
    Instead of a pitiful rummer[8]
    My Wine overbrims a whole Summer
    My bowl is the sky
    And I drink at my eye
    Till I feel in the brain
    A delphian[9] pain –
    Then follow my Caius[10] then follow
    On the Green of the Hill
    We will drink our fill
    Of golden sunshine
    Till our brains intertwine
    With the glory and grace of Apollo!

God of the Meridian
    And of the East and West[11]
To thee my soul is flown
    And my body is earthward press'd —
    It is an awful mission
    A terrible division
    And leaves a gulph austere
    To be filled with worldly fear.
    Aye, when the Soul is fled
    To high above our head,
    Affrighted do we gaze
    After its airy maze —
    As doth a Mother wild,
    When her young infant child
    Is in an eagle's claws —

[7]archaism: familiar (cf. uncouth).

[8]a large glass.

[9]poetic frenzy, as if a possessed prophetess, e.g., the oracle of Apollo at Delphi.

[10]Reynolds's pen name for articles in *The Yellow Dwarf*, a liberal periodical edited by John Hunt.

[11]noon, sunrise, and sunset (Apollo).

And is not this the cause
of Madness? God of Song
Thou bearest me along
Through sights I scarce can bear
O let me, let me share
With the hot Lyre and thee,
The staid Philosophy.
Temper my lonely hours,
And let me see thy bow'rs
More unalarmd! –

My Dear Reynolds, you must forgive all this ranting – but the fact is, I cannot write sense this Morning – however you shall have some. I will copy my last Sonnet.

When I have fears that I may cease to be[12]
    Before my pen has glean'd my teeming brain,
Before high piled Books in charactery
    Hold like rich garners the full ripen'd grain—
When I behold upon the night's starr'd face
    Huge cloudy symbols of a high romance,
And feel that I may never live to trace
    Their shadows with the magic hand of chance:
And when I feel, fair creature of an hour,
    That I shall never look upon thee more
Never have relish in the fairy power
    Of unreflecting Love: then on the Shore
        Of the wide world I stand alone and think
        Till Love and Fame to Nothingness do sink.—

I must take a turn, and then write to Teignmouth. Remember me to all, not excepting yourself.

Your sincere friend,
John Keats.

[12]K's Shakespearean sonnet (first published as Sonnet VII in *1848* [2.293]) opens in complexly blended echoes: Shakespeare's Sonnet 12, "When I do count the clock that tells the time"; Milton's (Petrarchan) sonnet, "When I consider how my light is spent / Ere half my days, in this dark world and wide . . ."; Wordsworth's "few could know / When Lucy ceased to be" (*Song*)—which by 1816 had been summoned in Shelley's sonnet-lament that the now Tory poet should "cease to be" his former self (*To Wordsworth*).

§ J. H. Reynolds's sonnets on Robin Hood (addressed to Keats)

Sent to Keats on 3 February, the text shown here was published in
Yellow Dwarf *(21 February 1818, p. 64).*

TO A FRIEND, ON ROBIN HOOD[1]

The trees in Sherwood forest are old and good,—
The grass beneath them now is dimly green;
Are they deserted all? Is no young mien,
With loose slung bugle, met within the wood?
No arrow found,—foil'd of its antler'd food,—
Struck in the oak's rude side?—Is there nought seen,
To mark the revelries which there have been,
In the sweet days of merry Robin Hood?
Go there, with Summer, and with evening,—go
In the soft shadows like some wandering man,—   10
And thou shalt far amid the Forest know
The archer men in green, with belt and bow,
Feasting on pheasant, river fowl, and swan,
With Robin at their head, and Marian.

TO THE SAME

With coat of Lincoln green and mantle too,
And horn of ivory mouth, and buckle bright,—
And arrows wing'd with peacock-feathers light,
And trusty bow well gather'd of the yew,—
Stands Robin Hood:—and near, with eyes of blue
Shining through dusk hair, like the stars of night,
And habited in pretty forest plight,
His greenwood beauty sits, young as the dew.[2]
Oh gentle-tressed girl! Maid Marian!
Are thine eyes bent upon the gallant game   10
That stray in the merry Sherwood: thy sweet fame
Can never, never die. And thou, high man,
Would we might pledge thee with thy silver can
Of Rhenish, in the woods of Nottingham!

[1]Folk hero Robin Hood was a political subject by the 19th c, a patriotic opponent of
tyranny, famous for robbing from the rich to give to the poor.
[2]ms to K] . . . sits, tender and true

Letter to John Hamilton Reynolds, 3 February 1818[1]

Along with his Robin Hood "answer," Keats conveys views of Words-worth's egotism and Hunt's self-infatuation.

My dear Reynolds, [. . .]
    The first is the best on account of the first line, and the "arrow—foil'd of its antler'd food" and moreover (and this is the only word or two I find fault with, the more because I have had so much reason to shun it as a quicksand) the last has "tender and true" – We must cut this,[2] and not be rattlesnaked[3] into any more of the like – It may be said that we ought to read our Contemporaries. that Wordsworth &c should have their due from us. but for the sake of a few fine imaginative or domestic passages, are we to be bullied into a certain Philosophy engendered in the whims of an Egotist – Every man has his speculations, but every Man does not brood and peacock[4] over them till he makes a false coinage and deceives himself – Many a man can travel to the very bourne of Heaven, and yet want confidence to put down his half-seeing. Sancho will invent a Journey heavenward as well as any body.[5] We hate poetry that has a palpable design upon us – and if we do not agree, seems to put its hand in its breeches pocket.[6] Poetry should be great & unobtrusive, a thing which enters into one's soul, and does not startle it or amaze it with itself– but with its subject. — How beautiful are the retired flowers! how would they lose their beauty were they to throng into the highway crying out, "admire me I am a violet!– dote upon me I am a primrose! [. . .] I will cut all this – I will have no more of Wordsworth or Hunt in particular [. . .] Why be teased with "nice Eyed wagtails," when we have in sight "the Cherub Contemplation"?[7]

[1]WLB 28–30.

[2]As the printed version shows, Reynolds did "cut this."

[3]A K-coined verb (*OED* give this as the first instance).

[4]*peacock*: strut ostentatiously; *OED* credits this as the first usage as a verb. *brood*: to hatch an egg (with pride), but also to give into emotional self-indulgence.

[5]Brooding Hamlet terms the afterlife as the "undiscovered country, from whose bourn / No traveler returns" (3.1.79–80); *bourn*: region. Sancho Panza is the practical squire to the idealistic hero of Cervantes' *Don Quixote*.

[6]refuse to engage; sulk

[7]The first is a phrase from Hunt's *The Nymphs* (K read it in ms); it was published in *Foliage: or, Poems Original and Translated* (1818): "little ponds that hold the rains, / Where the nice-eyed wagtails glance, / Sipping 'twixt their jerking dance" (2.168–70, p. xxxiii). The second phrase is from Milton's *Il Penseroso* (54; describing the angel cherubim contemplating God).

—Why with Wordsworths "Matthew with a bough of wilding in his hand" when we can have Jacques "under an oak &c"?[8] – The secret of the Bough of Wilding will run through your head faster than I can write it - Old Matthew spoke to him some years ago on some nothing, & because he happens in an Evening Walk to imagine the figure of the Old Man - he must stamp it down in black & white, and it is henceforth sacred - I don't mean to deny Wordsworth's grandeur &Hunt's merit, but I mean to say we need not be teazed with grandeur & merit - when we can have them uncontaminated &unobtrusive. Let us have the old Poets, and Robin Hood. Your letter and its sonnets gave me more pleasure than will the 4th Book of Childe Harold &the whole of any body's life &opinions.[9] In return for your Dish of filberts, I have gathered a few Catkins, I hope they'll look pretty.

To J.H.R. In answer to his Robin Hood Sonnets
[WLB cross-references his ms of the poem (published in *1820*). See § below.]

I hope you will like them they are at least written in the Spirit of Outlawry[10] [. . .] I will call on you at 4 tomorrow [. . .] I hope also to bring you my 2[d] book[11] – In the hope that these Scribblings will be some amusement for you this Evening – I remain copying on the Hill
Y[r] sincere friend and Coscribbler
John Keats –

§   To John H. Reynolds
In answer to his Robin Hood Sonnets

No! those days are gone away,
And their hours are old and grey,

---

[8]The poet of *The Two April Mornings* (*Lyrical Ballads*, 1800) remembers the village schoolmaster (long dead) holding a "bough / Of wilding in his hand" (the closing words; K is oddly untouched by the pained memory). In *As You Like It*, Jaques sits under an oak pitying a wounded hunted deer (2.1.31). Not only had Wordsworth been dismissive of an ode to Pan (*Endymion* Book I) when K eagerly recited it to him—"a Very pretty piece of Paganism" (reports a dismayed and angry Haydon)—but when K seemed eager to converse on some points of poetry, Mrs. Wordsworth put her hand on his arm and advised (so K later told Clarke), "Mr. Wordsworth is never interrupted."

[9]Byron's eagerly anticipated *Childe Harold's Pilgrimage* Canto IV would be out in April. Coleridge's *Biographia Literaria* ("life and opinions") was published in 1817.

[10]The spirit extends to poetic form, the 7-syllable couplets of 17th-c. verse—a swerve from the sonnets and couplets at which K was (too) adept. There are no sonnets in *1820*, and its one couplet-poem, *Lamia*, plays the form in a briskly new way, also with a 17th-c. (Dryden) reference.

[11]The fair copy of *Endymion* Book II.

And their Minutes buried all
Under the down-trodden pall
Of the leaves of many years:
Many times have winter's sheers,
Frozen North and chilling East,
Sounded tempests to the feast
Of the forest's whispering fleeces,
Since men paid no rent and leases.[12]

No, the Bugle sounds no more,
And the twanging bow no more;
Silent is the ivory[13] shrill
Past the heath and up the hill:
There is no mid-forest laugh,
Where lone Echo gives the half
To some wight, amaz'd to hear
Jesting, deep in forest drear.[14]

On the fairest time of June
You may go, with sun or moon,
Or the seven stars to light you,
Or the polar ray[15] to right you;
But you never may behold
Little John or Robin bold;
Never any of the clan
Thrumming on an empty can
Some old hunting ditty, while
He doth his green way beguile
To fair Hostess' Merriment
Down beside the pasture Trent,[16]
For he left the merry tale,
Messenger to spicy ale.

---

[12]Before the enclosure acts, there was a lot of open land, free for use by all.

[13]hunting horn

[14]An even more distant, mythological past, when the nymph Echo inhabited the woods; *wight*: archaic term for "poor fellow" (see *La Belle Dame sans Mercy*, p. 421).

[15]Northern star

[16]the river running through pastureland

Gone, the merry morris din;
Gone the song of Gamelyn;[17]
Gone the tough-belted outlaw
Idling in the "grenè shawe";[18]
All are gone away and past!
And if Robin <u>should be</u> cast
Sudden from his turfed grave;
And if Marian <u>should</u> have
Once again her forest days;
She would weep, and he would craze:
He would swear, for all his oaks,
Fall'n beneath the dockyard strokes,
Have rotted on the briny seas:
She would weep that her wild bees
Sang not to her—"Strange that honey
Can't be got without hard money!"[19]

So it is: yet let us sing,
Honour to the old bow-string!
Honour to the bugle-horn!
Honour to the woods unshorn!
Honour to the Lincoln green!
Honour to the archer keen!
Honour to tight little John,
And the horse he rode upon!
Honour to bold Robin Hood
Sleeping in the underwood!
Honor to maid Marian,
And to all the Sherwood-clan!
Though their days have hurried by
Let us two a burden[20] try.

[17]the music of the morris dance and the mid-14th-c. verse romance *The Tale of Gamelyn*, in which the hero becomes the king of an outlaw forest-band.

[18]Chaucerian diction (green grove).

[19]Another reference to modern commerce and the imperial business of ship-building.

[20]chorus

§ A sonnet-contest with Shelley and Hunt

Keats has just sent Endymion Book II *to his publishers. Around 4 February 1818 (he tells his brothers), "Shelley, Hunt & I, wrote each a sonnet on the River Nile." Timed to 15 minutes, the contest (like so many others) took place at Hunt's. There is some suspicion that Hunt preplanned his sonnet, then suggested the contest. At any rate, he promptly published his. Keats wasn't so eager; his sonnet first appeared in a weekly journal in 1838, then in 1848, with Hunt's and Shelley's* Ozymandias *(Hunt wrongly gave this to Milnes as Shelley's effort).*

TO THE NILE

Son of the old moon-mountains[1] African!
Stream of the Pyramid and Crocodile!
We call thee fruitful, and that very while
A desert fills our seeing's inward span:
Nurse of swart nations since the world began,
Art thou so fruitful? or dost thou beguile
Such men to honour thee, who, worn with toil,
Rest for a space 'twixt Cairo and Decan?[2]
O may dark fancies err! They surely do;
'Tis ignorance that makes a barren waste
Of all beyond itself. Thou dost bedew
Green rushes like our rivers, and dost taste
The pleasant sun-rise. Green isles hast thou too,
And to the sea as happily dost haste.

                                                                J.K.

THE NILE

It flows through old hush'd Egypt and its sands,
Like some grave mighty thought threading a dream;
And times and things, as in that vision, seem
Keeping along it their eternal stands,—
Caves, pillars, pyramids, the shepherd bands

---

[1] From Ethiopia's Mountains of the Moon descends the Nile.

[2] A common European route to India (Decan) tracked from the port of Alexandria, southward along the Nile to Cairo, then across the desert to the Red Sea and on east.

That roamed through the young earth, the glory extreme
Of high Sesostris, and that southern beam,
The laughing queen that caught the world's great hands.

Then comes a mightier silence, stern and strong,
As of a world left empty of its throng,
And the void weighs on us; and then we wake,
And hear the fruitful stream lapsing along
'Twixt villages, and think how we shall take
Our own calm journey on for human sake.

L. H.

Shelley's To the Nile *was first published in* St. James's Magazine, *1876.*
Text: The Poetical Works of Percy Bysshe Shelley, *ed. H. B. Forman*
(London: 1876–77) 3.410–11.

TO THE NILE

Month after month the gathered rains descend
Drenching yon secret Ethiopian dells,
And from the desert's ice-girt pinnacles
Where Frost and Heat in strange embraces blend
On Atlas,[3] fields of moist snow half depend.
Girt there with blasts and meteors Tempest dwells
By Nile's aëreal urn, with rapid spells
Urging those waters to their mighty end.

O'er Egypt's land of Memory floods are level,
And they are thine, O Nile—and well thou knowest
That soul-sustaining airs and blasts of evil
And fruits and poisons spring where'er thou flowest.
Beware, O Man—for knowledge must to thee,
Like the great flood to Egypt, ever be.—[4]

---

[3]mountains in northwest Africa
[4]The Nile floods and irrigates the plains every August.

Letter to John Hamilton Reynolds, 19 February 1818[1]

Keats has just seen a print-sheet of Endymion *Book I. Reynolds has been ill, and Keats amuses him with thoughts on indolence, passiveness, and* "O thou whose face hath felt the Winter's wind" *(first published in* 1848 *1.90).*

My dear Reynolds,

I have an idea that a Man might pass a very pleasant life in this manner— let him on a certain day read a certain Page of full Poesy or distilled Prose, and let him wander with it, and muse upon it, and reflect upon it, and bring home to it, and prophesy upon it, and dream upon it – until it becomes stale – but when will it do so? Never– When Man has arrived at a certain ripeness in intellect any one grand and spiritual passage serves him as a starting-post towards all "the two-and-thirty Palaces" How happy is such a voyage of conception! – what delicious diligent Indolence![2] A doze upon a Sofa does not hinder it, and a nap upon Clover engenders ethereal finger-pointings – the prattle of a child gives it wings, and the converse of middle age a strength to beat them – a strain of music conducts to 'an odd angle of the Isle' and when the leaves whisper it puts 'a girdle round the earth.'[3] Nor will this sparing touch of noble Books be any irreverance to their Writers – for perhaps the honors paid by Man to Man are trifles in comparison to the Benefit done by great Works to the 'Spirit and pulse of good' by their mere passive existence.[4]
Memory should not be called Knowledge – Many have original Minds who do not think it - they are led away by Custom. Now it appears to me that almost any Man may like the Spider spin from his own niwards[5] his own airy Citadel - the points of leaves and twigs on

[1]ALS, Robert H. Taylor collection, Princeton University.

[2]K will later write, but not publish, *Ode on Indolence*; "indolence" denotes a conscious luxuriating in passivity and receptivity, in relaxation from usual busy-ness.

[3]Sprite Ariel reports to magician Prospero that he has deposited the shipwrecked king's son, Ferdinand, thought drowned, "in an odd angle of the isle," where he sits in stunned sorrow (*The Tempest* 1.2.223). Sprite Puck assures Fairy King Oberon that he will "put a girdle round about the earth" in search for the herb "love-in-idleness" (*Midsummer Night's Dream* 2.1.175).

[4]It is striking to see K, who carped about Wordsworth's triviality and egotism to Reynolds just a couple of weeks earlier, quoting from one of the most didactic of the *Lyrical Ballads* (1798), *The Old Cumberland Beggar*: "'tis Nature's law / That none, . . . / . . . should exist / Divorced from good, a spirit and pulse of good" (75–77).

[5]This looks like "niwards'—as if K had started to write *nature*, then changed his mind.

1072/4

My dear Reynolds,

I have an idea that a Man might pass a very pleasant life in this manner - let him on any certain day read a certain Page of full Poesy or distilled Prose and let him wander with it, and muse upon it, and reflect from it, and bring home to it, and prophesy upon it, and dream upon it: untill it becomes stale - but when will it do so? Never. When Man has arrived at a certain ripeness in intellect any one grand and spiritual passage serves him as a starting post towards all "the two and thirty Pallaces" How happy is such a voyage of conception, what delicious diligent Indolence! A doze upon a sofa does not hinder it, and a nap upon Clover engenders ethereal finger-pointings - the prattle of a child gives it wings, and the converse of middle age a strength to beat them - a strain of musick conducts to 'an odd angle of the Isle' and when the leaves whisper it puts a girdle round the earth. Nor will this sparing touch of noble Books be any irreverance to their Writers - for perhaps the honors paid by Man to Man are trifles in comparison to the Benefit done by great Works to the 'Spirit and pulse of good' by their mere passive existence.

Manuscript of letter to Reynolds, 19 February 1818.

Memory should not be called Knowledge - Many have original
Minds who do not think it - they are led away by Custom.
Now it appears to me that almost any Man may like
the Spider spin from his own inwards his own airy
Citadel - the points of leaves and twigs on which the
Spider begins her work are few and she fills the
Air with a beautiful circuiting: man should
be content with as few points to tip with the fine
Web of his soul and weave a tapestry empyrean -
full of symbols for his spiritual eye, of softness
for his spiritual touch, of space for his wandering
of distinctness for his Luxury - But the Minds of
Mortals are so different and bent on such diverse
Journeys that it may at first appear impossible for
any common taste and fellowship to exist between
between two or three under these suppositions. It is
however quite the contrary. Minds would leave each
other in contrary directions, traverse each other in
numberless points, and all last greet each other at
the Journeys end. A old Man and a child would
talk together and the old Man be on his Path, and
the child left thinking - Man should not dispute or
assert but whisper results to his neighbour, and thus

page 2

by every germ of Spirit sucking the sap from mould
ethereal every human might become great, and
Humanity instead of being a wide heath of Furse
and Briars with here and there a remote Oak
or Pine, would become a grand democracy of
Forest Trees. It has been an old Comparison for
our urging on – the Bee hive – however it seems
to me that we should rather be the flower than the
Bee – for it is a false notion that more is gained
by receiving than giving – no the receiver and the
giver are equal in their benefits. The flower I doubt
not receives a fair guerdon from the Bee – its leaves
blush deeper in the next spring – and who shall say
between Man and Woman which is the most delighted?
Now it is more noble to sit like Jove than to fly
like Mercury – let us not therefore go hurrying about
and collecting honey-bee like, buzzing here and there
impatiently from a knowledge of what is to be arrived
at: but let us open our leaves like a flower and
be passive and receptive – budding patiently under
the eye of Apollo and taking hints from every noble
insect that favors us with a visit – sap will be

page 3

which the spider begins her work are few and she fills the Air with a beautiful circuiting: man should be content with as few points to tip with the fine Webb[6] of his Soul and weave a tapestry empyrean—full of Symbols for his spiritual eye, of softness for his spiritual touch, of space for his wandering of distinctness for his luxury – But the Minds of Mortals are so different and bent on such diverse Journeys that it may at first appear impossible for any common taste and fellowship to exist between two or three under these suppositions. It is however quite the contrary— Minds would leave each other in contrary directions, traverse each other in Numberless points, and all last greet each other at the Journeys end – A old Man and a child would talk together and the old Man be led on his Path, and the child left thinking – Man should not dispute or assert but whisper results to his neighbour and thus by every germ of Spirit sucking the Sap from mould ethereal every human might become great, and Humanity instead of being a wide heath of Furse and Briars with here and there a remote Oak or Pine, would become a grand democracy of Forest Trees. It has been an old Comparison for our urging on – the Bee hive – however it seems to me that we should rather be the flower than the Bee – for it is a false notion that more is gained by receiving than giving[7] – no the receiver and the giver are equal in their benefits – The fower I doubt not receives a fair guerdon[8] from the Bee – its leaves blush deeper in the next spring – and who shall say between Man and Woman which is the most delighted? Now it is more noble to sit like Jove that to fly like Mercury – let us not therefore go hurrying about and collecting honey bee-like, buzzing here and there impatiently from a Knowledge of what is to be arrived at: but let us open our leaves like a flower and be passive and receptive – budding patiently under the eye of Apollo and taking hints from every noble insect that favours us with a visit – sap will be given us for Meat and dew for drink – I was led into these thoughts, my dear Reynolds, by the beauty of the morning operating on a sense of Idleness – I have not read any Books – the Morning said I was right – I had no Idea but of the Morning, and the Thrush said I was right – seeming to say –

---

[6]The misspelling may betray brooding over Z's "Cockney School" papers, all headed by verse mocking K, attributed to Cornelius Webb (see p. 63).

[7]Jesus says, "It is more blessed to give than to receive" (Acts 20.35).

[8]reward

given up for Meat and dew for drink – I was led into
these thoughts, my dear Reynolds, by the beauty of the
morning operating on a sense of Idleness – I have not
read any Books – the Morning said I was right – I had
no Idea but of the Morning and the Thrush said I
was right – seeming to say

'O thou whose face hath felt the Winter's wind,
Whose eye has seen the snow clouds hung in Mist
And the black elm tops 'mong the freezing Stars
To thee the Spring will be a harvest time –
O thou whose only book has been the light
Of supreme darkness which thou feddest on
Night after night, when Phoebus was away
To thee the Spring shall be a Tripple morn.
O fret not after Knowledge – I have none
And yet my song comes native with the warmth
O fret not after Knowledge – I have none
And yet the Evening listens. He who saddens
At thought of Idleness cannot be idle,
And his awake who thinks himself asleep.'

Now I am sensible all this is a mere sophistication
however it may neighbour to any truths, to excuse

page 4

my own indolence – so I will not deceive myself that
Man should be equal with Jove – but think himself
very well off as a sort of scullion – Mercury or even
a humble Bee – It is not matter whether I am
right or wrong, either one way or another, if
there is sufficient to lift a little time from your
shoulders. Your affectionate friend
                    John Keats –

'O thou whose face hath felt the Winter's wind;[9]
　Whose eye has seen the Snow clouds hung in Mist
And the black elm-tops 'mong the freezing Stars
To thee the Spring will be a harvest-time –
O thou whose only book has been the light
Of supreme[10] darkness which thou feddest on
Night after night, when Phœbus was away
To thee the Spring shall be thipple[11] morn –
O fret not after knowledge – I have none
And yet my song comes native with the warmth
O fret not after knowledge – I have none
And yet the Evening listens. He who saddens
At thought of Idleness cannot he be idle,
And he's awake who thinks himself asleep.'

Now I am sensible all this is a mere sophistication, however it may neighbour to any truths, to excuse my own indolence – so I will not deceive myself that Man should be equal with Jove – but think himself very well off as a sort of scullion-Mercury or even a humble Bee – It is not matter whether I am right or wrong either one way or another, if there is sufficient to lift a little time from your Shoulders.

Your affectionate friend
John Keats —

Letter to John Taylor, 27 February 1818[1]

Having just finished the fair copy of Endymion *Book III, Keats is grateful for Taylor's advice on the wording and punctuation, and shares a few "axioms" about poetry.*

My dear Taylor, [. . .]
I am extremely indebted to you for this attention and also for your after admonitions – It is a sorry thing for me that any one should

---

[9]This is K's first experiment in an unrhymed sonnet (a quatorzain); he was moving away from the Petrarchan form, testing new possibilities with 41 exercises by the end of January 1818.

[10]This word is inserted (see p. 110).

[11]K probably started to write *third*, then *triple*, or maybe meant to coin this portmanteau.

---

[1]ALS, Pierpont Morgan Library.

have to overcome Prejudices in reading my Verses – that affects
me more than any hypercriticism on any particular Passage. In
<u>Endymion</u> I have most likely but moved into the Go-cart from the
leading strings. In Poetry I have a few Axioms, and you will see
how far I am from their Centre. 1st I think Poetry should surprise
by a fine excess and not by Singularity – it should strike the
Reader as a wording of his own highest thoughts, and appear
almost a Remembrance – 2nd Its touches of Beauty should never be
half way therby making the reader breathless instead of content:
the rise, the progress, the setting of imagery should like the Sun
come natural natural to him – shine over him and set soberly
although in magnificence leaving him in the Luxury of twilight –
but it is easier to think what Poetry should be than to write it –
and this leads me on to another axiom. That if Poetry comes not
as naturally as the Leaves to a tree it had better not come at all.[2]
However it may be with me I cannot help looking into new countries
with 'O for a Muse of fire to ascend!'[3] – If Endymion serves me as a
Pioneer perhaps I ought to be content. I have great reason to be
content, for thank God I can read and perhaps understand
Shakspeare to his depths, and I have I am sure many friends, who, if
I fail, will attribute any change in my Life and Temper to Humbleness
rather than to Pride – to a cowering under the Wings of great Poets
rather than to a Bitterness that I am not appreciated. I am anxious
to get <u>Endymion</u> printed that I may forget it and proceed. I have
coppied the 3rd Book and have begun the 4th. [. . .]
                    Your sincere and oblig^d friend
                              John Keats —
P.S. You shall have a shot <u>Preface</u> in good time[4] —

[2]Having heard these points in conversation with K, Woodhouse reports K also saying that "he never sits down to write unless he is full of ideas," an energy averse to
revision and self-correction: "My judgment, (he says), is as active while I am actually writing as my imagin^n In fact all my faculties are strongly excited, & in their full
play" (*KC* 1.128–29).

[3]The opening of the Prologue to *Henry V*; K assumes the full syntax, "ascend / The
brightest heaven of invention."

[4]Sent along with a "dedication, and the title page as I should wish it to stand" on 21
March (see p. 115). K may have meant *short* but the hostility makes *shot* seem a
plausible slip.

Letter to Benjamin Bailey, 13 March 1818[1]

An excerpt from the midst of a playful letter explaining delinquent correspondence and a failure to stop at Oxford on the way to George and Tom in Devonshire. Bailey was eager for Keats's thoughts on his sermon (published anonymously in 1817 by Taylor and Hessey) on the death of much-beloved Princess Charlotte in childbirth, late 1817, an occasion of national mourning. Addressing the issue of religion, Keats talks about "reality" as an effect of the mind's energies. He was preparing the last book of Endymion *for press.*

My dear Bailey, [. . .]
You know my ideas about Religion – I do not think myself more in the right than other people, and that nothing in this world is proveable. I wish I could enter into all your feelings on the subject merely for one short 10 Minutes and give you a Page or two to your liking. I am sometimes so very sceptical as to think Poetry itself a mere Jack a lanthen to amuse whoever may chance to be struck with its brilliance – As Tradesmen say every thing is worth what it will fetch, so probably every mental pursuit takes its reality and worth from the ardour of the pursuer – being in itself a nothing—Ethereal thing[s] may at least be thus real, divided under three heads- Things real — things semireal — and no things – Things real - such as existences of Sun Moon & Stars and passages of Shakspeare—Things semireal such as Love, the Clouds &c which require a greeting of the Spirit to make them wholly exist – and Nothings which are made Great and dignified by an ardent pursuit —which by the by stamps the burgundy mark on the bottles of our Minds, insomuch as they are able to "consecate whate'er they look upon"[2] [. . .] it is an old maxim of mine and of course must be well known that evey point of thought is the centre of an intellectual world – the two uppermost thoughts in a Man's mind are the two poles of his World he revolves on them and every thing is southward or northward to him through their means – We take but three steps from feathers to iron. Now my dear fellow I must once for all tell you I have not one Idea of the truth of any of my speculations – I shall never be a Reasoner because I care not to be in the right, when retired from bickering and

[1]ALS, Houghton Library, Harvard.
[2]Keats refracts Shelley's "Spirit of Beauty, that dost consecrate / With thine own hues all thou dost shine upon / Of human thought or form" (*Hymn to Intellectual Beauty* 13–15), to make this "greeting of the Spirit" (in K's phrase) the issue of "our Minds" instead of transcendent "Power."

*in a proper philosophical temper. [. . .] My Brother Tom desires to be
remember'd to you – he has just this moment had a spitting of blood
poor fellow. [. . .]*

    Your affectionate friend
    John Keats –

The first preface for *Endymion*[1]

*Keats finished copying Book IV on 14 March, drafted these front-texts
on the 19th, and sent them to his publishers on the 21st. The Preface
dismayed everyone, all urging Keats to try again, which he did on 10
April. The title page stayed the same, as did lines 1, 4, and 6 of the
dedication. The original draft, along with the title page and dedication, were first published in 1867 (a new edition of 1848).*

Title Page.

Endymion

a Romance

by John Keats —

The stretched metre of an antique song –
Shakespeare's Sonnets

[on a new page]

Inscribed,
with every feeling of pride and regret,
and with "a bowed mind,"
To the memory of
The most english of Poets except Shakspeare,
Thomas Chatterton—[2]

---

[1]K ms, Pierpont Morgan Library.

[2]For Shakespeare's sonnet, see letter to Reynolds, 22 Nov. 1817 (p. 72), and for
Chatterton, see p. 80, n. 1. The phrase "a bowed mind" is from the first stanza of the
1797 version of Coleridge's *Ode to the Departing Year* (K owned the 1797 2d edition of Coleridge's *Poems*).

[on a new page]

Preface

In a great nation, the work of an individual is of so little importance; his pleadings and excuses are so uninteresting; his 'way of life' such a nothing that ~~it nearly~~ a preface seems a sort of impertinent bow to ~~an~~ Strangers who care nothing about it — ~~However self-pride is the less offended, when~~

A preface however should be down in so many words; and such a one that by an eye glance over the type, the ~~Writer~~ Reader may catch an idea of an Author's modesty, and non opinion of himself — which I ~~hap~~ sincerely hope may be seen in the few lines I have to write, notwithstanding certain proverbs of many ages' ~~standing~~ old which men find a great pleasure in receiving for gospel.

About a twelvemonth since, I published a little book of verses; it was read by some dozen of my friends who lik'd it; and some dozen whom I was unacquainted with, who did not. Now when a dozen human beings, are at words with another dozen, it becomes a matter of anxiety to side with one's friends;—more especially when excited thereto by a great love of Poetry.

I fought under disadvantages. Before I began I had no inward feel of being able to finish; and as I proceeded my steps were all uncertain. So this Poem must rather be consider'd as an endeavour than a thing accomplish'd; a poor prologue to what, if I live, I humbly hope to do. In duty to the Public I should have kept it back for a year or two, knowing it to be so faulty: but I really cannot do ~~it~~ so:—by repetition my favorite Passages sound vapid in my ears, and I ~~as of such~~ would rather redeem myself with a new Poem should this one ~~create any interest~~ be found of any interest.

I have to apologise to the lovers of Simplicity for touching the spell of Loveliness that hung about Endymion: if any of my lines plead for me with such people I shall be proud.

It has been too much the fashion of late to consider men biggotted and adicted to every word that may chance to escape their lips: now I here declare that I have not any particular affection for any particular phrase, word or letter in the whole ~~matter~~ affair. I have written to please myself and in hopes to please others, and for a love of fame; if I neither please myself, nor others nor get fame of what consequence is Phraseology?

I would fain escape the bickerings that all Works, not exactly in chime bring upon their begetters:— but this is not fair to expect, there must be conversation of some sort and to object shows a Man's consequence. — In case of a London drizzle or a scotch Mist, the following quotation from Marston may perhaps stead me ~~for~~ as an umbrella for an hour or so: 'let it be the Curtesy of my peruser rather to pity my self hindering labours than to malice me'[3]

One word more.— for we cannot help seeing our own affairs in every point of view —. Should any one call my dedication to Chatterton affected I ~~say~~ answer as followeth:
> *"Were I dead Sir I should like a Book dedicated to me"—*

*Teignmouth March 19*th *1818 —*

Letter and verse-epistle to John Hamilton Reynolds, 25 March 1818[1]

Keats is in Teignmouth with Tom, who has had a setback. In London, Reynolds is suffering from rheumatic fever, in constant pain and depressed about his prospects in business (so George reported). The verse was first published in 1848 (1.113–16), without the last four lines and with several substantive variants. In 1848 the "prose" that here appears at the end was at the top of the letter, before the verse.

Dear Reynolds, as last night I lay in bed,
There came before my eyes that wonted thread
Of Shapes, and Shadows and Remembrances,
That every other minute vex and please:
Things all disjointed come from North and South,
Two witch's eyes above a cherub's mouth,
Voltaire with casque and shield and Habergeon,[2]

---

[3]The exhortation is preceded by ". . . since to satisfie others, I neglect my selfe, let it be . . ." etc.; from "To my equall Reader," Thomas Marston's Preface to *Parasitaster, or The Fawne* (1606), included in Charles Dilke's *Old English Plays* (1814–16), a collection K knew. A *Parasitaster* is a wretched, pathetic, fawning parasite.

---

[1]Woodhouse's transcript, Houghton Library, Harvard, from a now lost original.

[2]various pieces of medieval armor (a habergeon is a jacket of mail).

And Alexander with his night-cap on –
Old Socrates a tying his cravat;
And Hazlitt playing with Miss Edgworth's cat;[3]   10
And Junius Brutus pretty well so, so,
Making the best of 's way towards Soho.[4]
    Few are there who escape these visitings—
P'rhaps one or two, whose lives have patent[5] wings;
And through whose curtains peeps no hellish nose,
No wild boar tushes,° and no Mermaid's toes: (archaic) tusks
But flowers bursting out with lusty pride;
And young Æolian harps personified,
Some, Titian[6] colours touch'd into real life. —
The sacrifice goes on; the pontif knife   20
Gleams in the sun, the milk-white heifer lows,
The pipes go shrilly, the libation flows:
A white sail shews above the green-head cliff
Moves round the point, and throws her anchor stiff.
The Mariners join hymn with those on land. —
You know the Enchanted Castle it doth stand
Upon a Rock on the Border of a Lake
Nested in Trees, which all do seem to shake
From some old Magic like Urganda's sword.[7]
O Phœbus° that I had thy sacred word   Apollo 30

[3]During these months K was reading Voltaire and attending Hazlitt's lectures. Maria Edgeworth was a popular, commercially successful writer of novels, children's stories, and books on educational theory and practice. Hazlitt was public about his dislike of her writings.

[4]*so, so*: tipsy (there is a related transliteral punning into *'s sway*). *Soho*: a somewhat shady district of London. Junius Brutus Booth (b. 1796), America's star Shakespearean actor, was a rival to Kean. He played signature Kean roles such as Richard III and in 1817 played Iago to Kean's Othello. (His infamous son John Wilkes was born in 1838.)

[5]Editors like to emend to *patient*, noting *Endymion*'s "patient wing" (3.24) and the ms of *To Autumn* where, with a characteristic shorthand downstroke, K writes *patent* for *patient* (21); they also observe that the word *patent* never appears in K's poetry. Even so, *patent* (open, unobstructed) seems a possible reading to me.

[6]Painter of the Italian Renaissance famed for his rich colors. K had seen Claude Lorrain's *Landscape with the Father of Psyche Sacrificing at the Milesian Temple of Apollo* at the British institution in 1816, along with Titian's gorgeously colored *Europa*.

[7]To the hero of *Amadis of Gaul* (see p. 56, n. 3) enchantress Urganda the Unknown gave a lance. K likely knew Claude's *Landscape with Psyche and the Palace of Amor* ("The Enchanted Castle") from engravings and from Hazlitt's public admiration.

To shew this Castle in fair dreaming wise
Unto my friend, while sick and ill he lies.
    You know it well enough, where it doth seem
A mossy place, a Merlin's Hall,[8] a dream.
You know the clear Lake, and the little Isles,
The Mountains blue, and cold near neighbour rills —
All which elsewhere are but half animate
Here do they look alive to love and hate;
To smiles and frowns; they seem a lifted mound
Above some giant, pulsing underground.[9]   40
    Part of the building was a chosen See
Built by a banish'd Santon of Chaldee:[10]
The other part two thousand years from him
Was built by Cuthbert de Saint Aldebrim;[11]
Then there's a little wing, far from the Sun,
Built by a Lapland Witch[12] turn'd Maudlin nun –
And many other juts of aged stone
Founded with many a mason-devil's groan.
    The doors all look as if they oped themselves,
The windows as if latch'd by fays & elves —   50
And from them comes a silver flash of light
As from the Westward of a Summer's night;
Or like a beauteous woman's large blue eyes
Gone mad through olden songs and Poesies –
    See what is coming from the distance dim!
A golden galley all in silken trim!
Three rows of oars are lightening moment-whiles
Into the verdurous bosoms of those Isles.
Towards the Shade under the Castle Wall
It comes in silence – now 'tis hidden all.   60
The clarion sounds; and from a postern grate

[8]Merlin is the magician in the world of King Arthur.

[9]*giant* works as adjective or noun; as the latter, it refers to the underground imprisonment of the Titan gods by their successors (see *Hyperion* 2.22–28).

[10]*See*: the residence of a church official; *Santon*: Muslim holy man (a figure in oriental romances).

[11]K's playfully faux medievalism.

[12]"the night-hag . . . riding through the air she comes / Lured with the smell of infant blood, to dance / With Lapland witches" (*PL* 2.662–65); K underlined this passage.

An echo of sweet music doth create
A fear in the poor herdsman who doth bring
His beasts to trouble the enchanted spring:
He tells of the sweet Music and the spot
To all his friends, and they believe him not.
    O that our dreamings all of sleep or wake
Would all their colours from the sunset take:
From something of material[13] sublime,
Rather than shadow° our own Soul's daytime   *(verb)*   70
In the dark void of Night. For in the world
We jostle – but my flag is not unfurl'd
On the Admiral° Staff – and to philosophize   *lead ship*
I dare not yet! – Oh never will the prize,
High reason, and the lore[14] of good and ill
Be my award. Things cannot to the will
Be settled, but they tease us out of thought.[15]
Or is it that Imagination brought
Beyond its proper bound, yet still confined, —
Lost in a sort of Purgatory blind,   80
Cannot refer to any standard law
Of either earth or heaven? — It is a flaw
In happiness to see beyond our bourn° —   *terrain*
It forces us in Summer skies to mourn:
It spoils the singing of the Nightingale.
    Dear Reynolds. I have a mysterious tale
And cannot speak it. The first page I read
Upon a Lampit[16] Rock of green sea weed
Among the breakers – 'twas a quiet Eve;
The rocks were silent – the wide sea did weave   90
An untumultuous fringe of silver foam
Along the flat brown sand. I was at home,
And should have been most happy – but I saw
Too far into the sea; where every maw

---

[13]physical nature, thus verifiable. This last paragraph unfolds a serious meditation in terms that echo those of K's early poetry and forecast the themes of later work.

[14]The echo of *love* in *award* is lost in *1848*'s revision to "love of."

[15]See the last stanza of *Ode on a Grecian Urn* for a return to this effect (pp. 359–60).

[16]K's coinage combines *limpet* (a rock-browsing mollusk) and *limpid* (lucid, intelligible, serene).

The greater on the less feeds evermore:[17] —
But I saw too distinct into the core
Of an eternal fierce destruction,
And so from Happiness I far was gone.
Still am I sick of it: and though to day
I've gathered young spring-leaves, and flowers gay   100
Of Periwinkle and wild strawberry,
Still do I that most fierce destruction see,
The Shark at savage prey – the hawk at pounce,
The gentle Robin, like a pard or ounce,[18]
Ravening a worm — Away ye horrid moods,
Moods of one's mind![19] *You know I hate them well,*
You know I'd sooner be a clapping bell
To some Kamschatkan missionary church,
Than with these horrid moods be left in lurch[20] —
Do you get health – and Tom the same – I'll dance,   110
And from detested Moods in new Romance[21]
Take refuge — Of bad lines a Centaine dose[22]
Is sure enough — and so "here follows prose."[23] —
My dear Reynolds,

                In hopes of cheering you through a Minute or
two, I was determined nil-he will-he to send you some lines so you'll
excuse the unconnected subject, & careless verse – You know, I am sure,

[17]An adventurous morphing of and near rhyme with *every maw*. The "great ones eat up the little ones," observes a fisherman of the food-chain in *Pericles* (2.1).

[18]leopard or lynx

[19]A Wordsworthian mode: *Moods of my own mind* was a subsection in 1807 *Poems*.

[20]*1848* ends here. Christian missionaries had gone to the impossibly bleak peninsula of Kamschatka at the remote northeastern end of Russia (opposite Alaska).

[21]*Isabella; or, The Pot of Basil*, already begun. As a dark "romance," it is a "new" form of the genre for *Endymion*-sick K. This verse-epistle is virtually the last time K would write at such length in the loose "romance" couplets that had generated "I stood tip-toe," *Sleep and Poetry*, the verse epistles, and the 4,000 lines of *Endymion*.

[22]100 lines; K means medicinal dose, but the rhyme with *prose* retro-acts a pun on *doze*.

[23]Riffing on priggish steward Malvolio trying to decipher what he thinks may be a love-letter to him from his employer (it's a jest): "Soft! here follows prose," he murmurs, and then reads: "I am above thee, but be not afraid of greatness. Some are born great, some achieve greatness, and some have greatness thrust upon them" (*Twelfth Night* 2.5.141ff)—an implied continuation that may tacitly convey K's self-chastening.

Claude's Enchanted Castle, and I wish you may be pleased with my remembrance of it. The rain is come on again[24] I think with me Devonshire stands a very poor chance, I shall damn it up hill and down dale, if it keeps up to the average of 6 fine days in three weeks.[25] Let me have better news of you.

Your affectionate friend
John Keats.

Letter to Benjamin Robert Haydon, 8 April 1818[1]

Keats is in Teignmouth, planning to travel during the summer; he comments on Wordsworth's social manner in town.

My dear Haydon,
[. . .] Tom (who is getting greatly better) is anxious to be in Town therefore I put off my threading the County. I purpose within a Month to put my knapsack at my back and make a pedestrian tour through the North of England, and part of Scotland – to make a sort of Prologue to the Life I intend to pursue – that is to write, to study and to see all Europe at the lowest expence. I will clamber through the Clouds and exist. I will get such an accumulation of stupendous recollolections that as I walk through the suburbs of London I may not see them – I will stand upon Mount Blanc[2] and remember this coming Summer when I intend to straddle ben Lomond – with my Soul! – galligaskins[3] are out of the Question – I am nearer myself to hear your Christ is being tinted into immortality – Believe me Haydon your picture is a part of myself – I have ever been too sensible of the labyrinthian path to eminence in Art (judging from Poetry)

---

[24]A possible reference to a line in song that closes *Twelfth Night*: "the rain it raineth every day"—a world in which one has a choice whether to mourn, or dance and sing.
[25]Woodhouse's clerk puts this sentence in shorthand (perhaps suspecting profane punning on "damn"). I use the prose in WLB (which cross-references to the ms of the verse).

---

[1]ALS, Houghton Library, Harvard.
[2]The highest peak in the Alps (16,000 ft), a must-see on any Grand Tour. K's bravado is self-ironizing: the summit had been attained only a very few times by 1818.
[3]loose pants

ever to think I understood the emphasis of Painting. The innumerable compositions and decompositions which take place between the intellect and its thousand materials before it arrives at that trembling delicate and snail-horn perception of Beauty.[4] I know not you many havens of intenseness – nor ever can know them [. . .]

I am affraid Wordsworth went rather huff'd out of Town – I am sorry for it. he cannot expect his fireside Divan to be infallible he cannot expect but that every Man of worth is as proud as himself. [. . .]
Your affectionate friend
John Keats—

Letter to John Hamilton Reynolds, 9 April 1818[1]

From Teignmouth, Keats comments on the reaction to his draft of a Preface for Endymion.

My Dear Reynolds,
         Since you all agree that the thing is bad, it must be so – though I am not aware there is anything like Hunt in it, (and if there is, it is my natural way, and I have something in common with Hunt) look it over again and examine into the motives, the seeds from which any one sentence sprung – I have not the slightest feel of humility towards the Public – or to any thing in existence,—but the eternal Being, the Principle of Beauty, – and the Memory of great Men- When I am writing for myself for the mere sake of the Moment's enjoyment, perhaps nature has its course with me – but a Preface is written to the Public; a thing I cannot help looking upon as an Enemy, and which I cannot address without feelings of Hostility – If I write a Preface in a supple or subdued style, it will not be in character with me as a public speaker – I wo^d be subdued before my friends, and

---

[4]In his recent lecture, Hazlitt remarked that in a Shakespearean character "there is a continual composition and decomposition of its elements, a fermentation of every particle in the whole mass, by its alternate affinity or antipathy to other principles which are brought in contact with it" ("On Shakespeare and Milton," 1818 text, p. 100). The snail-horn image also evokes Shakespeare's imagery: see K's letter to Reynolds, 22 Nov. 1817 (p. 72).

---

[1]WLB 58–60.

thank them for subduing me — but among Multitudes of Men - I have no feel of stooping, I hate the idea of humility to them -

I never wrote one single Line of Poetry with the least Shadow of public thought. Forgive me for vexing you and making a Trojan Horse of such a Trifle, both with respect to the matter in Question, and myself—but it eases me to tell you - I could not live without the love of my friends - I would jump down Ætna for any great Public good[2] - but I hate a Mawkish Popularity. — I cannot be subdued before them — My glory would be to daunt and dazzle the thousand jabberers about Pictures and Books — I see swarms of Porcupines with their Quills erect "like lime-twigs set to catch my Winged Book"[3] and I would fright 'em away with a torch — You will say my preface is not much of a Torch. It would have been too insulting "to begin from Jove"[4] and I could not set a golden head upon a thing of clay — if there is any fault in the preface it is not affectation: but an under-song of disrespect to the Public. - if I write another preface. it must be done without a thought of those people — I will think about it. [. . .] Tom is getting better he hopes you may meet him at the top o' the hill— My Love to your nurses.[5] I am ever

Your affectionate Friend,
John Keats.

Letter to John Taylor, 27 April 1818[1]

From Teignmouth, Keats sends a sheet of corrections for Endymion, *with a report of his plans for the summer and the next phase of his intellectual development. He has been writing* Isabella.

---

[2]In emulation of Empedocles, 5th-c BCE philosopher, whose curiosity about the volcanic Mt. Etna in Sicily proved fatal.

[3]With a bad conscience about the murder of a rival, Cardinal Beaufort, dying in delirium, imagines the corpse's hair standing upright "like lime-twigs set to catch" his soul (*2 Henry VI* 3.3.16).

[4]Thus Robert Herrick begins "Evensong" (in *Hesperides*); K owned an 1813 edition.

[5]his sisters [Woodhouse's note]. Tom wasn't getting better; K's letter to Reynolds the next day reports him "quite low spirited" amid unrelenting rainy weather.

---

[1]ALS, Pierpont Morgan Library.

My dear Taylor, [. . .]
*I was purposing to travel over the north this Summer — there is but
one thing to prevent me - I know nothing I have read nothing and I
mean to follow Solomon's directions of 'get Wisdom - get understanding'*[2]
*I find cavalier days are gone by. I find that I can have no enjoyment
in the World but continual drinking of Knowledge - I find there is no
worthy pursuit but the idea of doing some good for the world - some
do it with their society - some with their wit - some with their
benevolence - some with a sort of power of conferring pleasure and
good humour on all they meet and in a thousand ways all equally
dutiful to the command of Great Nature - there is but one way for
me - the road lies through application study and thought. I will pursue
it and to that end purpose retiring for some years.*[3] *I have been
hovering for some time between an exquisite sense of the luxurious and
a love for Philosophy — were I calculated for the former I should be
glad — but as I am not I shall turn all my soul to the latter.
My Brother Tom is getting better and I hope I shall see both him
and Reynolds well before I retire from the World. I shall see you soon
and have some talk about what Books I shall take with me—*
Your very sincere friend
John Keats

Letter to John Hamilton Reynolds, 27 April 1818[1]

> *From Teignmouth, having finished* Isabella *and awaiting the publication of* Endymion, *Keats casts a curriculum of reading.*

My dear Reynolds.
     *It is an awful while since you have heard from me - I hope I
may not be punished, when I see you well, and so anxious as you always
are for me, with the remembrance of my so seldom writing when you
were so horribly confined - the most unhappy hours in our lives are
those in which we recollect times past to our own blushing - If we are*

---

[2]Proverbs (of Solomon) 4.5.

[3]K is telling his publisher that he won't be getting to work on anything new.

---

[1]WLB 62ff.

immortal that must be the Hell—If I must be immortal, I hope it will be after having taken a little of "that watery labyrinth"[2] in order to forget some of my school-boy days & others since those.

I have heard from George at different times how slowly you were recovering. It is a tedious thing – but all Medical Men will tell you how far a very gradual amendment is preferable; you will be strong after this, never fear. – We are here still enveloppd in clouds – I lay awake last night listening to the Rain with a sense of being drown'd and rotted like a grain of wheat – [. . .] Tom [. . .] I think is getting better – therefore I shall perhaps remain here some Months. I have written to George for some Books – shall learn Greek, and very likely Italian – and in other ways prepare myself to ask Hazlitt in about a years time the best metaphysical road I can take. – For although I take Poetry to be Chief, there is something else wanting to one who passes his life among Books and thoughts on Books – I long to feast upon old Homer as we have upon Shakespeare, and as I have lately upon Milton. If you understood Greek, and would read me passages, now and then, explaining their meaning, 't would be, from its mistiness, perhaps a greater luxury than reading the thing one's self. – I shall be happy when I can do the same for you. – I have written for my folio Shakespeare, in which there is the first few stanzas of my "Pot of Basil": I have the rest here finish'd, [. . .]

Your affectionate Friend,
John Keats

Letter to J. H. Reynolds, 3 May 1818[1]

Thinking again about the power of Wordsworth's modern poetry versus Milton's theological certainties, Keats continues to map his aspirations, with a simile of the mind as a set of apartments in a large, unknown building. He includes a May-day ode to Maia, "Mother of Hermes!"

My dear Reynolds.

What I complain of is that I have been in so an uneasy a state of Mind as not to be fit to write to an invalid. I cannot write to any length under a disguised feeling. I should have loaded you with

[2] A description of Lethe (*PL* 2.584, underlined by K).

---

[1] WLB 64–70. I accept Woodhouse's corrections of his clerk's transcript.

an addition of gloom, which I am sure you do not want. I am now thank God in a humour to give you a good groats worth - for Tom, after a Night without a Wink of sleep, and overburdened with fever, has got up after a refreshing day sleep and is better than he has been for a long time; and you I trust have been again round the Common without any effect but refreshment

[. . . ; Keats then speaks to Reynolds's gloominess about the effect of a legal career on his aspirations as poet]

I do not see why a Mind like yours is not capable of harbouring and digesting the whole Mystery of Law as easily as Parson Hugh does Pepins[2] - which did not hinder him from his poetic Canary - Were I to study physic or rather Medicine again, I feel it would not make the least difference in my Poetry; when the Mind is in its infancy a Bias is in reality a Bias, but when we have acquired more strength, a Bias becomes no Bias. Every department of Knowledge we see excellent and calculated towards a great whole. I am so convinced of this, that I am glad at not having given away my medical Books, which I shall again look over to keep alive the little I know thitherwards; [. . .] An extensive knowledge is needful to thinking people - it takes away the heat and fever; and helps, by widening speculation, to ease the Burden of the Mystery:[3] a thing I begin to understand a little, and which weighed upon you in the most gloomy and true sentence in your Letter. The difference of high Sensations with and without knowledge appears to me this - in the latter case we are falling continually ten thousand fathoms deep[4] and being blown up again without wings and with all horror of a bare shoulderd Creature - in the former case, our shoulders are fledge,[5] and we go thro' the same air and space without fear. This is running one's rigs[6] on the score of abstracted benefit - when we come to human   Life and the affections it is impossible to know how

[2]In *The Merry Wives of Windsor*, Sir Hugh Evans still means to have room for pippins (apples) and cheese, after a full meal (1.2).

[3]In *Tintern Abbey*, Wordsworth cherishes that "blessed mood, / In which the burthen of the mystery, / In which the heavy and the weary weight / Of all this unintelligible world / Is lighten'd" (38–42)—a solace amid "the fretful stir / Unprofitable, and the fever of the world" (53–54).

[4]Satan in the abyss beyond hell: "Fluttering his pennons vain, plumb down he drops / Ten thousand fathom deep" (*PL* 2.934–35, lines K underscored).

[5]Archangels have "shoulders (fledged with wings)" (*PL* 3.627; lines K underscored).

[6]going top speed; the next image of treading water suggests a shipwreck on abstract benefits.

a parallel of breast and head can be drawn – (you will forgive me for thus privately treading out my depth and take it for treading as schoolboys tread the water) – it is impossible to know how far Knowledge will console us for the death of a friend and the ill "that flesh is heir to"[7] – With respect to the affections and Poetry you must know by a sympathy my thoughts that way; and I dare say these few lines will be but a ratification: I wrote them on May-day – and intend to finish the ode[8] all in good time.-

    Mother of Hermes! and still youthful Maia!
        May I sing to thee
    As thou wast hymned on the shores of Baiæ?[9]
        Or may I woo thee
    In earlier Sicilian? or thy smiles
    Seek as they once were sought, in Grecian isles,
    By Bards who died content in pleasant sward,
    Leaving great verse unto a little clan?
    O give me their old vigour, and unheard,
    Save of the quiet Primrose, and the span
    Of Heaven and few ears rounded by thee
    My song should die away content as theirs
    Rich in the simple worship of a day. —

You may be anxious to know for fact to what sentence in your Letter I allude. You say "I fear there is little chance of any thing else in this life." You seem by that to have been going through with a more painful and acute zest the same labyrinth that I have – I have come to the same conclusion thus far. My Branchings out therefrom have been numerous: one of them is the consideration of Wordsworth's genius and as a help, in the manner of gold being the meridian Line[10] of worldly wealth,—how he differs from Milton.—And here I have nothing

---

[7]In his famous soliloquy, Hamlet imagines death as the end of "The heartache, and the thousand natural shocks / That flesh is heir to" (3.1.62–63).

[8]An experiment with form: the first 10 lines array a Petrarchan sonnet-rhyme with the metrical flexibility of an irregular ode. Woodhouse thought to sonnetize it all into 14 lines, resorting 11–13 into 4 lines: " . . . ears / Rounded . . . away / Content . . . theirs / Rich . . ."; though many editors from Milnes on accept this shaping, there is no Keatsian authority. Begun on 1 May, the "ode" halted at this state (first published in *1848*, 1.135).

[9]A famous Roman resort city on the Bay of Naples.

[10]high point

but surmises, from an uncertainty whether Miltons apparently less
anxiety for Humanity proceeds from his seeing further or no than
Wordsworth: And whether Wordsworth has in truth epic passion, and
martyrs himself to the human heart, the main region of his song[11] – In
regard to his genius alone – we find what he says true as far as we have
experienced and we can judge no further but by larger experience—for
axioms in philosophy are not axioms until they are proved upon our
pulses: We read fine —— things but never feel them to thee full until
we have gone the same steps as the Author. – I know this is not plain;
you will know exactly my meaning when I say, that now I shall relish
Hamlet more than I ever have done. Or, better – You are sensible no
Man can set down Venery[12] as a bestial or joyless thing until he is
sick of it and therefore all philosophizing on it would be mere wording.
Until we are sick, we understand not;—in fine, as Byron says,
"Knowledge is Sorrow"; and I go on to say that "Sorrow is Wisdom"-
and further for aught we can know for certainty! "Wisdom is folly"[13]
—So you see how I have run away from Wordsworth, and Milton;
and shall still run away from what was in my head [. . .] If I scribble
long letters I must play my vagaries. I must be too heavy, or too light,
for whole pages—I must be quaint and free of[14] Tropes and figures –
I must play my draughts as I please [. . .] with your patience, I will
return to Wordsworth – whether or no he has an extended vision or a
circumscribed grandeur—whether he is an eagle in his nest, or on the
wing—And to be more explicit and to show you how tall I stand by
the giant, I will putdown a simile of human life as far as I now perceive
it; that is, to the point to which I say we both have arrived at—' Well-
I compare human life to a large Mansion of Many Apartments, two
of which I can only describe, the doors of the rest being as yet shut upon
me – The first we step into we call the infant or thoughtless Chamber,
in which we remain as long as we do not think— We remain there a

---

[11]Wordsworth aligned *The Excursion* (1814) with *PL* but declared the modernity of
his taking "the Mind of Man" as the "haunt, and the main region of my song"
(Prospectus 40–41).

[12]sexual indulgence

[13]Either a misremembering or a reversing of the lament of Byron's occult scientist,
Manfred, "Sorrow is knowledge" (*Manfred* 1.1.10), mapped on Milton's view of
Adam and Eve's fatal error. K's equations also involve the famous end of Thomas
Gray's *Ode on a Distant Prospect of Eton College* (1747): "where ignorance is bliss, /
'Tis folly to be wise."

[14]i.e., "have the freedom of" (not "be rid of")

long while, and notwithstanding the doors of the Second Chamber remain wide open, showing a bright appearance, we care not to hasten to it; but are at length imperceptibly impelled by the awakening of this thinking principle – within us – we no sooner get into the second Chamber, which I shall call the Chamber of Maiden-Thought, than we become intoxicated with the light and the atmosphere, we see nothing but pleasant wonders, and think of delaying there for ever in delight: However among the effects this breathing is father of is that tremendous one of sharpening one's vision into the heart and nature of Man – of convincing ones nerves that the world is full of Misery and Heartbreak, Pain, Sickness and oppression – whereby This Chamber of Maiden Thought becomes gradually darken'd and at the same time on all sides of it many doors are set open – but all dark – all leading to dark passages – We see not the ballance of good and evil. We are in a Mist. We are now in that state – We feel the "burden of the Mystery,"[15] To this Point was Wordsworth come, as far as I can conceive when he wrote 'Tintern Abbey' and it seems to me that his Genius is explorative of those dark Passages. Now if we live, and go on thinking, we too shall explore them. he is a Genius and superior us, in sofar as he can, more than we, make discoveries, and shed a light in them – Here I must think Wordsworth is deeper than Milton – though I think it has depended more upon the general and gregarious advance of intellect, than individual greatness of Mind – From the Paradise Lost and the other Works of Milton, I hope it is not too presuming, even between ourselves to say, that his Philosophy, human and divine, may be tolerably understood by one not much advanced in years. In his time englishmen were just emancipated from a great superstition[16] and Men had got hold of certain points and resting places in reasoning which were too newly born to be doubted, and too much opposed by the Mass of Europe not to be thought etherial and authentically divine– who could gainsay his ideas on virtue, vice, and Chastity in Comus, just at the time of the dismissal of Cod-pieces and a hundred other disgraces?[17]

---

[15]Having thought of Wordsworth's declared "intent" in the Prospectus to *The Excursion*, "To weigh the good and evil of our mortal state," K reassesses the value of *Tintern Abbey*: instead of easing the burden of the mystery, he now sees Wordsworth registering its weight and pressure against reasoning.

[16]The Protestant view of Catholicism (see *Written in disgust of Vulgar Superstition*, p. 84).

[17]In *Comus* (1634), Milton depicts the temptation of a lady's virtue by an enchanter. A codpiece is a bag (often quite ostentatious) worn over the fly in a man's breeches.

who would not rest satisfied with his hintings at good and evil in the Paradise Lost, when just free from the inquisition and burning in Smithfield?[18] The Reformation produced such immediate and great benefits, that Protestantism was considered under the immediate eye of heaven, and its own remaining Dogmas and superstitions, then, as it were, regenerated, constituted those resting places and seeming sure points of Reasoning-from that I have mentioned, Milton, whatever he may have thought in the sequel,[19] appears to have been content with these by his writings - He did not think into the human heart, as Wordsworth has done - Yet Milton as a Philosopher, had sure as great powers as Wordsworth -   What is then to be inferr'd? O many things - It proves there is really a grand march of intellect—, It proves that a mighty providence subdues the mightiest Minds to the service of the time being, whether it be in human Knowledge or Religion - I have often pitied a Tutor who has to hear "Nom^e: Musa"—so often dinn'd into his ears—I hope you may not have the same pain in this scribbling - I may have read these things before, but I never had even a thus dim perception of them; and moreover I like to say my lesson to one who will endure my tediousness for my own sake [. . .]

Tom has spit a <u>leetle</u> blood this afternoon, and that is rather a damper - but I know - the truth is there is something real in the World Your third Chamber of Life shall be a lucky and a gentle one—stored with the wine of love - and the Bread of Friendship. When you see George if he should not have reced a letter from me tell him he will find one at home most likely - tell Bailey I hope soon to see him - Remember me to all The leaves have been out here, for mony a day — I have written to George for the first stanzas of my Isabel - I shall have them soon and will copy the whole out for you.

Your affectionate friend
John Keats.

[18]The medieval Catholic Church instituted the Inquisition to condemn heretics. Smithfield in London was a site of horrific public executions during the persecutions of the 16th and 17th centuries, as the "Protestant" Reformation contended with the upholders of Roman Catholicism.

[19]*Paradise Regained*

Further poetry from January–April 1818, posthumously published

(in order of publication)

from *Comic Annual*, 1830, p. 14[1]

SONNET TO A CAT

BY THE LATE JOHN KEATS

CAT! who hast pass'd thy grand climacteric,[2]
   How many mice and rats hast in thy days
   Destroy'd?—How many tit-bits stolen? Gaze
With those bright languid segments green, and prick
Those velvet ears—but pr'ythee do not stick
   Thy latent talons in me—and upraise
   Thy gentle mew—and tell me all thy frays
Of fish and mice, and rats and tender chick.
Nay, look not down, nor lick thy dainty wrists—
   For all the wheezy asthma,—and for all
Thy tail's tip is nick'd off—and though the fists
Of many a maid have given thee many a maul,
Still is that fur as soft as when the lists
In youth thou enter'dst on glass-bottled wall.

---

[1]Edited by Thomas Hood, who married J. H. Reynolds's sister Jane. K's ms dated this mock Petrarchan sonnet 16 Jan. 1818 with the title *To Mrs. Reynolds's Cat* (Mrs. Reynolds is J. H. Reynolds's mother).

[2]prime of life

from *Life, Letters, and Literary Remains* (1848): "Time's sea"[1]

To ———*

TIME'S sea hath been five years at its slow ebb;[2]
    Long hours have to and fro let creep the sand;
Since I was tangled in thy beauty's web,
    And snared by the ungloving of thine hand.
And yet I never look on midnight sky,
    But I behold thine eyes' well memoried light;
I cannot look upon the rose's dye,
    But to thy cheek my soul doth take its flight;
I cannot look on any budding flower,
    But my fond ear, in fancy at thy lips,   10
And hearkening for a love-sound, doth devour
    Its sweets in the wrong sense: — Thou dost eclipse
Every delight with sweet remembering,
And grief[3] unto my darling joys dost bring.

* A lady whom he saw for some few moments at Vauxhaull.[4]

"Blue!"[1]

ANSWER TO A SONNET ENDING THUS

"Dark eyes are dearer far
Than those that mock the hyacinthine bell;"[2]

By J. H. Reynolds.
Feb. 1818

[1]Written 4 Feb. 1818, K's second Shakespearian sonnet. First published in *Hood's Magazine* 2, 1844, p. 240; then *1848* (Sonnet XI; 2.297), a text that is closer to Woodhouse's transcript.

[2]*Hood's*] Life's sea hath been five times at its slow ebb,

[3]*Hood's*] sorrow

[4]Milnes's note, from Woodhouse's note. Vauxhall Gardens is a public entertainment park in London on the south bank of the Thames.

[1]Written 8 Feb. 1818, after reading Reynolds's sonnet (and in the midst of preparing *Endymion* for press); first published in *1848* (Sonnet IX; 2.295), the text here.

[2]*1848* prints *made* for *mock*; its errata list supplies the correction.

BLUE! 'tis the life of heaven,——the domain
   Of Cynthia,—the wide palace of the sun,—
The tent of Hesperus,° and all his train,——   *evening star*
   The bosomer of clouds, gold, grey and dun.
Blue! 'tis the life of waters—ocean
   And all its vassal streams: pools numberless
May rage, and foam, and fret, but never can
   Subside, if not to dark-blue nativeness.
Blue! Gentle cousin of the forest-green,
   Married to green in all the sweetest flowers—   10
Forget-me-not,—the blue bell,—and, that queen
   Of secrecy, the violet: what strange powers
Hast thou, as a mere shadow! But how great,
When in an Eye thou art, alive with fate!

§ John Hamilton Reynolds, *Sonnet*[1]

Sweet poets of the gentle antique line,
   That made the hue of beauty all eterne,
   And gave earth's melodies a silver turn,——
Where did you steal your art so right divine?——
Sweetly ye memoried every golden twine
   Of your ladies' tresses:——teach me how to spurn
   Death's lone decaying and oblivion stern
From the sweet forehead of a lady mine.
The golden clusters of enamouring hair
   Glow'd in poetic pictures sweetly well;——   10
Why should not tresses dusk, that are so fair
   On the live brow, have an eternal spell
In poesy?——dark eyes are dearer far
   Than orbs that mock the hyacinthine-bell.

---

[1]Written in early 1818; published in *The Garden of Florence*, 1821 (pp. 128–29).

§ Oscar Wilde, letter to Emma Speed on "Blue!"[1] with a fair copy of *Keats's Grave*

Wilde wrote to George Keats's daughter Emma Speed (1823–83) on 21 March 1882, thanking her for the gift of the original ms of Keats's sonnet, which he had quoted with warm admiration in a lecture in her hometown Louisville, Kentucky. He sends a fair copy of his sonnet, Keats's Grave, *an exchange he recounted in* Century Guild Hobby Horse, *July 1866, with a facsimile of the Keats ms. The original, sold at the forced auction of Wilde's effects in 1795, has since disappeared.*

What you have given me is more golden than gold, more precious than any treasure this great country could yield me [. . .] It is a sonnet I have loved always, and indeed who but the supreme and perfect artist could have got from a mere colour a motive so full of marvel: and now I am half enamoured of the paper that touched his hand, and the ink that did his bidding, grown fond of the sweet comeliness of his charactery, for since my boyhood I have loved none better than your marvellous kinsman, that godlike boy, the real Adonis of our age, who knew the silver-footed messages of the moon, and the secret of the morning, who heard in Hyperion's vale the large utterance of the early gods, and from the beechen plot the light-winged Dryad, who saw Madeline at the painted window, and Lamia in the house at Corinth, and Endymion ankle-deep in lilies of the vale, who drubbed the butcher's boy for being a bully, and drank confusion to Newton for having analysed the rainbow. In my heaven he walks eternally with Shakespeare and the Greeks [. . .] Let me send you my sonnet on Keats's grave[2]

§ Keats's Grave

Rid of the world's injustice and its pain
He rests at last beneath God's veil of blue;
Taken from life while life and love were new

---

[1] Letter text: Oxford UP, c. 1962, by Vyvyan Holland.

[2] Wilde sent this sonnet to Milnes in June 1877, to W. M. Rossetti (an editor of K and brother to Dante Gabriel and Christina), and to HBF. His article, *The Tomb of Keats*, based on a visit, appeared with this sonnet in *The Irish Monthly*, July 1877, the text here.

The youngest of the Martyrs here is lain,
Fair as Sebastian and as foully slain.[3]
No cypress shades his tomb, nor funeral yew,
But red-lipped daisies, violets drenched with dew,
And sleepy poppies, catch the evening rain.
O proudest heart that broke for misery!
O saddest poet that the world hath seen!
O sweetest singer of our English land!
Thy name was writ in water on the sand,
But our tears shall keep thy memory green,
And make it flourish like a Basil-tree.[4]

---

[3]St. Sebastian, tortured with an onslaught of arrows, like K, was an icon for homosexual affection; in the fable promulgated by Shelley's Adonais, K is slain by reviewers' arrows. A variant text reads "early slain."

[4]K asked that his epigraph read "Here lies one whose name was writ on water"; Wilde aligns himself and other Keatsians with K's Isabella, mourning for her murdered lover, whose basil-potted head nourishes the plant on which she dotes.

from *Endymion*

Written April–December 1817, Endymion *was revised through the winter and published on 19 May 1818 by Taylor and Hessey (Keats had an advance copy in late April) in an economic octavo, priced 9 shillings. Having allegorized poetic imagination in Endymion's romance with the moon in "I stood tip-toe" (181–93), Keats extends the myth in* Endymion *along several lines of purpose, from the practical and worldly to the ideal and imaginative. Eager to redeem the commercial and thus vocational disappointment of* Poems, *he set the completion of this long poem as a test of imagination—its ideals, its frustrations, its successes—that would also be poetically self-actualizing. Yet over the course of telling the story of dreamer Endymion, Keats's initial purposes and ideals—the function of poetry as an eternal "thing of beauty" in a dark world, the fulfillment of a visionary imagination infused with erotic fascination—dissipated. This self-appointed "trial of my Powers of Imagination and chiefly of my invention" (letter, 8 October 1818) produced not so much a professional epic as an array of poetic intensities, from the local image to the figural scene, from the lush to the grotesque, from the sensual to the philosophical, weaving a romance everywhere in love with "fine Phrases" (so Keats confessed this pleasure to Bailey, 14 August 1819). It is telling that in the same letter in which he outlines the heroics of a long poem, Keats says that he means to conceive 4,000 lines in which "Lovers of Poetry" will find "a little Region to wander in where they may pick and choose, and which the images are so numerous that many are forgotten and found new in a second Reading." This "Romance" of 4,050 lines, Keats's longest poem ever (and, at 207 pages, his longest publication), struck its first reviewers, both loving and unloving, as a too-rich jewel cabinet. Although some nineteenth-century critics tried to discern an allegory (a religion of Beauty in a Neo-Platonic answer to the erotic quest-death of Shelley's* Alastor), *what radiates is a Keatsian negative capability with a vengeance: an uncertainty about visionary desire, its erotic embodiments, it social and psychological fallout, its pathology, its self-indulgence, its comedy—and not the least, its poetry. Much of this effect accrues across repetitions of basic tropes: scenes of dreaming as inspiration, as obsession, as disease, as a romance with death; of bowers as paradise, as infant chambers, as parodies of paradise, as prisons, as tombs; and the array of young men who reflect and qualify one another, the poet-narrator, dedicatee Thomas Chatterton, the self-chastising young poet of the Preface, and within, hero Endymion, Adonis, Glaucus, and the young men and gods who populate similes, metaphors, myths, and legend, among them, Apollo, Ganymede, Hyacinth, Narcissus, Pan.*

Accepting Keats's invitation to pick and choose, I've selected passages under a variety of principles: the verses that present Keats's aspirations, the verses about which he cared most, the verses that focused the ire of Tory reviews and later Victorian ridicule of his boyish sensuality—but also the passages that trace a developing critical perspective on his initial ideals of imagination, nowhere more so than in the over-the-top exhaustion of the poem's conclusion. The dominant form is the "romance" couplet. Text: Endymion, 1818.

Preface

Knowing within myself the manner in which this Poem has been produced, it is not without a feeling of regret that I make it public.

What manner I mean, will be quite clear to the reader, who must soon perceive great inexperience, immaturity, and every error denoting a feverish attempt, rather than a deed accomplished. The two first books, and indeed the two last, I feel sensible are not of such completion as to warrant their passing the press; nor should they if I thought a year's castigation would do them any good;—it will not: the foundations are too sandy. It is just that this youngster should die away: a sad thought for me, if I had not some hope that while it is dwindling I may be plotting, and fitting myself for verses fit to live.

This may be speaking too presumptuously, and may deserve a punishment: but no feeling man will be forward to inflict it: he will leave me alone, with the conviction that there is not a fiercer

E N D Y M I O N :

A Poetic Romance.

BY JOHN KEATS.

" THE STRETCHED METRE OF AN ANTIQUE SONG."

LONDON:

PRINTED FOR TAYLOR AND HESSEY,

93, FLEET STREET.

1818.

Keats's epigraph is from Shakespeare's Sonnet 17; see his letter to Reynolds, 22 November 1817 (pp. 72–73).

hell than the failure in a great object. This is not written with the least atom of purpose to forestall criticisms of course, but from the desire I have to conciliate men who are competent to look, and who do look with a zealous eye, to the honour of English literature.

The imagination of a boy is healthy, and the mature imagination of a man is healthy; but there is a space of life between, in which the soul is in a ferment, the character undecided, the way of life uncertain, the ambition thick-sighted: thence proceeds mawkishness, and all the thousand bitters which those men I speak of must necessarily taste in going over the following pages.

I hope I have not in too late a day touched the beautiful mythology of Greece, and dulled its brightness: for I wish to try once more, before I bid it farewel.[1]

Teignmouth, April 10, 1818.

from BOOK I

With a now-famous first line, Keats begins with the principle of "beauty" and casts a schedule of composition along a calendar of nature, from spring budding to fall harvest. The Romance opens on a community of farmers, hunters, and shepherds in Latmos, a mountain in Caria, Asia Minor, ruled by Prince Endymion and dedicated to the worship of woodland god Pan. It is the morning of the day of a festival to honor Pan.

A thing of beauty is a joy for ever:
Its loveliness increases; it will never
Pass into nothingness; but still will keep
A bower quiet for us, and a sleep
Full of sweet dreams, and health, and quiet breathing.
Therefore, on every morrow, are we wreathing
A flowery band to bind us to the earth,
Spite of despondence, of the inhuman dearth
Of noble natures, of the gloomy days,
Of all the unhealthy and o'er-darkened ways   10

[1]A reference to *Hyperion* (see the letter to Haydon, 23 Jan. 1818 (p. 88).

Made for our searching: yes, in spite of all,
Some shape of beauty moves away the pall
From our dark spirits. Such the sun, the moon,
Trees old and young, sprouting a shady boon
For simple sheep; and such are daffodils
With the green world they live in; and clear rills
That for themselves a cooling covert make
'Gainst the hot season; the mid forest brake,
Rich with a sprinkling of fair musk-rose blooms:
And such too is the grandeur of the dooms   20
We have imagined for the mighty dead;
All lovely tales that we have heard or read:
An endless fountain of immortal drink,
Pouring unto us from the heaven's brink.

   Nor do we merely feel these essences
For one short hour; no, even as the trees
That whisper round a temple become soon
Dear as the temple's self, so does the moon,
The passion poesy, glories infinite,
Haunt us till they become a cheering light   30
Unto our souls, and bound to us so fast,
That, whether there be shine, or gloom o'ercast,
They alway must be with us, or we die.

   Therefore, 'tis with full happiness that I
Will trace the story of Endymion.
The very music of the name has gone
Into my being, and each pleasant scene
Is growing fresh before me as the green
Of our own vallies: so I will begin
Now while I cannot hear the city's din;[2]   40
Now while the early budders are just new,
And run in mazes of the youngest hue
About old forests; while the willow trails
Its delicate amber; and the dairy pails
Bring home increase of milk. And, as the year

[2]April 1817, on the Isle of Wight.

Grows lush in juicy stalks, I'll smoothly steer
My little boat, for many quiet hours,
With streams that deepen freshly into bowers.
Many and many a verse I hope to write,
Before the daisies, vermeil rimm'd and white,   50
Hide in deep herbage; and ere yet the bees
Hum about globes of clover and sweet peas,
I must be near the middle of my story.
O may no wintry season, bare and hoary,
See it half finished: but let Autumn bold,
With universal tinge of sober gold,
Be all about me when I make an end.[3]
And now at once, adventuresome, I send
My herald thought into a wilderness:
There let its trumpet blow, and quickly dress   60
My uncertain path with green, that I may speed
Easily onward, thorough flowers and weed.

    Upon the sides of Latmos was outspread
A mighty forest; for the moist earth fed
So plenteously all weed-hidden roots
Into o'er-hanging boughs, and precious fruits.
And it had gloomy shades, sequestered deep,
Where no man went; and if from shepherd's keep
A lamb strayed far a-down those inmost glens,
Never again saw he the happy pens   70
Whither his brethren, bleating with content,
Over the hills at every nightfall went.
Among the shepherds, 'twas believed ever,
That not one fleecy lamb which thus did sever
From the white flock, but pass'd unworried
By angry wolf, or pard° with prying head,   *leopard*
Until it came to some unfooted plains
Where fed the herds of Pan: ay great his gains
Who thus one lamb did lose. Paths there were many,
Winding through palmy fern, and rushes fenny,   80
And ivy banks; all leading pleasantly

[3]K did finish by the end of Nov. 1817; he revised through the winter and drafted the
Preface in April 1818.

To a wide lawn, whence one could only see
Stems thronging all around between the swell
Of turf and slanting branches: who could tell
The freshness of the space of heaven above,
Edg'd round with dark tree tops? through which a dove
Would often beat its wings, and often too
A little cloud would move across the blue.

   Full in the middle of this pleasantness
There stood a marble altar, with a tress   90
Of flowers budded newly; and the dew
Had taken fairy phantasies to strew
Daisies upon the sacred sward last eve,
And so the dawned light in pomp receive.
For 'twas the morn: Apollo's upward fire
Made every eastern cloud a silvery pyre
Of brightness so unsullied, that therein
A melancholy spirit well might win
Oblivion, and melt out his essence fine
Into the winds: rain-scented eglantine   100
Gave temperate sweets to that well-wooing sun;
The lark was lost in him; cold springs had run
To warm their chilliest bubbles in the grass;
Man's voice was on the mountains; and the mass
Of nature's lives and wonders puls'd tenfold,
To feel this sun-rise and its glories old.

[*A company of garlanded children, young damsels dancing, singing shepherds, proceeds to the festival for Pan.*]

         . . . After them appear'd,
Up-followed by a multitude that rear'd
Their voices to the clouds, a fair wrought car,°   *chariot*
Easily rolling so as scarce to mar
The freedom of three steeds of dapple brown:
Who stood therein did seem of great renown
Among the throng. His youth was fully blown,[4]

---

[4]in full bloom

Shewing like Ganymede[5] to manhood grown;   170
And, for those simple times, his garments were
A chieftain king's: beneath his breast, half bare,
Was hung a silver bugle, and between
His nervy knees there lay a boar-spear keen.[6]
A smile was on his countenance; he seem'd,
To common lookers on, like one who dream'd
Of idleness in groves Elysian:
But there were some who feelingly could scan
A lurking trouble in his nether lip,
And see that oftentimes the reins would slip   180
Through his forgotten hands: then would they sigh,
And think of yellow leaves, of owlets cry,
Of logs piled solemnly.[7]—Ah, well-a-day,
Why should our young Endymion pine away!

[*The festival goes on, with a hymn to Pan, a 74-line inset ode, the one Keats recited to Wordsworth. It was published separately in the* Yellow Dwarf *(Reynolds's venue) on 9 May 1818. In this scene, Endymion sits withdrawn among the elders, who talk of the bliss awaiting them in the afterlife.*]

                    Thus all out-told
Their fond imaginations,—saving him
Whose eyelids curtain'd up their jewels dim,
Endymion: yet hourly had he striven
To hid the cankering venom, that had riven
His fainting recollections. Now indeed
His senses had swoon'd off: he did not heed
The sudden silence, or the whispers low,
Or the old eyes dissolving at his woe,   400
Or anxious calls, or close of trembling palms,
Or maiden's sigh, that grief itself embalms:
But in the self-same fixed trance he kept,
Like one who on the earth had never stept—

[5]The beautiful boy whom Jupiter brought to Heaven to be a cup-bearer to the gods (Ovid's *Metamorphoses* X).
[6]Hunter Adonis was killed by a boar and mourned by Venus (see p. 72).
[7]fragmentary images of autumn, winter, death.

Aye, even as dead-still as a marble man,
Frozen in that old tale Arabian.[8]

[*Endymion's worried sister Peona leads him to a favorite bower, where she soothes him to sleep.*]

O magic sleep! O comfortable bird,
That broodest o'er the troubled sea of the mind
Till it is hush'd and smooth! O unconfin'd
Restraint! imprisoned liberty! great key
To golden palaces, strange minstrelsy,
Fountains grotesque, new trees, bespangled caves,
Echoing grottos, full of tumbling waves
And moonlight; aye, to all the mazy world   460
Of silvery enchantment!—who, upfurl'd
Beneath thy drowsy wing a triple hour,
But renovates and lives?—Thus, in the bower,
Endymion was calm'd to life again.
Opening his eyelids with a healthier brain,
He said: "I feel this thine endearing love
All through my bosom: thou art as a dove
Trembling its closed eyes and sleeked wings
About me; and the pearliest dew not brings
Such morning incense from the fields of May,   470
As do those brighter drops that twinkling stray
From those kind eyes,—the very home and haunt
Of sisterly affection. Can I want
Aught else, aught nearer heaven, than such tears?
Yet dry them up, in bidding hence all fears
That, any longer, I will pass my days
Alone and sad. No, I will once more raise
My voice upon the mountain-heights; once more
Make my horn parley from their foreheads hoar:
Again my trooping hounds their tongues shall loll   480
Around the breathed boar: again I'll poll
The fair-grown yew tree, for a chosen bow:
And, when the pleasant sun is getting low,
Again I'll linger in a sloping mead

[8]Editors cite *The History of the Young King of the Black Isles*, in *The Arabian Nights*.

To hear the speckled thrushes, and see feed
Our idle sheep. So be thou cheered sweet,
And, if thy lute is here, softly intreat
My soul to keep in its resolved course."

[*Seeing her brother refreshed, Peona drills him about his too-apparent malady.*]

"Brother, 'tis vain to hide
That thou dost know of things mysterious,
Immortal, starry; such alone could thus
Weigh down thy nature. Hast thou sinn'd in aught
Offensive to the heavenly powers? Caught
A Paphian dove upon a message sent?[9]   510
Thy deathful bow against some deer-herd bent,
Sacred to Dian? Haply,° thou hast seen   *perhaps*
Her naked limbs among the alders green;
And that, alas! is death.[10] No, I can trace
Something more high perplexing in thy face!"

[. . . *Endymion replies:*]
"Ah! thou hast been unhappy at the change   520
Wrought suddenly in me. What indeed more strange?
Or more complete to overwhelm surmise?
Ambition is no sluggard: 'tis no prize,
That toiling years would put within my grasp,
That I have sigh'd for: with so deadly gasp
No man e'er panted for a mortal love.
So all have set my heavier grief above
These things which happen. Rightly have they done:
I, who still saw the horizontal sun
Heave his broad shoulder o'er the edge of the world,   530
Out-facing Lucifer,[11] and then had hurl'd
My spear aloft, as signal for the chace——
I, who, for very sport of heart, would race

[9]the doves from Venus's temple in Paphos
[10]In punishment for seeing the goddess of the hunt Diana bathing, hunter Actaeon was turned into a stag, then torn apart by his own hounds (Ovid, *Metamorphoses* III).
[11]the morning star (literally, light-bearer)

With my own steed from Araby; pluck down
A vulture from his towery perching; frown
A lion into growling, loth retire——
To lose, at once, all my toil breeding fire,
And sink thus low! but I will ease my breast
Of secret grief, here in this bowery nest.

    This river does not see the naked sky,   540
Till it begins to progress silverly
Around the western border of the wood,
Whence, from a certain spot, its winding flood
Seems at the distance like a crescent moon:
And in that nook, the very pride of June,
Had I been used to pass my weary eves;
The rather for the sun unwilling leaves
So dear a picture of his sovereign power,
And I could witness his most kingly hour,
When he doth lighten up the golden reins,   550
And paces leisurely down amber plains
His snorting four.[12] Now when his chariot last
Its beams against the zodiac-lion° cast,   *constellation Leo*
There blossom'd suddenly a magic bed
Of sacred ditamy, and poppies red:°   *(sacred to Diana)*
At which I wondered greatly, knowing well
That but one night had wrought this flowery spell;
And, sitting down close by, began to muse
What it might mean. Perhaps, thought I, Morpheus,[13]
In passing here, his owlet pinions shook;   560
Or, it may be, ere matron Night uptook
Her ebon urn, young Mercury, by stealth,
Had dipt his rod in it: such garland wealth
Came not by common growth.[14] Thus on I thought,
Until my head was dizzy and distraught.
Moreover, through the dancing poppies stole
A breeze, most softly lulling to my soul;

[12] the horses that draw Apollo's chariot of the sun

[13] Poppy is sleep-inducing.

[14] Mercury's caduceus, a magic wand given to him by Apollo, has the power to restore life. Morpheus is the god of sleep.

And shaping visions all about my sight
Of colours, wings, and bursts of spangly light;
The which became more strange, and strange, and dim, 570
And then were gulph'd in a tumultuous swim:
And then I fell asleep. Ah, can I tell
The enchantment that afterwards befel?
Yet it was but a dream: yet such a dream
That never tongue, although it overteem[15]
With mellow utterance, like a cavern spring,
Could figure out and to conception bring
All I beheld and felt. Methought[16] I lay
Watching the zenith, where the milky way
Among the stars in virgin splendour pours; 580
And travelling my eye, until the doors
Of heaven appear'd to open for my flight,
I became loth and fearful to alight
From such high soaring by a downward glance:
So kept me stedfast in that airy trance,
Spreading imaginary pinions wide.
When, presently, the stars began to glide,
And faint away, before my eager view:
At which I sigh'd that I could not pursue,
And dropt my vision to the horizon's verge; 590
And lo! from opening clouds, I saw emerge
The loveliest moon, that ever silver'd o'er
A shell for Neptune's goblet: she did soar
So passionately bright, my dazzled soul
Commingling with her argent spheres did roll
Through clear and cloudy, even when she went
At last into a dark and vapoury tent—
Whereat, methought, the lidless-eyed train
Of planets all were in the blue again.
To commune with those orbs, once more I rais'd 600
My sight right upward: but it was quite dazed
By a bright something, sailing down apace,

---

[15]*OED* credits K with coining this verb.

[16]This is the diction of medieval dream allegory, a venture into a spiritual realm. The previous lines echo Bottom's effort to recount his dream in *A Midsummer's Night's Dream* (4.1).

Making me quickly veil my eyes and face:
Again I look'd, and, O ye deities,
Who from Olympus watch our destinies!
Whence that completed form of all completeness?
Whence came that high perfection of all sweetness?
Speak, stubborn earth, and tell me where, O where
Hast thou a symbol of her golden hair?
Not oat-sheaves drooping in the western sun;   610
Not——thy soft hand, fair sister! let me shun
Such follying before thee——yet she had,
Indeed, locks bright enough to make me mad;
And they were simply gordian'd up[17] and braided,
Leaving, in naked comeliness, unshaded,
Her pearl round ears, white neck, and orbed brow;
The which were blended in, I know not how,
With such a paradise of lips and eyes,
Blush-tinted cheeks, half smiles, and faintest sighs,
That, when I think thereon, my spirit clings   620
And plays about its fancy, till the stings
Of human neighbourhood envenom all.
Unto what awful power shall I call?
To what high fane?°——Ah! see her hovering feet,   *temple*
More bluely vein'd, more soft, more whitely sweet
Than those of sea-born Venus, when she rose
From out her cradle shell. The wind out-blows
Her scarf into a fluttering pavilion;
'Tis blue, and over-spangled with a million
Of little eyes, as though thou wert to shed,   630
Over the darkest, lushest blue-bell bed,
Handfuls of daisies."——"Endymion, how strange!
Dream within dream!"——"She took an airy range,
And then, towards me, like a very maid,
Came blushing, waning, willing, and afraid,
And press'd me by the hand: Ah! 'twas too much;

---

[17]The K-coined adjective (*OED*) is derived from the intricate Gordian knot, which only Alexander the Great can undo, with a swift cut from his sword; "gordian" will figure in Circe's enchantment of Glaucus (3.494). K will soon be writing to Bailey of his "gordian complication of feelings" about women (July 1818); and the word will convey Lamia's powers of enchantment (*Lamia* 1.47). All involve the serpent's "Gordian" writhing in *PL* (4.348).

Methought I fainted at the charmed touch,
Yet held my recollection, even as one
Who dives three fathoms where the waters run
Gurgling in beds of coral: for anon,   640
I felt upmounted in that region
Where falling stars dart their artillery forth,
And eagles struggle with the buffeting north
That balances the heavy meteor-stone;——
Felt too, I was not fearful, nor alone,
But lapp'd and lull'd along the dangerous sky.
Soon, as it seem'd, we left our journeying high,
And straightway into frightful eddies swoop'd;
Such as ay muster where grey time has scoop'd
Huge dens and caverns in a mountain's side: 650
There hollow sounds arous'd me, and I sigh'd
To faint once more by looking on my bliss——
I was distracted; madly did I kiss
The wooing arms which held me, and did give
My eyes at once to death: but 'twas to live,
To take in draughts of life from the gold fount
Of kind and passionate looks; to count, and count
The moments, by some greedy help that seem'd
A second self, that each might be redeem'd
And plunder'd of its load of blessedness.   660
Ah, desperate mortal! I ev'n dar'd to press
Her very cheek against my crowned lip,
And, at that moment, felt my body dip
Into a warmer air: a moment more,
Our feet were soft in flowers. There was store
Of newest joys upon that alp. Sometimes
A scent of violets, and blossoming limes,
Loiter'd around us; then of honey cells,
Made delicate from all white-flower bells;
And once, above the edges of our nest,   670
An arch face peep'd,——an Oread[18] as I guess'd.

   Why did I dream that sleep o'er-power'd me
In midst of all this heaven? Why not see,

[18]mountain nymph

Far off, the shadows of his pinions dark,
And stare them from me? But no, like a spark
That needs must die, although its little beam
Reflects upon a diamond, my sweet dream
Fell into nothing——into stupid sleep.
And so it was, until a gentle creep,
A careful moving caught my waking ears,   680
And up I started: Ah! my sighs, my tears,
My clenched hands;——for lo! the poppies hung
Dew-dabbled on their stalks, the ouzel° sung   *blackbird*
A heavy ditty, and the sullen day
Had chidden herald Hesperus away,
With leaden looks: the solitary breeze
Bluster'd, and slept, and its wild self did teaze
With wayward melancholy; and I thought,
Mark me, Peona! that sometimes it brought
Faint fare-thee-wells, and sigh-shrilled adieus!——   690
Away I wander'd——all the pleasant hues
Of heaven and earth had faded: deepest shades
Were deepest dungeons; heaths and sunny glades
Were full of pestilent light; our taintless rills
Seem'd sooty, and o'er-spread with upturn'd gills
Of dying fish; the vermeil rose had blown
In frightful scarlet, and its thorns out-grown
Like spiked aloe. If an innocent bird
Before my heedless footsteps stirr'd, and stirr'd
In little journeys, I beheld in it   700
A disguis'd demon, missioned to knit
My soul with under darkness; to entice
My stumblings down some monstrous precipice:
Therefore I eager followed, and did curse
The disappointment. Time, that aged nurse,
Rock'd me to patience. Now, thank gentle heaven!
These things, with all their comfortings, are given
To my down-sunken hours, and with thee,
Sweet sister, help to stem the ebbing sea
Of weary life."

         Thus ended he, and both   710
Sat silent: for the maid was very loth

To answer; feeling well that breathed words
Would all be lost, unheard, and vain as swords
Against the enchased crocodile, or leaps
Of grasshoppers against the sun. She weeps,
And wonders; struggles to devise some blame;
To put on such a look as would say, *Shame*
On this poor weakness! but, for all her strife,
She could as soon have crush'd away the life
From a sick dove. At length, to break the pause,   720
She said with trembling chance: "Is this the cause?
This all? Yet it is strange, and sad, alas!
That one who through this middle earth should pass
Most like a sojourning demi-god, and leave
His name upon the harp-string,[19] should achieve
No higher bard than simple maidenhood,
Singing alone, and fearfully,—how the blood
Left his young cheek; and how he used to stray
He knew not where; and how he would say, *nay*,
If any said 'twas love: and yet 'twas love;   730
What could it be but love? How a ring-dove
Let fall a sprig of yew tree in his path;
And how he died: and then, that love doth scathe,
The gentle heart, as northern blasts do roses;
And then the ballad of his sad life closes
With sighs, and an alas!——Endymion!
Be rather in the trumpet's mouth,—anon
Among the winds at large——that all may hearken!
Although, before the crystal heavens darken,
I watch and dote upon the silver lakes   740
Pictur'd in western cloudiness, that takes
The semblance of gold rocks and bright gold sands,
Islands, and creeks, and amber-fretted strands
With horses prancing o'er them, palaces
And towers of amethyst,——would I so tease
My pleasant days, because I could not mount
Into those regions? The Morphean fount
Of that fine element that visions, dreams,
And fitful whims of sleep are made of, streams

[19]be so famous for heroic deeds as to be honored in song

Into its airy channels with so subtle,   750
So thin a breathing, not the spider's shuttle,
Circled a million times within the space
Of a swallow's nest-door, could delay a trace,
A tinting of its quality: how light
Must dreams themselves be; seeing they're more slight
Than the mere nothing that engenders them!
Then wherefore sully the entrusted gem
Of high and noble life with thoughts so sick?
Why pierce high-fronted honour to the quick
For nothing but a dream?" Hereat the youth   760
Look'd up: a conflicting of shame and ruth
Was in his plaited brow: yet, his eyelids
Widened a little, as when Zephyr bids
A little breeze to creep between the fans
Of careless butterflies: amid his pains
He seem'd to taste a drop of manna-dew,
Full palatable; and a colour grew
Upon his cheek, while thus he lifeful spake.

    "Peona! ever have I long'd to slake
My thirst for the world's praises: nothing base,   770
No merely slumberous phantasm, could unlace
The stubborn canvas for my voyage prepar'd——
Though now 'tis tatter'd; leaving my bark° bar'd   *little boat*
And sullenly drifting: yet my higher hope
Is of too wide, too rainbow-large a scope,
To fret at myriads of earthly wrecks.
Wherein lies happiness?[20] In that which becks
Our ready minds to fellowship divine,
A fellowship with essence; till we shine,
Full alchemiz'd,[21] and free of space. Behold   780
The clear religion of heaven! Fold
A rose leaf round thy finger's taperness,
And soothe thy lips: hist, when the airy stress

---

[20]Writing to Taylor, 30 Jan. 1818, K tells him that the question and ensuing lines "set before me at once the gradations of Happiness even like a Kind of Pleasure Thermometer" of ascending intensity.

[21]Alchemy is the medieval pseudo-science of transmuting base metals to pure gold.

Of music's kiss impregnates the free winds,
And with a sympathetic touch unbinds
Eolian magic from their lucid wombs:
Then old songs waken from enc1ouded tombs;
Old ditties sigh above their father's grave;
Ghosts of melodious prophecyings rave
Round every spot were trod Apollo's foot;   790
Bronze clarions awake, and faintly bruit,°   *proclaim*
Where long ago a giant battle was;[22]
And, from the turf, a lullaby doth pass
In every place where infant Orpheus slept.
Feel we these things?——that moment have we stept
Into a sort of oneness, and our state[23]
Is like a floating spirit's. But there are
Richer entanglements, enthralments far
More self-destroying, leading, by degrees,
To the chief intensity: the crown of these   800
Is made of love and friendship, and sits high
Upon the forehead of humanity.
All its more ponderous and bulky worth
Is friendship, whence there ever issues forth
A steady splendour; but at the tip-top,
There hangs by unseen film, an orbed drop
Of light, and that is love: its influence,
Thrown in our eyes, genders° a novel sense,   *engenders*
At which we start and fret; till in the end,
Melting into its radiance, we blend,   810
Mingle, and so become a part of it,——
Nor with aught else can our souls interknit
So wingedly: when we combine therewith,
Life's self is nourish'd by its proper pith,
And we are nurtured like a pelican brood.[24]
Aye, so delicious is the unsating food,

[22]The rebellion of the Olympian generation against the elder Titans (the terrain of *Hyperion*).

[23]K left this line unrhymed.

[24]Young pelicans feed on digested food (sometimes fabled, the very blood) from their parents, often to the point of parental emaciation. King Lear complains of his pelican daughters, and K jokes about "these Pelican duns" to his publishers, 10 June 1817, as he asks for another advance.

That men, who might have tower'd in the van
Of all the congregated world, to fan
And winnow from the coming step of time
All chaff of custom,[25] wipe away all slime   820
Left by men-slugs and human serpentry,
Have been content to let occasion die,
Whilst they did sleep in love's elysium.
And, truly, I would rather be struck dumb,
Than speak against this ardent listlessness:
For I have ever thought that it might bless
The world with benefits unknowingly;
As does the nightingale, upperched high,
And cloister'd among cool and bunched leaves——
She sings but to her love, nor e'er conceives   830
How tiptoe Night holds back her dark-grey hood.
Just so may love, although 'tis understood
The mere commingling of passionate breath,
Produce more than our searching witnesseth:
What I know not: but who, of men, can tell
That flowers would bloom, or that green fruit would swell
To melting pulp, that fish would have bright mail,
The earth its dower of river, wood, and vale,
The meadows runnels, runnels pebble-stones,
The seed its harvest, or the lute its tones,   840
Tones ravishment, or ravishment its sweet,
If human souls did never kiss and greet?[26]

    Now, if this earthly love has power to make
Men's being mortal, immortal; to shake
Ambition from their memories, and brim
Their measure of content; what merest whim,

[25]K marked the passage in *Troilus and Cressida* in which Greek general Agamemnon urges his army to regard frustrations as a test of mettle: "in the wind and tempest of her frown, / Distinction, with a broad and powerful fan, / Puffing at all, winnows the light away, / And what hath mass or matter by itself / Lies high in virtue and un-mingled" (1.3.26–30).

[26]Bailey disliked this "abominable" Shelleyan principle "that <u>Sensual love</u> is the principle of <u>things</u>"—and thought that K's flux of imagination had led him uncon-sciously to this "false, delusive & dangerous conclusion" (*KC* 1.34–35). Byron thought the principle oddly "sentimental" and had no taste for K's "faun and satyr machinery" (Medwin's *Conversations*, 1824, 2d edn., p. 369).

Seems all this poor endeavour after fame,
To one, who keeps within his stedfast aim
A love immortal, an immortal too.
Look not so wilder'd; for these things are true,   850
And never can be born of atomies°   *tiny things*
That buzz about our slumbers, like brain-flies,
Leaving us fancy-sick. No, no, I'm sure,
My restless spirit never could endure
To brood[27] so long upon one luxury,
Unless it did, though fearfully, espy
A hope beyond the shadow of a dream.

[*Endymion relates more visionary adventures, leading to his sounding of the classical trope of* ubi sunt *(where are they gone?), in prelude to the conclusion of Book I.*]

        ——Ah! where   970
Are those swift moments? Whither are they fled?[28]
I'll smile no more, Peona; nor will wed
Sorrow the way to death; but patiently
Bear up against it: so farewel, sad sigh;
And come instead demurest meditation,
To occupy me wholly, and to fashion
My pilgrimage for the world's dusky brink.
No more will I count over, link by link,
My chain of grief: no longer strive to find
A half-forgetfulness in mountain wind   980
Blustering about my ears: aye, thou shalt see,
Dearest of sisters, what my life shall be;
What a calm round of hours shall make my days.
There is a paly flame of hope that plays
Where'er I look: but yet, I'll say 'tis naught——
And here I bid it die. Have not I caught,
Already, a more healthy countenance?
By this the sun is setting; we may chance
Meet some of our near-dwellers with my car."°   *chariot*

[27]nurture, dwell upon
[28]"Whither is fled the visionary gleam? / Where is it now the glory and the dream?" (Wordsworth, *Ode: Intimations of Immortality*, stanza 4).

This said, he rose, faint-smiling like a star   990
Through autumn mists, and took Peona's hand:
They stept into the boat, and launch'd from land.

from BOOK II

Keats models this book and the next on the underworld quest motif of classical epic.

O sovereign power of love! O grief! O balm!
All records,[1] saving thine, come cool, and calm,
And shadowy, through the mist of passed years:
For others, good or bad, hatred and tears
Have become indolent; but touching thine,
One sigh doth echo, one poor sob doth pine,
One kiss brings honey-dew from buried days.
The woes of Troy, towers smothering o'er their blaze,
Stiff-holden shields, far-piercing spears, keen blades,
Struggling, and blood, and shrieks—all dimly fades   10
Into some backward corner of the brain;
Yet, in our very souls, we feel amain[2]
The close[3] of Troilus and Cressid sweet.
Hence, pageant history! hence, gilded cheat!
Swart° planet in the universe of deeds!   *black*
Wide sea, that one continuous murmur breeds
Along the pebbled shore of memory!
Many old rotten-timber'd boats there be
Upon thy vaporous bosom, magnified
To goodly vessels; many a sail of pride,   20
And golden keel'd, is left unlaunch'd and dry.
But wherefore this? What care, though owl did fly
About the great Athenian admiral's mast?[4]

---

[1] A pun on the etymology, "re-cord" (on the heart).

[2] with full force

[3] embrace; conclusion

[4] Editors identify Plutarch's *Life of Themosticles*: he is urging his officers to risk a sea battle; when an owl lights upon their shipmast, they take it as a good omen.

What care, though striding Alexander past
The Indus with his Macedonian numbers?[5]
Though old Ulysses tortured from his slumbers
The glutted Cyclops, what care?[6]——Juliet leaning
Amid her window-flowers,——sighing,——weaning
Tenderly her fancy from its maiden snow,[7]
Doth more avail than these: the silver flow   30
Of Hero's tears, the swoon of Imogen,
Fair Pastorella in the bandit's den,[8]
Are things to brood on with more ardency
Than the death-day of empires. Fearfully
Must such conviction come upon his head,
Who, thus far, discontent, has dared to tread,
Without one muse's smile, or kind behest,
The path of love and poesy. But rest,
In chaffing restlessness, is yet more drear
Than to be crush'd, in striving to uprear   40
Love's standard on the battlements of song.
So once more days and nights aid me along,
Like legion'd soldiers.

                    Brain-sick[9] shepherd prince,
What promise hast thou faithful guarded since
The day of sacrifice? Or, have new sorrows
Come with the constant dawn upon thy morrows?
Alas! 'tis his old grief. For many days,
Has he been wandering in uncertain ways:
Through wilderness, and woods of mossed oaks;
Counting his woe-worn minutes, by the strokes   50
Of the lone woodcutter; and listening still,
Hour after hour, to each lush-leav'd rill.

[5]Alexander the Great crossed the Indus river with his army in 326 BCE.
[6]Ulysses blinds sleeping Cyclops, enabling his ship and crew to escape (*Odyssey* IX).
[7]Juliet at her balcony over the garden, yearning for Romeo (*Romeo and Juliet* 2.2).
[8]In Marlowe's *Hero and Leander*, Leander dies attempting to swim the Hellespont to his lover Hero. Hero is also the jilted woman in *Much Ado About Nothing*. Virtuous Imogen swoons into seeming death in *Cymbeline* 4.2; Pastorella winds up in a bandit's den in *FQ* VI.xi.
[9]draft] Fainting

Now he is sitting by a shady spring,
And elbow-deep with feverous fingering
Stems the upbursting cold: a wild rose tree
Pavilions him in bloom, and he doth see
A bud which snares his fancy: lo! but now
He plucks it, dips its stalk in the water: how!
It swells, it buds, it flowers beneath his sight;
And, in the middle, there is softly pight[10]   60
A golden butterfly; upon whose wings
There must be surely character'd[11] strange things,
For with wide eye he wonders, and smiles oft.

    Lightly this little herald flew aloft,
Follow'd by glad Endymion's clasped hands:
Onward it flies. From languour's sullen bands
His limbs are loosed, and, eager, on he hies[12]
Dazzled to trace it in the sunny skies.

[*Endymion ventures into the underworld and arrives at the Bower of Adonis, where Venus's slain love sleeps for six months of the year, then is awakened to return to earth with her every spring.*]

    And down some swart abysm he had gone,
Had not a heavenly guide benignant led
To where thick myrtle branches, 'gainst his head
Brushing, awakened: then the sounds again
Went noiseless as a passing noontide rain   380
Over a bower, where little space he stood;
For as the sunset peeps into a wood
So saw he panting light, and towards it went
Through winding alleys; and lo, wonderment!
Upon soft verdure saw, one here, one there,
Cupids a slumbering on their pinions fair.
After a thousand mazes overgone,
At last, with sudden step, he came upon

[10]pitched (archaic)

[11]patterned, inscribed

[12]The subtle internal rhyme with *flies* sounds the binding of Endymion's path to this herald's.

A chamber, myrtle wall'd, embowered high,[13]
Full of light, incense, tender minstrelsy,   390
And more of beautiful and strange beside:
For on a silken couch of rosy pride,
In midst of all, there lay a sleeping youth
Of fondest beauty; fonder, in fair sooth,
Than sighs could fathom, or contentment reach:
And coverlids gold-tinted like the peach,
Or ripe October's faded marigolds,
Fell sleek about him in a thousand folds——
Not hiding up an Apollonian curve
Of neck and shoulder, nor the tenting swerve   400
Of knee from knee, nor ankles pointing light;
But rather, giving them to the filled sight
Officiously. Sideway his face repos'd
On one white arm, and tenderly unclos'd,
By tenderest pressure, a faint damask° mouth   *(rich silk)*
To slumbery pout; just as the morning south
Disparts° a dew-lipp'd rose. Above his head,   *opens up*
Four lily stalks did their white honours wed
To make a coronal; and round him grew
All tendrils green, of every bloom and hue,   410
Together intertwin'd and trammel'd[14] fresh:
The vine of glossy sprout; the ivy mesh,
Shading its Ethiop berries; and woodbine,
Of velvet leaves and bugle-blooms divine;
Convolvulus in streaked vases flush;
The creeper, mellowing for an autumn blush;
And virgin's bower,° trailing airily;   *clematis*
With others of the sisterhood. Hard by,
Stood serene Cupids watching silently.
One, kneeling to a lyre, touch'd the strings,   420
Muffling to death the pathos with his wings;
And, ever and anon, uprose to look
At the youth's slumber; while another took
A willow-bough, distilling odorous dew,

---

[13]The description is threaded with Spenser's imagination of the Garden of Adonis in *FQ* III.vi and the bower of the Bower of Bliss (II.xii).

[14]netted, entangled

And shook it on his hair; another flew
In through the woven roof, and fluttering-wise
Rain'd violets upon his sleeping eyes.

   At these enchantments, and yet many more,
The breathless Latmian wonder'd o'er and o'er;
Until, impatient in embarrassment,   430
He forthright pass'd, and lightly treading went
To that same feather'd lyrist, who straightway,
Smiling, thus whisper'd: "Though from upper day
Thou art a wanderer, and thy presence here
Might seem unholy, be of happy cheer!
For 'tis the nicest touch of human honour,
When some ethereal and high-favouring donor
Presents immortal bowers to mortal sense;
As now 'tis done to thee, Endymion. Hence
Was I in no wise startled. So recline   440
Upon these living flowers. Here is wine,
Alive with sparkles——never, I aver,
Since Ariadne was a vintager,[15]
So cool a purple: taste these juicy pears,
Sent me by sad Vertumnus, when his fears
Were high about Pomona:[16] here is cream,
Deepening to richness from a snowy gleam;
Sweeter than that nurse Amalthea[17] skimm'd
For the boy Jupiter: and here, undimm'd
By any touch, a bunch of blooming plums   450
Ready to melt between an infant's gums:[18]
And here is manna pick'd from Syrian trees,
In starlight, by the three Hesperides.[19]
Feast on, and meanwhile I will let thee know
Of all these things around us." He did so,
Still brooding o'er the cadence of his lyre;

[15]as Bacchus's associate

[16]Fruit god Vertumnus was rejected by orchard-nymph Pomona.

[17]This Princess of Crete nursed infant Jupiter on goat's milk.

[18]Victorian poet Alexander Smith ridiculed this line (a "style of babyish effeminacy") in his article on K for *Encyclopedia Britannica*.

[19]These three daughters of Hesperus guarded the golden apples give to Juno by Jupiter on their wedding; for *manna*, see *Endymion* 1.766.

And thus:[20] "I need not any hearing tire
By telling how the sea-born goddess pin'd
For a mortal youth, and how she strove to bind
Him all in all unto her doting self.   460
Who would not be so prison'd? but, fond elf,[21]
He was content to let her amorous plea
Faint through his careless arms; content to see
An unseiz'd heaven dying at his feet;
Content, O fool! to make a cold retreat,
When on the pleasant grass such love, lovelorn,
Lay sorrowing; when every tear was born
Of diverse passion; when her lips and eyes
Were clos'd in sullen moisture, and quick sighs
Came vex'd and pettish through her nostrils small.   470
Hush! no exclaim——yet, justly mightst thou call
Curses upon his head.——I was half glad,
But my poor mistress went distract and mad,
When the boar tusk'd him: so away she flew
To Jove's high throne, and by her plainings[22] drew
Immortal tear-drops down the thunderer's beard;
Whereon, it was decreed he should be rear'd
Each summer time to life. Lo! this is he,
That same Adonis, safe in the privacy
Of this still region all his winter-sleep.   480
Aye, sleep; for when our love-sick queen did weep
Over his waned corse, the tremulous shower
Heal'd up the wound, and, with a balmy power,
Medicined death to a lengthened drowsiness:
The which she fills with visions, and doth dress
In all this quiet luxury; and hath set
Us young immortals, without any let,
To watch his slumber through. 'Tis well nigh pass'd,
Even to a moment's filling up, and fast

[20]The story that follows draws on Shakespeare's *Venus and Adonis*, which K was
reading at the time (see his letter to Reynolds, 22 Nov. 1817, p. 72), *FQ* III, and
Ovid's *Metamorphoses* X.

[21]A slightly sarcastic use of Spenser's term for his fairy knights, often used by K,
partly for the convenience of its rhyme with, and internal residence in, *self*.

[22]complainings (laments)

She scuds with summer breezes, to pant through   490
The first long kiss, warm firstling, to renew
Embower'd sports in Cytherea's° isle.   *Venus's*
Look! how those winged listeners all this while
Stand anxious: see! behold!"——This clamant[23] word
Broke through the careful silence; for they heard
A rustling noise of leaves, and out there flutter'd
Pigeons and doves:[24] Adonis something mutter'd,
The while one hand, that erst upon his thigh
Lay dormant, mov'd convuls'd and gradually
Up to his forehead. Then there was a hum   500
Of sudden voices, echoing, "Come! come!
Arise! awake! Clear summer has forth walk'd
Unto the clover-sward, and she has talk'd
Full soothingly to every nested finch:
Rise, Cupids! or we'll give the blue-bell pinch
To your dimpled arms. Once more sweet life begin!"
At this, from every side they hurried in,
Rubbing their sleepy eyes with lazy wrists,
And doubling over head their little fists
In backward yawns. But all were soon alive: 510
For as delicious wine doth, sparkling, dive
In nectar'd clouds and curls through water fair,
So from the arbour roof down swell'd an air
Odorous and enlivening; making all
To laugh, and play, and sing, and loudly call
For their sweet queen: when lo! the wreathed green
Disparted,° and far upward could be seen   *opened up*
Blue heaven, and a silver car, air-borne,
Whose silent wheels, fresh wet from clouds of morn,
Spun off a drizzling dew,——which falling chill   520
On soft Adonis' shoulders, made him still
Nestle and turn uneasily about.
Soon were the white doves plain, with necks stretch'd out,
And silken traces lighten'd in descent;
And soon, returning from love's banishment,

[23]clamorous
[24]Venus's heralds

Queen Venus leaning downward open arm'd:
Her shadow fell upon his breast, and charm'd
A tumult to his heart, and a new life
Into his eyes.

[*Witnessing this reunion, Endymion is stung anew by his own misery;
Venus reassures him.*]

" . . . Endymion! one day thou wilt be blest:
So still obey the guiding hand that fends
Thee safely through these wonders for sweet ends.
'Tis a concealment needful in extreme;
And if I guess'd not so, the sunny beam
Thou shouldst mount up to with me. Now adieu!
Here must we leave thee."——At these words up flew
The impatient doves, up rose the floating car,   580
Up went the hum celestial. High afar
The Latmian saw them minish into nought;
And, when all were clear vanish'd, still he caught
A vivid lightning from that dreadful bow.
When all was darkened, with Etnean throe[25]
The earth clos'd——gave a solitary moan——
And left him once again in twilight lone.

    He did not rave, he did not stare aghast,
For all those visions were o'ergone, and past,
And he in loneliness; he felt assur'd   590
Of happy times, when all he had endur'd
Would seem a feather to the mighty prize.
So, with unusual gladness, on he hies . . .

[*Conveyed to a "jasmine bower, all bestrown / With golden moss"
(670–71), Endymion sinks into a dream of embracing the "naked waist"
of his Moon-goddess; the following passage was praised by some for its
luxurious sensuality ("Those lips, O slippery blisses"), was ridiculed by
others, and was censured by the* British Critic *(June 1820) for "retailing"
language "better adapted to the stews" (brothels).*]

---

[25]Typhon, a Titan imprisoned by Jupiter in the earth, breathes fires through the vol-
cano of Mt. Etna.

These lovers did embrace, and we must weep   730
That there is no old power left to steep
A quill immortal in their joyous tears.
Long time in silence did their anxious fears
Question that thus it was; long time they lay
Fondling and kissing every doubt away;
Long time ere soft caressing sobs began
To mellow into words, and then there ran
Two bubbling springs of talk from their sweet lips.
"O known Unknown! from whom my being sips
Such darling essence, wherefore may I not   740
Be ever in these arms? in this sweet spot
Pillow my chin for ever? ever press
These toying hands and kiss their smooth excess?
Why not for ever and for ever feel
That breath about my eyes? Ah, thou wilt steal
Away from me again, indeed, indeed——
Thou wilt be gone away, and wilt not heed
My lonely madness. Speak, my kindest[26] fair!
Is——is it to be so? No! Who will dare
To pluck thee from me? And, of thine own will,   750
Full well I feel thou wouldst not leave me. Still
Let me entwine thee surer, surer——now
How can we part? Elysium! who art thou?
Who, that thou canst not be for ever here,
Or lift me with thee to some starry sphere?
Enchantress! tell me by this soft embrace,
By the most soft completion of thy face,
Those lips, O slippery blisses, twinkling eyes,
And by these tenderest, milky sovereignties——
These tenderest, and by the nectar-wine,   760
The passion"——

[26]draft] delicious

from BOOK III

These opening lines were zapped by Z as "lisp[ing] sedition" (p. 199), the epitome of "Cockney politics" in "Cockney poetry." Keats's over-arching question is whether, in an era of restored monarchies, love is a cherished liberty, or whether love's dynamics of power and thraldom might be another form of tyranny—and, moreover, whether erotic tyranny is the engine of political tyranny, or political tyranny is the corrupting determinant of erotic relations.

There are who lord it o'er their fellow-men
With most prevailing tinsel: who unpen
Their baaing vanities, to browse away
The comfortable green and juicy hay
From human pastures; or, O torturing fact!
Who, through an idiot blink, will see unpack'd
Fire-branded foxes to sear up and singe
Our gold and ripe-ear'd hopes.[1] With not one tinge
Of sanctuary splendour, not a sight
Able to face an owl's, they still are dight°   *arrayed*   10
By the blear-eyed nations in empurpled vests,[2]
And crowns, and turbans. With unladen breasts,
Save of blown self-applause, they proudly mount
To their spirit's perch, their being's high account,
Their tiptop nothings, their dull skies, their thrones—
Amid the fierce intoxicating tones
Of trumpets, shoutings, and belabour'd drums,
And sudden cannon. Ah! how all this hums,
In wakeful ears, like uproar past and gone—
Like thunder clouds that spake to Babylon,   20
And set those old Chaldeans to their tasks.—
Are then regalities all gilded masks?
No, there are throned seats unscalable

---

[1]Samson sends 300 foxes with firebrands tied to their tails into the Philistines' corn-fields and vineyards (Judges 15.4–5).

[2]The anti-monarchal discourse ("purple" is the garb of royalty, especially tyrants, from Nero on) is patent *Examiner*-ese aimed at the repressive Regency that had im-prisoned the Hunts, at the restored Bourbon monarchy in France (1814), and at other reactionary European monarchies, recharged after the defeat of Napoleon (1815).

But by a patient wing, a constant spell,
Or by ethereal° things that, unconfin'd,   *spiritual*
Can make a ladder of the eternal wind,
And poise about in cloudy thunder-tents
To watch the abysm-birth of elements.
Aye, 'bove the withering of old-lipp'd Fate
A thousand Powers keep religious state,   30
In water, fiery realm, and airy bourne;°   *circumference*
And, silent as a consecrated urn,
Hold sphery sessions for a season due.
Yet few of these far majesties, ah, few!
Have bared their operations to this globe——
Few, who with gorgeous pageantry enrobe
Our piece of heaven——whose benevolence
Shakes hand with our own Ceres; every sense
Filling with spiritual sweets to plenitude,
As bees gorge full their cells. And, by the feud   40
'Twixt Nothing and Creation, I here swear,
Eterne Apollo! that thy Sister fair°   *the Moon*
Is of all these the gentlier-mightiest.
When thy gold breath is misting in the west,
She unobserved steals unto her throne,
And there she sits most meek and most alone;
As if she had not pomp subservient;
As if thine eye, high Poet! was not bent
Towards her with the Muses in thine heart;
As if the ministering starts kept not apart,   50
Waiting for silver-footed messages.
O Moon! the oldest shades 'mong oldest trees
Feel palpitations when thou lookest in:
O Moon! old bough lisp forth a holier din
The while they feel think airy fellowship.
Thou dost bless every where, with silver lip
Kissing dead things to life. The sleeping kine,°   *cattle*
Couched in thy brightness, dream of fields divine:
Innumerable mountains rise, and rise,
Ambitious for the hallowing of thine eyes;   60
And yet thy benediction passeth not
One obscure hiding-place, one little spot

Where pleasure may be sent: the nested wren
Has thy fair face within its tranquil ken,
And from beneath a sheltering ivy leaf
Takes glimpses of thee; thou art a relief
To the poor patient oyster, where it sleeps
Within its pearly house.—The mighty deeps,
The monstrous sea is thine—the myriad sea!
O Moon! far-spooming[3] Ocean bows to thee,   70
And Tellus feels his forehead's cumbrous load.[4]

[*Endymion finds another twin-in-destiny who seems to have been expecting him: the superannuated Glaucus, whose erotic quest had led to a bower with a difference. His story of himself, a fisherman grown restless with the quiet life of social usefulness, draws on Ovid's* Metamorphoses, *XIII–XIV.*]

Why was I not contented? Wherefore reach
At things which, but for thee, O Latmian!
Had been my dreary death? Fool! I began
To feel distemper'd longings: to desire
The utmost privilege that ocean's sire
Could grant in benediction: to be free
Of all his kingdom. Long in misery
I wasted, ere in one extremest fit
I plung'd for life or death. To interknit   380
One's senses with so dense a breathing stuff
Might seem a work of pain; so not enough
Can I admire how crystal-smooth it felt,
And buoyant round my limbs. At first I dwelt
Whole days and days in sheer astonishment;
Forgetful utterly of self-intent;
Moving but with the mighty ebb and flow.
Then, like a new fledg'd bird that first doth shew
His spreaded feathers to the morrow chill,
I tried in fear the pinions of my will.   390
'Twas freedom! and at once I visited
The ceaseless wonders of this ocean-bed.

[3]foaming; *OED* credits K with making this verb from an archaic noun for *foam*.
[4]moon-caused tides

No need to tell thee of them, for I see
That thou hast been a witness——it must be——
For these I know thou canst not feel a drouth,
By the melancholy corners of that mouth.
So I will in my story straightway pass
To more immediate matter. Woe, alas!
That love should be my bane! Ah, Scylla fair!
Why did poor Glaucus ever——ever dare   400
To sue thee to his heart? Kind stranger-youth!
I lov'd her to the very white of truth,
And she would not conceive it. Timid thing!
She fled me swift as sea-bird on the wing,
Round every isle, and point, and promontory,
From where large Hercules wound up his story⁵
Far as Egyptian Nile. My passion grew
The more, the more I saw her dainty hue
Gleam delicately through the azure clear:
Until 'twas too fierce agony to bear;   410
And in that agony, across my grief
It flash'd, that Circe might find some relief——
Cruel enchantress! So above the water
I rear'd my head, and look'd for Phoebus' daughter.°   *(Circe)*
Æa's isle° was wondering at the moon:——   *(Circe's domain)*
It seem'd to whirl around me, and a swoon
Left me dead-drifting to that fatal power.

    When I awoke, 'twas in a twilight bower;
Just when the light of morn, with hum of bees,
Stole through its verdurous matting of fresh trees.   420
How sweet, and sweeter! for I heard a lyre,
And over it a sighing voice expire.
It ceased——I caught light footsteps; and anon
The fairest face that morn e'er look'd upon
Push'd through a screen of roses. Starry Jove!
With tears, and smiles, and honey-words she wove
A net whose thraldom was more bliss than all
The range of flower'd Elysium. Thus did fall⁶

⁵Hercules burnt himself on a pyre on Greek's Mt. Oeta.
⁶The rhyme *all/fall* is spun out of thr*al*dom.

The dew of her rich speech: "Ah! Art awake?
O let me hear thee speak, for Cupid's sake!   430
I am so oppress'd with joy! Why, I have shed
An urn of tears, as though thou wert cold dead;
And now I find thee living, I will pour
From these devoted eyes their silver store,
Until exhausted of the latest drop,
So it will pleasure thee, and force thee stop
Here, that I too may live: but if beyond
Such cool and sorrowful offerings, thou art fond
Of soothing warmth, of dalliance supreme;
If thou art ripe to taste a long love dream;   440
If smiles, if dimples, tongues for ardour mute,
Hang in thy vision like a tempting fruit,
O let me pluck it for thee." Thus she link'd
Her charming syllables, till indistinct
Their music came to my o'er-sweeten'd soul;
And then she hover'd over me, and stole
So near, that if no nearer it had been
This furrow'd visage thou hadst never seen.

     Young man of Latmos! thus particular
Am I, that thou may'st plainly see how far   450
This fierce temptation went: and thou may'st not
Exclaim, How then, was Scylla quite forgot?

     Who could resist?[7] Who in this universe?
She did so breathe ambrosia;° so immerse   *food of the gods*
My fine existence in a golden clime.
She took me like a child of suckling time,
And cradled me in roses. Thus condemn'd,
The current of my former life was stemm'd,
And to this arbitrary° queen of sense   *tyrannous*
I bow'd a tranced vassal: nor would thence   460
Have mov'd, even though Amphion's harp had woo'd[8]

---

[7]In Ovid's tale Glaucus does resist, and Circe punishes him by changing Scylla into a monster.

[8]Akin to Orpheus, Amphion, fabled inventor of music, with his lyre coaxed stones to move and build the walls of Thebes.

Me back to Scylla o'er the billows rude.
For as Apollo each eve doth devise
A new appareling for western skies;
So every eve, nay every spendthrift hour
Shed balmy consciousness[9] within that bower.
And I was free of haunts umbrageous;
Could wander in the mazy forest-house
Of squirrels, foxes shy, and antler'd deer,
And birds from coverts innermost and drear   470
Warbling for very joy mellifluous sorrow——
To me new born delights!

      Now let me borrow,
For moments few, a temperament as stern
As Pluto's sceptre, that my words not burn
These uttering lips, while I in calm speech tell
How specious heaven was changed to real hell.

 "One morn she left me sleeping: half awake
I sought for her smooth arms and lips, to slake
My greedy thirst with nectarous camel-draughts;
But she was gone. Whereat the barbed shafts   480
Of disappointment stuck in me so sore,
That out I ran and search'd the forest o'er.
Wandering about in pine and cedar gloom
Damp awe assail'd me; for there 'gan to boom
A sound of moan, an agony of sound,
Sepulchral from the distance all around.
Then came a conquering earth-thunder, and rumbled
That fierce complain[10] to silence: while I stumbled
Down a precipitous path, as if impell'd.
I came to a dark valley.——Groanings swell'd   490
Poisonous about my ears, and louder grew,
The nearer I approach'd a flame's gaunt blue,
That glar'd before me through a thorny brake.

---

[9]draft] nectarous Influence. (K may have wanted to save "nectarous" for the comedy of line 479.)

[10]Keats-coined noun

This fire, like the eye of gordian[11] snake,
Bewitch'd me towards; and I soon was near
A sight too fearful for the feel of fear:
In thicket hid I curs'd the haggard[12] scene——
The banquet of my arms, my arbour queen,
Seated upon an uptorn forest root;
And all around her shapes, wizard and brute,   500
Laughing, and wailing, groveling, serpenting,[13]
Shewing tooth, tusk, and venom-bag, and sting!
O such deformities! Old Charon's self,
Should he give up awhile his penny pelf,
And take a dream 'mong rushes Stygian,[14]
It could not be so phantasied. Fierce, wan,
And tyrannizing was the lady's look,
As over them a gnarled staff she shook.
Oft-times upon the sudden she laugh'd out,
And from a basket emptied to the rout[15]   510
Clusters of grapes, the which they raven'd quick
And roar'd for more; with many a hungry lick
About their shaggy jaws.[16] Avenging, slow,
Anon she took a branch of mistletoe,
And emptied on't a black dull-gurgling phial:
Groan'd one and all, as if some piercing trial
Was sharpening for their pitiable bones.
She lifted up the charm: appealing groans
From their poor breasts went sueing to her ear
In vain; remorseless as an infant's bier   520
She whisk'd against their eyes the sooty oil.
Whereat was heard a noise of painful toil,
Increasing gradual to a tempest rage,

---

[11]See p. 149, n. 17.

[12]bewitched, depleted

[13]Keats-coined verb

[14]Charon charges a fee to ferry the souls of the dead across the river Styx in the underworld.

[15]party

[16]Critic Karen Swann comments that while this scene is an extended metaphor for male passion-anxiety, in the Ovidian perspective it has the look of an actual metamorphosis ("*Endymion*'s Beautiful Dreamers"). See *Metamorphoses* XIV and Homer's *Odyssey* X.

Shrieks, yells, and groans of torture-pilgrimage;
Until their grieved bodies 'gan to bloat
And puff from the tail's end to stifled throat:
Then was appalling silence: then a sight
More wildering than all that hoarse affright;
For the whole herd, as by a whirlwind writhen,°   *writhed*
Went through the dismal air like one huge Python[17]   530
Antagonizing Boreas,°——and so vanish'd.   *North wind*
Yet there was not a breath of wind: she banish'd
These phantoms with a nod. Lo! from the dark
Came waggish fauns, and nymphs, and satyrs stark,
With dancing and loud revelry,——and went
Swifter than centaurs after rapine bent.——
Sighing an elephant appear'd and bow'd
Before the fierce witch, speaking thus aloud
In human accent: "Potent goddess! chief
Of pains resistless! make my being brief,   540
Or let me from this heavy prison fly:
Or give me to the air, or let me die!
I sue not for my happy crown again;
I sue not for my phalanx on the plain;
I sue not for my lone, my widow'd wife;
I sue not for my ruddy drops of life,
My children fair, my lovely girls and boys!
I will forget them; I will pass these joys;
Ask nought so heavenward, so too——too high:
Only I pray, as fairest boon, to die,   550
Or be deliver'd from this cumbrous flesh,
From this gross, detestable, filthy mesh,
And merely given to the cold bleak air.
Have mercy, Goddess! Circe, feel my prayer!"

　　That curst magician's name fell icy numb
Upon my wild conjecturing: truth had come
Naked and sabre-like against my heart.
I saw a fury whetting a death-dart;
And my slain spirit, overwrought with fright,

[17]serpent killed by Apollo

Fainted away in that dark lair of night.   560
Think, my deliverer, how desolate
My waking must have been! disgust, and hate,
And terrors manifold divided me
A spoil amongst them. I prepar'd to flee
Into the dungeon core of that wild wood:
I fled three days—when lo! before me stood
Glaring the angry witch. O Dis,° even now,   *Pluto*
A clammy dew is beading on my brow,
At mere remembering her pale laugh, and curse.
"Ha! ha! Sir Dainty! there must be a nurse   570
Made of rose leaves and thistledown, express,
To cradle thee my sweet, and lull thee: yes,
I am too flinty-hard for thy nice touch:
My tenderest squeeze is but a giant's clutch.
So, fairy-thing, it shall have lullabies
Unheard of yet; and it shall still its cries
Upon some breast more lily-feminine.
Oh, no——it shall not pine, and pine, and pine
More than one pretty, trifling thousand years;
And then 'twere pity, but fate's gentle shears   580
Cut short its immortality. Sea-flirt!
Young dove of the waters! truly I'll not hurt
One hair of thine: see how I weep and sigh,
That our heart-broken parting is so nigh.
And must we part? Ah, yes, it must be so.
Yet ere thou leavest me in utter woe,
Let me sob over thee my last adieus,
And speak a blessing: Mark me! Thou hast thews[18]
Immortal, for thou art of heavenly race:
But such a love is mine, that here I chase   590
Eternally away from thee all bloom
Of youth, and destine thee towards a tomb.
Hence shalt thou quickly to the watery vast;
And there, ere many days be overpast,
Disabled age shall seize thee; and even then
Thou shalt not go the way of aged men;

[18]physical strength

But live and wither, cripple and still breathe
Ten hundred years: which gone, I then bequeath
Thy fragile bones to unknown burial.
Adieu, sweet love, adieu!"——As shot stars fall,   600
She fled ere I could groan for mercy. Stung
And poisoned was my spirit: despair sung
A war-song of defiance 'gainst all hell.
A hand was at my shoulder to compel
My sullen steps; another 'fore my eyes
Moved on with pointed finger. In this guise
Enforced, at the last by ocean's foam
I found me; by my fresh, my native home.
Its tempering coolness, to my life akin,
Came salutary as I waded in;   610
And, with a blind voluptuous rage, I gave
Battle to the swollen billow-ridge, and drave
Large froth before me, while there yet remain'd
Hale strength, nor from my bones all marrow drain'd.

    Young lover, I must weep——such hellish spite
With dry cheek who can tell? While thus my might
Proving upon this element, dismay'd,
Upon a dead thing's face my hand I laid;
I look'd—'twas Scylla! Cursed, cursed Circe!
O vulture-witch, hast never heard of mercy?   620
Could not thy harshest vengeance be content,
But thou must nip this tender innocent
Because I lov'd her?——Cold, O cold indeed
Were her fair limbs, and like a common weed
The sea-swell took her hair. Dead as she was
I clung about her waist, nor ceas'd to pass
Fleet as an arrow through unfathom'd brine,
Until there shone a fabric° crystalline,   *building*
Ribb'd and inlaid with coral, pebble, and pearl.
Headlong I darted; at one eager swirl   630
Gain'd its bright portal, enter'd, and behold!
'Twas vast, and desolate, and icy-cold;
And all around——But wherefore this to thee
Who in few minutes more thyself shalt see?——
I left poor Scylla in a niche and fled.

My fever'd parchings up, my scathing dread
Met palsy half way: soon these limbs became
Gaunt, wither'd, sapless, feeble, cramp'd, and lame.

from BOOK IV

Beginning with an invocation to the muse of his "native land," the narrator resumes Endymion's story with his discovery of an Indian (eastern) Maid abandoned by Bacchus. The poem's denouement has struck some readers as contrived, while others, noting Keats's own disenchantment with his Romance, discern a critical (even satirical) turn against the genre.

[. . .] Great Muse, thou know'st what prison,   20
Of flesh and bone, curbs, and confines, and frets
Our spirit's wings: despondency besets
Our pillows; and the fresh to-morrow morn
Seems to give forth its light in very scorn
Of our dull, uninspired, snail-paced lives.
Long have I said, how happy he who shrives[1]
To thee! But then I thought on poets gone,
And could not pray:——nor can I now——so on
I move to the end in lowliness of heart.————

"Ah, woe is me! that I should fondly part   30
From my dear native land! Ah, foolish maid!
Glad was the hour, when, with thee, myriads bade
Adieu to Ganges and their pleasant fields!
To one so friendless the clear freshet yields
A bitter coolness; the ripe grape is sour:
Yet I would have, great gods! but one short hour
Of native air——let me but die at home."

Endymion to heaven's airy dome
Was offering up a hecatomb° of vows,   *100 tombs*
When these words reach'd him. Whereupon he bows   40

[1]makes confession

His head through thorny-green entanglement
Of underwood, and to the sound is bent,
Anxious as hind towards her hidden fawn.

"Is no one near to help me? No fair dawn
Of life from charitable voice? No sweet saying
To set my dull and sadden'd spirit playing?
No hand to toy with mine? No lips so sweet
That I may worship them? No eyelids meet
To twinkle on my bosom? No one dies
Before me, till from these enslaving eyes   50
Redemption sparkles!——I am sad and lost."

Thou, Carian lord, hadst better have been tost
Into a whirlpool. Vanish into air,
Warm mountaineer! for canst thou only bear
A woman's sigh alone and in distress?
See not her charms! Is Phœbe[2] passionless?
Phœbe is fairer far——O gaze no more:——
Yet if thou wilt behold all beauty's store,
Behold her panting in the forest grass!
Do not those curls of glossy jet surpass   60
For tenderness the arms so idly lain
Amongst them? Feelest not a kindred pain,
To see such lovely eyes in swimming search
After some warm delight, that seems to perch
Dovelike in the dim cell lying beyond
Their upper lids?——Hist!

[*Hearing her lament, Endymion falls hard, but not without conflict about
his first love, the dream-goddess.*]

                        Upon a bough
He leant, wretched. He surely cannot now
Thirst for another love: O impious,
That he can even dream upon it thus![3]——

[2]The first instance of this (yet another) name for the Moon-goddess.
[3]The first draft was less sarcastic] The Latmian lean'd his arm upon a bough, / A
wretched mortal: what can he do now? / Must he another Love?"

Thought he, "Why am I not as are the dead,
Since to a woe like this I have been led   90
Through the dark earth, and through the wondrous sea?
Goddess! I love thee not the less: from thee
By Juno's smile I turn not——no, no, no——
While the great waters are at ebb and flow.——
I have a triple soul![4] O fond pretence——
For both, for both my love is so immense,
I feel my heart is cut in twain for them."

    And so he groan'd, as one by beauty slain.
The lady's heart beat quick, and he could see
Her gentle bosom heave tumultuously.   100
He sprang from his green covert: there she lay,
Sweet as a muskrose upon new-made hay;
With all her limbs on tremble, and her eyes
Shut softly up alive. To speak he tries.
"Fair damsel, pity me! forgive that I
Thus violate thy bower's sanctity!
O pardon me, for I am full of grief——
Grief born of thee, young angel! fairest thief!
Who stolen hast away the wings wherewith
I was to top the heavens. Dear maid, sith   110
Thou art my executioner, and I feel
Loving and hatred, misery and weal,
Will in a few short hours be nothing to me,
And all my story that much passion slew me;
Do smile upon the evening of my days:
And, for my tortur'd brain begins to craze,
Be thou my nurse; and let me understand
How dying I shall kiss that lily hand.——
Dost weep for me? Then should I be content."
                    [. . .]
Endymion could not speak, but gazed on her;
And listened to the wind that now did stir
About the crisped oaks full drearily,
Yet with as sweet a softness as might be

[4]The Moon, the dream-goddess Cynthia, and now the Indian Maid (do the math).

Remember'd from its velvet summer song.
At last he said: "Poor lady, how thus long
Have I been able to endure that voice?
Fair Melody! kind Syren! I've not choice;   300
I must be thy sad servant evermore:
O cannot choose but kneel here and adore.
Alas, I must not think—by Phœbe, no!
Let me not think, soft Angel! shall it be so?
Say, beautifullest, shall I never think?
O thou could'st foster me beyond the brink
Of recollection! make my watchful care
Close up its bloodshot eyes, not see despair!
Do gently murder half my soul, and I
Shall feel the other half so utterly!——   310
I'm giddy at that cheek so fair and smooth;
O let it blush so ever! let it soothe
My madness!"

[*Endymion surrenders to this Indian Maid; they soar high on mysterious celestial horses, then fall asleep. He dreams of Cynthia and awakes to a rapturous view of the moon. In despair, he enters the Cave of Quietude.*]

The moon put forth a little diamond peak,
No bigger than an unobserved star,
Or tiny point of fairy scymetar;[5]
Bright signal that she only stoop'd to tie   500
Her silver sandals, ere deliciously
She bow'd into the heavens her timid head.
Slowly she rose, as though she would have fled,
While to his lady meek the Carian turn'd,
To mark if her dark eyes had yet discern'd
This beauty in its birth—Despair! despair!
He saw her body fading gaunt and spare
In the cold moonshine. Straight he seiz'd her wrist;
It melted from his grasp: her hand he kiss'd,
And, horror! kiss'd his own—he was alone.   510

[5]curved sword

Her steed a little higher soar'd, and then
Dropt hawkwise to the earth.

                  There lies a den,[6]
Beyond the seeming confines of the space
Made for the soul to wander in and trace
Its own existence, of remotest glooms.
Dark regions are around it, where the tombs
Of buried griefs the spirit sees, but scarce
One hour doth linger weeping, for the pierce
Of new-born woe it feels more inly smart:
And in these regions many a venom'd dart   520
At random flies; they are the proper home
Of every ill: the man is yet to come
Who hath not journeyed in this native hell.
But few have ever felt how calm and well
Sleep may be had in that deep den of all.
There anguish does not sting; nor pleasure pall:
Woe-hurricanes beat ever at the gate,
Yet all is still within and desolate.
Beset with plainful gusts, within ye hear
No sound so loud as when on curtain'd bier   530
The death-watch tick[7] is stifled. Enter none
Who strive therefore: on the sudden it is won.
Just when the sufferer begins to burn,
Then it is free to him; and from an urn,
Still fed by melting ice, he takes a draught——
Young Semele[8] such richness never quaft
In her maternal longing. Happy gloom!
Dark Paradise! where pale becomes the bloom
Of health by due; where silence dreariest
Is most articulate; where hopes infest;   540
Where those eyes are the brightest far that keep
Their lids shut longest in a dreamless sleep.
O happy spirit-home! O wondrous soul!
Pregnant with such a den to save the whole

[6]This den is shadowed by Spenser's Cave of Despair (*FQ* I.ix.39ff).

[7]either a watch, or an insect-sound like it

[8]Bacchus's mother

In thine own depth. Hail, gentle Carian!
For, never since thy griefs and woes began,
Hast thou felt so content: a grievous feud
Hath led thee to this Cave of Quietude.
Aye, his lull'd soul was there, although upborne
With dangerous speed: and so he did not mourn   550
Because he knew not whither he was going.
So happy was he, not the aerial blowing
Of trumpets at clear parley from the east
Could rouse from that fine relish, that high feast.

[*Frustrated unto exhaustion, Endymion moans, "I have clung / To nothing, lov'd a nothing, nothing seen / Or felt but a great dream!" (636–38). He decides his palpable "Indian bliss" (663) is his best hope for "some tranquility" (723), only to hear from her, suddenly, "I may not be thy love: I am forbidden" (752). At this nadir, Peona appears, wondering at Endymion's sadness on the eve of a festival to "Cynthia, queen of light" (the moon). Beyond repair, he decides to live as a hermit, asking her to accept the Indian Maid as a sister, and to visit him alone, from time to time, to hear "the wonders I shall tell" (862). The Indian Maid not only agrees, but decides herself to become a chaste votary to "Dian's sisterhood" (the cult of the Moon-goddess). Endymion sighs in melancholy.*]

[. . .] So he inwardly began
On things for which no wording can be found;
Deeper and deeper sinking, until drown'd
Beyond the reach of music: for the choir
Of Cynthia he heard not, though rough briar
Nor muffling thicket interpos'd to dull
The vesper hymn, far swollen, soft and full,
Through the dark pillars of those sylvan aisles.
He saw not the two maidens, nor their smiles,
Wan as primroses gather'd at midnight   970
By chilly finger'd spring. "Unhappy wight!°   *Poor guy!*
Endymion!" said Peona, "we are here!
What wouldst thou ere we all are laid on bier?"⁹
Then he embrac'd her, and his lady's hand
Press'd, saying: "Sister, I would have command,

⁹funeral wagon

If it were heaven's will, on our sad fate."
At which that dark-eyed stranger stood elate
And said, in a new voice, but sweet as love,
To Endymion's amaze: "By Cupid's dove,
And so thou shalt! and by the lily truth   980
Of my own breast thou shalt, beloved youth!"
And as she spake, into her face there came
Light, as reflected from a silver flame:
Her long black hair swell'd ampler, in display
Full golden; in her eyes a brighter day
Dawn'd blue and full of love. Aye, he beheld
Phœbe, his passion! joyous she upheld
Her lucid bow,[10] continuing thus: "Drear, drear
Has our delaying been; but foolish fear
Withheld me first; and then decrees of fate;   990
And then 'twas fit that from this mortal state
Thou shouldst, my love, by some unlook'd for change
Be spiritualiz'd. Peona, we shall range
These forests, and to thee they safe shall be
As was thy cradle; hither shalt thou flee
To meet us many a time." Next Cynthia bright
Peona kiss'd, and bless'd with fair good night:
Her brother kiss'd her too, and knelt adown
Before his goddess, in a blissful swoon.
She gave her fair hands to him, and behold,   1000
Before three swiftest kisses he had told,
They vanish'd far away!——Peona went
Home through the gloomy wood in wonderment.

THE END.

⁓

[10]revealed Moon-goddess

Letter to Benjamin Bailey, 21 and 25 May 1818[1]

Bailey wanted Keats to visit him at Oxford; George is about to depart for America.

My dear Bailey,   Hampstead Thursday —
                 I should have answered your letter on the moment -
if I could have said yes to your invitation. What hinders me is
insuperable; I will tell it at a little length. You know my Brother
George has been out of employ for some time. it has weighed very much
upon him, and driven him to scheme and turn over things in his Mind.
the result has been his resolution to emigrate to the back Settlements
of America, become farmer and work with his own hands after
purchacing 1400 hundred Acres of the American Government. This
for many reasons has met with my entire consent - and the chief one
is this - he is of too independant and liberal a Mind to get on in trade
in this Country - in which a generous Man with a scanty recourse
must be ruined. I would sooner he should till the ground than bow to
a Customer - there is no choice with him; he could not bring himself to
the latter. I would not consent to his going alone - no; but that objection
is done away with - he will marry before he sets sail a young Lady he
has known some years - of a nature liberal and highspirited enough
to follow him to the Banks of the Mississipi. He will set off in a month
or six weeks, and you will see how I should wish to pass that time with
him — and then I must set out on a journey of my own. Brown and
I are going a pedestrian tour through the north of England and
Scotland as far a John o Grots. I have this morning such a Lethargy
that I cannot write - the reason of my delaying is oftentimes from this
feeling - I wait for a proper temper. Now you ask for an immediate
answer I do not like to wait even till tomorrow However I am now so
depressed that I have not an Idea to put to paper— my hand feels like
lead - and yet it is and unpleasant numbness it does not take away
the pain of existence. I don't know what to write—
Monday [25 May] - You see how I have delayed — and even now I
have but a confused idea of what I should be about my intellect must
be in a degenating state - it must be for when I should be writing about
god knows what I am troubling you with Moods of my own Mind[2] or

[1]ALS, Houghton Library, Harvard.

[2]Wordsworthian self-absorption; see the verse letter to Reynolds, 25 March 1818
(p. 121).

rather body—for Mind there is none. I am in that temper that if I
were under Water I would scarcely kick to come to the top. I know
very well 'tis all nonsense. In a short time I hope I shall be in a temper
to fell sensibly your mention of my Book[3] - in vain have I waited till
Monday to have any interest in that or in any thing else. I feel no
spur at my Brothers going to America, and am almost stony-hearted
about his wedding. All this will blow over [. . .] Yesterday I dined with
Hazlitt, Barnes, and Wilkie at Haydon's. The topic was the Duke of
Wellington very amusingly pro and con'd - Reynolds has been getting
much better [. . .] I hope I shall soon see you for we must have many
new thoughts and feelings to analize, and to discover whether a little
more knowledge has not made us more ignorant

Your's affectionately John Keats—

Letter to Benjamin Bailey, 10 June 1818[1]

Endymion *was ridiculed in the orthodox* British Critic, *one of the
first reviews. Bailey's notice on the poem, urging support for "this
rising genius," appeared in* Oxford University and City Herald,
*across the issues of 30 May and 6 June. After talking about his
closeness to his brothers, his admiration of George's wife, and
Reynolds's and Rice's returns to health, Keats mentions his coming
abuse in* Blackwood's.

My dear Bailey,

I have been very much gratified and very much
hurt by your Letters in the Oxford Paper: because independant of
that unlawful and mortal feeling of pleasure at praise, there is a glory
in enthusiam; and because the world is malignant enough to chuckle
at the most honorable Simplicity. [. . .] were it in my choice I would
reject a petrarchal coronation[2] - on accout of my dying day, and
because women have Cancers. I should not by rights speak in this tone
to you - for it is an incendiary spirit that would do so. Yet I am not
old enough or magnanimous enough to anihilate self - and it would
perhaps be paying you an ill compliment. I was in hopes some little

[3]*Endymion*, published 19 May.

---

[1]ALS, Houghton Library, Harvard.
[2]Italian Renaissance poet Petrarch was honored with a laurel crown.

time back to be able to releive your dullness by my spirits - to point
out things in the world worth your enjoyment - and now I am never
alone without rejoicing that there is such a thing as death - without
placing my ultimate in the glory of dying for a great human purpose.
Perphaps if my affairs were in a different state I should not have
written the above - you shall judge - I have two Brothers one is driven
by the 'burden of Society' to America the other, with an exquisite love
of Life, is in a lingering State. My Love for my Brothers from the
early loss of our parents and even for earlier Misfortunes has grown
into a affection 'passing the Love of Women'[3]— I have been ill temper'd
with them, I have vex'd them - but the thought of them has always
stifled the impression that any woman might otherwise have made
upon me. I have a Sister too[4] and may not follow them, either to
America or to the Grave — Life must be undergone, and I certainly
derive a consolation from the thought of writing one or two more Poems
before it ceases. [. . .] I am not certain whether I shall be able to go
my Journey on account of my Brother Tom and a little indisposition
of my own - If I do not you shall see me soon –if no on my return - or
I'll quarter myself upon you in Scotland next Winter. I had know my
sister in Law some time before she was my Sister and was very fond of
her. I like her better and better - she is the most disinterrested[5] woman I
ever knew - that is to say she goes beyond degree in it. To see an entirely
disinterrested Girl quite happy is the most pleasant and extraordinary
thing in the world- it depends upon a thousand Circumstances - on
my word 'tis extraordinary. Women must want[6] Imagination and they
may thank God for it -and so my we that a delicate being can feel
happy without any sense of crime. It puzzles me and I have no sort of
Logic to comfort me. I shall think it over. [. . .] I felt that passage of
Dante - if I take any book with me it shall be those minute volumes of
carey[7] for they will go into the aptest corner - Reynolds is getting I
may say robust — his illness has been of service to him - like eny one
just recoverd he is high-spirited - I hear also good accounts of Rice.

[3]"My brother Jonathan," laments King David of his death, "thy love to me was
wonderful, passing the love of women" (2 Samuel 1.26).

[4]K feels responsible to Fanny, who is still under the control of her legal guardian
Richard Abbey.

[5]not self-interested or self-absorbed; devoted to the welfare of others

[6]be lacking in

[7]Henry F. Carey's 3-vol. *Divine Comedy* (rpt. Taylor & Hessey, 1814) was issued in
an economical form, 32mo (32 pages printed per sheet, yielding very small pages).

*With respect to domestic Literature—the Endinburgh Magasine in
another blow up against Hunt calls me 'the amiable Mister Keats'
and I have more than a Laurel from the Quarterly Reviewers for
they have <u>smothered</u> me in 'Foliage'[8] I want to read you my 'Pot of
Basil' if you go to scotland I should much like to read it there to you
among the Snows of next Winter. My Brothers' remembrances to you.*

*Your affectionate friend
John Keats—*

Letter to Fanny Keats, 2–5 July 1818, with "There was a naughty Boy" [3 July][1]

My dear Fanny, [. . .]

*I have so interruptions
that I cannot manage to fill
a Letter in one day— since
I scribbled the Song we have
walked through a beautiful
— Country to Kirkudbright —
at which place I will write
you a song about mys elf[2] -
There was a naughty Boy
A naughty boy was he,
He would not stop at home
He could not quiet be -
He took
In his Knapsack*

---

[8]Punning the name of the magazine of Z's career-ending assaults, K refers to "Letter from Z. to Leigh Hunt, King of the Cockneys" (May 1818), which ridiculed "amiable but infatuated bardling, Mister John Keats" composing a "Cockney Poem" in honor of Hunt (p. 197). Though K was not named in the *Quarterly*'s review of Hunt's *Foliage; or Poems Original and Translated* (January; published June), he is implied in the smirk at its "leafy luxuries" (a near phrase in his dedicatory sonnet to Hunt in *1817*) and Hunt's "infant sect" (p. 327)—and perhaps in its quotation (p. 328) of Hunt's ode to his son ("Ah, little ranting Johnny, / For ever blithe, and bonny, / And singing nonny nonny").

---

[1]ALS Morgan library; first published HBF (1883), 2.290–94. K writes the song after some prose, but the letter's page column, which I transcribe, makes the prose seem like a poetic prologue—especially with the warm-up of *Kirkudbright / I will write*.

[2]K's script divides the word thus.

A Book
Full of vowels
And a shirt
With some towels –
A slight cap
For night cap —
A hair brush,
Comb ditto,
New Stockings
For old ones
Would split O!
This Knapsack
Tight at 's back
He rivetted close
And followéd his Nose
To the North,
To the North,
And follow'd his nose
To the North –

There was a naughty boy
And a naughty boy was he,
For nothing would he do
But scribble poetry—
He took
An ink stand
In his hand
And a Pen
Big as ten
In the other,
And away
In a Pother
He ran
To the mountains
And fountains
And ghostes
And Postes
And witches
And ditches
And wrote

In his coat
When the wather
Was ~~warm~~ cool –
   Fear of gout,
And without
When the weather
   Was ~~cool~~ warm—
Och the charm
When we choose
To follow ones nose
   To the north,
   To the north,
To follow one's nose to the
        north!

There was a naughty boy
   And a naughty boy we he,
He kept little fishes
   In washing tubs three
      In spite
      Of the might
      Of the Maid
      Nor affraid
      Of his Granny-good –
        He often would
        Hurly burly
        Get up early
      And go
        By hook or crook
      To the brook
      And bring home
      Miller's thumb
      Tittlebat
      Not over fat
      Minnows small
      As the stall
      Of a glove
      Not above
      The size

Of a nice
Little Baby's
Little fingers —
O he made
'Twas his trade
Of Fish a pretty Kettle
A Kettle - A Kettle
Of Fish a pretty Kettle
A Kettle!
There was a naughty Boy
And a naughty Boy was he
He ran away to Scotland
The people for to see —
Then he found
That the ground
Was as hard,
That a yard
Was as long,
That a song
Was as merry,
That a cherry
Was as red -
That lead
Was as weighty,
That fourscore
Was as eighty
That a door
Was as wooden
As in england -
So he stood in
His shoes
And he wonderd
He wonderd
He stood in his
Shoes and he
wonder'd —
My dear Fanny I
am ashamed of
writing you such

stuff, nor would
I if it were not
for being tired after
my days walking,
and ready to

tumble into bed
so fatigued that
when I am asleep
you might sew
my nose to my
great toe and
trundle me round
the town like a
Hoop without wa-
king me – Then
I get so hungry –
a Ham goes but
a very little way –
and fowls are
like Larks to me –
A Batch of Bread
I make no more
ado with than a
sheet of parliament;
and I can eat a
Bull's head as easily

as I used to do Bull's eyes– I take a whole string of Pork Sausages
down as easily as a Pen'orth of Lady's fingers – Oh dear I must soon
be contented with an acre or two of oaten cake a hogshead of Milk
and a Cloaths basket of Eggs morning noon and night when I get
among the Highlanders – Before we see them we shall pass into Ireland
and have a chat with the Paddies, and look at the Giant's Cause-way
which you must have heard of – I have not time to tell you particularly
for I have to send a Journal to Tom of whom you shall hear all
particulars or from me when I return. Since I began this we have
walked sixty miles to newton stewart at which place I put in this
Letter [. . .] God bless you—

Your affectionate Brother John—

Letter to Benjamin Bailey, 18 and 22 July 1818[1]

Keats confesses his social discomfort with women, with some self-analysis.

[18 July] *My dear Bailey,* [. . .]
I will say a few words written in a sane and sober Mind, a very scarce thing with me, for they may hereafter save you a great deal of trouble about me, which you do not deserve, and for which I ought to be batinadoed. I carry all matters to an extreme – so that when I have any little vexation it grows in five Minutes into a theme for Sophocles – then and in that temper if I write to any friend I have so little selfpossession that I give him matter for grieving at the very time perhaps when I am laughing at a Pun. Your last Letter made me blush for the pain I had given you – I know my own disposition so well that I am certain of writing many times hereafter in the same strain to you – now you know how far to believe in them – you must allow for imagination. [. . .] *Yet further I will confess to you that I cannot enjoy Society small or numerous. I am certain that our fair friends*[2] *are glad I should come for the mere sake of my coming; but I am certain I bring with me a Vexation they are better without – If I can possibly at any time feel my temper coming upon me I refrain even from a promised visit. I am certain I have not a right feeling towards Women – at this moment I am striving to be just to them but I cannot – Is it because they fall so far beneath my Boyish imagination? When I was a Schoolboy I though a fair Woman a pure Goddess, my mind was a soft nest in which some one of them slept, though she knew it not – I have no right to expect more than their reality. I thought them etherial above Men – I find them perhaps equal – great by comparison is very small – Insult may be inflicted in more ways than by Word or action – one who is tender of being insulted does not like to think an insult against another – I do not like to think insults in a Lady's Company – I commit a Crime with her which absence would have not known – Is it not extraordinary? When among Men I have no evil thoughts, no malice, no spleen – I feel free to speak or to be silent – I can listen and from every one I can learn – my hands are*

---

[1]ALS, Houghton Library, Harvard.
[2]Reynolds's sisters; Bailey was visiting the family and seemed to be courting Mariane.

in my pockets I am free from all suspicion and comfortable. When I am among Women I have evil thoughts, malice spleen – I cannot speak or be silent – I am full of Suspicions and therefore listen to nothing – I am in a hurry to be gone – You must be charitable and put all this perversity to my being disappointed since Boyhood – Yet with such feelings I am happier alone among Crowds of men, by myself or with a friend or two – With all this trust me – Bailey I have not the least idea that Men of different feelings and inclinations are more short sighted than myself – I never rejoiced more than at my Brother's Marriage and shall do so at that of any of my friends – I must absolutely get over this – but how? The only way is to find the root of evil, and so cure it "with backward mutters of dissevering Power"[3] That is a difficult thing; for an obstinate Prejudice can seldom be produced but from a gordian complication of feelings, which must take time to unravell and care to keep unravelled.[4] I could say a good deal about this but I will leave it in hopes of better and more worthy dispositions – and also content that I am wronging no one, for after all I do think better of Womankind than to suppose they care whether Mister John Keats five feet hight likes them or not. You appeard to wish to avoid any words on this subject – dont think it a bore my dear fellow – it shall be my Amen — I should not have consented to myself these four Months tramping in the high lands but that I thought it would give me more experience, rub off more Prejudice, use to more hardship, identify finer scenes load me with grander Mountains, and strengthen more my reach in Poetry, than would stopping at home among Books even though I should reach Homer. By this time I am comparitively a a[5] mountaineer [. . . 22 July] Your affectionate friend

John Keats —

---

[3]In Milton's masque, the means to free a virtuous lady from an enchanter with designs on her virtue: "without his rod revers't, / And backwards mutters of dissevering power, / We cannot free the Lady that sits here / In stony fetters fixt and motionless" (*Comus* 816–19).

[4]For the she-sexualizing of Gordias's intricate knot, see also *Endymion* (1.614) and *Lamia* (1.47).

[5]K repeats this word at the start of a new line.

§ *Blackwood's Edinburgh Magazine*, August 1818, 519–24

> *With this skewering of Keats impending (it appeared in early Septem-*
> *ber), his friends tried to pre-empt it with praising notices to greet*
> Endymion. *Bailey met Lockhart (Z) during the summer, and tried to*
> *endear him with reports of Keats's perseverance during his surgeon's*
> *apprenticeship; when Z used this information for ridicule, Bailey was*
> *mortified. Bailey's letters of advertisement (see p. 184) were followed by*
> The Champion's *review (7 and 14 June, by either Reynolds or Wood-*
> *house), but none helped with sales or reception. Z's attacks on Hunt*
> *persisted in his "Cockney School" papers II (November 1817) and III*
> *(July 1818); "Letter from Z. to Leigh Hunt" (May 1818) included*
> *ridicules of "young Mister Keats" (Keats reported to Bailey, 10 June).*

Cockney School of Poetry, No IV.

————————OF KEATS,

THE MUSES' SON OF PROMISE, AND WHAT FEATS

HE YET MAY DO, &c.

CORNELIUS WEBB.

OF all the manias of this mad age, the most incurable, as well as the most common, seems to be no other than the *Metromanie*.[1] The just celebrity of Robert Burns and Miss Baillie[2] has had the melancholy effect of turning the heads of we know not how many farm-servants and unmarried ladies; our very footmen compose tragedies, and there is scarcely a superannuated governess in the island that does not leave a roll of lyrics behind her in her band-box.[3] To witness the disease of any human understanding, however feeble, is distressing; but the spectacle of an able mind reduced to a state of insanity is of course ten times more afflicting. It is with such sorrow as this that we have contemplated the case of Mr John Keats. This young man appears to have received from nature talents of an excellent, perhaps even of a superior order—talents which, devoted to the purposes of any useful profession, must have

[1]Meter-mania (poetry-writing fever), initiating the recurrent medical sarcasm, and evoking William Gifford's satire of "this pernicious pest, / This metromania" in *The Baviad* (1791).

[2]Two Scots poets spared Z's abuse: much loved Robert Burns (dead when Z wrote), also a champion of Scottish independence and the French Revolution; widely admired Joanna Baillie (then still alive).

[3]cardboard box for hats and other head-accessories; a footman is a low-order servant.

rendered him a respectable, if not an eminent citizen. His friends, we understand, destined him to the career of medicine, and he was bound apprentice some years ago to a worthy apothecary in town. But all has been undone by a sudden attack of the malady to which we have alluded. Whether Mr John had been sent home with a diuretic or composing draught[4] to some patient far gone in the poetical mania, we have not heard. This much is certain, that he has caught the infection, and that thoroughly. For some time we were in hopes, that he might get off with a violent fit or two; but of late the symptoms are terrible. The phrenzy of the "Poems" was bad enough in its way; but it did not alarm us half so seriously as the calm, settled, imperturbable drivelling idiocy of "Endymion." We hope, however, that in so young a person, and with a constitution originally so good, even now the disease is not utterly incurable. Time, firm treatment, and rational restraint, do much for many apparently hopeless invalids; and if Mr Keats should happen, at some interval of reason, to cast his eye upon our pages, he may perhaps be convinced of the existence of his malady, which, in such cases, is often all that is necessary to put the patient in a fair way of being cured.

The readers of the Examiner newspaper were informed, some time ago, by a solemn paragraph, in Mr Hunt's best style, of the appearance of two new stars of glorious magnitude and splendour in the poetical horizon of the land of Cockaigne.[5] One of these turned out, by and by, to be no other than Mr John Keats. This precocious adulation confirmed the wavering apprentice in his desire to quit the gallipots,[6] and at the same time excited in his too susceptible mind a fatal admiration for the character and talents of the most worthless and affected of all the versifiers of our time. One of his first productions was the following sonnet, "*written on the day when Mr Leigh Hunt left prison.*" It will be recollected, that the cause of Hunt's confinement was a series of libels against his sovereign, and that its fruit was the odious and incestuous "Story of Rimini."

[4]urine-maker or sedative

[5]Actually three new stars (Z also had Shelley in his crosshairs). With a pun on "Cockney" pretension, *Cockaigne* is a country renowned in medieval fable for luxury and idleness.

[6]apothecaries' pots, or a metonym for the profession itself

[Z quotes the sonnet, with *Kind Hunt, In Spenser's walls!* and
With daring Milton! in outraged italics and added exclamations]
The absurdity of the thought in this sonnet is, however, if possible,
surpassed in another, "*addressed to Haydon*" the painter, that
clever, but most affected artist, who as little resembles Raphael in
genius as he does in person, notwithstanding the foppery of having
his hair curled over his shoulders in the old Italian fashion. In this
exquisite piece it will be observed, that Mr Keats classes together
WORDSWORTH, HUNT, and HAYDON, as the three greatest spirits of
the age, and that he alludes to himself, and some others of the rising
brood of Cockneys, as likely to attain hereafter an equally honourable elevation. Wordsworth and Hunt! what a juxta-position!
The purest, the loftiest, and, we do not fear to say it, the most classical of living English poets, joined together in the same compliment
with the meanest, the filthiest, and the most vulgar of Cockney
poetasters. No wonder that he who could be guilty of this should
class Haydon with Raphael, and himself with Spencer.
    [Z quotes "Great spirits" with outraged italicizing on 5–6 and
    12 (from *Hear ye not*) to 14]
The nations are to listen and be dumb! And why, good Johnny
Keats? because Leigh Hunt is editor of the Examiner, and Haydon
has painted the judgment of Solomon, and you and Cornelius
Webb, and a few more city sparks, are pleased to look upon yourselves as so many future Shakspeares and Miltons! The world has
really some reason to look to its foundations! Here is a *tempestas
in matulâ*[7] with a vengeance. At the period when these sonnets were
published, Mr Keats had no hesitation in saying, that he looked on
himself as "*not yet* a glorious denizen of the wide heaven of poetry,"[8]
but he had many fine soothing visions of coming greatness, and
many rare plans of study to prepare him for it. The following we
think is very pretty raving.
    [Z quotes *Sleep and Poetry* 96–121]
Having cooled a little from this "fine passion," our youthful poet
passes very naturally into a long strain of foaming abuse against
a certain class of English Poets, whom, with Pope at their head, it
is much the fashion with the ignorant unsettled pretenders of the

[7]tempest in a pisspot
[8]*Sleep and Poetry* 47–49.

present time to undervalue. Begging these gentlemens' [*sic*] pardon, although Pope was not a poet of the same high order with some who are now living, yet, to deny his genius, is just about as absurd as to dispute that of Wordsworth, or to believe in that of Hunt. Above all things, it is most pitiably ridiculous to hear men, of whom their country will always have reason to be proud, reviled by uneducated and flimsy striplings, who are not capable of understanding either their merits, or those of any other *men of power—* fanciful dreaming tea-drinkers, who, without logic enough to analyse a single idea, or imagination enough to form one original image, or learning enough to distinguish between the written language of Englishmen and the spoken jargon of Cockneys, presume to talk with contempt of some of the most exquisite spirits the world ever produced, merely because they did not happen to exert their faculties in laborious affected descriptions of flowers seen in window-pots, or cascades heard at Vauxhall;[9] in short, because they chose to be wits, philosophers, patriots, and poets, rather than to found the Cockney school of versification, morality, and politics, a century before its time. After blaspheming himself into a fury against Boileau, &c. Mr Keats comforts himself and his readers with a view of the present more promising aspect of affairs; above all, with the ripened glories of the poet of Rimini. Addressing the manes of the departed chiefs of English poetry, he informs them, in the following clear and touching manner of the existence of "him of the Rose," &c.

[Z quotes *Sleep and Poetry* 226–29]

From this he diverges into a view of "things in general." We smile when we think to ourselves how little most of our readers will understand of what follows.

[Z quotes *Sleep and Poetry* 248–69, italicizing the *thorns / fawns* rhyme]

From some verses addressed to various amiable individuals of the other sex, it appears, notwithstanding all this gossamer-work, that Johnny's affections are not entirely confined to objects purely etherial. Take, by way of specimen, the following prurient and vulgar lines, evidently meant for some young lady east of Temple-bar.

[Z quotes another poem in *1817*, italicizing *higher* and *Thalia*]

---

[9]Musical concerts at the public entertainment park on the south bank of the Thames.

Who will dispute that our poet, to use his own phrase (and rhyme),
  "Can mingle music fit for the soft *ear*
  Of lady *Cytherea*."[10]
So much for the opening bud; now for the expanded flower. It is
time to pass from the juvenile "Poems," to the mature and elaborate "Endymion, a Poetic romance." The old story of the moon
falling in love with a shepherd, so prettily told by a Roman Classic,
and so exquisitely enlarged and adorned by one of the most elegant
of German poets, has been seized upon by Mr John Keats, to be
done with as might seem good unto the sickly fancy of one who
never read a single line either of Ovid or of Wieland.[11] If the quan-
tity, not the quality, of the verses dedicated to the story is to be
taken into account, there can be no doubt that Mr John Keats may
now claim Endymion entirely to himself. To say the truth, we do
not suppose either the Latin or the German poet would be very
anxious to dispute about the property of the hero of the "Poetic
Romance." Mr Keats has thoroughly appropriated the character, if
not the name. His Endymion is not a Greek shepherd, loved by a
Grecian goddess; he is merely a young Cockney rhymester dreaming a fantastic dream at the full of the moon. Costume, were it
worthwhile to notice such a trifle, is violated in every page of this
goodly octavo.[12] From his prototype Hunt, John Keats has acquired
a sort of vague idea, that the Greeks were a most tasteful people,
and that no mythology can be so finely adapted for the purposes of
poetry as theirs. It is amusing to see what a hand the two Cockneys
make of this mythology: the one confesses that he never read the
Greek Tragedians, and the other knows Homer only from Chapman;[13] and both of them write about Apollo, Pan, Nymphs, Muses,
and Mysteries, as might be expected from persons of their education. We shall not, however, enlarge at present upon this subject, as
we mean to dedicate an entire paper to the classical attainments
and attempts of the Cockney poets. As for Mr Keats' "Endymion,"

---

[10]From the hymn to Neptune at the end of *Endymion* (3.974–75); "goddess" (not
the sarcastic "Lady") Cytherea is Venus's name on one of the Aegean islands.

[11]In William Sotheby's translation (1798), K read the extremely popular epic poem
Oberon (1780) by the celebrated German poet C. M. Wieland (1733–1813).

[12]The inexpensive print form of *Endymion*.

[13]A snide reference to the sonnet featured in Hunt's "Young Poets" and republished
in Keats's *Poems* (1817).

it has just as much to do with Greece as it has with "old Tartary the
fierce";[14] no man, whose mind has ever been imbued with the
smallest knowledge or feeling of classical poetry or classical history, could have stooped to profane and vulgarise every association
in the manner which has been adopted by this "son of promise."
Before giving any extracts, we must inform our readers, that this
romance is meant to be written in English heroic rhyme.[15] To those
who have read any of Hunt's poems, this hint might indeed be
needless. Mr Keats has adopted the loose, nerveless versification,
and Cockney rhyme of the poet of Rimini; but in fairness to that
gentleman, we must add, that the defects of the system are tenfold
more conspicuous in his disciple's work than in his own. Mr Hunt
is a small poet, but he is a clever man. Mr Keats is a still smaller
poet, and he is a boy of pretty abilities, which he has done every
thing in his power to spoil.

The poem sets out with the following exposition of the reasons
which induced Mr Keats to compose it.

[Z quotes 1–35, italicizing *Therefore* (34) and adding !!! to 35]

After introducing his hero to us in a procession, and preparing us,
by a few mystical lines, for believing that his destiny has in it some
strange peculiarity, Mr Keats represents the beloved of the moon as
being conveyed by his sister Peona into an island in a river. This
young lady has been alarmed by the appearance of the brother, and
questioned him thus

[Z quotes 1.505–15]

Endymion replies in a long speech, wherein he describes his first
meeting with the Moon. We cannot make room for the whole of it,
but shall take a few pages here and there.

[Z quotes 544–67; 598–616; 633–45]

Not content with the authentic love of the Moon, Keats makes his
hero captivate another supernatural lady, of whom no notice oc-
curs in any of his predecessors.

[Z quotes 2.98–130]

But we find we really have no patience for going over four books
filled with such amorous scenes as these, with subterraneous journeys equally amusing, and submarine processions equally beautiful;
but we must not omit the most interesting scene of the whole piece

[14]*Endymion* 4.262 (in the Indian Maid's "sorrow" song).
[15]rhymed iambic couplets

[Z quotes 2.706–41]
After all this, however, the "modesty," as Mr Keats expresses it, of the Lady Diana prevented her from owning in Olympus her passion for Endymion. Venus, as the most knowing in such matters, is the first to discover the change that has taken place in the temperament of the goddess. [. . .] The inamorata, to vary the intrigue, carries on a romantic intercourse[16] with Endymion, under the disguise of an Indian damsel. At last, however, her scruples, for some reason or other, are all overcome, and the Queen of Heaven owns her attachment.

[Z quotes the last four lines of *Endymion*]
And so, like many other romances, terminates the "poetic Romance" of Johnny Keats, in a patched-up wedding.

We had almost forgot to mention, that Keats belongs to the Cockney School of Politics, as well as the Cockney School of Poetry.

It is fit that he who holds Rimini to be the first poem, should believe the Examiner to be the first politician of the day. We admire consistency, even in folly. Hear how their bantling[17] has already learned to lisp sedition.

[Z quotes *Endymion* 3.1–23]
And now, good-morrow to "the Muses' son of Promise;" as for "the feats he yet may do," as we do not pretend to say, like himself, "Muse of my native land am I inspired," we shall adhere to the safe old rule of *pauca verba*.[18] We venture to make one small prophecy, that his bookseller will not a second time venture £50 upon any thing he can write.[19] It is a better and a wiser thing to be a starved apothecary than a starved poet; so back to the shop Mr John, back to "plasters, pills, and ointment boxes," &c. But, for Heaven's sake, young Sangrado, be a little more sparing of extenuatives and soporifics in your practice than you have been in your poetry.[20]

Z.

---

[16]The primary meaning is romantic relationship, but the sexual sense is also involved; hence the joke about the "patched-up wedding" that ensues.

[17]baby (in its German origin, bastard); *sedition*: illegal incitement of revolt

[18]few words; the quotation is a parody of the opening of Book IV.

[19]The advance against expected earnings (probably Bailey's information).

[20]Sangrado is a medical quack in Le Sage's novel *Gil Blas* (1715–35); *extenuatives* are diet potions; *soporifics* are sleep potions.

Letter to Charles Wentworth Dilke, 20–21 September 1818[1]

Reports of Tom's illness amidst Keats's ambitions for Hyperion *and recent erotic raptures.*

My dear Dilke,

According to the Wentworth place Bulletin you have left Brighton much improved: therefore now a few lines will be more of a pleasure than a bore – [. . .] I suppose you will have heard Hazlitt has on foot a prosecution against Blackwood[2] – I dined with him a few days since at Hessey's – there was not a word said about, though I understand he is excessively vexed – [. . .] my throat has become worse after getting well [. . .] I was going to Town tomorrow with M^rs D, but I though it best to ask her excuse this morning – I wish I could say Tom was any better. His identity presses upon me so all day that I am obliged to go out– and although I intended to have given some time to study alone I am obliged to write, and plunge into abstract images to ease myself of his countenance his voice and feebleness — so that I live now in a continual fever. it must be poisonous to life although I feel well. Imagine 'the hateful siege of contraries"[3] – if I think of fame of poetry it seems a crime to me, and yet I must do so or suffer – –I am sorry to give you pain – I am almost resolv'd to burn this — but I really have not self possession and magninimity enough to manage the thing otherwise — after all it may be a nervousness proceeding from the Mercury—

[. . .] I have just had a Letter from Reynolds - he is going on gloriously. The following is a translation of a Line of Ronsard:

'Love poured her Beauty into my warm veins' —[4]

You have passed your Romance and I never gave into it or else I think this line a feast for one of your Lovers— How goes it with Brown?

Your sincere friend

John Keats –

[1] ALS, transcribed from plates xix–xxi in G. Williamson, ed., *The Keats Letters, Papers, & c* (1914); first published in 1875.

[2] *Blackwood's* had viciously insulted Hazlitt in the same issue (Aug. 1818) that had just skewered Keats. *Blackwood's* settled the suit for libel and it was dropped in Feb. 1819 (Rollins 1.368).

[3] K underlined and margin-marked this phrase in *PL* (9.121–22); admiring the beauty of Eden, Satan laments: "But I in none of these / Find place or refuge; and the more I see / Pleasures about me, so much more I feel / Torment within me, as from the hateful siege / Of contraries."

[4] See the next letter to Reynolds.

Letter to J. H. Reynolds 22(?) September 1818[1]

My dear Reynolds,

    Believe me I have rather rejoiced in your happiness than fretted at your silence. Indeed I am grieved on your account that I am not at the same time happy – But I conjure you to think at present of nothing but pleasure "Gather the rose, &'c"[2] *Gorge the honey of life. I pity you as much that it cannot last for ever, as I do myself now drinking bitters.—Give yourself up to it – you cannot help it – and I have a consolation in thinking so – I never was in love — yet the voice and the shape of a Woman has haunted me these two days – at such a time when the relief, the feverous relief of Poetry seems a much less crime – This morning Poetry has conquered – I have relapsed into those abstractions which are my only life – I feel escaped from a new strange and threatening sorrow.— and I am thankful for it — There is an awful warmth about my heart like a load of Immortality.*

    Poor Tom[3] *— that woman — and Poetry were ringing changes in my senses – now I am in comparison happy — I am sensible this will distress you — you must forgive me. Had I known you would have set out so soon I could have sent you the 'Pot of Basil' for I had copied it out ready. - Here is a free translation of a Sonnet of Ronsard, which I think will please you – I have the loan of his works – they have great Beauties.*

    Nature withheld Cassandra in the skies &'c &'c
[. . .] Tom is not up yet – I can not say he is better. I have not heard from George.

                  *Y*ʳ *affect*ᵗᵉ *friend*   *John Keats*

---

[1] WLB 18–19.

[2] A *carpe diem* ("seize the day") sentiment, voiced in books K owned: "Gather therefore the rose of love, whilest yet is prime" (Spenser, *FQ* II.xii.75); "Gather ye rosebuds while ye may, / Old time is still a-flying; / And this same flower that smiles today, / Tomorrow will be dying" (Herrick, *To the Virgins, to Make Much of Time*).

[3] K underlined "Poor Tom" in *King Lear* and wrote next to it "Sunday evening, Oct. 4, 1818."

§ Pierre de Ronsard, *Les Amours de Cassandre, Sonet II*[1]

> Nature ornant Cassandre, qui devoit
> De sa douceur forcer les plus rebelles,
> Lui fit présent des beautez nouvelles,
> Que dés mille ans en epargne elle avoit.—
> De tous les biens qu' Amour au Ciel couvoit
> Comme vu tresor cherement sous ses ailes,
> Elle enrichit les Graces immortelles
> De son bel œil, qui les Dieux esmouvoit.—
> Du ciel à peine elle estait descenduë
> Quand je la vey, quand mon ame esperduë
> En devint folle, et d'un si poignant trait
> Amour couler ses beautez en mes veines,
> Q' autres plaisirs je ne sense que mes peines,
> Ny autre bien qu' adorer son portrait.

Keats's "free translation" of Ronsard's sonnet

> Nature withheld Cassandra in the skies
> For more adornment, a full thousand years;
> She took their cream of Beauty's fairest dyes,
> And shap'd and tinted her above all Peers:
> Meanwhile Love kept her dearly with his wings,
> And underneath their shadow fill'd her eyes
> With such a richness that the cloudy Kings
> Of high Olympus utter'd slavish sighs.
> When from the Heavens I saw her first descend,
> My heart took fire, and only burning pains,
> They were my pleasures—they my Life's sad end;
> Love pour'd her beauty into my warm veins.

---

[1]1552; K had the loan of *Amours* in a 1584 text from Woodhouse. I use the text in *1848* (1.241, converting the *u* that signifies *v* to *v*, and silently correcting obvious typos); *1848* is also my text for K's translation, minus the couplet Milnes attached to make a 14-line sonnet.

§ Article on *Endymion, Quarterly Review* XIX
(published around 27 September)[1]

REVIEWERS have been sometimes accused of not reading the works which they affected to criticise. On the present occasion we shall anticipate the author's complaint, and honestly confess that we have not read his work. Not that we have been wanting in our duty—far from it—indeed, we have made efforts almost as super-human as the story itself appears to be, to get through it; but with the fullest stretch of our perseverance, we are forced to confess that we have not been able to struggle beyond the first of the four books of which this Poetic Romance consists. We should extremely lament this want of energy, or whatever it may be, on our parts, were it not for one consolation—namely, that we are no better acquainted with the meaning of the book through which we have so painfully toiled, than we are with that of the three which we have not looked into.

It is not that Mr. Keats, (if that be his real name, for we almost doubt that any man in his sense would put his real name to such a rhapsody,) it is not, we say, that the author has not powers of lan-guage, rays of fancy, and gleams of genius—he has all these; but he is unhappily a disciple of the new school of what has been some-where[2] called Cockney poetry; which may be defined to consist of the most incongruous ideas in the most uncouth language.

Of this school, Mr. Leigh Hunt, as we observed in a former Number,[3] aspires to be the hierophant. Our readers will recollect the pleasant recipes for harmonious and sublime poetry which he gave us in his preface to 'Rimini,' and the still more facetious in-stances of his harmony and the sublimity in the verses themselves; and they will recollect above all the contempt of Pope, Johnson, and such like poetasters and pseudo-critics, which so forcibly con-trasted itself with Mr. Leigh Hunt's self-complacent approbation of

---

[1]Dated April 1818; 204–8; unsigned. The reviewer is notoriously nasty John Wilson Croker, whom Shelley cited in *Adonais* for hastening the death of sensitive K. Pub-lished by John Murray and edited by William Gifford (another acid satirist), and with the patronage of the Monarchy and the Church, the Tory *Quarterly* had such wide circulation that it could make or break a career.

[2]Croker is being disingenuous; Murray was a close associate of William Blackwood, and Z's "Cockney School" papers were a well-known series of abuses.

[3]With Gifford, Croker had skewered Hunt's *Rimini* in the January 1816 *Quarterly*.

————'all the things itself had wrote,
Of special merit though of little note.'[4]
This author is a copyist of Mr. Hunt; but he is more unintelligible, almost as rugged, twice as diffuse, and ten times more tiresome
and absurd than his prototype, who, though he impudently pre-
sumed to seat himself in the chair of criticism, and to measure his
own poetry by his own standard, yet generally had a meaning. But
Mr. Keats had advanced no dogmas which he was bound to support by examples: his nonsense therefore is quite gratuitous; he
writes it for its own sake, and, being bitten by Mr. Leigh Hunt's in-
sane criticism, more than rivals the insanity of his poetry.

Mr. Keats's preface hints that his poem was produced under peculiar circumstances

[quotes the first two sentences, italicizing *quite clear*]

We humbly beg his pardon, but this does not appear to us to be
quite so clear—we really do not know what he means—but the
next passage is more intelligible

[quotes K saying none of it should have gone to press . . .]

we have a clear and, we believe, a very just estimate of the entire work.

Mr. Keats, however, deprecates criticism on this 'immature and
feverish work' in terms which are themselves sufficiently feverish; and
we confess that we should have abstained from inflicting upon him
any of the tortures of the *'fierce hell'* of criticism, which terrify his
imagination, if he had not begged to be spared in order that he might
write more; if we had not observed in him a certain degree of talent
which deserves to be put in the right way, or which, at least, ought to
be warned of the wrong; and if, finally, he had not told us that he is of
an age and temper which perilously require mental discipline.

Of the story we have been able to make out but little it seems to
be mythological, and probably relates to the loves of Diana and
Endymion; but of this, as the scope of the work has altogether escaped us, we cannot speak with any degree of certainty; and must
therefore content ourselves with giving some instances of its diction
and versification:—and here again we are perplexed and puzzled.—
At first it appeared to us, that Mr. Keats had been amusing himself

[4]"Much did it talk, in its own pretty phrase, / Of genius and of taste, of players and
plays; / Much too of writings which itself had wrote, / Of special merit though of little note; / For fate in a strange humour had decreed / That what it wrote, none but
itself should read," writes Charles Churchill of a sexually ambiguous playwright in
The Rosciad (1761).

and wearying his readers with an immeasurable game at *bouts-rimés*;[5] but, if we recollect rightly, it is an indispensable condition at this play, that the rhymes when filled up shall have a meaning; and our author, as we have already hinted, has no meaning. He seems to use to write a line at random, and then he follows not the thought excited by this line, but that suggested by the rhyme with which it concludes. There is hardly a complete couplet inclosing a complete idea in the whole book. He wanders from one subject to another, from the association, not of ideas but of sounds, and the work is composed of hemistichs[6] which, it is quite evident, have forced themselves upon the author by the mere force of the catchwords on which they turn.

We shall select, not as the most striking instance, but as that least liable to suspicion, a passage from the opening of the poem.
[quotes 13 ("Such the sun . . .")–21]
Here it is clear that the word, and not the idea, *moon* produces the simple sheep and their shady *boon*, and that 'the *dooms* of the mighty dead' would never have intruded themselves but for the '*fair musk-rose blooms.*'

Again. [quotes 95–106]
Here Apollo's *fire* produces a *pyre*, a silvery pyre of clouds, *where* a spirit might *win* oblivion and melt his essence *fine*, and scented *eglantine* gives sweets to the *sun*, and cold springs had *run* into the *grass*, and then the pulse of the *mass* pulsed *tenfold* to feel the glories *old* of the new-born day, &c.

One example more. [quotes the hymn to Pan, 293–98]
Lodge, dodge—heaven, leaven—earth, birth; such in six words, is the sum and substance of six lines. [. . .]

By this time our readers must be pretty well satisfied as to the meaning of his sentences and the structure of his lines: we now present them with some of the new words with which, in imitation of Mr. Leigh Hunt, he adorns our language.[7]

We are told that 'turtles *passion* their voices,' that 'an arbour was *nested*,' and a lady's locks '*gordian'd* up,' and to supply the place of the nouns thus verbalized Mr. Keats, with great fecundity, spawns new ones; such as 'men-slugs and human *serpentry*,' the '*honey-feel* of bliss,' wives prepare *needments*,'—and so forth.

[5]The game is to compose a rhymed poem from randomly assigned words.

[6]decorative embroidery wrought from threads already in the fabric

[7]I omit Croker's page-number references. The Keatsian coinages that he mocks are a genre of poetic invention practiced by Shakespeare, Milton, Wordsworth, and others.

Then he has formed new verbs by the process of cutting off their natural tails, the adverbs, and affixing them to their foreheads; thus 'the wine out-sparkled,' 'the multitude up-followed,' and 'night up-took.' 'The wind up-blows,' and the 'hours are down-sunken.'

But if he sinks some adverbs in the verbs he compensates the language with adverbs and adjectives which he separates from the parent stock. Thus, a lady 'whispers *pantingly* and close,' makes '*hushing* signs,' and steers her skiff into a '*ripply* cove'; a shower falls '*refreshfully*'; and a vulture has a '*spreaded* tail.'

But enough of Mr. Leigh Hunt and his simple neophyte.— If any one should be bold enough to purchase this 'Poetic Romance,' and so much more patient, than ourselves, as to get beyond the first book, and so much more fortunate as to find a meaning, we entreat him to make us acquainted with his success; we shall then return to the task which we now abandon in despair, and endeavour to make all due amends to Mr. Keats and to our readers.

Letter to James Hessey, 8 October 1818[1]

Writing from Hampstead to his publisher Hessey's offices in London, Keats thanks him for sending some positive notices (among them Reynolds's, which Hunt reprinted in The Examiner), *and promises to write poetry with more control and judgment.*

My dear Hessey,

          You are very good in sending me the letter from the Chronicle - and I am very bad in not acknowledging such a kindness sooner [. . .] I cannot but feel indebted to those Gentlemen who have taken my part[2] - As for the rest, I begin to get a little acquainted with my own strength and weakness. - Praise or blame has but a momentary effect on the man whose love of beauty in the abstract makes him a severe critic on his own Works. My own domestic criticism has given me pain without comparison beyond what Blackwood or the

[1]WLB 13–14.
[2]Initial-signed letters to the Editor of the *Morning Chronicle* (K read it regularly) appeared 3 and 8 Oct., protesting the partisan rancor of the *Quarterly*'s notice of *Endymion*, and praising many "beauties of the highest order" amid passages of seeming "haste and carelessness."

Quarterly could possibly inflict. and also when I feel I am right, no external praise can give me such a glow as my own solitary reperception & ratification of what is fine. J.S. is perfectly right in regard to the slip-shod Endymion. That it is so is no fault of mine. — No! — though it may sound a little paradoxical. It is as good as I had power to make it - by myself - Had I been nervous about its being a perfect piece, &with that view asked advice, &trembled over evey page, it would not have been written; for it is not in my nature to fumble— I will write independantly.— I have written independently without Judgment - I may write independently, &with judgement hereafter. — The Genius of Poetry must work out its own salvation in a man: It cannot be matured by law & precept, but by sensation & watchfulness in itself — That which is creative must create itself — In Endymion, I leaped headlong into the Sea, and thereby have become better acquainted with the Soundings, the quicksands, &the rocks, than if I had stayed upon the green shore, and piped a silly pipe, and took tea &comfortable advice.— I was never afraid of failure; for I would sooner fail than not be among the greatest — But I am nigh getting into arant.[3] So, with remembrances to Taylor & Woodhouse &c I am

Yrs very sincerely
John Keats.

Letter to George and Georgiana Keats, 14–31 October 1818[1]

Tom's decline, bad reviews, two enchanting women, a determination never to marry, a love of solitude: all occupy Keats's report to George and Georgiana across the last half of October.

[14 October] My dear George; There was a part in your Letter which gave me a great deal of pain, that where you lament not receiving Letters from England - I intended to have written immediately on my return from Scotland (which was two Months earlier than I had intended on account of my own as well as Tom's health) but then I was told [. . .] you had said you would not wish any one to write till

---

[3]K probably means "a rant" but he writes the letters close enough together as to suggest a pun on *arrant* (an older form of *errant*): outstandingly bad.

---

[1]ALS, Houghton Library, Harvard.

we had heard from you. [. . .] you could have had no good news of Tom and I have been withheld on his account from beginning these many days; I could not bring myself to say the truth, that he is no better, but much worse – However it must be told and you must my dear Brother and Sister take example frome me and bear up against any Calamity for my sake as I do for your's. Our's are ties which independent of their own Sentiment are sent us by providence to prevent the deleterious effects of one great, solitary grief. I have Fanny and I have you – three people whose Happiness to me is sacred – and it does annul that selfish sorrow which I should otherwise fall into, living as I do with poor Tom who looks upon me as his only comfort – the tears will come into your Eyes – let them – and embrace each other – thank heaven for what happiness you have and after thinking a moment or two that you suffer in common with all Mankind hold it not a Sin to regain your cheerfulness—

I will relieve you of one uneasiness of overleaf:[2] I returned I said on account of my health – I am now well from a bad sore throat which came of bog trotting in the Island of Mull [. . .] Your content in each other is a delight to me which I cannot express – the Moon is now shining full and brilliant – she is the same to me in Matter, what you are to me in Spirit – If you were here my dear Sister I could not pronounce the words which I can write to you from a distance: I have a tenderness for you, and an admiration which I feel to be as great and more chaste than I can have for any woman in the world. You will mention Fanny — her character is not formed; her identity does not press upon me as yours does. I hope from the bottom of my heart that I may one day feel as much for her as I do for you – I know not how it is, but I have never made any acquaintance of my own – nearly all through your medium my dear Brother – through you I know not only a Sister but a glorious human being – And now I am talking of those to whom you have made me known I cannot forbear mentioning Haslam as a most kind and obliging and constant friend – His behaviour to Tom during my absence and since my return has endeared him to me for ever – besides his anxiety about you. [. . .] Reynolds has returned from a six weeks enjoyment in Devonshire, he is well and persuades me to publish my pot of Basil as an answer to the attacks made on me in Blackwood's Magazine and the Quarterly

[2]K has turned over the leaf of paper to continue the letter.

Review. There have been two Letters in my defence in the Chronicle and one in the Examiner, coppied from the Alfred Exeter paper and written by Reynolds[3] – –I do not know who wrote those in the ~~Quarterly~~ Chronicle – this is a mere matter of the moment – I think I shall be among the English Poets after my death. ~~The~~ Even as a Matter of present interest the attempt to crush me in the ~~Chro~~ Quarterly has only brought me more into notice and it is a common expression among book men "I wonder the Quarterly should cut its own throat.' It does me not the least harm in Society to make me appear little and rediculous:[4] I know when a Man is superior to me and give him all due respect – he will be the last to laugh at me and as for the rest I feel that I make an impression upon them which insures me personal respect ~~whic~~ while I am in sight whatever they may say when my back is turned—[. . .]

The Miss Reynoldses are very kind to me – but they have lately displeased me much and in this way [. . .] On my return, the first day I called they were in a sort of taking or bustle about a Cousin of theirs who having fallen out with her Grandpapa in a serious manner, was invited by M^rs R — to take Asylum in her house – She is an east indian and ought to be her Grandfather's Heir. At the time I called Mrs R. was in conference with her up stairs and the young Ladies were warm in her praises down stairs, calling her genteel, interesting and a thousand other pretty things to which I gave no heed, not being partial to 9 days wonders – Now all is completely changed— they hate her; and from what I hear she is not without faults — of a real kind: but she has othrs which are more apt to make women of inferior charms hate her. She is not a Cleopatra, but she is at least a Charmian.[5] She has a rich eastern look; she has fine eyes and fine manners. When she comes into a room she makes an impression the same as the Beauty of a Leopardess. She is too fine and too concious of her Self to repulse any Man who may address her – from habit she thinks that nothing <u>particular</u>.[6] I always find myself more at ease

---

[3]See the letter to Hessey, 8 Oct. (p. 206) about *The Chronicle*; Reynolds's defense appeared in the *Alfred, West of England Journal* on 6 Oct., reprinted by Hunt in *The Examiner* on 12 Oct.

[4]In K's habit of spelling the word this way critic Christopher Ricks sees punning on the blush of ridicule (*Keats and Embarrassment*).

[5]One of Cleopatra's female attendants. The cousin is Jane Cox.

[6]i.e., he is not hitting on her.

with such a woman; the picture before me always gives me a life and animation which I cannot possibly feel with any thing inferiour— I am at such times too much occupied in admiring to be awkward or on a tremble. I forget myself entirely because I live in her. You will by this time think I am in love with her; so before I go any further I will tell you I am not — she kept me awake one Night as a tune of Mozart's might do – I speak of the thing as a passtime and an amuzement than which I can feel none deeper than a conversation with an imperial woman the very 'yes' and 'no' of whose Lips is to me a Banquet. I dont cry to take the moon home with me in my Pocket not do I fret to leave her behind me. I like her and her like because one has no <u>sensations</u> – what we both are is taken for granted — You will suppose I have by this had much talk with her - no such thing— there are the Miss Reynoldses on the look out— They think I dont admire her because I did not stare at her-
They call her a flirt to me — What a want of Knowledge? She walks across a room in such a manner that a Man is drawn towards her with a magnetic Power. This they call flirting! they do not know things. They do not know what a Woman is. I believe tho' she has faults - the same as Charmian and Cleopatra might have had. Yet she is a fine thing speaking in a worldly way: for there are two distinct tempers of mind in which we judge of things — the worldly, theatrical and pantomimical; and the unearthly, spiritual and ethereal — in the former Buonaparte, Lord Byron and this Charmian hold the first place in our Minds; in the latter John Howard, Bishop Hooker rocking his child's cradle[7] and you my dear Sister are the conquering feelings. As a Man in the world I love the rich talk of a Charmian; as an eternal Being I love the thought of you. I should like her to ruin me, and I should like you to save me. Do not think my dear Brother from this that my Passions are headlong or likely to be ever of any pain to you—no
   "I am free from Men of Pleasure's cares
   By dint of feelings far more deep than theirs"[8]
This is Lord Byron, and is one of the finest things he has said— [. . .]

---

[7]John Howard, philanthropist and devoted prison reformer. Izaak Walton's biography of 16th-c. theologian Richard Hooker (not a bishop) may have been K's source.

[8]K has slightly misremembered the lines and their author (as K recalls them, they do seem Byronic). The source is Hunt's *Story of Rimini* (1816) describing young Paolo, who in his reverence for virtue, "had been kept from men of pleasure's cares / By dint of feelings still more warm that theirs" (p. 50; canto 3.121–22).

[24 Oct.] *Since I wrote thus far I have met with that same Lady again, whom I saw at Hastings and whom I met when we were going to the English Opera.*[9] *It was in a street which goes from Bedford Row to Lamb's Conduit Street – I passed her and turrned back – she seemed glad of it; glad to see me and not offended at my passing her before We walked on towards Islington where we called on a friend of her's who keeps a Boarding School. She has always been an enigma to me – she has ~~new~~ been in a Room with you and with Reynolds and wishes we should be acquainted without any of our common acquaintance knowing it. As we went along, some times through shabby, sometimes through decent Street I had my guessing at work, not knowing what it would be and prepared to meet any surprise – First it ended at this House at Islington: on parting from which I pressed to attend her home. She consented, and then again my thoughts were at work what it might lead to, tho' now they had received a sort of genteel hint from the Boarding School. Our Walk ended in 34 Gloucester Street, Queen Square – not exactly so for we went up stairs into her sitting room – a very tasty sort of place with Books, Pictures a bronze statue of Buonaparte, Music, æolian Harp; a Parrot a Linnet – a Case of choice Liquers &c &c &. she behaved in the kindest manner – made me take home a Grouse for Tom's dinner – Asked for my address for the purpose of sending more game – As I had warmed with her before and kissed her – I though it would be living backwards not to do so again – she had a better taste: she perceived how much a thing of course it was and shrunk from it – not in a prudish way but in as I say a good taste. She contrived to disappoint me in a way which made me feel more pleasure than a simple Kiss could do – She said I should please her much more if I would only press her hand and go away. Whether she was in a different disposition when I saw her before – or whether I have in fancy wrong'd her I cannot tell.   I expect to pass some pleasant hours with her now and then: in which I feel I shall be of service to her in matters of knowledge and taste: if I can I will. I have no libidinous thought about her — she and your George are the only women à peu près de mon age*[10] *whom I would be content to know for their mind and friendship alone. I shall in a short time write you as far as I know how I intend to pass my Life — I cannot think of those things now*

[9]Mrs. Isabella Jones, a friend of Taylor.

[10]French: close to my own age

Tom is so unwell and weak. Notwithstand your Happiness and your recommendation I hope I shall never marry. Though the most beautiful Creature were waiting for me at the end of a Journey or a Walk; though the carpet were of Silk, the Curtains of the morning Clouds; the chairs and Sofa stuffed with Cygnet's down; the food Manna, the Wine beyond Claret, the Window opening on Winander mere,[11] I should not feel – or rather my Happiness would not be so fine, ands my Solitude is sublime. Then instead of what I have described, there is a Sublimity to welcome me home. The roaring of the wind is my wife and the Stars through the window pane are my Children. The mighty abstract Idea I have of Beauty in all things stifles the more divided and minute domestic happiness – an amiable wife and sweet Children I contemplate as a part of that Beauty. but I must have a thousand of those beautiful particles to fill up my heart. I feel more and more every day, as my imagination strengthens, that I do not live in this world alone but in a thousand worlds. No sooner am I alone than shapes of epic greatness are stationed around me, and serve my Spirit the office of which is equivalent to a King's body guard – then 'Tragedy with scepter'd pall, comes sweeping by."[12] According to my state of mind I am with Achilles shouting in the Trenches,[13] or with Theocritus in the Vales of Sicily. Or I throughw my whole being into Triolus, and repeating those lines, 'I wander, like a lost Soul upon the stygian Banks staying for waftage",[14] I melt into the air with a voluptuousness so delicate that I am content to be alone. These things combined with the opinion I have of the generallity of women – who appear to me as children to whom I would rather give a Sugar Plum than my time, form a barrier against Matrimony which I rejoice in. I have written this that you might see I have my share of the highest pleasures and that though I may choose to pass my days alone I shall be no Solitary.[15] You see there is nothing spleenical in all this. The only thing that can ever effect me personally for more than one short passing day, is any doubt about my powers for poetry – I seldom have any, and I look withhope to the nighing time when I shall have none. I am

[11]One of the lakes of Wordsworth-country, a popular tourist destination.

[12]Paraphrasing Milton, *Il Penseroso* 97–98.

[13]See Pope's *Iliad* 18.241–70—an amazing rally.

[14]Troilus, dying of anticipation of a first tryst with Cressida (*Troilus and Cressida* 3.2.7–9).

[15]The despondent, world-battered recluse of Wordsworth's *Excursion*.

as happy as a Man can be – that is in myself I should be happy if Tom was well, and I knew you were passing pleasant days. Then I should be most enviable – with the yearning Passion I have for the beautiful, connected and made one with the ambition of my intellect. Thnk of my Pleasure in Solitude, in comparison of my commerce with the world – there I am a child -there they do not know me not even my most intimate acquaintance – I give into their feelings as though I were refraining from irritating a little child – Some think me middling, others silly, others foolish – every one thinks he sees my weak side against my will; when in truth it is with my will. — I am content to be thought all this because I have in my own breast so great a resource. This is one great reason why they like me so; because they can all show to advantage in a room, and eclipse from a certain tact one who is reckoned to be a good Poet – I hope I am not here playing tricks 'to make the angels weep':[16] I think not: for I have not the least contempt for my species; and though it may sound paradoxical: my greatest elevations of soul leave me every time more humbled – Enough of this – [. . . 31 October] Think of me and for my sake be cheerful. Believe me my dear Brother and sister
Your anxious and affectionate Brother
John—

This day is my Birth day —

Letter to Richard Woodhouse, 27 October 1818[1]

Keats defines his poetic character as "camelion," not egotistical, and values speculation over philosophy.

My dear Woodhouse,

　　　　　　　　Your Letter gave me a great satisfaction; more on account of its friendliness, than any relish of that matter in it which is accounted so acceptable in the 'genus irritabile'[2] The best answer

---

[16]More than God, it is man, laments Isabella to tyrannical regent Angelo, who "plays such fantastic tricks before high heaven / As makes the angels weep" (*Measure for Measure* 2.2.117–22).

---

[1]ALS, Houghton Library, Harvard.

[2]Roman poet Horace called poets "the irritable tribe" (*Epistles* 2.2.102). K is replying to a long, affectionately supportive letter, 21 Oct., expressing dismay at the *Quarterly* and K's saying that there seemed to be nothing new to be done in poetry, so he would give it up.

I can give you is in a clerklike manner to make some observations on
two principle points, which seem to point like indices into the midst of
the whole pro and con, about genius, and views and atchievements and
ambition and cætera.³ 1ˢᵗ As to the poetical Character itself, (I mean
that sort of which, if I am any thing, I am a Member; that sort
distinguished from the wordsworthian or egotistical sublime; which is
a thing per se and stands alone⁴) it is not itself – it has no self – it is
every thing and nothing –It has no character – it enjoys light and
shade; it lives in gusto, be it foul or fair, high or low, rich or poor,
mean or elevated – It has as much delight in conceiving an Iago
as an Imogen.⁵ What shocks the virtuous philosopher, delights the
camelion⁶ Poet. It does no harm from its relish of the dark side of
things any more than from its taste for the bright one; because they
both end in speculation. A Poet is the most unpoetical of any thing
in existence; because he has no Identity – he is continually infor–⁷
and filling some other Body – The Sun, the Moon, the Sea and Men
and Women who are creatures of impulse are poetical and have about
them an unchangeable attribute – the poet has none; no identity – he
is certainly the most unpoetical of all God's Creatures. If then he has
no self, and if I am a Poet, where is the Wonder that I should say I
would ~~right~~ write no more? Might I not at that very instant have
been cogitating on the Characters of Saturn and Ops?⁸ It is a wretched
thing to confess; but is a very fact that not one word I ever utter can
be taken for granted as an opinion growing out of my identical nature –
how can it, when I have no nature? When I am in a room with People

³Latin: the rest.

⁴"I am sorry that Wordsworth has left a bad impression where-ever he visited in town by his egotism, Vanity, and bigotry," K wrote his brothers on 21 Feb. 1818; "Yet he is a great poet if not a philosopher." By "poetic Character," K means both a persona and the signature of a poet (his identity, views, philosophy, etc.) in his work. Shakespeare was celebrated by Coleridge and Hazlitt as the antitype, for being, said Hazlitt in his lecture of early 1818, "the least of an egoist that it was possible to be. He was nothing in himself; but . . . all that others were."

⁵Iago is the villain of *Othello*; Imogen is the virtuous heroine of *Cymbeline*. Hazlitt's *On Gusto* (*Examiner*, May 1816) begins: "Gusto in art is power or passion defining any object." See K's review of Kean for another reference to "gusto" (p. 75).

⁶A chameleon instinctively adapts to the coloring of its situation.

⁷This is the last script on the page, as if K had begun to write a word he forgot to finish when he turned over the leaf.

⁸K jokes that he might have been inhabiting the consciousness of the defeated gods of *Hyperion*.

if I ever am free from speculating on creations of my own brain, then not myself goes home to myself: but the identity of every one in the room begins to so press upon me that I am in a very little time anhilated – not only among Men; it would be the same in a Nursery of children: I know not whether I make myself wholly understood: I hope enough so to let you see that no dependence is to be placed on what I said that day.

In the second place I will speak of my views, and of the life I purpose to myself – I am ambitious of doing the world some good: if I should be spared that may be the work of maturer years – in the interval I will assay to reach to as high a summit in Poetry as the nerve bestowed upon me will suffer. The faint conceptions I have of Poems to come brings the blood frequently into my forehead – All I hope is that I may not lose all interest in human affairs – that the solitary indifference I feel for applause even from the finest Spirits, will not blunt any acuteness of vision I may have. I do not think it will – I feel assured I should write from the mere yearning and fondness I have for the Beautiful even if my night's labours should be burnt every morning and no eye ever shine upon them. But even now I am perhaps not speaking from myself: but from some character in whose soul I now live – I am sure however that this next sentence is from myself. I feel your anxiety, good opinion and friendliness in the highest degree, and am

Your's most sincerely
John Keats

§ Oscar Wilde calls on Keats to defend the aesthetics of *Dorian Gray*, 12 July 1890

When this novel first appeared in Lippincott's Monthly Magazine, *July 1890, an anonymous reviewer in* Scot's Observer *(5 July) found its dubious morality unworthy of Wilde's talents. Wilde fired back a letter to the editor, published on 12 July, in which he summons Keats to the defense.*

from MR. WILDE'S REJOINDER

Your critic then, sir, commits the absolutely unpardonable crime of trying to confuse the artist with his subject-matter. For this, sir, there is no excuse at all. Of one who is the greatest figure in the world's literature since Greek days Keats remarked that he had as much pleasure in conceiving the evil as he had in conceiving the good. Let your reviewer, sir, consider the bearings of Keats's fine criticism, for it is under these conditions that every artist works. One stands remote from one's subject-matter. One creates it, and one contemplates it. The further away the subject-matter is, the more freely can the artist work. Your reviewer suggests that I do not make it sufficiently clear whether I prefer virtue to wickedness or wickedness to virtue. An artist, sir, has no ethical sympathies at all. Virtue and wickedness are to him simply what the colours on his palette are to the painter. They are no more, and they are no less. He sees that by their means a certain artistic effect can be produced, and he produces it. Iago may be morally horrible and Imogen stainlessly pure. Shakespeare, as Keats said, had as much delight in creating the one as he had in creating the other.

Sonnet to Ailsa Rock

This poem appeared in Leigh Hunt's Literary Pocket Book; or, Companion for the Lover of Nature and Art *(1819, pub. November 1818), p. 225, just below another sonnet by Keats,* The Human Seasons, *both signed "I." Keats wrote it on the tour with Brown. From the sea near the Ayrshire coast, Ailsa Rock rises over 1,100 feet. Keats sets the scene for Tom in the letter of 10 July 1818, in which he drafted the sonnet: "we had a gradual ascent and got among the tops of the Mountains whence In a little time I descried in the Sea Ailsa Rock 940 feet hight – it was 15 Miles distant and seemed close upon us – The effect of ailsa with the peculiar perspective of the Sea in connection with the ground we stood on, and the misty rain then falling gave me a complete Idea of a deluge. Ailsa struck me very suddenly—really I was a little alarmed —"; just after the sonnet he writes, "This is the only Sonnet of any worth I have of late written"——*

Hearken, thou craggy ocean pyramid!
    Give answer from thy voice, the sea-fowls' screams!
    When were thy shoulders mantled in huge streams?[1]
When, from the sun, was thy broad forehead hid?
How long is't since the mighty power bid
    Thee heave to airy sleep from fathom dreams?
    Sleep in the lap of thunder or sunbeams,
    Or when grey clouds are thy cold coverlid.

Thou answer'st not; for thou art dead asleep;
    Thy life is but[2] two dead eternities—   10
The last in air, the former in the deep;
    First with the whales, last with the eagle-skies—
Drown'd wast thou till an earthquake made thee steep,
    Another cannot wake thy giant size.

[1]K delighted in Spenser's "sea-shouldring Whales" (*FQ* II.xii.23; Charles and Mary Cowden Clarke, *Recollections of Writers*, London, 1878) and noted a similar figure in Milton's God creating the earth from the ocean: "Immediately the mountains huge appear / Emergent, and their broad bare backs upheave / Into the clouds; their tops ascend the sky" (*PL* 7.85–87, underlined by K).

[2]K's letter draft shows him testing "has been" and "will be" for "is but."

Posthumous Publications of Poems Written in 1818

Lines Written in the Scotch Highlands

§ from "Mountain Scenery," *New Monthly Magazine*, 4 March 1822, pp. 247–52[1]

[p. 252] The poet Keats walked in the Highlands, not with the joyousness, the rapture of the young Rousseau, but in that hallowed pleasure of the soul, which, in its fulness, is a-kin to pain. The following extract of a poem, not published in his works, proves his intensity of feeling, even to the dread of madness. It was written while on his journey, soon after his pilgrimage to the birth-place of Burns, not for the gaze of the world, but as a record for himself of the temper of his mind at the time. It is a sure index to the more serious traits in his character; but Keats, neither in writing nor in speaking, could affect a sentiment,—his gentle spirit knew not how to counterfeit. I leave it, without comment on its beauties, to the reader,—and to his melancholy, as he thinks upon so young a poet dying of a broken heart.[2]

---

[1]The article, signed S., is by Charles Brown, with whom Keats toured Scotland.

[2]By 1822 this sentence encompasses both K and Burns. Brown then arranges K's quasi-heroic iambic heptameter (7-beat) couplets (though with clearly weighted medial caesurae) 1–6, 25–26, and 41–48 into more ballad-like units of alternating tetrameter and trimeter.

from *The Examiner*, 14 July 1822, p. 445

LINES WRITTEN IN THE SCOTCH HIGHLANDS

{The following piece by KEATS,—or rather portions of it,—appeared in a late Number of the *New Monthly Magazine*. That the Editor (it having been forwarded to him entire) should have sent it forth mutilated,[3] is altogether unaccountable to us, as, exclusive of its rare poetic merits, it is valuable as an index to the mind of the lamented Author, while under the excitation of the powerful scenery of the Highlands.}

THERE is a charm in footing slow across a silent plain,
Where patriot battle has been fought, where glory had the gain;
There is a pleasure on the heath, where Druids old have been,
Where mantles grey have rustled by, and swept the nettles green;
There is a joy in every spot made known in days of old,
New to the feet, although each tale a hundred times be told;
There is a deeper joy than all, more solemn in the heart,
More parching to the tongue than all, of more divine a smart,
When weary steps forget themselves upon a pleasant turf,
Upon hot sand, or flinty road, or sea-shore iron scurf,[4]   10
Toward the castle or the cot, where long ago was born
One who was great through mortal days, and died of fame unshorn!

Light heather-bells may tremble then,—but they are far away;
Wood-lark may sing from sandy fern,——the sun may hear his lay;
Runnels may kiss the grass on shelves and shallows clear,—
But their low voices are not heard, though come on travels drear;
Blood-red the sun may set behind black mountain peaks,
Blue tides may sluice and drench their time in caves and weedy creeks,
Eagles may seem to sleep wing-wide upon the air,
Ring-doves may fly convulsed across to some high-cedar'd lair,—   20
But the forgotten eye is still fast lidded to the ground,
As Palmer's[5] that with weariness mid-desert shrine hath found.

[3]Brown's excerpting and the re-lineation.
[4]crust
[5]Pilgrim's

At such a time the soul's a child, in childhood is the brain,
Forgotten is the worldly heart——alone, it beats in vain!
Aye, if a madman could have leave to pass a healthful day,
To tell his forehead swoon and faint when first began decay,
He might make tremble many a one, whose spirit had gone forth
To find a Bard's[6] low cradle-place about the silent North!

Scanty the hour, and few the steps, beyond the bourn[7] of care,
Beyond the sweet and bitter world,——beyond it unaware!   30
Scanty the hour and few the steps,——because a longer stay
Would bar return, and make a man forget his mortal way.
O horrible! to lose the sight of well remember'd face,
Of brother's eyes, of sister's brow,——constant to every place;
Filling the air, as on we move, with portraiture intense,
More warm than those heroic tints that pain a painter's sense,
When shapes of old come striding by, and visages of old,
Locks shining black, hair scanty grey, and passions manifold!

No, no,——that horror cannot be! for at the cable's length,
Man feels the gentle anchor pull, and gladdens in its strength.   40
One hour half-ideot he stands by mossy waterfall,
But in the very next he reads his soul's memorial;
He reads it on the mountain's height, where chance he may sit down
Upon rough marble diadem,——that hill's eternal crown!
Yet be his anchor e'er so fast, room is there for a prayer
That man may never lose his mind on mountains black and bare,
That he may stray, league after league, some great birth-place to find,
And keep his vision clear from speck, his inward sight unblind!

[6]Burns [*Examiner*]; "One of the pleasantest bouts we have had was our walk to Burns's Cottage," K wrote to Bailey on 22 July about the occasion; "I wrote some lines [. . .] which I will transcribe or rather cross scribe in the front of this" (i.e., write on top of the letter at right angles). This letter appeared with these lines in *1848* (1.178–81).
[7]limit

from *Life, Letters and Literary Remains* (1848)
On Visiting the Tomb of Burns and "This mortal body"

1: 156–59, *the first publication of these sonnets, originally drafted in a journal letter to Tom Keats.*

July 2nd

ON VISITING THE TOMB OF BURNS

The town, the church-yard, and the setting sun,
The clouds, the trees, the rounded hills all seem,
Though beautiful, cold—strange—as in a dream,
I dreamed long ago, now new begun.
The short-liv'd, paly, Summer is but won
From Winter's ague, for one hour's gleam;
Though sapphire-warm, their stars do never beam:
All is cold Beauty; pain is never done:
For who has mind to relish, Minos-wise,
The Real of Beauty, free from that dead hue
Sickly imagination and sick pride
Cast wan upon it![1] Burns! with honor due
I oft have honor'd thee. Great shadow, hide
Thy face; I sin against thy native skies.

[. . .] Burns's tomb is in the church-yard corner, not very much to my taste, though on a scale large enough to show they wanted to honor him. [. . .] This sonnet I have written in a strange mood, half-asleep. I know not how it is, the clouds, the sky, the houses, all seem anti-Grecian and anti-Charlemagnish.[2] [. . .] Then we went to the cottage where Burns was born; there was a board to that effect by the door's side; it had the same effect as the same sort of memorial at Stratford on Avon.[3] We drank some toddy to Burns's memory

---

[1]Echoing Hamlet's soliloquy: "the native hue or resolution / Is sicklied o'er with the pale cast of thought" (3.1). Minos is the judge who decides the punishments in Dante's *Inferno*; in Canto V (the second circle, where abide Paolo and Francesca) he ushers the poet into this "abode of pain."

[2]inimical to the aesthetics of Greek art and medieval romance (with hero Charlemagne).

[3]Shakespeare's residence.

with an old man who knew him. There was something good in his description of Burns's melancholy the last time he saw him. I was determined to write a sonnet in the cottage; I did, but it was so bad I cannot venture it here.[4]

SONNET.

This mortal body of a thousand days
    Now fills, O Burns, a space in thine own room,
Where thou didst dream alone on budded bays,[5]
    Happy and thoughtless of thy day of doom!
My pulse is warm with thine own Barley-bree,
    My head is light with pledging[6] a great soul,
My eyes are wandering, and I cannot see,
    Fancy is dead and drunken at its goal;
Yet can I stamp my foot upon thy floor,
    Yet can I ope thy window-sash to find
The meadow thou hast tramped o'er and o'er——
    Yet can I think of thee till thought is blind,——
Yet can I gulp a bumper[7] to thy name,——
O smile among the shades, for this is fame!

"Sonnet I wrote on the top of Ben Nevis" ("Read me a lesson")[8]

Keats mounted Ben Nevis. When on the summit a cloud enveloped him, and sitting on the stones, as it slowly wafted away, showing a tremendous precipice into the valley below, he wrote these lines:—

Read me a lesson, Muse, and speak it loud
Upon the top of Nevis, blind in mist!

---

[4]K didn't send it to Tom but Brown preserved a copy, noting that the cottage was now a whiskey shop presided over by a drunken, talkative bore. Burns's misery and poverty, K told Reynolds, depressed him deeply.

[5]bay laurel, the emblem of poetic fame

[6]drinking a toast; whisky is made from barley.

[7]large toasting-glass

[8]"'T was the most vile descent," K wrote to Tom 6 Aug.; "—shook me all to pieces — Over leaf you will find a Sonnet I wrote on the top of Ben Nevis" (2 Aug.). It was first published in 1838 in a regional journal, then in *1848* (1.189), without the letter, and with the introduction by Milnes.

I look into the chasms, and a shroud
Vaporous doth hide them,—just so much I wist
Mankind do know of hell; I look o'erhead,
And there is sullen mist,—even so much
Mankind can tell of heaven; mist is spread
Before the earth, beneath me,—even such,
Even so vague is man's sight of himself!
Here are the craggy stones beneath my feet,—
Thus much I know that, a poor witless elf,
I tread on them,—that all my eye doth meet
Is mist and crag, not only on this height,
But in the world of thought and mental might!

Fragment ("Where's the Poet?") and *Modern Love*

[1.282–83] [T]he following pieces are so fragmentary as more becomingly to take their place in the narrative of the author's life, than to show as substantive productions. Yet it is, perhaps, just in verses like these that the individual character pronounces itself most distinctly, and confers a general interest which more care of art at once elevates and diminishes. The occasional verses of a great poet are records, as it were of his poetical table-talk,[9] remembrances of his daily self and its intellectual companionship, more delightful from what they recall, than for what they are—more interesting for what they suggest, than for what they were ever meant to be.

FRAGMENT

Where's the Poet? show him! show him!
Muses nine! that I may know him!
'Tis the man who with a man
Is an equal, be he King,
Or poorest of the beggar-clan,
Or any other wondrous thing

---

[9]A popular publication genre of conversation and incidental writing; Hazlitt published under this title (1821), and Coleridge's *Table Talk* was a popular posthumous publication. These two poems, written in 1818, were first published in *1848*, with titles by Milnes.

A man may be 'twixt ape and Plato;
'Tis the man who with a bird,
Wren or Eagle, finds his way to
All its instincts; he hath heard   10
The Lion's roaring, and can tell
What his horny throat expresseth;
And to him the Tiger's yell
Comes articulate and presseth
On his ear like mother-tongue.

MODERN LOVE

And what is love? It is a doll dress'd up
For idleness to cosset, nurse, and dandle;
A thing of soft misnomers, so divine
That silly youth doth think to make itself
Divine by loving, and so goes on
Yawning and doting a whole summer long,
Till Miss's comb is made a pearl tiara,
And common Wellingtons[10] turn Romeo boots;
Then Cleopatra lives at number seven,
And Antony resides in Brunswick Square.   10
Fools! if some passions high have warm'd the world,
If Queens and Soldiers have play'd deep for hearts,
It is no reason why such agonies
Should be more common than the growth of weeds.
Fools! make me whole again that weighty pearl
The Queen of Egypt melted,[11] and I'll say
That ye may love in spite of beaver hats.

---

[10]fashionable high boots, named for the military hero, the Duke of Wellington.

[11]Cleopatra was reputed to have dissolved a pearl in wine, which she drank in pledge to Antony. Not yet in love himself (though smitten with the exotic Reynolds-cousin and the lady from Hastings), K was amused in 1818 at the behavior of his love-smitten friends.

ANNOTATIONS ON *PARADISE LOST*

These annotations were first published, partially, in an American literary-philosophical periodical, The Dial *(1843), then in 1848 (vol. 1), then with improvements and additions by HBF (vol. 3), working directly from Keats's two-volume Edinburgh edition of 1808. Because of the historical importance of HBF's report, I present his transcription, with two modifications: I revert his italics to Keats's underlining, and sometimes supply in internal brackets a correction agreed upon by subsequent editors (who also reverse his tidying up of Keats's writing). Footnotes are mine unless otherwise noted; my brackets give locations in Keats's edition and PL (1808 text). The most complete, scrupulous, and durably valuable account of the marginalia, graced with several photo-plates, is Beth Lau's* Keats's Paradise Lost.

[*on the half title page*]

The Genius of Milton, more particularly in respect to its span in immensity, calculated him, by a sort of birthright, for such an 'argument' as the Paradise Lost: he had an exquisite passion for what is properly, in the sense of ease and pleasure, poetical Luxury; and with that it appears to me he would fain have been content, if he could, so doing, have preserved his self-respect and feel of duty performed; but there was working in him as it were that same sort of thing as operates in the great world to the end of a Prophecy's being accomplish'd: therefore he devoted himself rather to the ardours than the pleasures of Song, solacing himself at intervals with cups of old wine; and those are with some exceptions the finest parts of the Poem. With some exceptions—for the spirit of mounting and adventure can never be unfruitful or unrewarded: had he not broken through the clouds which envelope so deliciously the Elysian field of verse and committed himself to the Extreme, we never should have seen Satan as described—
> "But his face
> Deep scars of thunder had entrench'd," &c.[1]

[*above the Argument to Book 1*]

There is a greatness which the Paradise Lost possesses over every other Poem—<u>the Magnitude of Contrast</u>, and that is softened by the contrast being ungrotesque to a degree. Heaven moves on like music

---

[1] 1.600–601, from the sublime description of "Arch Angel ruin'd."

throughout. *Hell is also peopled with angels; it also moves on like music, not grating and harsh,*[2] *but like a grand accompaniment in the Base to Heaven.*

[*above 1.1–22*]

There is always a great charm in the openings of great Poems, more particularly where the action begins—that of Dante's Hell [—of] *Hamlet. the first step must be heroic and full of power; and nothing can be more impressive and shaded than the commencement of the action here—* '*Round he throws his baleful eyes*'

[*1.44–67*]

<u>Him the Almighty Power</u>
<u>Hurl'd headlong flaming from the ethereal sky,</u>
<u>With hideous ruin and combustion, down</u>
<u>To bottomless perdition, there to dwell</u>
<u>In adamantine chains and penal fire,</u>
<u>Who durst defy the Omnipotent to Arms.</u>
Nine times the Space that measures Day and Night   50
To mortal men, he with his horrid crew
Lay vanquish'd, rowling in the fiery Gulfe
Confounded though immortal: But his doom
Reserv'd him to more wrath; for now the thought
Both of lost happiness and lasting pain
Torments him; <u>round he throws his baleful eyes,</u>
That witness'd huge affliction and dismay
Mix'd with obdurate pride and stedfast hate:
<u>At once, as far as Angels' ken, he views</u>
<u>The dismal situation waste and wilde,</u>   60
A dungeon horrible, on all sides round
As one great furnace flam'd, yet from those flames
No light, but rather darkness visible
Serv'd only to discover <u>sights of woe,</u>
<u>Regions of sorrow, doleful shades, where peace</u>
<u>And rest can never dwell; hope never comes</u>
<u>That comes to all;</u> but torture without end

---

[2]K evokes what Wordsworth hears in *Tintern Abbey*: "the still, sad music of human-ity, / Not harsh nor grating, though of ample power / To chasten and subdue" (92–94).

[*in the margins next to 1.59–94*, "Satan, with bold words /
Breaking the horrid silence thus began / 'If thou beest he;
but O how fall'n! how chang'd / . . . / who knew / The force
of those dire Arms?'"]

*One of the most mysterious of semi-speculations is, one would suppose,
that of one Mind's imagining into another. Things may be described
by a Man's self in parts so as to make a grand whole which that Man
himself would scarcely inform to its excess. A Poet can seldom have justice
done to his imagination—for men are as distinct in their conceptions of
material shadowings as they are in matters of spiritual understanding:
it can scarcely be conceived how Milton's Blindness might here aid³ the
magnitude of his conceptions as a bat in a large gothic vault.*

[**1.318–21**: *Satan wonders at the repose of the defeated
band of fallen angels in hell*]

> have ye chosen this place
> After the toil of battle to repose
> Your wearied virtue, for the ease you find
> <u>To slumber here, as in the vales of Heaven?</u>

*There is a cool pleasure in the very sound of vale. The [e]nglish word
is of the happiest chance. Milton has put vales in heaven and hell with
the very utter affection and yearning of a great Poet. It is a sort of
Delphic Abstraction—a beautiful thing made more beautiful by being
reflected and put in a Mist. The next mention of Vale is one of the
most pathetic in the whole range of Poetry. 'Others more mild, retreated
in a silent Valley &c.⁴ How much of the charm is in the Valley!—*

[**1.535–69**: *Satan rallies his comrades, trumpets and clarions
sound, and Azazel*]

. . . forthwith from <u>the glittering staff unfurl'd</u>
<u>The imperial ensign, which full high advanced</u>

---

³K wrote *here ade*, in such a way that it might be read for *pervade*; but his manuscript
is full of slips of this kind; and the sense leaves no doubt that *here aid* is what he meant.
[. . .] Milton's blindness might so sharpen his imagination as to give him the same advantage in the realm of the unseen as a bat has in the darkness of a gothic vault. [HBF 3.21]

⁴2.546 (to *mild*)–47; K underscores this passage, with another marginal note (see p.
231). Apollo's oracular communications at Delphi often involved mist; *Delphic* thus
means "obscure."

Shone like a meteor streaming to the wind,
With gems and golden lustre rich emblazed,
Seraphic arms and trophies; all the while
Sonorous metal blowing martial sounds: 540
At which the universal host up-sent
A shout, that tore Hell's concave, and beyond
Frighted the reign of Chaos and old Night.
All in a moment through the gloom were seen
Ten thousand banners rise into the air
With orient colours waving: with them rose
A forest huge of spears, and thronging helms
Appear'd, and serried shields in thick array
Of depth immeasurable: anon they move
In perfect phalanx to the Dorian mood   550
Of flutes and soft recorders; such as raised
To height of noblest temper heroes old
Arming to battle, and instead of rage
Deliberate valour breath'd, firm and unmoved
With dread of death to flight or foul retreat;
Nor wanting power to mitigate and swage
With solemn touches, troubled thoughts, and chase
Anguish, and doubt, and fear, and sorrow, and pain,
From mortal or immortal minds. Thus they
Breathing united force with fixed thought   560
Moved on in silence to soft pipes, that charm'd
Their painful steps o'er the burnt soil; and now
Advanced in view they stand, a horrid front
Of dreadful length and dazzling arms, in guise
Of warriors old with order'd spear and shield,
Awaiting what command their mighty chief
Had to impose:[5] He through the armed files
Darts his experienced eye, and soon <u>traverse</u>
The whole battalion views . . .

The light and shade—the sort of black brightness—the ebon diamonding—the Ethiop Immortality—the sorrow, the pain. the sad-sweet Melody—the P[h]alanges of Spirits so depressed as to be

[5]HBF's transcription stops here; Lau provides the rest.

"uplifted beyond hope"—the short mitigation of Misery—the thousand Melancholies and Magnificences of this Page—leaves no room for anything to be said thereon but "so it is."

[*1.591–600: the sublimity of fallen Satan*]

> his form had not yet lost
> All her original brightness, nor appear'd
> Less than Arch-Angel ruin'd, and the excess
> Of glory obscured; as when the sun new risen
> Looks through the horizontal misty air
> Shorn of his beams; or from behind the moon
> In dim eclipse disastrous twilight sheds
> On half the nations, and with fear of change
> Perplexes monarchs. Darken'd so, yet shone
> Above them all the Arch-Angel: but his face   600
> Deep scars of thunder had intrench'd, and care
> Sat on his faded cheek, but under brows
> Of dauntless courage, and considerate pride
> Waiting revenge: cruel his eye, but cast
> Signs of remorse and passion to behold
> The fellows of his crime, the followers rather
> (Far other once beheld in bliss) condemn'd
> For ever now to have their lot in pain;
> Millions of spirits for his fault amerced
> Of Heaven, and from eternal splendours flung   610
> For his revolt, yet faithful how they stood,
> Their glory wither'd: as when Heaven's fire
> Hath scath'd the forest oaks, or mountain pines,
> With singed top their stately growth though bare
> Stands on the blasted heath.[6]

How noble and collected an indignation against Kings, "*and for fear of change perplexes Monarchs*" &c. His very wishing should have had power to pull that feeble animal Charles [II] from his

---

[6]HBF prints K's marking to 567. Lau supplies the rest, with the vertical line down the left margin next to 609–15. In the anger against kings, "blasted heath" may relay K's interest in King Lear, exiled to the blasted heath, where he confronts his pompous neglect of his poor subjects.

bloody throne. "The evil days"[7] *had come to him; he hit the new System of things a mighty mental blow; the exertion must have had or is yet to have some sequences.*

[*1.701–30: the creation of the city in Hell, Pandemonium*]

veins of liquid fire
Sluiced from the lake, a second multitude
With wondrous art founded the massy ore,
Severing each kind, and scumm'd the bullion dross;
A third as soon had form'd within the ground
A various mould, and from the boiling cells
By strange conveyance fill'd each hollow nook,
As in an organ[8] from one blast of wind
To many a row of pipes the sound-board breathes.[9]
Anon out of the earth a fabric huge   710
Rose like an exhalation, with the sound
Of dulcet symphonies and voices sweet,
Built like a temple, where pilasters round
Were set, and Doric pillars overlaid
With golden architrave; nor did there want
Cornice or frieze, with bossy sculptures graven;
The roof was fretted gold. Not Babylon,
Nor great Alcairo such magnificence
Equall'd in all their glories, to inshrine
Belus or Serapis their Gods, or seat   720
Their kings, when Egypt with Assyria strove
To wealth and luxury. The ascending pile
Stood fix'd her stately height; and straight the doors
Opening their brazen folds, discover, wide
Within, her ample spaces, o'er the smooth
And level pavement: from the arched roof
Pendent by subtle magic many a row

[7]"On evil days though fall'n and evil tongues, / In darkness and with dangers compassed round" (7.26–27), blind and financially ruined, but still an opponent of monarchy, Milton went into hiding, then was arrested, imprisoned, and faced execution; though he was spared that sentence, his blindness made him vulnerable to vigilante justice.

[8]The introduction to K's edition reports that Milton often consoled his blindness by playing the organ.

[9]Lau supplies the information for 702–9 and notes a vertical line down the left margin next to 706–9.

Of starry lamps and blazing cressets, fed
With Naptha and Asphaltus, yielded light
As from a sky.   730

What creates the intense pleasure of not knowing? A sense of
independence, of power from the fancy's creating a world of its own
by the sense of probabilities. We have read the Arabian Nights and
hear there are thousands of those sort of Romances lost—we imagine
after them[10]*—but not their realities if we had them nor our fancies in*
their strength can go further than this Pandemonium

"Straight the doors opening" &c.
"rose like an exhalation".

[2.546–61: *the recreations of the fallen angels in Hell*]

        Others more mild,
Retreated in a silent valley, sing
With notes angelical to many a harp
Their own heroic deeds and hapless fall
By doom of battle; and complain that fate   550
Free virtue should inthrall to force or chance.
Their song was partial, but the harmony
(What could it less when Spirits immortal sing?)
Suspended Hell, and took with ravishment
The thronging audience. In discourse more sweet
(For eloquence the soul, song charms the sense,)
Others apart sat on a hill retired,
In thoughts more elevate, and reason'd high
On providence, foreknowledge, will, and fate,
Fix'd fate, free will, foreknowledge absolute,   560
And found no end, in wandering mazes lost.

Milton is godlike in the sublime pathetic.[11] *In Demons, fallen Angels,*
and Monsters the delicacies of passion, living in and from their
immortality, is of the most softening and dissolving nature. It is
carried to the utmost here—"Others more mild"—nothing can express

[10]A rich layering of meanings of *after*: our imagination is chronologically later;
strains to grasp them; takes their pattern.

[11]At the Surrey-Institution lecture, Hazlitt remarked of this passage, "the most perfect example of mingled pathos and sublimity" (1818 edition; p. 130). Keats draws
a vertical line in the margin next to 558–60 (Lau).

the sensation one feels at 'Their song was partial'"[12] &c. Examples of
this nature are divine to the utmost in other poets—in Caliban
"<u>Sometimes a thousand twangling instruments</u>"[13] &c. [. . .] There are
numerous other instances in Milton—where Satan's progeny is called
his "<u>daughter dear</u>,"and where this same Sin, a female, and with a
feminine instinct for the showy and martial, is in pain least death
should sully his bright arms, "<u>nor vainly hope to be invulnerable in
those bright arms</u>." Another instance is "<u>Pensive 1 sat</u> alone."[14] We
need not mention "<u>Tears such as Angels weep</u>."[15]

> **[*the opening of Book 3*: *blind Milton's address to "holy
> Light." Keats marks 1–22 down the left margin, underlining
> some, then continuously 26–50; HBF's report is very incom-
> plete; I rely on Beth Lau.*]**

<u>Or hearest thou rather, pure ethereal stream,</u>
<u>Whose fountain who shall tell?</u>   8
                [. . .]
<u>Thee I revisit now with bolder wing,</u>
<u>Escaped the Stygian pool, though long detain'd</u>
<u>In that obscure sojourn,</u> while in my flight
Through utter and through middle darkness borne,
<u>With other notes than to the Orphéan lyre,</u>
<u>I sung of Chaos and eternal Night.</u>
Taught by the heavenly Muse to venture down
The dark descent, and up to re-ascend,   20
Though hard and rare: thee I revisit safe,
And feel <u>thy sovereign vital lamp</u>; but thou
Revisitst not these eyes, that roll in vain
To find thy piercing ray, and find no dawn;
So thick a drop serene hath quench'd their orbs,
Or dim suffusion veil'd. <u>Yet not the more</u>
<u>Cease I to wander, where the Muses haunt</u>

---

[12] biased to their own cause or "party."

[13] *The Tempest* 3.2 (Caliban's love of the magical noises of the island).

[14] Exiting from Hell, Satan learns that Sin is his daughter (2.817); she has just
warned him that for all his bright armor, he is vulnerable to Death (811–12), the son
(fathered by Satan) she felt stirring while she sat pensive in her new station
as gatekeeper of hell (277–78). K underlined this last passage.

[15] About to address his fallen comrades, Satan weeps "tears such as Angels weep"
(1.620; in genuine grief, or a theatrical performance?)—a sublime pathetic in both
situation and simile.

Clear spring, or shady grove, or sunny hill,
Smit with the love of sacred song; but chief
Thee, Sion, and the flowery brooks beneath,   30
That wash thy hallow'd feet, and warbling flow,
Nightly I visit: nor sometimes forget
Those other two equall'd with me in fate,
So were I equall'd with them in renown,
Blind Thamyris, and blind Maeonides,
And Tiresias and Phineus, prophets old:
Then feed on thoughts, that voluntary move
Harmonious numbers; as the wakeful bird
Sings darkling, and in shadiest covert hid
Tunes her nocturnal note. Thus with the year   40
Seasons return, but not to me returns
Day, or the sweet approach of even or morn,
Or sight of vernal bloom, or summer's rose,
Or flocks, or herds, or human face divine;
But cloud instead, and ever-during dark
Surrounds me, from the cheerful ways of men
Cut off, and for the book of knowledge fair
Presented with a universal blank
Of nature's works, to me expunged and rased,
And wisdom at one entrance quite shut out.   50

The management of this Poem is Apollonian. Satan first "throws
round his baleful eyes". the[n] awakes his legions, he consults, he sets
forward on his voyage—and just as he is getting to the end of it we see
the Great God and our first parent, and that same Satan all brought
in one's vision—we have the invocation to light before we mount to
heaven—we breathe more freely—we feel the great Author's consolations
coming thick upon him at a time when he complains most—we are
getting ripe for diversity—the immediate topic of the Poem opens
with a grand Perspective of all concerned.

[*3.131–56: God in Heaven. HBF gives only 135–37, but*
Lau reports that Keats's note is written in the right margin
of the page on which all these lines are printed. God has
just allowed man to find grace for his sin, and the Son of
God elaborates the argument.]

Hell is finer than this

[*3.487–89: Milton's skill with sound*]

A violent cross wind from either coast
Blows them traverse ten thousand leagues awry
Into the devious air;

[*with* **X** *next to 488*] *This part of its sound is unaccountably expressive of the description.*

[*3.606–17: Satan's first view of Heaven. Lau reports that Keats's comment is written next to 610–17, which he marked in the left margin.*]

What wonder then if fields and regions here
<u>Breathe forth Elixir pure,</u> and rivers run
Po[r]table gold, <u>when, with one virtuous touch,</u>
<u>The arch-chemic Sun,</u> so far from us remote,
Produces with terrestrial humour mix'd,   610
Here in the dark so many precious things
Of colour glorious and effects so rare?
Here matter new to gaze the Devil met
Undazzled, far and wide his eye commands,
For sight no obstacle found here, nor shade,
But all sunshine, <u>as when his beams at noon</u>
<u>Culminate from the Equator,</u>

A Spirits eye . . .

[***above Book 4,*** *when Adam and Eve in Eden appear*]

A friend of mine[16] *says this Book has the finest opening of any—the point of time is gigantically critical—the wax is melted, the seal is about to be applied—and Milton breaks out "*<u>O for that warning voice,</u>*" &c. There is moreover an opportunity for a Grandeur of Tenderness. The opportunity is not lost. Nothing can be higher— nothing so more than Delphic.*

[*4.268–71: the beauty of Eden*]

<u>Not that fair field</u>
<u>Of Enna, where Proserpine gathering flowers,</u>

---

[16]Bailey said it was he; Lau proposes Dilke, whose copy of *PL* has a similar note.

Herself a fairer flower, by gloomy Dis
Was gather'd, which cost Ceres all that pain
To seek her through the world;

There are two specimens of a very extraordinary beauty in the
Paradise Lost, they are of a nature as far as I have read, unexampled
elsewhere—they are entirely distinct from the brief pathos of Dante—
and they are not to be found even in Shakespeare—they are according
to the great prerogative of poetry better described in themselves than
by a volume the one is in this fol[lowing]—"which cost Ceres all that
pain"—the other is that ending "Nor could the Muse defend her
son"—they appear exclusively Miltonic without the Shadow of
another mind ancient or modern.[17]

[**6.58–59:** *Milton's power with words*]

reluctant flames, the sign
Of wrath awaked; . . .

"Reluctant" with its original and modern meaning combined and woven
together,[18] *with all its shades of signification has a powerful effect.*

[**7.420–23:** *Milton's stationing of his figures*]

Their callow young, but feather'd soon and fledge
They summ'd their pens, and, soaring the air sublime

---

[17]The second passage, Book VII, lines 32–8, is entirely underlined in Keats's copy. [HBF]. Milton asks his muse to "drive far off the barbarous dissonance / Of Bacchus and his revelers; the race / Of that wild rout that tore the Thracian bard / In Rhodope, where woods, and rocks, had ears / To rapture, till the savage clamour drown'd / Both harp and voice; not could the Muse defend / Her Son." Musician Orpheus (whose music could move the very rocks) is torn apart by female Bacchantes, in an ecstatic fury. K underlines much more of the passage in Book 4 than HBF presents: Lau shows all but continuous underscoring from 237 to 281, with a rare double underlining of "all that pain" (and K's comments filling all the outer margins of pp. 92–93 in his copy of *PL*).

[18]The Latin etymology of *reluctant* is "struggle against"; the modern meaning is "unwilling, averse, disinclined." OED cites this instance for the modern meaning only and cites 10.514–16 for the older: turning into a snake, Satan falls "on his Belly prone / Reluctant but in vaine: a greater pow'r / Now ruled him, punished in the shape he sinned." See also another instance K underlined: the way Milton imagines Eve submitting to Adam's will with "sweet reluctant, amorous delay" (4.311). K's "woven together" may have been drawn from the part of the line he didn't underline: "So spake the Sovran voice, and Clouds began / To darken all the Hill, and smoke to roll / In dusky wreaths, reluctant flames, the sign of wrath awak't," a rolling into wreathes, in which, too, the *wreaths* seems literally to awake *wrath*.

> With clang despised the ground, under a cloud
> In prospect;

Milton in every instance pursues his imagination to the utmost—he is "sagacious of his Quarry,"[19] *he sees Beauty on the wing, pounces upon it and gorges it to the producing his essential verse. "So from the root the springs lighten the green stalk,"*[20] *&c. But in no instance is this sort of perseverance more exemplified than in what may be called his* stationing or statuary. *He is not content with simple description, he must station,— thus here we not only see how the Birds "*with clang despised the ground,*" but we see them "*under a cloud in prospect*" So we see Adam "*Fair indeed and tall—under a plantane*"—and so we see Satan "*disfigured on the Assyrian Mount.*"*[21] *This last with all its accompaniments, and keeping in mind the Theory of Spirits' eyes and the simile of Galileo,*[22] *has a dramatic vastness and solemnity fit and worthy to hold one amazed in the midst of this Paradise Lost.*

[9.41–47: *Milton on his inspiration*]

> Me, of these
> Nor skill'd nor studious, higher argument
> Remains, sufficient of itself to raise
> That name, unless an age too late, or cold
> Climate, or years, damp my intended wing
> Depress'd; and much they may, if all be mine,
> Not hers who brings it nightly to my ear.

Had not Shakespeare liv'd?[23]

[9.179–91: *Satan's night in Eden, before the temptation of man; he must hide himself from detection by the angel guards*]

> So saying, through each thicket, dark or dry,
> Like a black mist low creeping, he held on   180

---

[19]Carrion-feeding fowl, anticipating a battle-field slaughter (10.273ff).

[20]Archangel Raphael's description to Adam of divinely ordered nature (5.479–80).

[21]Eve's recollection of her first sight of Adam, 4.477–78; Satan beheld by Uriel, 4.126–27.

[22]Spirits' eyes are the angelic guards of Eden; the simile of Galileo, a metonymy for his telescope, has 3 instances: 1.287–91, 3.588–90 (just after the passage on which K comments, "A Spirit's eye"), and 5.260–63.

[23]Lau reports that K made a vertical line from 43 to 47 and an X at 47, keyed to this protest.

His <u>midnight search,</u> where soonest he might find
The serpent: <u>him fast sleeping soon he found</u>
<u>In labyrinth of many a round self-roll'd,</u>
<u>His head the midst, well stored with subtle wiles.</u>
<u>Not yet in horrid shade or dismal den,</u>
<u>Nor nocent° yet, but, on the grassy herb</u>   *(in-nocent)*
<u>Fearless, unfear'd he slept: in at his mouth</u>
<u>The Devil enter'd, and his brutal sense,</u>
<u>In heart or head, possessing, soon inspired</u>
<u>With act intelligential; but his sleep</u>   190
<u>Disturb'd not, waiting close the approach of morn.</u>

*Satan having entered the Serpent, and inform'd his brutal sense—
might seem sufficient—but Milton goes on "<u>but his sleep disturb'd
not</u>." Whose spirit does not ache at the smothering and confinement—
the unwilling stillness—the "<u>waiting close</u>"? Whose head is not dizzy
at the possible[24] speculations of Satan in the serpent prison—no
passage of poetry ever can give a greater pain of suffocation.*

$\backsim$

Letter to George and Georgiana Keats, 14 February–3 May 1819[1]

**"Why did I laugh tonight?" "As Hermes once" (on a dream of
Dante's Paolo and Francesca), *La belle dame sans merci,*
sonnets on Fame, *To Sleep,* "If by dull rhymes"**

*With news of his own fluxes of writing and health, an amusing anec-
dote of Bailey in love, a meditation on indolence, on the difference between philosophy and poetry, an encounter with Coleridge, a sketch of
life as a vale of soul-making, Keats includes drafts of several poems.*

[14 February from his lodgings with Brown at Wentworth Place]

*My dear Brother & Sister —
[. . .] I have kept in doors lately. resolved if possible to rid myself of my
sore throat - [. . .] Miss Brawne and I have every now and then a*

---

[24]K actually wrote "prosiable," a coinage seeming to combine, or to be uncertain
about writing, "possible," "probable," "prosy" (wearisome).

---

[1]ALS Houghton Library, Harvard.

chat and a tiff. [. . .] *The Literary world I know nothing about –
There is a Poem from Rogers dead born – and another Satire is expected
from Byron call'd Don Giovanni[2] –* [. . .]
*I have not seen M͟r Lewis lately for I have shrunk from going up the
hill – M͟r Lewis went a few morning ago to town with M͟rs Brawne
they talked about me – and I heard that M͟r L said a thing I am not
at all contented with – Says he 'O, he is quite the little Poet' now this
is abominable – you might as well say Buonaparte is quite the little
Soldier – You see what it is to be under six foot and not a lord—— There
is a long fuzz to day in the examiner about a young Man who delighted
a young woman with a Valentine – I think it must be Ollier's[3] –*
[. . .]
*I was surprised to hear from Taylor the amount of Muray the
Booksellers last sale – what think you of £25,000? He sold 4000 coppies
of Lord Byron.[4] I am sitting opposite the Shakspeare I brought from
the Isle of wight* [. . .] *I shall send you the Pot of Basil, S͟t Agnes eve,
and if I should have finished it a little thing call'd the 'eve of St Mark'
you see what fine mother Radcliff names I have[5] – it is not my fault –
I did not search for them – I have not gone on with Hyperion – for to
tell the truth I have not been in great cue for writing lately – I will
wait for the sping to rouse me up a little –* [. . .]
*[19 February . . .] I have not said in any Letter yet a word about my
affairs – in a word I am in no despair about them – my poem[6] has
not at all succeeded – in the course of a year or so I think I shall try
the public again – in a selfish point of view I should suffer my pride
and my contempt of public opinion to hold me silent – but for your's
and fanny's sake I will pluck up a spirit and try again – I have no
doubt of success in a course of years if I persevere – but it must be
patience – for the Reviews have enervated and made indolent mens*

---

[2]The first installment of *Don Juan* (Cantos I–II) appeared 15 July 1819, though as K makes clear, it was already a topic of conversation in literary circles.

[3]This gentle satire in *The Examiner* wasn't by K's former publisher; Charles Lamb was the author of "Valentine's Day—(14th of February)."

[4]*Childe Harold's Pilgrimage IV*, the latest and last canto, appeared to sensational success in April 1818. K is recalling news that advance sales by Feb. numbered 4,000; the first edition was a print run of 10,000.

[5]With *The Mysteries of Udolpho* and *The Italian*, Ann Radcliffe had prodigious success in the 1790s in the genre of the gothic novel, threaded with terror and the supernatural.

[6]*Endymion*

minds – few think for themselves – These Reviews too are getting more
and more powerful and especially the Quarterly – They are like a
superstition which the more it prostrates the Crowd and the longer it
continues the more powerful it becomes just in proportion to their
increasing weakness – I was in hopes that when people saw, as they must
do now, all the trickery and iniquity of these Plagues they would scout
them, but no they are like the spectators at the Westminster cock-pit –
they like the battle and do not care who wins or who looses. [. . .]
I have a long Story to tell you about Bailey – I will say first the
circumstances as plainly and as well as I can remember, and then I
will make my comment. You know that Bailey was very much cut up
about a little Jilt in the country somewhere; I thought he was in a dying
state about it when at Oxford with him: little supposing as I have since
heard, that he was at that very time making impatient Love to[7] Marian
Reynolds – and guess my astonishment at hearing after this that he
had been trying at Miss Martin – So matters have been. So Matters
stood – when he got ordained and went to a Curacy near Carlisle
where the family of the Gleigs reside – There his susceptible heart was
conquered by Miss Gleig – and thereby all his connections in town
have been annulled – both male and female I do not now remember
clearly the facts – These however I know – He showed his correspondence
with Marian to Gleig – returnd all her Letters and asked for his own –
he also wrote very abrubt Letters to Mrs Reynolds – I do not know
any more of the Martin affair than I have written above – No doubt
his conduct has been verry bad. The great thing to be considered is –
whether it is want of delicacy and principle or want of Knowledge and
polite experience – And again Weakness – yes that is it – and the want
of a Wife – yes that is it – and then Marian made great Bones of him
although her Mother and Sister have teased her very much about it.
Her conduct has been very upright throughout the whole affair – She
liked Bailey as a Brother – but not as a Husband – especially as he used
to woo her with the Bible and Jeremy Taylor[8] under his arm – they
walked in no grove but Jeremy Taylors – Marians obstinacy is some
excuse – but his so quickly taking to miss Gleig can have no excuse –
except that of a Ploughmans who wants a wife – The thing which
sways me more against him than any thing else is Rice's conduct on

[7]courting; "Marian" is Reynold's sister Mariane (b. 1795).
[8]17th-c. theologian, intensely admired by Bailey; the work at hand is *The Golden
Grove*.

the occasion; Rice would not make an immature resolve: he was ardent in his friendship for Bailey, he examined the whole for and against minutely; and he has abandoned Bailey entirely. All this I am not supposed by the Reynoldses to have any hint of – It will be a good Lesson to the Mother and Daughters – nothing would serve but Bailey – If you mentioned the word Tea pot – some one of them came out with an a propos about Bailey – noble fellow – fine fellow! was always in their mouths – this may teach them that the man who redicules[9] romance is the most romantic of Men – that he who abuses women and slights them – loves them the most – that he who talks of roasting a Man alive would not do it when it came to the push – and above all that they are very shallow people who take every thing literal a Man's life of any worth is a continual allegory – and very few eyes can see the Mystery of his life – a life like the scriptures, figurative – which such people can no more make out than they can the hebrew Bible. Lord Byron cuts a figure – but he is not figurative – Shakspeare led a life of Allegory; his works are the comments on it – [. . .]
I have been at different times turning it in my head whether I should go to Edinburgh & study for a physician; I am afraid I should not take kindly to it; I am sure I could not take fees – & yet I should like to do so: it's not worse than writing poems, and hanging them up to be flyblown on the Reviewshambles. [. . .]
[12 March . . .] the candles are burnt down and I am using the wax taper– which has a long snuff on it – the fire is at its last click – I am sitting with my back to it with one foot rather askew upon the rug and the other with the heel a little elevated from the carpet – I am writing this on the Maid's tragedy which I have read since tea with Great pleasure [. . .] I require nothing so much of you as that you will give me a like description of yourselves, however it may be when you are writing to me – Could I see the same thing done of any great Man long since dead it would be a great delight: as to know in what position Shakspeare sat when he began 'To be or not to be" [. . .]
[13 March . . .] I know not why Poetry and I have been so distant lately I must make some advances soon or she will cut me entirely. [. . .]
[17 March . . .] On sunday I went to Davenports' were I dined – and had a nap. I cannot bare a day anhilated in that mannner – there is

---

[9]A punning respelling admired by Christopher Ricks (*Keats and Embarrassment*); cf. letter to G&GK in Sept. 1819 (p. 271).

a great difference between an easy and an uneasy indolence[10] – An indolent day – fill'd with speculations even of an unpleasant colour – is bearable and even pleasant alon[e]– when one's thoughts cannot find out any thing better in the world; and experience has told us that locomotion is no change: but to have nothing to do, and tobe surrounded with unpleasant human identities; who press upon one just enough to prevent one getting into a lazy position; and not enough to interest or rouse one; is a capital punishment of a capital crime: for is not giving up, through goodnature, one's time to people who have no light and shade a capital crime? Yet what can I do? – they have been very kind and attentive to me. I do not know what I did on monday – nothing – nothing – nothing – I wish this was any thing extraordinary. [. . .] [19 March][11] Yesterday I got a black eye – the first time I took a Cricket bat. Brown who is always onesfriend in a disaster applied a leech to the eyelid,[12] and there is no inflammation this morning though the ball hit me directly on the sight — twas a white ball – I am glad it was not a clout. This is the second black eye I have had since leaving school – during all my school days I never had one at all – we must eat a peck before we die – This morning I am in a sort of temper indolent and supremely careless: I long after a stanza or two of Thompson's Castle of indolence.[13] My passions are all alseep from my having slumbered till nearly eleven and weakened the animal fibre all over me to a delightful sensation about three degrees on this side of faintness – if I had teeth of pearl and the breath of lillies I should call it languor – but as I am + I must call it Laziness. In this state of effeminacy the fibres of the brain are relaxed in common with the rest of the body, and to such a happy degree that pleasure has no show of enticement and pain no unbearable frown. Neither Poetry, nor Ambition, nor Love have any alertness of countenance as they pass by me: they seem rather like three figures on a greek vase – a Man and two women whom no one but myself could distinguish in their

+ especially as I have a black eye

[10]See K's letter to Reynolds in Feb. 1818 on "delicious diligent Indolence" (p. 105).

[11]I follow editorial tradition in filling in likely letters, lost to tears, in some half dozen words.

[12]Leeches, used to suck out "bad blood," were a common household medicinal item.

[13]In the first part of James Thomson's *The Castle of Indolence* (1748), wizard Indolence entices weary wayfarers into his castle, where they sink into pleasurable languor.

disguisement.[14] This is the only happiness; and is a rare instance of advantage in the body overpowering the Mind. I have this moment received a note from Haslam in which he expects the death of his Father – who has been for some time in a state of insensibility – his mother bears up he says very well – I shall go to twon tommorrow to see him. This is the world – thus we cannot expect to give way many hours to pleasure – Circumstances are like Clouds continually gathering and bursting – While we are laughing the seed of some trouble is put into ~~he~~ the wide arable land of events – while we are laughing it sprouts is grows and suddenly bears a poison fruit which we must pluck – Even so we have leisure to reason on the misfortunes of our friends; our own touch us too nearly for words. Very few men have ever arrived at a complete disinterestedness[15] of Mind: very few have been influenced by a pure desire of the benefit of others – in the greater part of the Benefactors ~~of~~ & to Humanity some meretricious motive has sullied their greatness – some melodramatic scenery has facinated them – From the manner in which I feel Haslam's misfortune I perceive how far I am from any humble standard of disinterestedness – Yet this feeling ought to be carried to its highest pitch as there is no fear of its ever injuring Society – which it would do I fear pushed to an extremity – For in wild nature the Hawk would loose his Breakfast of Robins and the Robin his of Worms – the Lion must starve as well as the swallow – The greater part of Men make their way with the same instinctiveness, the same unwandering eye from their purposes, the same animal eagerness as the Hawk – The Hawk wants a Mate, so does the Man – look at them both they set about it and procure[16] on in the same manner. They want both a nest and they both set about one in the same manner – they get their food in the same manner – The noble animal Man for his amusement smokes his pipe – the Hawk balances about the Clouds – that is the only difference of their leisures. This it is that makes the Amusement of Life – to a speculative Mind. I go among the Fields and catch a glimpse of a Stoat or a fieldmouse peeping out of the withered grass – the creature hath a purpose and its eyes are bright with it. I go amongst the buildings of a city and I see a Man hurrying along – to what? the Creature has a purpose and

[14]This is the genesis of a dreamy *Ode on Indolence* (see p. 282), which K did not think to publish. In the ode it is not clear that "Ambition" is male.

[15]not motivated by self-interest; the opposite of meretricious.

[16]get; but with a more specific sense of "seek to satisfy sexual longing."

his eyes are bright with it. But then as Wordsworth says, "we have all one human heart"[17] —there is an ellectric fire in human nature tending to purify – so that among these human creature there is continully some birth of new heroism. The pity is that we must wonder at it: as we should at finding a pearl in rubbish – I have no doubt that thousands of people never heard of have had hearts competely disinterested: I can remember but two – Socrates and Jesus – their Histories evince it – What I heard a little time ago, Taylor observe with respect to Socrates may be said of Jesus— That he was so great as man that though he transmitted no writing of his own to posterity, we have his Mind and his sayings and his greatness handed to us by others.[18] It is to be lamented that the history of the latter was written and revised by Men interested in the pious frauds of Religion.[19] Yet through all this I see his splendour. Even here though I myself am pursueing the same instinctive course as the veriest human animal you can think of – I am however young writing at random – straining at particles of light in the midst of a great darkness – without knowing the bearing of any one assertion of any one opinion. Yet may I not in this be free from sin? May there not be superior beings amused with any graceful, though instinctive attitude my mind my fall into, as I am entertained with the alertness of a Stoat or the anxiety of a Deer? Though a quarrel in the Streets is a thing to be hated, the energies displayed in it are fine; the commonest Man shows a grace in his quarrel – By a superior being our reasoning may take the same tone – though erroneous they may be fine – This is the very thing in which consists poetry; and if so it is not so fine a thing as philosophy – For the same reason that an eagle is not so fine a thing as a truth – Give me this credit – Do you not think I strive – to know myself? Give me this credit – and you will not think that on my own accout I repeat Milton's lines
    "How charming is divine Philosophy
    Not harsh and crabbed as dull fools suppose
    But musical as is Apollo's lute"[20] –

[17]*The Old Cumberland Beggar* (1800) 146: the recognition that motivates charity even in "the poorest of the poor" (140–46).

[18]Neither was known as an author; their teachings were published by their students. And each willingly embraced death on the principles of his philosophy.

[19]K has been reading skeptic Voltaire, who wields such phrases (critic Robert Ryan).

[20]One brother's response to another's long praise of chastity and disgust of "carnal sensuality" (*Comus* 475–77) as they assure themselves about their captive sister's virtue; for another reference to this masque, see K's letter to Bailey, 18 July 1818 (p. 192).

No - no for myself - feeling grateful as I do to have got into a state of mind to relish them properly - Nothing ever becomes real till it is experienced - Even a Proverb is no proverb to you till your Life has illustrated it. I am ever affraid that your anxiety for me will lead you to fear for the violence of my temperament continually smothered down: for that reason I did not intend to have sent you the following sonnet - but look over the two last pages and ask yourselves whether I have not that in me which will well bear the buffets of the world. It will be the best comment on my sonnet; it will show you that it was written with no Agony but that of ignorance; with no thirst of any thing but Knowledge when pushed to the point though the first steps to it were through my human passions - they went away, and I wrote with my Mind - and perhaps I must confess a little bit of my heart -
P   Why did I laugh tonight? No voice will tell:[21]

     No God no Deamon of severe response
Deigns to reply from heaven or from Hell - -
     Then to my human heart I turn at once - -
Heart! thou and I are here sad and alone;
     Say, wherefore did I laugh? O mortal pain!
O Darkness! Darkness! ever must I moan
     To question Heaven and Hell and Heart in vain!
Why did I laugh? I know this being's lease
     My fancy to its utmost blisses spreads:
Yet could I on this very midnight cease
     and the world's gaudy ensigns see in shreds.
Verse, fame and Beauty are intense indeed
     But Death intenser - Deaths is Life's high mead."[22]

I went to ~~bead~~ bed, and enjoyed an uninterrupted Sleep - Sane I went to bed and sane I ~~rose~~ arose. || This the 15th of April - you see what a time it is since I wrote - all that time I have been day by day expecting Letters from you. I write quite in the dark - In the hopes of a Letter daily I have deferred that I might write in the light. [. . .]
Last Sunday [11 April] I took a Walk towards highgate and in the lane that winds by the side of Lord Mansfield's park I met Mr Green

---

[21]K didn't think to publish this either; it was first printed in *1848*, Sonnet XV (2.301). The stray P on the page is inexplicable.

[22]reward. K's punctuation makes the intended sense uncertain: he may mean "Death is Life's high mead (the reward of life is death—the end of 'mortal pain')"; or he may mean "Death's high mead is Life's high mead (the rewards earned in life are claimed ultimately by Death as his trophies)."

our Demonstrator at Guy's in conversation with Coleridge[23] – I joined them, after enquiring by a look whether it would be agreeable – I walked with him a his alderman-after dinner pace for near two miles I suppose In those two Miles he broached a thousand things – let me see if I can give you a list – Nightingales,[24] Poetry – on Poetical Sensation – Metaphysics – Different genera and species of Dreams – Nightmare – a dream accompanied ~~with~~ by a sense of touch – single and double touch – A dream related – First and second consciousness – the difference explained between will and Volition – so my metaphysicians from a want of smoking[25] the second consciousness – Monsters – the Kraken[26] – Mermaids – Southey[27] believes in them – Southey's belief too much diluted – A Ghost story – Good morning – I heard his voice as he came towards me – I heard it as he moved away – I had heard it all the interval – if it may be called so. He was civil enough to ask me to call on him at Highgate Good night! [. . .]

[16 April] I have been looking over the correspondence of the pretended Amena and Wells this evening[28] – I now see the whole cruel deception – I think Wells must have had an accomplice in it – Amena's Letters are in a Man's language, and in a Man's hand imitating a woman's – The instigations to this diabolical scheme were vanity, and the love of intrigue. It was no thoughtless hoax – but a cruel deception on a sanguine Temperament, with every show of friendship. I do not think death too bad for the villain – The world ~~will~~ would look upon it in a different light should I expose it – they would call it a frolic – so I must be wary – but I consider it my duty to be prudently revengeful. I will hang over his head like a sword by a hair. I will be opium to his vanity – if I cannot injure his – He is a rat and he shall have ratsbane to his vanity – I will harm him all I possibly can – I have no doubt I shall be able to do so – Let us leave him to his misery alone except

[23]By this time, Coleridge was living with his doctor in Highgate (near the Heath); Joseph Henry Green was his literary executor; Kenwood is the residence of the Earl of Mansfield, lord chief justice.

[24]*The Nightingale* (disputing the literary association with melancholy) was one of Coleridge's poems in the 1798 *Lyrical Ballads*.

[25]finding fault with; "my" (just prior) is shorthand for "many."

[26]an underwater beast (later the title of an apocalyptic lyric by Alfred Tennyson).

[27]Coleridge's brother-in-law, and by this point, Poet Laureate.

[28]Wells is the friend whose gift of roses K commemorates in a sonnet in 1817. In a jest in 1816, he sent Tom a series of love letters from "Amena Bellefila"; falling for the ruse, Tom was humiliated when it was exposed, and K ended his friendship with Wells.

when we can throw in a little more — The fifth canto of Dante pleases me more and more - it is that one in which he meets with Paulo and Franchesca - I had passed many days in rather a low state of mind, and in the midst of them I dreamt of being in that region of Hell. The dream was one of the most delightful enjoyments I ever had in my life - I floated about the whirling atmosphere as it is described with a beautiful figure to whose lips mine were joined at it seem'd for an age - and in the midst of all this cold and darkness I was warm - even flowery tree tops sprung up and we rested on them sometimes with the lightness of a cloud till the wind blew us away again—I tried a Sonnet upon it[29]— there are fourteen lines but nothing of what I felt in it— O that I could dream it every night—

> As Hermes once took to his feathers light
> When lulled Argus, baffled, swoon'd and slept
> So on a delphic reed my idle spright
> So play'd, so charm'd so conquer'd, so bereft
> The dragon world of all its hundred eyes[30]
> And seeing it asleep so fled away: —
> Not to pure Ida with its ~~snow~~clad cold skies,[31]
> Nor unto Tempe where Jove grieved that day,
> But to that second circle of sad hell,
> Where in the gust, the whirlwind[32] and the flaw
> Of Rain and hailstones lovers need not tell

[29]Leigh Hunt published this in *The Indicator* 38 (28 June 1820, p. 301), over the signature that K used for *La Belle Dame* (*Indicator*, 10 May 1820): CAVIARE; it was titled *A Dream, After Reading Dante's Episode of Paolo and Francesca* (the subject of his own *Story of Rimini*, a target of abuse since 1816).

[30]Smitten with nymph Io (from Tempe), Jove changed her into a heifer to mask her from Juno, but this still suspicious wife set the hundred-eyed Argus to guard her from Jove (in the disguise of a bull). Jove sent Hermes to lull Argus to sleep with his music (a tale in Ovid's *Metamorphoses* Book I). K underlined Milton's description of the "watchful cherubim" guarding the gates of Eden: "Spangled with eyes more numerous than those / Of Argus, and more wakeful than to drowse, / Charm'd with Arcadian pipe, the pastoral reed / Of Hermes, or his opiate rod" (*PL* 11.130–33).

[31]The mountain near Troy where Paris awarded the golden apple to Venus, who then assisted his abduction of the Greek queen Helen to Troy (and the rest is history).

[32]*Indicator*] world-wind;

There is a debate about this variant: is *world* an error, or a deliberate revision? The word *world* does evoke the antagonism of worldly spies and jesters; it may pun on *whirl'd*—a verb in Cary's translation (1814, which K owned) of *Inferno* V: "The stormy blast of hell / With restless fury drives the spirits on / Whirl'd round and dash'd amain with sore annoy" (32–34), as well as the word *whirling* in K's letter.

> Their sorrows – Pale were the sweet lips I saw
> Pale were the lips I kiss'd and fair the form[33]
> I floated with about that melancholy storm—

[. . .]
[21 April]

> La belle dame sans merci —[34]

> O what can ail thee Knight at arms
>   Alone and palely loitering?[35]
> The sedge has wither'd from the Lake
>   And no birds sing!

> O what can ail thee knight at arms
>   So haggard[36] and so woe begone?
> The squirrels granary is full
>   And the harvest's done –

>   a
> I see ~~death's~~ lilly on thy brow
>   With anguish moist and fever dew,
>   a
> And on thy cheeks ~~death's~~ fading rose
> Fast Withereth too –

---

[33]The last two lines are written at right angles up the left margin of the page.

[34]French: *The beautiful lady without mercy*—i.e., one who denies a lover's petition. Both *merci* and *mercy* derive from the medieval French *merces*, price or wages, suggesting an erotic economy: the granting of sexual favor for gifts and service. Women were expected to honor this tacit contract or suffer a charge of being "sans merci." K's Belle Dame joins a long tradition of "femmes fatales." After this version was published, tidied up, in *1848*, it became the preferred one, in part because it could be shorn of association with Hunt. For the version in Hunt's *Indicator*, see p. 419.

[35]K marked a passage about Arcite's love-lorn grief from Chaucer's *Knight's Tale* in Burton's *Anatomy of Melancholy*, where it is quoted: "His hewe falow and pale as asshen colde, / And solitarie he was and evere alone, / And wailynge al the nyght, makynge his mone" (1364–66); K will make this moan originally the lady's. The imagery of the knight's ailment is also threaded with Hunt's descriptors for lovelorn Paolo in the final canto of *Rimini*: "moist anguish," "woe," "wan," "pallid."

[36]The word *haggard* implies the effects of commerce with a witch ("hag").

I met a Lady in the ~~Wilds~~ Meads[37]
   Full beautiful, a faery's child
Her hair was long, her foot was light
   And her eyes were wild –
I made a Garland for her head,
   And bracelets too, and fragrant ~~Zones~~
She look'd at me as she'd did love
   And made sweet moan —

I set her on my pacing steed
   And nothing else saw all day long
For sidelong would she bend, and sing
   A faerys song –
She found me roots of relish sweet,
              manna[38]
   And honey wild and ~~honey~~ dew
And sure in language strange she said
   I love thee true -
She took me to her elfin grot,
          and sigh'd full sore
And there she wept ~~and there she sighed full sore~~
And there I shut her wild wild eyes
   With kisses four.

And there she Lulled me asleep,
   And there I dream'd Ah woe betide!
The latest dream I ever dreamt
   On the cold hill side

I saw pale Kings and Princes too
   Pale warriors death pale were they all
They cried - La belle dame sans merci
   Thee hath in thrall -

[37]Although this stanza seems to begin the knight's reply, the syntactic parallels with the preceding stanza, and the absence of punctuation to discriminate a second speaker, allow for the possibility that the questioning is self-addressed.

[38]K underlined "his tongue / Dropped manna" in Milton's description of Belial's seductive rhetoric (*PL* 2.112–13). For manna, see the glossary and cf. *The Eve of St. Agnes* 268 (p. 348), and *Endymion, Book* 1.766.

I saw their starv'd lips in the gloam
~~All tremble~~   gaped
    With horrid warning ˏ wide ~~agape~~
And I awoke and found me here
    On the cold hill's side.

And this is way I ~~wither~~ sojourn here,
    Alone and palely loitering,
Though the sedge is wither'd from the Lake,
    And no birds sing — – . . . .

Why four Kisses – you will say – why four because I wish to restrain
the headlong impetuousity of my Muse – she would have fain said 'score'
without hurting the rhyme— but we must temper the Imagination as
the Critics say with Judgment. I was obliged to choose an even number
that both eyes might have fair play: and to speak truly I think two a
piece quite sufficient – Suppose I had said seven; there would have
been three and a half a piece – a very awkward affair – and well got
out of on my side —[. . .]

I have been reading lately two very different books Robertson's
America and Voltaire's *Siecle De Louis XIV*. It is like walking arm
and arm between Pizarro and the great little Monarch.[39] In How
lementabl a case do we see the great body of the people in both
instances: in the first, where Men might seem to inherit quiet of Mind
from unsophisticated senses; from uncontamination of civilisation;
and especially from their being as it were estranged from the mutual
helps of Society and its mutual injuries – and thereby more immediately
under the Protection of Providence – even there they had mortal pains
to bear as bad; or even worse than Baliffs, Debts and Poverties of
civilised Life – The whole appears to resolve into this – that Man is
originally 'a poor forked creature'[40] subject to the same mischances as

---

[39]Scots minister William Robertson's *History of the Discovery and Settlement of
America* (1777) was the first account in English to bring a sympathetic view to the
Spanish conquistadors, including Cortez (see *On First Looking into Chapman's
Homer*, p. 8) and Pizarro (c. 1475–1541), vanquisher of the Incan empire in Peru.
Voltaire's *Le Siècle de Louis XIV* (1751) included a new focus on culture and com-
merce (in addition to war and politics). One of the epithets of this Sun King
(1638–1715), builder of Versailles Palace, was "Le Grand Monarque."

[40]Lear's shocked realization when he encounters "Poor Tom" on the heath (*King
Lear* 3.4.109–10).

the beasts of the forest, destined to hardships and disquietude of some kind or other. If he improves by degrees his bodily accomodations and comforts – at each stage, at each accent there are waiting for him a fresh set of annoyances – he is mortal and there is still a heaven with its Stars above his head. The most interesting question that can come before us is How far by the persevering endeavours of a seldom appearing Socrates Mankind may be made happy – I can imagine such happiness carried to an extreme – but what must it end in? –Death – and who could in such a case bear with death – the whole troubles of life which are now frittered away in a series of years, would the be accumulated for the last days of a being who instead of hailing its approach, would leave this world as Eve left Paradise – But in th truth I do not at all believe in this sort of perfectibility – the nature of the world will not admit of it – the inhabitants of the world will correspond to itself. – Let the fish philosophise the ice away from the Rivers in winter time and they shall be at continual play in the tepid delight of summer. Look at the Poles and at the Sands of Africa, Whirlpools and volcanoes – Let men exterminate them and I will say that they may arrive at earthly Happiness– The point at which Man may arrive is as far as the paralel state in inanimate nature and no further – For instance suppose a rose to have sensation, it blooms on a beautiful morning it enjoys itself – but there comes a cold wind, a hot sun – it can not escape it, it cannot destroy its annoyances – they are as native to the world as itself: no more can man be happy in spite, the worldy elements will prey upon his nature – The common cognomen of this world among the misguided and superstitious is 'a vale of tears'[41] from which we are to be redeemed by a certain arbitary interposition of God and taken to Heaven – What a little circumscribe straightened notion! Call the world if you Please "The vale of Soul-making" Then you will find out the use of the world (I am speaking now in the highest terms for human nature admitting it to be immortal which I will here take for granted for the purpose of showing a thought which has struck me concerning it) I say 'Soul making' Soul as distinguished from an Intelligence – There may be intelligences or sparks of the divinity in millions—but they are not

---

[41]In his platonic *Hymn to Intellectual Beauty* (*Examiner* 1817), Percy Shelley, drawing on St. Paul, describes "our state" in mortal life as a "dim vast vale of tears" (16–17).

Souls ~~the~~ till they acquire identities, till each one is personally itself. Itelligences are atoms of perception – they know and they see and they are pure, in short they are God – How then are Souls to be made? How then are these sparks which are God to have identity given them – so as ever to possess a bliss peculiar to each ones individual existence? How, but by the medium of a world like this?[42] This point I sincerely wish to consider because I think it a grander system of salvation than the chrystean religion – or rather it is a system of Spirit-creation – This is effected by three grand materials acting the one upon the other for a series of years – These three Materials are the Intelligence — the human heart (as distinguished from intelligence or Mind) and the World or Elemental space suited for the proper action of Mind and Heart on each other for the purpose of forming the Soul or Intelligence destined to possess the sense of Identity. I can scarcely express what I but dimly perceive – and yet I think I perceive it – that you may judge the more clearly I will put it in the most homely form possible – I will call the world a School instituted for the purpose of teaching little children to read – I will call the human heart the horn Book[43] used in that School – and I will call the Child able to read, the Soul made from that school and its hornbook. Do you not see how necessary a World of Pains and troubles is to school an Intelligence and make it a Soul? A Place where the heart must feel and suffer in a thousand diverse ways! Not merely is the Heart a Hornbook, It is the Minds Bible, it is the Minds experience, it is the teat from which the Mind or intelligence sucks its identity – As various as the Lives of Men are – so various become their souls, and thus does God make individual beings, Souls, Identical Souls of the Sparks of his own essence. This appears to me a faint Sketch of a system of Salvation which does not affront our reason and humanity – I am convinced that many difficulties which christians labour under would vanish before it – There is one which even now Strikes me – the Salvation of Children – In them the Spark or intelligence returns to God without any identity —it having had no time to learn of, and be altered by, the heart – or

---

[42]In contrast to the Platonic/Christian theology of a pre-existing immortal soul (Wordsworth's thesis in *Ode: Intimation of Immortality* [1815]), K proposes an experiential soul, matured by the adversities of mortal life. *Itelligences* seems an inadvertent pun on this potential for the thinking "I."

[43]a child's primer for spelling, reading, arithmetic (bound in horn-skin for durability)

seat of the human Passions[44] [. . .] If what I have said should not be plain enough, as I fear it may not be, I will but you in the place where I began in this series of thoughts – I mean, I began by seeing how man was formed by circumstances – and what are circumstances? – but touchstones of his heart—? and what are touchstones? but proovings of his heart?—and what are proovings of his heart but fortifiers or alterers of his nature? and what is his altered nature but his Soul?— and what was his Soul before it came into the world and had these provings and alterations and perfectionings?—An intelligence – without Identity – and how is this Identity to be made? Through the medium of the Heart? and how is the heart to become this Medium but in a world of Circumstances? There now I think what with Poetry and Theology you may thank your Stars that my pen is not very long winded [. . .] Friday – April 30 – Brown has been rummaging up some of my old sins – that is to say sonnets. I do not think you remember them, so I will copy them out as well as two or three lately written – I have just written one on Fame which Brown is transcribing and he has his book and mine. I must employ myself perhaps in a sonnet on the same subject[45] –

On Fame
<u>You cannot eat your Cake and have it too</u>

Proverb.

How fever'd is that Man ~~misled~~ who cannot look
    Upon his mortal days with temperate blood
Who vexes all the leaves of his Life's book
    And robs his fair name of its maidenhood
It is as if the rose should pluck herself
    Or the ripe plum~~b~~ finger its misty bloom
As if a clear Lake meddling with itself
    Should ~~fill~~ cloud its pureness with a muddy gloom
But the rose leaves herself upon the Briar
    For winds to kiss and grateful Bees to ~~taste~~ feed

[44]A dispute with the thesis of Wordsworth's *Ode*, in which children's souls are represented as purest because still "trailing clouds of glory" from God, Heaven, and Eternity, the soul's true "home."

[45]The first one was first published in *1848* as Sonnet XIV, titled *On Fame*; the second was first published in 1838 and then a couple of times more, before appearing in *1848* as Sonnet XIII.

And the ripe plumb ~~still will~~ still wears its dim attire
   The undisturbed Lake has crystal space
                      teasing the world for grace
   Why then should man ~~his own bright name deface~~
~~And spoil burn our pleasure in his selfish fire.~~
Spoil his salvation by a fierce miscreed

Another on Fame

Fame like a wayward girl will still be coy
   To those who woo her with too slavish knees
   But makes surrender to some thoughtless boy
And dotes the more upon a heart at ease –
She is a Gipsey will not speak to those
   Who have not learnt to be content without her
A Jilt whose ear was never whisper'd close
   Who think they scandal her who talk about her
A very Gipsey is she Nilus born,[46]
Sister in law to jealous Potiphar:[47]
Ye lovesick Bards, repay her scorn for scorn.
Ye lovelorn Artists madmen that ye are,
Make your best bow to her and bid adieu
Then if she likes it she will follow you.

To Sleep[48]

O soft embalmer of the still midnight
   Shutting with careful fingers and benign
   Our gloom-pleas'd eyes embowered from the light,
   Enshaded in forgetfulness divine —
O soothest sleep, if so it please the close
   In midst of this thine hymn my willing eyes,
Or wait the amen, ere thy poppy throws
   Around my bed it dewy Charities —
Then save me or the passed day will shine

[46]By a false etymology, gypsies were thought to come from Egypt (the site of the Nile river).

[47]Potiphar, the wife of an Egyptian officer who has bought David, takes a shine to him and pesters him for sex; frustrated by his refusals, she frames him for attempted rape, and her husband has him thrown into prison (Genesis 39).

[48]First published in *1848*. K drafted and revised another, probably earlier version on the flyleaf of vol. 2 of his *PL* (see Lau 130–31). K later revised *dewy* (8) to *lulling*, and *lords* (11) to *hoards*.

Upon my pillow breeding many woes;
Save me from curious conscience that still lords
　Its strength for darkness, borrowing like ~~the~~ a Mole –
　Turn the key deftly in the oiled wards
　And seal the hushed Casket of my soul –

[*Then follows Keats's prologue to and text of* Ode to Psyche *(see p. 360 for these)*]

Incipit altera Sonneta–[49]

—

I have been endeavouring to discover a better Sonnet Stanza than we have. The legitimate does not suit the language over-well from the pouncing rhymes – the other kind appears too elegiac[50] — and the couplet at the end of it has seldom a pleasing effect – I do not pretend to have succeeded – it will explain itself—

If by dull rhymes our english must be chaind
And, like Andromeda,[51] the Sonnet sweet
Fetterd in spite of pained Loveliness . .
Let us find out, if we must be constrain'd,
Sandals more interwoven and complete
　To fit the naked foot of Poesy[52] –
　Let us inspect the Lyre,[53] and weigh the stress
　Of every chord,[54] and see what may be gain'd

---

[49]Latin: *Here begins another sonnet.* K's *another* means *the next* but also relates to his experiments with "other" arrays of form. While every sonnet evokes the traditions, K's "Incipit," like Wordsworth's "Nuns fret not at their Convent's narrow room" (1807), is explicit. K had written about 60 sonnets by spring 1819 but would write very few after this.

[50]The *legitimate* is the older Petrarchan pattern, *abba / abba // cdecde*, with 3 couplets in the first 8 lines; the quatrains of the "other" Shakespearean pattern (*abab / cdcd / efef*) came to be called *elegiac* after their use in Thomas Gray's immensely popular *Elegy Written in a Country Churchyard* (1751). In the alteration of K's *sonneta*, rhymes are interwoven through a syntactic structure of 4 tercets and a couplet: *abc / abd / cdb / cde / de.*

[51]In Ovid's *Metamorphoses*, a beautiful woman chained to a rock, to be ravished by a sea-serpent. She was rescued by Medusa-slayer Perseus, riding Pegasus, an emblem of poetic energy.

[52]Punning on metrical fect; *Poesy*, the first of the *d* chord, is the sonnet's weakest rhyme-word.

[53]the harp of Apollo, and classical poets

[54]Punning on a binding cord.

> By ear industrious, and attention meet.[55]
>   Misers of sound and syllable, no less
>   Than Midas of his coinage,[56] let us be
>   Jealous of dead leaves in the bay wreath crown;[57]
>   So, if we may not let the muse be free,
>   She will be bound with Garlands of her own.

Here endeth the other Sonnet —
This is the 3ʳᵈ of May and every thing is in delightful forwardness;
the violets are not witherd before the peeping of the first rose. – [. . .]
[4 May . . .]
God bless you, my dear Brother & Sister   Your ever affectionate
Brother John Keats.

Letter to Miss Jeffery, 31 May 1819[1]

The Jefferys were very kind to Tom in Teignmouth; Keats is writing from Hampstead, with Wordsworth's "Immortality" Ode still in his thoughts, and contending with melancholy prospects. He has just returned all borrowed books and burned old letters (alas!).

My dear Lady,
[. . .] I want you to do me a Favor; which I will first ask and then tell you the reasons. Enquire in the Villages round Teignmouth if there is any Lodging commodious for its cheapness; and let me know where it is and what price. I have the choice as it were of two Poisons (yet I ought not to call this a Poison) the one is voyaging to and from India for a few years;[2] the other is leading a fevrous life

---

[55]appropriate, with a punning hint of "meter."

[56]The miserly king in *Metamorphoses* got his wish that all he touched would turn to gold, only to find that he has killed his daughter and is unable to feed himself (he starves to death).

[57]The bay-laurel wreath honors military heroes and poets (hence Poet Laureate). In *Metamorphoses*, when nymph Daphne pleas to the gods to help her escape Apollo's rapacious pursuit, they change her into a laurel tree; Apollo claims the laurel as his emblem of praise.

---

[1]Text: the first publication, A. Forbes Sieveking, "Some Unedited Letters of John Keats," *Fortnightly Review* 54 (1893), pp. 732–33.

[2]As a ship-surgeon for the East India Company.

alone with Poetry—This latter will suit me best; for I cannot resolve to give up my Studies—It strikes me it would not be quite so
proper for you to make such inquiries—so give my love to your
Mother and ask her to do it. Yes, I would rather conquer my indolence and strain my nerves at some grand Poem – than be in a dun-
derheaded indiaman – [. . .] I have been always till now almost as
careless of the world as a fly—my troubles were all of the Imagination. My Brother George always stood between me and any deal-
ings with the world—Now I find I must buffet it—I must take my
stand upon some vantage ground and begin to fight—I must choose
between despair and Energy—I choose the latter—though the
world has taken on a quakerish look with me, which I once
thought was impossible.
     'Nothing can bring back the hour
     Of splendour in the grass and glory in the flower.'³
I once thought this a Melancholist's dream — [. . .]

Your sincere friend
John Keats

Letter to Miss Jeffery, 9 June 1819¹

> *His amusing but now unwell friend, James Rice, has invited him to the
> Isle of Wight; Keats muses on philosophy versus versifying, the plea-
> sures of indolence.*

My Dear young Lady, [. . .]
Your advice about the Indiaman is a very wise advice, because it
just suits me, though you are a little in the wrong concerning its de-
stroying the energies of Mind: on the contrary it would be the finest
thing in the world to strengthen them—To be thrown among people who care not for you, with whom you have no sympathies

³Wordsworth's "Intimations" *Ode* 181–82; the syntax subordinates this phrase in a "though" clause, the main one stating a determination to "find strength in what re-mains behind." K's ensuing reference to Melancholist suggests that *Ode on Melancholy* may have been drafted around this time.

¹Text: Sieveking, 734–35; the first publication.

forces the Mind upon its own recources [resources?], and leaves it free to make its speculations of the differences of human character and to class them with the calmness of a Botanist. An Indiaman is a little world. One of the great reasons that the english have produced the finest writers in the world; is, that the English world has ill-treated them during their lives and foster'd them after their deaths. They have in general been trampled aside into the bye paths of life and seen the festerings of Society. [. . .] The middle age of Shakspeare was all couded over; his days were not more happy than Hamlet's who is perhaps more like Shakspeare himself in his common every day Life than any other of his Characters—Ben Johnson was a common soldier and in the Low countries [. . .] For all this I will not go on board an Indiaman, nor for examples sake run my head into dark alleys: I dare say my discipline is to come, and plenty of it too. I have been very idle lately, very averse to writing; both from the overpowering idea of our dead poets and from abatement of my love of fame. I hope I am a little more of a Philosopher than I was, consequently a little less of a versifying Pet-lamb.[2] I have put no more into print or you should have had it. You will judge of my 1819 temper when I tell you that the thing I have most enjoyed this year has been writing an ode to Indolence. [. . .]

Ever sincerely yours'

John Keats.

Letters to Fanny Brawne, July 1819

Keats writes from the Isle of Wight to Fanny in Hampstead. The letters to Fanny Brawne, written from this July to September 1820, were first published by HBF in a little ornamented volume in 1877, scandalizing many, including Matthew Arnold and Charles Algernon Swinburne, as unseemly, unmanly. My text here is a subsection in HBF 1883, vol. 4, dedicated to Joseph Severn, the young artist whom John and George met in 1816, whose miniature of Keats was exhibited at the Royal Academy in late March 1819 and who was persuaded to accompany Keats to Rome when Brown could not be located. His now famous

---

[2]See *Ode on Indolence* 54; here, "a versifying" puns on "averse" in the sentence prior.

sketch of dying Keats's pillowed head, late January 1821, is the frontispiece for HBF's edition of the letters, in both 1877 and 1883.

My dearest Lady,   [1 July[1]]
    I am glad I had not an opportunity of sending off a Letter which I wrote for you on Tuesday night—'twas too much like one out of Rosseau's Heloise.[2] I am more reasonable this morning. The morning is the only proper time for me to write to a beautiful Girl whom I love so much: for at night, when the lonely day has closed, and the lonely, silent, unmusical Chamber is waiting to receive me as into a Sepulchre, then believe me my passion gets entirely the sway, then I would not have you see those Rapsodies which I once thought it impossible I should ever give way to, and which I have often laughed at in another, for fear you should either too unhappy or perhaps a little mad. I am now at a very pleasant Cottage window, looking onto a beautiful hilly country, with a glimpse of the sea; the morning is very fine. I do not know how elastic my spirit might be, what pleasure I might have in living here and breathing and wandering as free as a stag about this beautiful Coast if the remembrance of you did not weigh so upon me. I have never known any unalloy'd Happiness for many days together: the death or sickness of some one has always spoilt my hours—and now when none such troubles oppress me, it is you must confess very hard that another sort of pain should haunt me. Ask yourself my love whether you are not very cruel to have so entrammelled me, so destroyed my freedom. Will you confess this in the Letter you must write immediately and do all you can to console me in it—make it rich as a draught of poppies to intoxicate me—write the softest words and kiss them that I may at least touch my lips where yours have been. For myself I know not how to express my devotion to so fair a form: I want a brighter word than bright, a fairer word than fair. I almost wish we were butterflies and liv'd but three summer days— three such days with you I could fill with more delight than fifty common years could ever contain. But however selfish I may feel, I am sure I could never act selfishly: as I told you a day or two before

---

[1]HBF 4.125–27; this is K's first letter to her.

[2]K owned J.-J. Rousseau's popular version of the Paolo and Francesca story, *Julie; ou, La Nouvelle Héloise* (1761), in which the heroine falls passionately in love with her tutor, remains faithful to her marriage, and confesses her true love only on her deathbed.

I left Hampstead, I will never return to London if my Fate does not turn up Pam or at least a Court-card.[3] Though I could centre my Happiness in you, I cannot expect to engross your heart so entirely—indeed if I thought you felt as much for me as I do for you at this moment I do not think I could restrain myself from seeing you again tomorrow for the delight of one embrace. But no—I must live upon hope and Chance. In case of the worst that can happen, I shall still love you—but what hatred shall I have for another! Some lines I read the other day are continually ringing a peal in my ears:

> To see those eyes I prize above mine own
> Dart favors on another——
> And those sweet lips (yielding immortal nectar)
> Be gently press'd by any but myself——
> Think, think Francesca, what a cursed thing
> It were beyond expression![4]

J.

Do write immediately [. . .] I know before night I shall curse myself having sent you so cold a Letter; yet it is better to do it as much in my senses as possible. Be as kind as the distance will permit your

J. Keats

[. . .]

My sweet Girl, July 8th[5]

Your Letter gave me more delight than any thing in the world but yourself could do; indeed I am almost astonished that any absent one should have that luxurious power over my senses which I feel. Even when I am not thinking of you I receive your influence and a tenderer nature steeling upon me. All my thoughts, my unhappiest days and nights have I find not at all cured me of my love of Beauty, but made it so intense that I am miserable that you are not with me: or rather breathe in that dull sort of patience that

---

[3]Pam is the jack of clubs, the highest trump card in the game of Loo; the court-cards are picture cards.

[4]The Duke in Philip Massinger's *Duke of Milan: A Tragedie* (1623), confessing his jealous torments to his faithful wife Marcelia (not Francesca; K is thinking of Paolo's beloved): "Am I to live / To see those Eyes I prize above mine owne, / Dart favours (though compel'd) upon another? / Or those sweet Lips (yielding Immortall Nectar) / Be gently touch'd by any but my selfe? / Thinke, thinke Marcelia, what a cursed thing / I were, beyond expression" (Act I).

[5]HBF 4.128–29.

cannot be called Life. I never knew before, what such a love as you have made me feel, was; I did not believe in it; my Fancy was afraid of it, lest it should burn me up. But if you will fully love me, though there may be some fire, 'twill not be more than we can bear when moistened and bedewed with Pleasures. You mention "horrid people" and ask me whether it depend upon them, whether I see you again. Do understand me, my love, in this. I have so much of you in my heart that I must turn Mentor when I see a chance of harm beffaling you. I would never see any thing but Pleasure in your eyes, love on your lips, and Happiness in your steps. I would wish to see you among those amusements suitable to your inclinations and spirits; so that our loves might be a delight in the midst of Pleasures agreeable enough, rather than a resource from vexations and cares. But I doubt much, in case of the worst, whether I shall be philosopher enough to follow my own Lessons: if I saw my resolution give you a pain I could not. Why may I not speak of your Beauty since without that I could never have lov'd you?—I cannot conceive any beginning of such love as I have for you but Beauty. There may be a sort of love for which, without the least sneer at it, I have the highest respect and can admire it in others: but it has not the richness, the bloom, the full form, the enchantment of love after my own heart. So let me speak of you Beauty, though to my own endangering; if you could be so cruel to me as to try elsewhere its Power. You say you are afraid I shall think you do not love me—in saying this you make me ache the more to be near you. I am at the diligent use of my faculties here, I do not pass a day without sprawling some blank verse or tagging some rhymes; and here I must confess, that (since I am on that subject) I love you the more in that I believe you have liked me for my own sake and for nothing else. I have met with women whom I really think would like to be married to a Poem and to be given away by a Novel. I have seen your Comet, and only wish it was a sign that poor Rice would get well whose illness makes him rather a melancholy companion: and the more so as so to conquer his feelings and hide them from me, with a forc'd Pun. I kiss'd your writing over in the hope you had indulg'd me by leaving a trace of honey. What was your dream? Tell it me and I will tell you the interpretation thereof.

Ever yours, my love!
John Keats.

Do not accuse me of delay—we have not here an opportunity of sending letters every day. Write speedily.

My love,   [15 July[6]]
    I have been in so irritable a state of health these two or three last days, that I did not think I should be able to write this week. Not that I was so ill, but so much so as only to be capable of an unhealthy teasing letter. To night I am greatly recovered only to feel the languor I have felt after you touched with ardency. You say you perhaps might have made me better: you would then have made me worse: now you could quite effect a cure: What fee my sweet Physician would I not give you to do so. Do not call it folly, when I tell you I took your letter last night to bed with me. In the morning I found your name on the sealing wax obliterated. I was startled at the bad omen till I recollected that it must have happened in my dreams, and they you know fall out by contraries. You must have found out by this time I am a little given to bode ill like the raven; it is my misfortune not my fault; it has proceeded from the general tenor of the circumstances of my life, and rendered every event suspicious. However I will no more trouble either you or myself with sad Prophecies; though so far I am pleased at it as it has given me opportunity to love your disinterestedness[7] towards me. I can be a raven no more; you and pleasure take possession of me at the same moment. I am afraid you have been unwell. If through me illness have touched you (but it must be with a very gentle hand) I must be selfish enough to feel a little glad at it. Will you forgive me this? I have been reading lately an oriental tale of a very beautiful color[8] — It is of a city of melancholy men, all made so by this circumstance. Through a series of adventures each one of them by turns reach some gardens of Paradise where they meet with a most enchanting Lady; and just as they are going to embrace her, she bids them shut their eyes—they shut them—and on opening their eyes again find themselves descending to the earth in a magic basket. The remembrance of

[6]HBF 4.130–33.

[7]selflessness; the opposite of selfishness/self-interest.

[8]A tale derived from *The Thousand and One Nights*; Rollins cites "The History of the Basket," in a book K was reading, *Henry Weber's Tales of the East* (Edinburgh, 1812), 2.666–74, in which the memory of the enchanted garden "renders all the pleasures of the world insipid" (677).

this Lady and their delights lost beyond all recovery render them melancholy ever after. How I applied this to you, my dear; how I palpitated at it; how the certainty that you were in the same world with myself, and though as beautiful, not so talismanic as that Lady; how I could not bear you should be so you must believe because I swear it by yourself. I cannot say when I shall get a volume ready. I have three or four stories half done, but as I cannot write for the mere sake of the press, I am obliged to let them progress or lie still as my fancy chooses. By Christmas perhaps they may appear, but I am not yet sure they ever will. 'Twill be no matter, for Poems are as common as newspapers and I do not see why it is a greater crime in me than in another to let the verses of an half-fledged brain tumble into the reading-rooms and drawing room windows. [. . .]

your letters keep me alive. My sweet Girl I cannot speak my love for you. Good night! and

Ever yours

John Keats.

My sweet Girl,   Sunday Night   [25 July][9]
              I hope you did not blame me much for not obeying your request of a Letter on Saturday; we have had four in our small room playing at cards night and morning leaving me no undisturb'd opportunity to write. Now Rice and Martin are gone I am at liberty. Brown[10] to my sorrow confirms the account you give of your ill health. You cannot conceive how I ache to be with you: how I would die for one hour——for what is in the world? I say you cannot conceive; it is impossible you should look with such eyes upon me as I have upon you: it cannot be. Forgive me if I wander a little this evening, for I have been all day employ'd in a very abstrct Poem[11] and I am in deep love with you—two things which must excuse me. I have, believe me, not been an age in letting you take possession of me; the very first week I knew you I wrote myself your vassal; but burnt the Letter as the very next time I saw you I thought you manifested some dislike to me. If you should ever feel for Man at the first sight what I did for you, I am

[9]HBF 4.133–35.

[10]He arrived around the 22d.

[11]Maybe the unfinished *Hyperion* project; maybe a poem to/about being in love.

lost. Yet I should not quarrel with you, but hate myself if such a thing were to happen—only I should burst if the thing were not as fine as a Man as you are as a Woman. Perhaps I am too vehement, then fancy me on my knees, especially when I mention a part of your Letter which hurt me; you say speaking of Mr Severn "but you must be satisfied in knowing that I admired you much more than your friend." My dear love, I cannot believe there ever was or ever could be any thing to admire in me especially as far as sight goes—I cannot be admired, I am not a thing to be admired. You are, I love you; all I can bring you is a swooning admiration of your Beauty. I hold that place among Men which snub-nos'd brunettes with meeting eyebrows do among women—they are trash to me—unless I should find one among them with a fire in her heart like the one that burns in mine. You absorb me in spite of myself——you alone: for I look not forward with any pleasure to what is call'd being settled in the world; I tremble at domestic cares—yet for you I would meet them, though if it would leave you the happier I would rather die than do so. I have two luxuries to brood over in my walks, your Loveliness and the hour of my death. O that I could have possession of them both in the same minute. I hate the world: it batters too much the wings of my self-will, and would I could take a sweet poison from your lips to send me out of it. From no others would I take it. I am indeed astonish'd to find myself so careless of all charms but yours—remembring as I do the time when even a bit of ribband was a matter of interest with me. What softer words can I find for you after this— what it is I will not read. Nor will I say more here, but in a Postscript answer any thing else you may have mentioned in your Letter in so many words——for I am distracted with a thousand thoughts. I will imagine you Venus tonight and pray, pray, pray to your star like a Hethen.

Your's ever, fair Star,
John Keats

My seal is mark'd like a family table cloth with my Mother's initial F for Fanny: put between my Father's initials. You will soon hear from me again [. . .]

Letter to Benjamin Bailey, 14 August 1819[1]

Bailey is in Scotland; Keats is with Brown in Winchester, musing on his ambitions, Milton, Shakespeare, and bluestocking women.

We removed to Winchester for the convenience of a Library and find it an exceeding pleasant Town, enriched with a beautiful Cathedrall and surrounded by a fresh-looking country. We are in tolerably good and cheap Lodgings. Within these two Months I have written 1500 Lines, most of which besides many more of prior composition you will probably see by next Winter. I have written two Tales, one from Boccacio call'd the Pot of Basil; and another call'd St Agnes' Eve on a popular superstition; and a third call'd Lamia ——— [. . .] I sincerely hope you will be pleased when my Labours since we last saw each other shall reach you – One of my Ambitions is to make as great a revolution in modern dramatic writing as Kean has done in acting – another to upset the drawling of the bluestocking literary world[2] – if in the course of a few years I do these two things I ought to die content – and my friends should drink a dozen of Claret on my Tomb – I am convinced more and more every day that (excepting the human friend Philosopher) a fine writer is the most genuine Being in the World – Shakspeare and the paradise Lost every day become greater wonders to me. I look upon fine Phrases like a Lover — [. . .]

Ever your sincere friend
John Keats.

Letter to John Taylor, 23 August 1819[1]

Keats is in Winchester, asking for an advance from his publisher in London.

My dear Taylor –

You will perceive that I do not write you till I am forced by necessity: that I am sorry for. You must forgive me for entering abruptly on the subject, merely pefixing an intreaty that

[1]ALS, Houghton Library, Harvard.
[2]On K's animosity to literary women, see the letter to Reynolds, 21 Sept. 1817 (p. 59).

[1]ALS, Houghton Library, Harvard; first printed in 1925 by Amy Lowell in *John Keats* 2.295–97.

you will not consider my business manner of wording and proceeding any distrust of, or stirrup standing against you; but put it to the account of a desire of order and regularity – I have been rather unfortunate lately in money concerns [. . .] For these three Months Brown has 'advanced' me money: he is not at all flush and I am anxious to get some elsewhere – We have together been engaged (this I should wish to remain secret) in a Tragedy which I have just finish'd; and from which we hope to share moderate Profits. Being thus far connected, Brown proposed to me, to stand with me responsible for any money you may advance to me to drive through the summer[2] – I must observe again that it is not from want of reliance on you readiness to assist me that I offer a ~~Bondill~~; but as a relief to myself from a too lax sensation of Life— which ought to be responsible which requires chains for its own sake—[. . .] I feel every confidence that if I choose I may be a popular writer; that I will never be; but for all that I will get a livelihood – I equally dislike the favour of the public with the love of a woman – they are both a cloying treacle to the wings of independence. I shall ever consider them (People) as debtors to me for verses, not myself to them for admiration—which I can do without. [. . .]

Ever yours sincerely
John Keats

Letter to J. H. Reynolds, 24 August 1819[1]

Reynolds is in London; Keats is still in Winchester, reading Paradise Lost, *hating the public and loving poetry.*

My dear Reynolds, [. . .]

I am convinced more and more day by day that fine writing is next to fine doing, the top thing in the world; the Paradise Lost becomes a greater wonder – The more I know what my diligence may in time probably effect; the more does my heart distend with Pride and Obstinacy[2] – I

[2]On 5 Sept. K thanked his publishers for "Bank post Bill of 30£——." (sent by Taylor's partner Hessey); he also received £30–40 from his friend Haslam.

---

[1]ALS, Berg collection, New York Public Library.
[2]Viewing his defeated troops rallying in hell, Satan's "heart / Distends with pride and, hard'ning in his strength, / Glories" (*PL* 1.571–73).

feel it in my power to become a popular writer – I feel it in my strength
to refuse the poisonous suffrage of a public – [. . .] I think if I had a
free and healthy and lasting organisation of heart and Lungs as
strong as an oxe's – so as to be able unhurt the shock of extreme
thought and sensation without weariness, I could pass my Life very
nearly alone though it should last eighty years. But I feel my Body
too weak to support me to the height; I am obliged continually to check
myself and strive to be nothing. [. . .] If you should have any reason
to regret this sate of excitement in me, I will turn the tide of your
feelings in the right channel by mentioning that it is the only state
for the best sort of Poetry – that is all I care for, all I live for. [. . .]

Ever your affectionate friend
John Keats

Letter to J. H. Reynolds, 21 September 1819[1]

*Reynolds is visiting the Woodhouse home, in the resort town of Bath.
Keats in Winchester is thinking about Milton, Chatterton, his dissatis-
faction with his* Hyperion *project, and the autumn season.*

My dear Reynolds, [. . .]
How beautiful the season is now – How fine the air. A temperate
sharpness about it. Really, without joking, chaste weather – Dian skies –
I never lik'd stubble fields so much as now – Aye better than the chilly
green of the Spring. Somehow a stubble plain looks warm – in the same
way that some pictures look warm. this struck me so much in my
Sunday's walk that I composed upon it.[2] I hope you are better employed
than in gaping after weather. I have been at different times so happy
as not to know what weather it was – No I will not copy a parcel of verses.
I always somehow associate Chatterton with autumn. He is the purest
writer in the English Language. He has no French idiom, or particles
like Chaucers — 'tis genuine English Idiom in English Words. I have
given up Hyperion – there were too many Miltonic inversions[3] in it –

[1]WLB 34–37.
[2]Woodhouse identifies *To Autumn.*
[3]Milton's Latinate poetic syntax, e.g., "to the level of his ear / Leaning with parted
lips some words she spake" (*Hyperion* 1.46–47).

Miltonic verse cannot be written but in an artful or rather artist's humour. I wish to give myself up to other sensations. English ought to be kept up. It may be interesting to you to pick out some lines from Hyperion and put a mark X to the false beauty proceeding from art, and one // to the true voice of feeling. Upon my soul 'twas imagination I cannot make the distinction – Every now &then there is a Miltonic intonation – But I cannot make the division properly. [. . .] To-night I am all in a mist; I scarcely know what's what. But you knowing my unsteady & vagarish[4] disposition, will guess that all this turmoil will be settled by tomorrow morning. It strikes me tonight that I have led a very odd sort of life for the two or three last years – Here &there – No anchor – I am glad of it. [. . .]

Ever your affectionate friend
John Keats —

Letter to Richard Woodhouse, 21–22 September 1819[1]

> Woodhouse is also in Bath; Keats in Winchester is feeling critical of the poetry he has been writing.

Dear Woodhouse, [. . .]

I will give you a few reasons why I shall persist in not publishing The Pot of Basil. It is too smokeable.[2] I can get it smoak'd at the Carpenters shaving chimney much more cheaply – There is too much inexperience of live, and simplicity of Knowledge in it – which might do very well after one's death – but not while one is alive. There are very few would look to the reality. I intend to use more finesse with the Public. It is possible to write fine things which cannot be laugh'd at in any way. Isabella is what I should call were I a reviewer 'A weak-sided Poem' with an amusing sober-sadness about it. Not that I do not think Reynolds and you are quite right about it[3] – it is enough for me.

---

[4]wandering, erratic, whimsical (*OED*); for "mist," see the letter to Reynolds, 3 May 1818 (p. 130).

---

[1]ALS, Houghton Library, Harvard; first printed by Amy Lowell in *The John Keats Memorial Volume*, ed. George Williamson (London: John Lane, 1921), pp. 115–20.

[2]easy to see through and ridicule

[3]Both liked it, and thought it would answer the bad reviews of *Endymion*.

268 • *Isabella* and *Lamia*

But this will not do to be public – If I may so say, in my dramatic capacity I enter fully into the feeling: but in Propria Persona[4] I should be apt to quiz[5] it myself – There is no objection of this kind to Lamia—A good deal to St Agnes Eve – only not so glaring – [. . .] Let me know how you pass your times and how you are -

Your sincere friend
John Keats —

Hav'nt heard from Taylor[6] —

Letter to C. W. Dilke, 22 September 1819[1]

Dilke is in London. Keats is back in Winchester, alone, having spent a month in London; he is (still) thinking about writing for the periodicals.

My dear Dilke, [. . .]

I have taken to endeavour to acqure something by temporary writing in periodical works. You must agree with me how unwise it is to keep feeding upon hopes, which depending so much on the state of temper and imagination, appear gloomy or bright, near or afar off just as it happens - Now an act has three parts - to act, to do, and to perform[2] - I mean I should <u>do</u> something for my immediate welfare - Even if I am swept away like a Spider from a drawing room I am determined to spin - home spun any thing for sale. Yea I will trafic. Any thing but Mortgage my Brain to Blackwood.[3] I am determined not to ~~layie~~ like a dead lump. [. . .] It is fortunate I have not before this been tempted to venture on the common.[4] I should a year or two

---

[4]"My Own Person" (not a literary character—say, a "Romance" narrator).

[5]make fun of, ridicule.

[6]Suffering from London's oppressive, dirty air, Taylor had gone to visit his father in Nottingham; Keats had closed his letter of 5 Sept. thanking him for the loan with wishes that he would send news of his health.

---

[1]Transcribed from K's ms, published in G. Williamson, ed. *The Keats Letters, Papers, & c* (1914), plates xxx–xxxiii.

[2]Two rustics, discussing the question of Ophelia's drowning (*Hamlet* 5.1.11–13).

[3]*Blackwood's Edinburgh Magazine* hosted Z's diatribes on the "Cockney School."

[4]become a street-walking prostitute

ago have spoken my mind on every subject with the utmost simplicity. I hope I have learnt a little better and am confident I shall be able to cheat as well as any literary Jew of the Market and shine up an article on any thing without much knowlege of the subject, aye like an orange. I would willingly have recourse to other means. I cannot; I am fit for nothing but literature. [. . .] If better events supersede this necessity what harm will be done? I have no trust whatever on Poetry – I dont wonder at it – the mavel it to me how people read so much of it. I think you will see the reasonableness of my plan. To forward it I purpose living in cheap Lodgng in Town, that I may be in the reach of books and information, of which there is here a plentiful lack.[5] If I can any place tolerably comfitable I will settle myself and fag[6] till I can affrad to buy Pleasure – which if never can afford I must go without – Talking of Pleasure, this moment I was writing with one hand, and with the other holding to my Mouth a Nectarine – good god how fine – It went down soft pulpy, slushy, oozy – all its delicious embonpoint melted down my throat like a large beatified Strawberry. I shall certainly breed. Now I come to my request. Should you like me for a neighbour again? Come, plump it out, I wont blush. [. . .] Notwithstand my aristocratic temper I cannot help being very much pleas'd with the present public proceedings.[7] I hope sincerely I shall be able to put a Mite of help to the Liberal side of the Question before I die [. . .]

Ever your sincere friend

John Keats –

Letter to Charles Brown, 23 September 1819[1]

[. . .] I assure you, I am as far from being unhappy as possible. Imaginary grievances have always been more my torment than real ones. You know this well. Real ones will never have any other effect upon me than to stimulate me to get out of or avoid them. This is easily accounted for. Our imaginary woes are conjured up by our

[5]Old men have "a plentiful lack" of wit, says Hamlet to Polonius (2.2).

[6]work away

[7]The agitation for Parliamentary reform, most spectacularly in the "Peterloo" events of August and the continuing reports in *The Examiner.*

[1]*1848* 2.30–31. K is still in Winchester, making plans.

passions, and are fostered by passionate feeling: our real ones come of themselves, and are opposed by an abstract exertion of mind. Real grievances are displacers of passion. The imaginary nail a man down for a sufferer, as on a cross; the real spur him up into an agent. I wish, at one view, you would see my heart towards you. 'Tis only from a high tone of feeling that I can put that word upon paper— out of poetry. [. . .] I am convinced, out and out, that by prosing for a while in periodical works, I may maintain myself decently.

Letter to George (and Georgiana) Keats, 17–27 September 1819, with "Pensive they sit"[1]

Still in Winchester, Keats confesses his low moods, his desire for financial security, the discourse of letter-writing and writing to distant correspondents, Chatterton's vs. Milton's English, Dilke's obsessiveness and illiberal intellect. He includes his poetic satire on lovers, "Pensive they sit."

My dear George, [. . .]

Mine I am sure is a tolerable tragedy[2] – it would have been a bank to me, if just as I had finish'd it I had not heard of Kean's resolution to go to America. That was the worst news I could have had. There is no actor can do the principal character besides Kean At Covent Garden there is a great chance of its being damn'd. Were it to succeed even there it would lift me out of the mire. I mean the mire of a bad reputation which is continually rising against me. My name with the literary fashionables is vulgar – I am a weaver boy to them – a Tragedy would lift me out of this mess. And mess it is as far as it regards our Pockets. But be not cast down any more than I am; I feel I can bear real ills better than imaginary ones. Whenever I find myself growing vapourish, I rouse myself, wash and put on a clean shirt brush my hair and clothes, tie my shoestrings neatly and in fact adonize as I were going out – then all clean and comfortable I sit down to write. This I find the greatest relief – Besides I am becoming accustom'd to

---

[1] ALS, Pierpont Morgan Library; GK is addressed, but K knows that G's wife will be reading along.

[2] *Otho the Great*; K and Brown had hoped Kean would act the part of mad, passionate Ludoph and they wrote the part with him in mind; *Otho* was first published in *1848* (2.111–203).

the privations of the pleasures of sense. In the midst of the world I live like a Hermit. I have forgot how to lay plans for enjoyment of any Pleasure. I feel I can bear any thing any misery, even imprisonment – so long as I have neither wife nor child. [. . .]
I saw Haslam he is very much occupied with love [. . .] Lover to a young woman. He show'd me her Picture by Severn– I think she is, though not very cunning, too cunning for him. Nothing strikes me so forcibly with a sense of the rediculous[3] as love. A Man in love I do think cuts the sorryest figure in the world. Even when I know a poor fool tobe really in pain about it, I could burst out laughing in his face – His pathetic visage becomes irrisistable. Not that I take Haslam as a pattern for Lovers – he is a very worthy man and a good friend. His love is very amusing. Somewhere in the Spectator is related an account of a Man inviting a party of stutterrs and squinters to his table– 't would please me more to scrape together a party of Lovers, not to dinner – not to tea. The would be no fighting as among Knights of old –

> Pensive they sit, and roll their languid eyes[4]
> Nibble their tosts, and cool their tea with sighs,
> Or else forget the purpose of the night
> Forget their tea – forget their appetite.
> See with cross'd arms they sit – ah hapless crew
> The fire is going out, and no one rings
> For coals, and therefore no coals betty[5] brings.
> A Fly is in the milk pot – must he die
> Circled by a humane Society?[6]
> No no there m^r Werter[7] takes his spoon
> Inverts it – dips the handle and lo, soon
> The little struggler sav'd from perils dark
> Across the teaboard draws a long wet mark.
> Romeo! Arise! take Snuffers by the handle
> There's a large Cauliflower in each candle.

[3]A punning *reddening* of *ridiculous* (passion-blush).

[4]First published in a U.S. newspaper, 1877, then in HBF, 1883.

[5]generic name for a servant girl

[6]The Royal Humane Society was founded in 1774 to rescue suicidal drowners.

[7]The hero of Goethe's sensational novel (1773), trans. D. Malthus as *The Sorrows of Werter* (1783), kills himself in despair of love—a fiction that set off a wave of imitations across Europe.

A winding-sheet[8] – Ah me! I must away
To no 7 just beyond the Circus gay.[9]
'Alas' my friend! your Coat sits very well:
Where may your Taylor live'?' 'I may not tell –
'O pardon me – I'mabsent: now and then."
Where <u>might</u> my Taylor live?[10] – I say again
I cannot tell – let me no more be teas'd –
He lives in wapping[11] <u>might</u> live where he pleasd.

You see I cannot get on without writing as boys do at school a few nonsense verses. [. . .]

[18 September] With my inconstant disposition it is no wonder that this morning, amid all our bad times and misfortunes, I should feel so alert and well spirited. At this moment you are perhaps in a very different State of Mind. It is because my hopes are very paramount to my despair. I have been reading over a part of a short poem I have composed lately call'd 'Lamia' - and I am certain there is that sort of fire in it which must take hold of people in some way – give them either pleasant or unpleasant sensation. What they want is a sensation of some sort. [. . .]

I have been reading lately Burton's Anatomy of Melancholy; and I think you will be very much amused with a page I here coppy for you. I call it a Feu de joie [. . .] Band playing "Amo, Amas &c"[12] "Every Lover admires his Mistress, though she be very deformed of herself, ill-favored, wrinkled, pimpled, pale, red, yellow, tann'd, tallow-fac'd, have a swoln juglers platter face, or a thin, lean, chitty face, have clouds in her face, be crooked, dry, bald, goggle-eyed, blear-eyed or with staring eyes, she looks like a squis'd cat, hold her head still awry, heavy, dull, hollow-eyed, black or yellow about the eyes, or squint-eyed, sparrow-mouth'd, Persean hook-nosed, have a sharp fox nose, a red nose, China flat, great nose, nare simo patuloque,[13] a nose like a promontory, gubber-tush'd, rotten teeth, black, uneven, brown teeth,

---

[8]The wax drippings, looking like funerary wrapping for a corpse, are superstitiously regarded as an omen of death.

[9]Picadilly Circus (circle) in London is a district with fashionable tailors.

[10]It's hard to imagine K is not punning on his publisher.

[11]East London dock-district, where cheap, ready-made clothing is sold.

[12]*Amo, amas, amat* (I love, you love, he loves) is one of the first lessons of Latin. K copies the passage (from *Anatomy* III.2.iii.i) very carefully.

[13]nose flat and spreading.

beetle-brow'd, a witches beard, her breath stink all over the room, her
nose drop winter and summer, with a Bavarian poke under her chin,
a sharp chin, lave-eared, with a long crane's neck, which stands awry
too, pendulis mammis,[14] her dugs like two double jugs, or else no dugs
in the other extream, bloody-falln fingers, she have filthy, long, unpaired,
nails, scabbed hands or wrists, a tan'd skin, a rotton carcass, crooked
back, she stoops, is lame, splea footed, as slender in the middle as a cow
in the wast, gowty legs, her ankles hang over her shooes, her feet stink,
she breed lice, a meer changeling, a very monster, anaufe imperfect,[15]
her whole complexion savors, an harsh voice, incondite gesture, vile gate,
a vast virago, or an ugly tit, a slug, a fat fustilugs, a trusse, a long
lean rawbone, a Skeleton, a Sneaker (si qua patent meliora puta[16])
and to thy Judgement looks like a maid in a Lanthorn, whom thou
couldst not fancy for a world, but hatest, loathest, and wouldst have
spit in her face, or blow thy nose in her bosom, remedium amoris[17] to
another man, a dowdy, a Slut, a scold, a nasty rank, rammy, filthy,
beastly quean,[18] dishonest peradventure, obscene, base, beggarly, rude,
foolish, untaught–peevish, Irus' daughter, Thersite's sister, Grobian's
Scholler;[19] if he love her once, he admires her for all this, he takes no
notice of any such errors or imperfections of boddy or mind." There's
a dose for you – fine!! I would give my favorite leg to have written this
as a speech in a Play: with what effect could Matthews[20] pop-gun it at
the pit! This I think will amuse you more than so much Poetry [. . .]
[20 September] I must take an opportunity here to observe that though
I am writing <u>to</u> you I am all the while writing <u>at</u> your Wife – This
explanation will account for my speaking sometimes <u>hoity-toityishly.</u>
Whereas if you were alone I should sport a little more sober sadness.
I am like a squintng gentleman who saying soft things to one Lady

[14]hanging tits

[15]half wit

[16]think whether better things lie open (instead of *patent* Burton has *latent*: what hidden things. . .).

[17]love-remedy; following his *Ars Amatoria* (The Arts of Love), Ovid wrote a volume of elegiac poetry, *Remedia Amoris.*

[18]prostitute

[19]A Grobian is a slut; Irus is a beggar in *The Odyssey*; Thersites, a scurrilous Greek officer in *Troilus and Cressida*, wields a detailed vocabulary of contempt for humanity, especially the lovers.

[20]Charles Matthews (1776–1835), friend of Coleridge and Lamb, was a celebrated comedian (a forerunner of stand-up comics). The pit has the cheapest seats, nearest the stage.

ogles another – or what is as bad in arguing with a person on his left hand appeals with his eyes to one one the right. His Vision is elastic he bends it to a certain object but having a patent spring it flies off. Writing has this disadvange of speaking – one cannot <u>write</u> a wink, or a nod, or a grin, or a purse of the Lips, or a <u>smile</u> – O law! One can-[not[21]] put ones pinger to one's nose, or yerk ye in the ribs,[22] or lay hold of your button in writing – but in all the most lively and titterly parts of my Letter you must not fail to imagine me as the epic poets say – now here, now there, now with one foot pointed at the ceiling, now with another – now with my pen on my ear, now with my elbow in my mouth. O my friends you loose the action – and attitude is every thing as Fusili said when he took up his leg like a Musket to shoot a Swallow just darting behind his shoulder.[23] [. . .]

[21 September . . .] there can be nothing so remembrancing and enchaining as a good long letter be it composed of what it may – From the time you left me, our friends say I have altered completely – am not the same person – perhaps in this letter I am for in a letter one takes up one's existence from the time we last met – I dare say you have altered also – every man does – Our bodies every seven years are completely fresh-materiald – seven years ago it was not this hand that clench'd itself against Hammond.[24] We are like the relict garments of a Saint: the same and not the same: for the careful Monks patch it and patch it: till there's not a thread of the original garment left, and still they show it for Sᵗ Anthony's shirt. This is the reason why men who had been bosom friends, on being separated for any number of years, afterwards meet coldly, neither of them knowing why – The fact is they are both altered – Men who live together have a silent ~~p~~ moulding, and influencing power over each other. They interassimulate.[25] 'T is an uneasy thought that in seven years the same hands cannot greet each other–again. All this may be obviated by a willful and dramatic exercise of our Minds towards each other. Some think I have lost that poetic ardour and fire 'tis said I once had – the fact is perhaps I have: but instead of that I hope I shall substitute a more thoughtful and

---

[21]K began this word at the end of the line but didn't complete it on the new line.

[22]Iago to Othello, on the prospect of stabbing some rival (*Othello* 1.2.5).

[23]Swiss painter Henri Fuseli (1714–1825), with a pun on *fusil* (musket); the whole is a farcical application of K's admiration of Miltonic "stationing" (see p. 236).

[24]K was apprenticed to surgeon Thomas Hammond for three years, starting in 1811.

[25]K-coinage, combining *inter-*, *assimilate*, and *simulate*.

quiet power. I am more frequently, now, contented to read and think –
but now & then, haunted with ambitious thoughts. Quiter in my pulse,
improved in my digestion; exerting myself against vexing speculations –
scarcely content to write the best verses for the fever they leave behind.
I want to compose without this fever. I hope I one day shall. You
would scarcely imagine I could live alone so comfortably "Kepen in
solitarinesse"[26] I told Anne, the servant here, the other day, to say I
was not at home[27] if any one should call. I am not certain how I
should endue loneliness and bad weather together. Now the time is
beautiful. I take a walk every day for one hour before dinner[28] [. . .]
In the course of a few months I shall be as good an Italian Scholar as
I am a french one. I am reading Ariosto at present: not managing
more than six or eight stanzas at a time. When I have done this
language so as tobe able to read it tolerably well – I shall set myself
to get complete in latin, and there my learning must stop. I do not
think of venturing upon Greek. I would not go even so far if I were not
persuaded of the power the knowlege of any language gives one. the
fact is I like to be acquainted with foreign languages. It is besides a nice
way of filling up intervals &c Also the reading of Dante in well worth
the while. And in latin there is a fund of curious literature of the
middle ages. [. . .] I shall never become attach'd to a foreign idiom so
as to put it into my writings. The Paradise lost though so fine in itself
is a curruption of our Language – it should be kept as it is unique –
a curiosity. a beautiful and grand Curiosity. The most remarkable
Production of the world. A northern[29] dialect accommodating itself to
greek and latin inversions and intonations. The purest english I think –
or what ought to be the purest – is Chatterton's. The Language had
existed long enough to be entirely uncorrupted of Chaucer's gallicisms,[30]
and still the old words are used – Chatterton's language is entirely
northern – I prefer the native music of it to Milton's ~~cult~~ cut by feet.[31]

---

[26]A self-quotation from *The Eve of St. Mark*, which K had transcribed earlier in the letter.

[27]not receiving visitors (he doesn't mean for her to lie)

[28]midday meal

[29]not Frenchified, native to the British Isles

[30]From the Norman conquest in 1066 into the 14th c., the language of court and culture was French.

[31]Dr. Johnson famously complained that Milton's blank verse was prose cut into in meters.

I have but lately stood on my guard against Milton. Life to him would be death to me – Miltonic verse cannot be written but ~~it~~ the vein of art – I wish to devote myself to another sensation – [24 September . . .] I wrote to Brown a comment [. . .] wherein I explained what I thought of Dilke's Character. Which resolved itself into this conclusion. That Dilke was a Man who cannot feel he has a personal identity unless he has made up his Mind about every thing. The only means of strengthening one's intellect is to make up ones mind about nothing – to let the mind be a thoroughfare for all thoughts. Not a select party. The genus is not scarce in population. All the stubborn arguers you meet with are of the same brood— They never begin upon a subject they have not preresolved on. They want to hammer their nail into you and if you turn the point, still they think you wrong. Dilke will never come at a truth as long as he lives; because he is always trying at it. He is a Godwin-methodist[32] [. . .] Believe me my dear brother and Sister –

Your affectionate and anxious Brother

Letter to Fanny Brawne, 13 October 1819[1]

Brown visited in Winchester, then both returned to London on 8 October. On the 10th, Keats saw Fanny in Hampstead.

My dearest Girl,

This moment I have set myself to copy some verses out fair. I cannot proceed with any degree of content. I must write you a line or two and see if that will assist in dismissing you from my Mind for ever so short a time. Upon my Soul I can think of nothing else. The time is passed when I had power to advise and warn you against the unpromising morning of my Life. My love has made me selfish. I cannot exist without you. I am forgetful of every thing but seeing you again – my

---

[32]Like Shelley, Dilke was a fan of William Godwin's *Political Justice* (1793), an "anarchist" tract against government institutions and a brief for the power of reasoning men.

---

[1]K's ms is transcribed from the photo-facsimile ALS in A. E. Hancock, *John Keats* (Boston: Houghton Mifflin, 1908), after p. 188.

Life seems to stop there – I see no further. You have absorb'd me. I have a sensation at the present moment as though I was dissolving – I should be exquisitely miserable without the hope of soon seeing you. I should be affraid to separate myself far from you. My sweet Fanny, will your heart never change? My love, will it? I have no limit now to my love – You note came in just here – I cannot be happier away from you. 'Tis richer than an Argosy of Pearles. Do not threat me even in jest. I have been astonished that Men could die Martyrs for religion – I have shudder'd at it. I shudder no more— I could be martyr'd for my Religion – Love is my religion – I could die for that. I could die for you. My Creed is Love and you are its only tenet. You have ravish'd me away by a Power I cannot resist; and yet I ~~can~~could resist till I saw you; and even since I have seen you I have endeavoured often 'to reason against the reasons of my Love"[2] I can do that no more – the pain would be too great – My love is selfish – I cannot breathe without you.

Yours for ever
John Keats.

Letter to Fanny Brawne, 19 October 1819[1]

Keats, in London, has decided to move back to Wentworth Place, in Hampstead.

My sweet Fanny,

    *On awakening from my three days dream ("I cry to dream again")[2] I find one and another astonish'd at my idleness and thoughtlessness. I was miserable last night – the morning is always restorative – I must be busy, or try to be so. I have several things to speak to you of tomorrow morning. M*rs *Dilke I should think will tell you that I purpose living at Hampstead – I must impose chains upon*

---

[2]In John Ford's *'Tis Pity She's a Whore* (1633), Giovanni confesses his passion to his sister Annabella: "I have . . . / Ran over all my thoughts, despised my fate, / Reasoned against the reasons of my love, / . . . But found all bootless: 'tis my destiny / That you must either love, or I must die" (1.2.219–25).

---

[1]ALS, Houghton Library, Harvard.

[2]Echoing Caliban's longing for the music of his dream: "when I wak'd / I cried to dream again" (*Tempest* 3.2).

myself – I shall be able to do nothing. I shold like to cast the die for Love or death – I have no Patience with any thing else – if you ever intend to be cruel to me as you say in jest now but perhaps may sometimes be in earnest be so now – and I will – my mind is in a tremble, I cannot tell what I am writing.

Ever my love yours
John Keats

"The day is gone"[1]

The day is gone, and all its sweets are gone!
 Sweet voice, sweet lips, soft hand, and softer breast
Warm breath, tranc'd whisper, tender semi tone,
 Bright eyes, accomplish'd shape, and lang'rous waist!
Vanish'd unseasonably at shut of eve[2]
 When the dusk Holiday, or Holinight
Of fragrant-curtain'd Love begins to weave
 The ~~texture thick of darkness~~
  woof of darkness, thick, for hid delight
   and all its budded charms
Faded the flower ~~of beuty from my eyes gaze~~
  sight Beauty ~~sad~~ eyes
 Faded the ~~voice~~ of ~~Love~~ from my ~~sad ears~~
Faded the shape of beauty from my arms,
 Faded the voice, ~~the Whiteness~~
   warmth, whiteness, ~~brilliance~~ paradise
  But, as I have read love's Missal through to day,
  He'll let me sleep – seeing I fast and pray –

[1]Autograph ms, Pierpont Morgan Library. First published in 1838, then, tidied up with reference to Charles Brown's copy, in *1848* (Sonnet XVIII; 2.304), there dated "1819" (reported by Brown and Woodhouse). That Fanny Brawne had a ms suggests K may have sent this to her, as a poem-letter souvenir of a day together, shortly after their reunion in October.

[2]end of the evening, but with a ghost of Milton's pun on Eve's return to Adam "at shut of evening flowers" (*PL* 9.278)—underlined by K; note "paradise" in line 12.

Letter to John Taylor, 17 November 1819[1]

From Hampstead, Keats writes to the Fleet Street office, London, about his career so far.

My dear Taylor,
    I have come to a determination not to publish any thing I have now ready written; but for all that to publish a Poem before long and that I hope to make a fine one. As the marvellous is the most enticing and the surest guarantee of harmonious numbers[2] I have been endeavouring to persuade myself to untether Fancy and let her manage for herself[3] – I and myself cannot agree about this at all. Wonders are no wonders to me. I am more at home amongst Men and women. I would rather read Chaucer than Ariosto[4] – The little dramatic skill I may as yet have, however badly it might show in a Drama, would I think be sufficient for a Poem – I wish to diffuse the colouring of St Agnes eve throughout a Poem in which Character and Sentiment would be the figures to such drapery – Two or three such Poems, if God should spare me, written in the course of the next six years, would be a famous gradus ad Parnassum altissimum[5] – I mean they would nerve me up to the writing of a few fine Plays – my greatest ambition – when I do feel ambitious. I am sorry to say that is very seldom. The subject we have once or twice talked of appears a promising one, the Earl of Leicester's history. I am this morning reading Holingshed's Elisabeth.[6] You had some books awhile ago, you promised to lend me, illustrative of my Subject. If you can lay hold of them or any others which may be serviceable to me I know you will encourage my low-spirited Muse by sending them – or rather by letting me know when our Errand cart Man shall call with my little Box. I will endeavour to set my self selfishly at work on this Poem that is to be –
                                  Your sincere friend
                                    John Keats —

[1] ALS, Pierpont Morgan Library.
[2] Milton's description of the verse of *PL* (3.38), a phrase K underlined.
[3] See *Fancy* in *1820* (p. 363).
[4] Epic poet of the Italian Renaissance.
[5] Latin: step toward highest Parnassus (home of the muses).
[6] The Earl of Leicester was a favorite of Elizabeth I; Raphael Holinshed's *Chronicles of England, Scotland, and Ireland* (1577) was a source for Shakespeare's history plays.

Posthumously published poetry from 1819

from *Life, Letters, and Literary Remains* (1848)

Milnes gives a report of Keats newly moved to the Westminster district of London in early October as prelude to the ode "What can I do . . . ?"; 1848 is its only source (2.33–35), perhaps from Charles Brown's copy of the original sent to Fanny Brawne.

Keats took possession of his new abode. But he had miscalculated his own powers of endurance: the enforced absence from his friends was too much for him, and a still stronger impulse drew him back again to Hampstead. She, whose name

"Was ever on his lips
But never on his tongue,"

exercised too mighty a control over his being for him to remain at a distance, which was neither absence nor presence, and he soon returned to where at least he could rest his eyes on her habitation, and enjoy each chance opportunity of her society. I find a fragment written about this date, and under this inspiration, but it is still an interesting study of the human heart, to see how few traces remain in his outward literary life of that passion which was his real existence.

TO ———————.

What can I do to drive away
Remembrance from my eyes? for they have seen,
Aye, an hour ago, my brilliant Queen!
Touch has a memory. O say, love, say,

What can I do to kill it and be free
In my old liberty?
When every fair one that I saw was fair,
Enough to catch me in but half a snare,
Not keep me there:
When, howe'er poor or particolour'd things,   10
My muse had wings,
And ever ready was to take her course
Whither I bent her force,
Unintellectual, yet divine to me;——
Divine, I say!——What sea-bird o'er the sea
Is a philosopher the while he goes
Winging along where the great water throes?

How shall I do
To get anew
Those moulted feathers, and so mount once more   20
Above, above
The reach of fluttering Love,
And make him cower lowly while I soar?
Shall I gulp wine? No, that is vulgarism,
A heresy and schism,
Foisted into the canon law of love;——
No,——wine is only sweet to happy men;
More dismal cares
Seize on me unawares,——
Where shall I learn to get my peace again?[1]   30
To banish thoughts of that most hateful land,
Dungeoner of my friends, that wicked strand
Where they were wreck'd and live a wrecked life;
That monstrous region, whose dull rivers pour,
Ever from their sordid urns unto the shore,
Unown'd of any weedy-haired gods;
Whose winds, all zephyrless, hold scourging rods,
Iced in the great lakes, to afflict mankind;
Whose rank-grown forests, frosted, black, and blind,
Would fright a Dryad; whose harsh herbag'd meads   40

[1]The ode now turns 14 iambic pentameter lines, mostly rhymed, a memory of K's
sonnet-writing, and a performance of the formal exercise, pouncing couplets and all.

Make lean and lank the starv'd ox while he feeds;
There bad flowers have no scent, birds no sweet song,
And great unerring Nature once seems wrong.[2]

O, for some sunny spell
To dissipate the shadows of this hell!
Say they are gone,——with the new dawning light
Steps forth my lady bright!
O, let me once more rest
My soul upon that dazzling breast!
Let once again these aching arms be plac'd,   50
The tender gaolers° of thy waist!   *jailers*
And let me feel that warm breath here and there
To spread a rapture in my very hair,——
O, the sweetness of the pain!
Give me those lips again!
Enough! Enough! it is enough for me
To dream of thee!

ODE ON INDOLENCE.[1]

1819.

"They toil not, neither do they spin."[2]

I.

One morn before me were three figures seen,
    With bowed necks, and joined hands, side-faced;

---

[2]In K's imagination of anti-romantic America, his final couplet evokes Pope's *Essay on Man*: "All Nature is but Art, unknown to thee; / All Chance, Direction, which thou canst not see; / All Discord, Harmony, not understood; / All partial Evil, universal Good: / And, spite of Pride, in erring Reason's spite, / One truth is clear, "Whatever IS, is RIGHT" (1.289–94).

---

[1]First published in *1848* (2.276–78), this is the only ode of spring 1819 not in *1820*. K refuses the standard view of "Indolence" as culpable laxity. Even Thomson's iconic *Castle of Indolence* (1748) luxuriates in the pleasures before applying a moral. K cultivates the mood as a relaxation from normal cares and business. See his letters to Reynolds ("diligent Indolence"; 19 Feb. 1818, p. 105), Miss Jeffery (on this ode, 9 June 1819, p. 257), and G&GK (19 March 1819, p. 241) on its genesis.

[2]It is not indolence but spiritual nurture that Jesus exhorts in his Sermon on the Mount: "Take no thought for your life, what ye shall eat, or what ye shall drink; nor yet for your body, what ye shall put on. Is not the life more than meat, and the

And one behind the other stepp'd serene,
  In placid sandals, and in white robes graced;
    They pass'd, like figures on a marble urn,
  When shifted round to see the other side;
They came again; as when the urn once more
    Is shifted round, the first seen shades return;
  And they were strange to me, as may betide
With vases, to one deep in Phidian lore.[3]   10

II.

How is it, Shadows![4] that I knew ye not?
  How came ye muffled in so hush a mask?[5]
Was it a silent deep-disguised plot
  To steal away, and leave without a task
    My idle days? Ripe was the drowsy hour;
  The blissful cloud of summer-indolence
Benumb'd my eyes; my pulse grew less and less;
    Pain had no sting, and pleasure's wreath no flower:
  O, why did ye not melt, and leave my sense
Unhaunted quite of all but—nothingness?   20

III.

A third time pass'd they by, and, passing, turn'd
  Each one the face a moment whiles to me;
Then faded, and to follow them I burn'd
  And ached for wings, because I knew the three;
    The first was a fair Maid, and Love her name;
  The second was Ambition, pale of cheek,
And ever watchful with fatigued eye;
    The last, whom I love more, the more of blame

---

body than raiment . . . why take ye thought for raiment? Consider the lilies of the field, how they grow; they toil not, neither do they spin: And yet I say unto you, That even Solomon in all his glory was not arrayed like one of these" (Matthew 6.26–29). The spinning of garments obliquely relates to working at texts, through a tacit pun on *textum* (Latin: something woven).

[3]Phidias (5th c. BCE) sculpted the Elgin Marbles.

[4]Insubstantial figures, phantoms, ghosts.

[5]A ms has "masque," a formal, court-theater genre; K allows the pun (see l. 56).

Is heap'd upon her, Maiden most unmeek,—
I knew to be my demon[6] Poesy.   30

IV.

They faded, and, forsooth! I wanted° wings: *lacked, desired*
   O folly! What is Love? and where is it?
And for that poor Ambition! it springs
      From a man's little heart's short fever-fit;
         For Poesy! —no,—she has not a joy,—
      At least for me,—so sweet as drowsy noons,
And evenings steep'd in honied indolence;
         O, for an age so shelter'd from annoy,[7]
      That I may never know how change the moons,
Or hear the voice of busy common-sense!   40

V.

And once more came they by;—alas! wherefore?
   My sleep had been embroider'd with dim dreams;
My soul had been a lawn besprinkled o'er
      With flowers, and stirring shades, and baffled beams:
         The morn was clouded, but no shower fell,
      Tho' in her lids hung the sweet tears of May;
The open casement press'd a new-leaved vine,
      Let in the budding warmth and throstle's lay;[8]
         O Shadows! 'twas a time to bid farewell!
Upon your skirts had fallen no tears of mine.   50

VI.

So, ye three Ghosts, adieu! Ye cannot raise
   My head cool-bedded in the flowery grass;
For I would not be dieted with praise,
   A pet-lamb in a sentimental farce![9]

---

[6]In Greek mythology a *demon* or *daemon* is a semi-divine spirit; the word also allows the post-classical sense of evil spirit. K burns in his anti-indolent love of poesy (he is working at this ode) and his harsh judgment in the reviews.

[7]A Keats-coined noun.

[8]thrush's song, but with an oblique pun related to the epigraph (a *throstle* is a frame for spinning).

[9]For a related image, see the letter to Miss Jeffrey, 9 June 1819 (p. 257).

Fade softly from my eyes, and be once more
In masque-like figures on the dreamy urn;
Farewell! I yet have visions for the night,
    And for the day faint visions there is store;
Vanish, ye Phantoms! from my idle spright,[10]
Into the clouds, and never more return!   60

To—— ("I cry your mercy")[1]

I CRY your mercy—pity—love!—aye, love!
    Merciful love that tantalises not,
One-thoughted, never wand'ring, guileless love,
    Unmask'd, and being seen—without a blot!
O, let me have thee whole,—all—all—be mine!
    That shape, that fairness, that sweet minor zest
Of love, your kiss,—those hands, those eyes divine,
    That warm, white, lucent, million-pleasured breast,—
Yourself—your soul—in pity give me all,
    Withhold no atom's atom or I die,
Or living on perhaps, your wretched thrall,
    Forget, in the mist of idle misery,
Life's purposes,—the palate of my mind
Losing its gust, and my ambition blind.

"This living hand"[1]

Editors date this mysterious manuscript fragment as late 1819; first published in the sixth edition of H. B. Forman's Poetical Works of John Keats *(1898, p. 417). Not just the grasping, writing hand, "hand"*

---

[10]Archaic term for spirit, but also a diminutive ghost, elf, fairy.

---

[1]*1848*, Sonnet XIX; untitled, dated 1819 (2.305). The opening phrase is a formal begging of pardon. K summons a literary genealogy of treachery: to Desdemona's protest of chaste and honest love, Othello answers: "I cry your mercy, / I took you for that cunning whore of Venice" (*Othello* 4.2.90–91). Hazlitt echoed Othello in the *Quarterly*, in his attack on Gifford's political bias (*A Letter to William Gifford, Esq. from William Hazlitt, Esq.* [1819], partly republished in *Examiner*, 7 and 14 March). After a long list of charges, Hazlitt writes, "You, sir, do you not [do] all this? I cry your mercy then: I took you for the Editor of the Quarterly Review!"— among the passages K transcribed for G&GK in his journal letter of spring 1819.

---

[1]K ms, Houghton Library, Harvard.

*also means one's identifiable handwriting; for the relation of these two
senses, see* The Fall of Hyperion 1.16–18.

This living hand, now warm and capable
Of earnest grasping, would, if it were cold
and in the icy silence of the tomb,
So haunt thy days and chill thy dreaming nights
                                    heat²
That thou would wish thine / own dry of blood
So in my veins red life might stream again,
and thou be conscience-calm'd – see here it is 4
I hold it towards you –

²K inserted *heat*; his characteristic compression of "r" in handwriting makes it possible that he meant *heart*, which fits the context (though *heat* is relevant).

Lamia, Isabella, The Eve of St. Agnes, and Other Poems

The title page identifies "John Keats, Author of Endymion.*" Endymion was Taylor and Hessey's first venture with Keats.* Lamia & c *was published in late June 1820, in duodecimo, an even less expensive format than* Endymion. *Among those "other poems" are the great odes for which Keats would become famous. Seriously ill since February, Keats relied on Woodhouse and Taylor to help prepare the volume, and some of their decisions grated: he wanted to open with* The Eve of St. Agnes; *they thought* Lamia, *with its strong swerve from* Endymion, *would be better. They also admired the fragment of* Hyperion (*Keats did not want to publish an incomplete effort*) *and put it at the back of the volume, with a separate title page. Keats was even unhappier with the front notice, drafted by Woodhouse, tweaked by Taylor, and not shown to Keats at all. In a volume he gave to an acquaintance, he crossed it out, writing at the top of the page, "This is none of my doing – I was ill at the time," and after the last sentence: "This is a lie."*

ADVERTISEMENT.

If any apology be thought necessary for the appearance of the unfinished poem of HYPERION, the publishers beg to state that they alone are responsible, as it was printed at their particular request, and contrary to the wish of the author. The poem was intended to have been of equal length with ENDYMION, but the reception given to that work discouraged the author from proceeding.

Fleet-Street, June 26, 1820

LAMIA,

ISABELLA,

THE EVE OF ST. AGNES,

AND

OTHER POEMS.

BY JOHN KEATS,

AUTHOR OF ENDYMION.

LONDON:

PRINTED FOR TAYLOR AND HESSEY,

FLEET-STREET.

1820.

Title page of *Lamia, Isabella, The Eve of St. Agnes, and Other Poems*, 1820.

LAMIA.

The three tales named in 1820's title all had separate title pages. Keats wrote the first named, Lamia, *last, in summer 1819, with his eye on the public: "I am certain there is that sort of fire in it which must take hold of people in some way—give them either pleasant or unpleasant sensation. What they want is sensation of some sort" (he reported to George and Georgiana in September). It is the volume's longest work: of its 200 pages, it commanded 46. Disenchanted with* Endymion *as he readied it for press, and thinking even* Isabella *and* The Eve of St. Agnes *"too smokeable" (see pp. 267–68), Keats invested* Lamia *as the antidote. "I have great hopes of success, because I make use of my Judgment more deliberately than I yet have done," he wrote in July 1819 to Reynolds, feeling he had written* Endymion *"without Judgment." He was enjoying Dryden's verse fables and legends, their crisp heroic couplets spiced with triple rhymes and calculated alexandrine extravagances (six-beat lines in the five-beat pattern). Not just in these measures, but also in key characterizations and circumstances,* Lamia *is saturated with ironic corrosives to "golden Romance": Corinth was a well-known site of slavery and erotic hedonism (an ancient-world Vegas); philosopher Apollonius is a deformation of Apollo; Keats-age Lycius is a blind visionary, then a tyrant, then a subject of catastrophic discipline; and Lamia is a gordian complication. Her name indicates the fabled sisterhood of African-descended she-vampires: seeming modest women above the waist, but below, serpents who tempt, then strangle and devour their victims. Keats was in love with Fanny Brawne and anxious about the surrender of his sense of self-possession, but there are suggestions that the enchantress herself may also be a victim of a spell. The vignette in Robert Burton's baroque seventeenth-century treatise,* Anatomy of Melancholy, *which Keats identified as his source and inspiration, was set as an endnote in the 1820 volume, as it is here.*

PART I.

UPON a time, before the faery broods
Drove Nymph and Satyr from the prosperous woods,
Before King Oberon's[1] bright diadem,°   *crown*
Sceptre, and mantle, clasp'd with dewy gem,
Frighted away the Dryads and the Fauns   5

---

[1]The king of this little tale of war-torn faeryland shares a name with the tyrant of Shakespeare's fairy world in *A Midsummer Night's Dream.*

From rushes green, and brakes,° and cowslip'd lawns,   *thickets*
The ever-smitten Hermes[2] empty left
His golden throne, bent warm on amorous theft:
From high Olympus had he stolen light,
On this side of Jove's clouds, to escape the sight   10
Of his great summoner, and made retreat
Into a forest on the shores of Crete.
For somewhere in that sacred island dwelt
A nymph, to whom all hoofed Satyrs knelt;
At whose white feet the languid Tritons[3] poured   15
Pearls, while on land they wither'd[4] and adored.
Fast by the springs where she to bathe was wont,
And in those meads[5] where sometime she might haunt,
Were strewn rich gifts, unknown to any Muse,
Though Fancy's casket were unlock'd to choose.   20
Ah, what a world of love was at her feet!
So Hermes thought, and a celestial heat
Burnt from his winged heels to either ear,
That from a whiteness, as the lily clear,
Blush'd into roses 'mid his golden hair,   25
Fallen in jealous curls about his shoulders bare.[6]
From vale to vale, from wood to wood, he flew,
Breathing upon the flowers his passion new,
And wound with many a river to its head,
To find where this sweet nymph prepar'd her secret bed: 30
In vain; the sweet nymph might nowhere be found,
And so he rested, on the lonely ground,
Pensive, and full of painful jealousies
Of the Wood-Gods, and even the very trees.
There as he stood, he heard a mournful voice,   35
Such as once heard, in gentle heart, destroys
All pain but pity: thus the lone voice spake:

---

[2]By force of the line break and a slight grammatical ambiguity in "From high Olympus had he stolen light" (9), K wittily poses Hermes as a junior Prometheus as well.

[3]sea gods or mermen

[4]for lack of water

[5]meadows

[6]The first of many alexandrine or otherwise hypermetrical lines (often thematically relevant).

"When from this wreathed tomb shall I awake!
 When move in a sweet body fit for life,
 And love, and pleasure, and the ruddy strife   40
 Of hearts and lips! Ah, miserable me!"
The God, dove-footed, glided silently
Round bush and tree, soft-brushing, in his speed,
The taller grasses and full-flowering weed,
Until he found a palpitating snake,   45
Bright, and cirque-couchant[7] in a dusky brake.

 She was a gordian shape[8] of dazzling hue,
Vermilion-spotted, golden, green, and blue;
Striped like a zebra, freckled like a pard,°   *leopard*
Eyed like a peacock,[9] and all crimson barr'd;   50
And full of silver moons, that, as she breathed,
Dissolv'd, or brighter shone, or interwreathed
Their lustres with the gloomier tapestries—
So rainbow-sided, touch'd with miseries,
She seem'd, at once, some penanced lady elf,   55
Some demon's mistress, or the demon's self.
Upon her crest she wore a wannish fire
Sprinkled with stars, like Ariadne's tiar:[10]
Her head was serpent, but ah, bitter-sweet!
She had a woman's mouth with all its pearls[11] complete: 60
And for her eyes: what could such eyes do there
But weep, and weep, that they were born so fair?
As Proserpine still weeps for her Sicilian air.
Her throat was serpent, but the words she spake
Came, as through bubbling honey, for Love's sake, 65

---

[7]K-invented faux-heraldic word for *lying in circular coils.*

[8]Like the intricate Gordian knot, impossible to untie; see n. 17 to *Endymion*, p. 149, and K's own reference to this legend in his letter to Bailey about his complicated feelings about women (18 July 1818), p. 192. K underlined Milton's verbally sinuous and slippery description of Satan in Eden: "the serpent sly / Insinuating wove with Gordian twine / His braided train" (*PL* 4.347–49).

[9]peacock's tail

[10]Bacchus gave Ariadne a tiara of seven stars—an association nicely sounded by the sliding *s* of "Ariadne's *tiar.*"

[11]In Renaissance love poetry, a standard compliment for teeth.

And thus; while Hermes on his pinions lay,
Like a stoop'd° falcon ere he takes his prey.   *ready to swoop*

    "Fair Hermes, crown'd with feathers, fluttering light,
    I had a splendid dream of thee last night:
    I saw thee sitting, on a throne of gold,   70
    Among the Gods, upon Olympus old,
    The only sad one; for thou didst not hear
    The soft, lute-finger'd Muses chaunting clear,
    Nor even Apollo when he sang alone,
    Deaf to his throbbing throat's long, long melodious moan.[12] 75
    I dreamt I saw thee, robed in purple flakes,
    Break amorous through the clouds, as morning breaks,
    And, swiftly as a bright Phoebean dart,[13]
    Strike for the Cretan isle; and here thou art!
    Too gentle Hermes, hast thou found the maid?"   80
Whereat the star of Lethe[14] not delay'd
His rosy eloquence, and thus inquired:
"Thou smooth-lipp'd serpent, surely high inspired!
    Thou beauteous wreath,[15] with melancholy eyes,
    Possess whatever bliss thou canst devise,   85
    Telling me only where my nymph is fled,——
    Where she doth breathe!" "Bright planet, thou hast said,"
Return'd the snake, "but seal with oaths, fair God!"
"I swear," said Hermes, "by my serpent rod,°   *caduceus*
    And by thine eyes, and by thy starry crown!"   90
Light flew his earnest words, among the blossoms blown.
Then thus again the brilliance feminine:
"Too frail of heart! for this lost nymph of thine,
    Free as the air, invisibly, she strays
    About these thornless wilds; her pleasant days   95
    She tastes unseen; unseen her nimble feet
    Leave traces in the grass and flowers sweet;

---

[12]An extraordinarily long metrical line—to evoke the moan.

[13]ray from the sun god, Phoebus Apollo.

[14]One of Hermes's tasks, as psychopomp, was to lead the souls of the dead across Lethe.

[15]One of several verbal affinities with Satan, who "curl'd many a wanton wreath in sight of *Eve*" as he begins his seduction (*PL* 9.517).

From weary tendrils, and bow'd branches green,
She plucks the fruit unseen, she bathes unseen:
And by my power is her beauty veil'd   100
To keep it unaffronted, unassail'd
By the love-glances of unlovely eyes,
Of Satyrs, Fauns, and blear'd Silenus' sighs.[16]
Pale grew her immortality, for woe
Of all these lovers, and she grieved so   105
I took compassion on her, bade her steep
Her hair in weïrd syrops,[17] that would keep
Her loveliness invisible, yet free
To wander as she loves, in liberty.
Thou shalt behold her, Hermes, thou alone,   110
If thou wilt, as thou swearest, grant my boon!"
Then, once again, the charmed God began
An oath, and through the serpent's ears it ran
Warm, tremulous, devout, psalterian.[18]
Ravish'd, she lifted her Circean head,[19]   115
Blush'd a live damask,[20] and swift-lisping said,
"I was a woman, let me have once more
  A woman's shape, and charming as before.
  I love a youth of Corinth——O the bliss!
  Give me my woman's form, and place me where he is.   120
  Stoop, Hermes, let me breathe upon thy brow,
  And thou shalt see thy sweet nymph even now."
The God on half-shut feathers sank serene,
She breath'd upon his eyes, and swift was seen
Of both the guarded nymph near-smiling on the green.   125
It was no dream; or say a dream it was,
Real are the dreams of Gods, and smoothly pass
Their pleasures in a long immortal dream.
One warm, flush'd moment, hovering, it might seem
Dash'd by the wood-nymph's beauty, so he burn'd;   130

[16]a satyr, usually depicted drunk, who tutored Bacchus
[17]magical syrups
[18]like a psalm; or sounding like a psaltery (a stringed instrument, like a zither).
[19]like Circe's. Hermes helped Ulysses recover his crew from her enchantment, which had turned men into beasts. Cf. *Endymion* 3.490–554.
[20]big pink rose of Asia Minor

Then, lighting on the printless verdure, turn'd
To the swoon'd serpent, and with languid arm,
Delicate, put to proof the lythe Caducean charm.
So done, upon the nymph his eyes he bent
Full of adoring tears and blandishment,   135
And towards her stept: she, like a moon in wane,
Faded before him, cower'd, nor could restrain
Her fearful sobs, self-folding like a flower
That faints into itself at evening hour:
But the God fostering her chilled hand,
She felt the warmth, her eyelids open'd bland,°   *unperturbed*
And, like new flowers at morning song of bees,
Bloom'd, and gave up her honey to the lees.°   *depths*
Into the green-recessed woods they flew;
Nor grew they pale, as mortal lovers do.   145

    Left to herself, the serpent now began
To change; her elfin blood in madness ran,
Her mouth foam'd, and the grass, therewith besprent,[21]
Wither'd at dew so sweet and virulent;°   *poisonous*
Her eyes in torture fix'd, and anguish drear,
Hot, glaz'd, and wide, with lid-lashes all sear,°   *scorched*
Flash'd phosphor and sharp sparks, without one cooling tear.
The colours all inflam'd throughout her train,
She writh'd about, convuls'd with scarlet pain:
A deep volcanian[22] yellow took the place   155
Of all her milder-mooned body's grace;
And, as the lava ravishes the mead,
Spoilt all her silver mail, and golden brede;[23]
Made gloom of all her frecklings, streaks and bars,
Eclips'd her crescents, and lick'd up her stars: 160
So that, in moments few, she was undrest
Of all her sapphires, greens, and amethyst,
And rubious-argent:° of all these bereft,   *silver*

---

[21]sprinkled. The word holds all the letters of "serpent."

[22]K coined this adjective (*OED*).

[23]*mail*: metal-mesh coat; *brede*: embroidery

Nothing but pain and ugliness were left.
Still shone her crown; that vanish'd, also she   165
Melted and disappear'd as suddenly;
And in the air, her new voice luting soft,
Cried, "Lycius! gentle Lycius!"——Borne aloft
With the bright mists about the mountains hoar
These words dissolv'd: Crete's forests heard no more.   170

    Whither fled Lamia, now a lady bright,[24]
A full-born beauty new and exquisite?
She fled into that valley they pass o'er
Who go to Corinth[25] from Cenchreas' shore;
And rested at the foot of those wild hills,   175
The rugged founts of the Peræan rills,
And of that other ridge whose barren back
Stretches, with all its mist and cloudy rack,
South-westward to Cleone.° There she stood   *(a village)*
About a young bird's flutter from a wood,   180
Fair, on a sloping green of mossy tread,
By a clear pool, wherein she passioned
To see herself escap'd from so sore ills,
While her robes flaunted with the daffodils.

    Ah, happy Lycius!——for she was a maid   185
More beautiful than ever twisted braid,
Or sigh'd, or blush'd, or on spring-flowered lea°   *meadow*
Spread a green kirtle° to the minstrelsy: *dress*
A virgin purest lipp'd, yet in the lore
Of love deep learned to the red heart's core: 190
Not one hour old, yet of sciential° brain   *knowing*
To unperplex bliss from its neighbour pain;
Define their pettish° limits, and estrange   *contested*
Their points of contact, and swift counterchange;
Intrigue with the specious° chaos, and dispart   *seeming*
Its most ambiguous atoms with sure art;
As though in Cupid's college she had spent

---

[24]A witty sonnet-stanza presents Lamia's debut as a lady-bright to love.
[25]harbor of the southern Grecian city of Corinth

Sweet days a lovely graduate, still unshent,°   *unspoiled*
And kept his rosy terms[26] in idle languishment.

Why this fair creature chose so fairily   200
By the wayside to linger, we shall see;
But first 'tis fit to tell how she could muse
And dream, when in the serpent prison-house,[27]
Of all she list,° strange or magnificent: *wished*
How, ever, where she will'd, her spirit went;   205
Whether to faint Elysium, or where
Down through tress-lifting waves the Nereids[28] fair
Wind into Thetis' bower by many a pearly stair;[29]
Or where God Bacchus drains his cups divine,
Stretch'd out, at ease, beneath a glutinous pine;   210
Or where in Pluto's gardens palatine
Mulciber's columns gleam in far piazzian line.[30]
And sometimes into cities she would send
Her dream, with feast and rioting to blend;
And once, while among mortals dreaming thus,   215
She saw the young Corinthian Lycius
Charioting foremost in the envious race,
Like a young Jove with calm uneager face,
And fell into a swooning love of him.
Now on the moth-time of that evening dim   220
He would return that way, as well she knew,
To Corinth from the shore; for freshly blew
The eastern soft wind, and his galley now

---

[26]*kept his rosy terms* puns triply: cherished his erotic terminology; honored an amorous contract; hewed to a temporal sequence (G. Stewart, "Language of Metamorphosis," 6). The triple rhyme, reinforced by the near ensuing couplet *magnificent / went* (204–5), flirts with *serpent* as a rhyme but keeps it in abeyance, as if to signal Lamia's successful transformation; but the fact that this word appears in line 203 as an internal rhyme also suggests an inner identity only repressed, not effaced.

[27]See K's marginalia to Satan insinuating himself into a serpent's body for disguise (*PL* 9.179–91).

[28]sea-nymphs

[29]Thetis is the mother of Achilles, the semi-divine Greek general of the Trojan War, invulnerable, except in the heel by which she held him when she dipped him in magical waters.

[30]*piazza*: open courtyard with rows of columns; *Mulciber*: Vulcan god of metalwork and architect of Pandemonium in Milton's hell (*PL* 1).

Grated the quaystones with her brazen prow
In port Cenchreas, from Egina isle   225
Fresh anchor'd; whither he had been awhile
To sacrifice to Jove, whose temple there
Waits with high marble doors for blood and incense rare.
Jove heard his vows, and better'd his desire;
For by some freakful chance he made retire   230
From his companions, and set forth to walk,
Perhaps grown wearied of their Corinth talk:
Over the solitary hills he fared,
Thoughtless at first, but ere eve's star appeared
His phantasy was lost, where reason fades,   235
In the calm'd twilight of Platonic shades.[31]
Lamia beheld him coming, near, more near—
Close to her passing, in indifference drear,
His silent sandals swept the mossy green;
So neighbour'd to him, and yet so unseen   240
She stood: he pass'd, shut up in mysteries,[32]
His mind wrapp'd like his mantle, while her eyes
Follow'd his steps, and her neck regal white
Turn'd——syllabling thus, "Ah, Lycius bright,
  And will you leave me on the hills alone?   245
  Lycius, look back! and be some pity shown."
He did; not with cold wonder fearingly,
But Orpheus-like at an Eurydice;[33]
For so delicious were the words she sung,
It seem'd he had lov'd them a whole summer long: 250
And soon his eyes had drunk her beauty up,
Leaving no drop in the bewildering cup,
And still the cup was full,——while he, afraid
Lest she should vanish ere his lip had paid
Due adoration, thus began to adore;   255
Her soft look growing coy, she saw his chain so sure:
"Leave thee alone! Look back! Ah, Goddess, see
  Whether my eyes can ever turn from thee!

[31]The otherworldly ideals of Plato's metaphysics; human knowledge, in Plato's famous "Allegory of the Cave," tends to mistake mere shadows for these truths.
[32]abstruse religion
[33]The nymph Eurydice was killed by snakebite.

For pity do not this sad heart belie°——   *lie to*
Even as thou vanishest so I shall die.   260
Stay! though a Naiad of the rivers, stay!
To thy far wishes will thy streams obey:
Stay! though the greenest woods be thy domain,
Alone they can drink up the morning rain:
Though a descended Pleiad,[34] will not one   265
Of thine harmonious sisters keep in tune
Thy spheres, and as thy silver proxy shine?
So sweetly to these ravish'd ears of mine
Came thy sweet greeting, that if thou shouldst fade
Thy memory will waste me to a shade:——   270
For pity do not melt!"——"If I should stay,"
Said Lamia, "here, upon this floor of clay,
   And pain my steps upon these flowers too rough,
What canst thou say or do of charm enough
To dull the nice[35] remembrance of my home?   275
Thou canst not ask me with thee here to roam
Over these hills and vales, where no joy is,——
Empty of immortality and bliss!
Thou art a scholar, Lycius, and must know
That finer spirits cannot breathe below   280
In human climes, and live: Alas! poor youth,
What taste of purer air hast thou to soothe
My essence? What serener palaces,
Where I may all my many senses please,
And by mysterious sleights a hundred thirsts appease?   285
It cannot be——Adieu!" So said, she rose
Tiptoe with white arms spread. He, sick to lose
The amorous promise of her lone complain,[36]
Swoon'd, murmuring of love, and pale with pain.
The cruel lady, without any show   290
Of sorrow for her tender favourite's woe,
But rather, if her eyes could brighter be,
With brighter eyes and slow amenity,

---

[34]One of the seven daughters of Atlas, all constellated as the Pleiades after their death.

[35]highly detailed

[36]An obsolete noun (for *complaint, lament*); *OED* cites this line as the sole instance since 1485.

Put her new lips to his, and gave afresh
The life she had so tangled in her mesh: 295
And as he from one trance was wakening
Into another, she began to sing,
Happy in beauty, life, and love, and every thing,
A song of love, too sweet for earthly lyres,
While, like held breath, the stars drew in their panting fires.   300
And then she whisper'd in such trembling tone,
As those who, safe together met alone
For the first time through many anguish'd days,
Use other speech than looks; bidding him raise
His drooping head, and clear his soul of doubt,   305
For that she was a woman, and without
Any more subtle fluid in her veins
Than throbbing blood, and that the self-same pains
Inhabited her frail-strung heart as his.
And next she wonder'd how his eyes could miss   310
Her face so long in Corinth, where, she said,
She dwelt but half retir'd, and there had led
Days happy as the gold coin could invent
Without the aid of love; yet in content
Till she saw him, as once she pass'd him by,   315
Where 'gainst a column he leant thoughtfully
At Venus' temple porch, 'mid baskets heap'd
Of amorous herbs and flowers, newly reap'd
Late on that eve, as 'twas the night before
The Adonian feast;[37] whereof she saw no more,   320
But wept alone those days, for why should she adore?
Lycius from death awoke into amaze,[38]
To see her still, and singing so sweet lays;
Then from amaze into delight he fell
To hear her whisper woman's lore so well;   325
And every word she spake entic'd him on
To unperplex'd delight and pleasure known.
Let the mad poets say whate'er they please
Of the sweets of Fairies, Peris,° Goddesses,   *Persian fairies*

[37]Annual fertility rite, celebrating the return of Adonis to Venus (see *Endymion* Book II).
[38]A verb transformed into a noun to evoke *a maze*, or labyrinth.

There is not such a treat among them all,   330
Haunters of cavern, lake, and waterfall,
As a real woman, lineal indeed
From Pyrrha's pebbles[39] or old Adam's seed.
Thus gentle Lamia judg'd, and judg'd aright,
That Lycius could not love in half a fright,   335
So threw the goddess off, and won his heart
More pleasantly by playing woman's part,
With no more awe than what her beauty gave,
That, while it smote, still guaranteed to save.
Lycius to all made eloquent reply,   340
Marrying to every word a twinborn sigh;
And last, pointing to Corinth, ask'd her sweet,
If 'twas too far that night for her soft feet.
The way was short, for Lamia's eagerness
Made, by a spell, the triple league decrease   345
To a few paces; not at all surmised
By blinded Lycius, so in her comprized.°   *enrapt*
They pass'd the city gates, he knew not how,
So noiseless, and he never thought to know.

    As men talk in a dream, so Corinth all,   350
Throughout her palaces imperial,
And all her populous streets and temples lewd,[40]
Mutter'd, like tempest in the distance brew'd,
To the wide-spreaded night above her towers.
Men, women, rich and poor, in the cool hours,   355
Shuffled their sandals o'er the pavement white,
Companion'd or alone; while many a light
Flared, here and there, from wealthy festivals,
And threw their moving shadows on the walls,
Or found them cluster'd in the corniced shade   360
Of some arch'd temple door, or dusky colonnade.[41]

---

[39]In a Greek-myth analogue to Noah's ark, Jupiter punishes mankind with a flood, survived only by Deucalion (a son of Prometheus) and his wife Pyrrha, who repopulate the earth with life-engendering pebbles.

[40]In *Anatomy of Melancholy* Burton reports of Corinth: "every day strangers came in, at each gate, from all quarters. In that one temple of Venus a thousand whores did prostitute themselves . . . all nations resorted thither as to a school of Venus."

[41]row of columns

Muffling his face, of greeting friends in fear,
Her fingers he press'd hard, as one came near
With curl'd gray beard, sharp eyes, and smooth bald crown,
Slow-stepp'd, and robed in philosophic gown: 365
Lycius shrank closer, as they met and past,
Into his mantle, adding wings to haste,
While hurried Lamia trembled: "Ah," said he,
"Why do you shudder, love, so ruefully?
  Why does your tender palm dissolve in dew?"——   370
"I'm wearied," said fair Lamia: "tell me who
  Is that old man? I cannot bring to mind
  His features:——Lycius! wherefore did you blind[42]
  Yourself from his quick eyes?" Lycius replied,
"'Tis Apollonius sage, my trusty guide   375
  And good instructor; but to-night he seems
  The ghost of folly haunting my sweet dreams."

    While yet he spake they had arrived before
A pillar'd porch, with lofty portal door,
Where hung a silver lamp, whose phosphor glow   380
Reflected in the slabbed steps below,
Mild as a star in water; for so new,
And so unsullied was the marble hue,
So through the crystal polish, liquid fine,
Ran the dark veins, that none but feet divine   385
Could e'er have touch'd there. Sounds Æolian
Breath'd from the hinges, as the ample span
Of the wide doors disclos'd a place unknown
Some time to any, but those two alone,
And a few Persian mutes, who that same year   390
Were seen about the markets: none knew where
They could inhabit; the most curious
Were foil'd, who watch'd to trace them to their house:
And but[43] the flitter-winged verse must tell,
For truth's sake, what woe afterwards befel,   395

---

[42]Make it difficult for yourself to be seen by (for this unusual usage, *OED* cites this line); there is also the sense of "avert your eyes from meeting his gaze."
[43]but for the fact that

'Twould humour many a heart to leave them thus,
Shut from the busy world of more incredulous.[44]

PART II.

LOVE in a hut, with water and a crust,
Is—Love, forgive us!—cinders, ashes, dust;
Love in a palace is perhaps at last
More grievous torment than a hermit's fast:——
That is a doubtful tale from faery land,   5
Hard for the non-elect to understand.
Had Lycius liv'd to hand his story down,
He might have given the moral a fresh frown,
Or clench'd it quite:[45] but too short was their bliss
To breed distrust and hate, that make the soft voice hiss.   10
Besides, there, nightly, with terrific glare,
Love,° jealous grown of so complete a pair,   *Cupid*
Hover'd and buzz'd his wings, with fearful roar,
Above the lintel[46] of their chamber door,
And down the passage cast a glow upon the floor.   15

   For[47] all this came a ruin: side by side
They were enthroned, in the even tide,
Upon a couch, near to a curtaining
Whose airy texture, from a golden string,
Floated into the room, and let appear   20
Unveil'd the summer heaven, blue and clear,
Betwixt two marble shafts:—there they reposed,
Where use had made it sweet, with eyelids closed,
Saving a tythe[48] which love still open kept,
That they might see each other while they almost slept;   25

---

[44]The final adjective (unbelieving, skeptical) may modify both *them* (the lovers believe only in their own reality and let the rest of the busy world go by), and the romance-reader's heart, happy to indulge such fantasy, unable to believe any other outcome.
[45]really nailed it
[46]weight-bearing beam
[47]In spite of / Because of
[48]tithe, tenth part

When from the slope side of a suburb[49] hill,
Deafening the swallow's twitter, came a thrill
Of trumpets——Lycius started——the sounds fled,
But left a thought, a buzzing in his head.
For the first time, since first he harbour'd in   30
That purple-lined palace of sweet sin,
His spirit pass'd beyond its golden bourn
Into the noisy world almost forsworn.
The lady, ever watchful, penetrant,
Saw this with pain, so arguing a want   35
Of something more, more than her empery°   empire
Of joys; and she began to moan and sigh
Because he mused beyond her, knowing well
That but a moment's thought is passion's passing bell.[50]
"Why do you sigh, fair creature?" whisper'd he: 40
"Why do you think?" return'd she tenderly:
"You have deserted me;——where am I now?
 Not in your heart while care weighs on your brow:
 No, no, you have dismiss'd me; and I go
 From your breast houseless: ay, it must be so."   45
He answer'd, bending to her open eyes,
Where he was mirror'd small in paradise,
"My silver planet, both of eve and morn![51]
 Why will you plead yourself so sad forlorn,
 While I am striving how to fill my heart   50
 With deeper crimson, and a double smart?
 How to entangle, trammel up and snare
 Your soul in mine, and labyrinth[52] you there
 Like the hid scent in an unbudded rose?
 Ay, a sweet kiss——you see your mighty woes.   55
 My thoughts! shall I unveil them? Listen then!
 What mortal hath a prize, that other men
 May be confounded and abash'd withal,

[49]a conscious archaism
[50]death knell
[51]Venus, both the morning and the evening star. K innovated this use of *mirror* as transitive verb (*OED*).
[52]*OED* cites this instance of *labyrinth* as its first use as active verb. The reciprocal of the noun *amaze* in Part I, it prepares for the punning of the crowd *maz'd* (156) by Lamia's splendidly transformed chamber.

But lets it sometimes pace abroad majestical,
And triumph, as in thee I should rejoice   60
Amid the hoarse alarm of Corinth's voice.
Let my foes choke, and my friends shout afar,
While through the thronged streets your bridal car
Wheels round its dazzling spokes."——The lady's cheek
Trembled; she nothing said, but, pale and meek,   65
Arose and knelt before him, wept a rain
Of sorrows at his words; at last with pain
Beseeching him, the while his hand she wrung,
To change his purpose. He thereat was stung,
Perverse, with stronger fancy to reclaim   70
Her wild and timid nature to his aim:
Besides, for all his love, in self despite,
Against his better self, he took delight
Luxurious in her sorrows, soft and new.
His passion, cruel grown, took on a hue   75
Fierce and sanguineous as 'twas possible
In one whose brow had no dark veins to swell.
Fine was the mitigated fury, like
Apollo's presence when in act to strike
The serpent[53]——Ha, the serpent! certes,° she   *certainly*
Was none. She burnt, she lov'd the tyranny,[54]
And, all subdued, consented to the hour
When to the bridal he should lead his paramour.
Whispering in midnight silence, said the youth,
"Sure some sweet name thou hast, though, by my truth,   85
    I have not ask'd it, ever thinking thee
    Not mortal, but of heavenly progeny,
    As still I do. Hast any mortal name,
    Fit appellation for this dazzling frame?
    Or friends or kinsfolk on the cited earth,   90
    To share our marriage feast and nuptial mirth?"
"I have no friends," said Lamia, "no, not one;
    My presence in wide Corinth hardly known:

[53]The sea-serpent Python, engendered from the mud left after the great flood (see p. 300, n. 39), was slain by Apollo at Delphi.

[54]"Women love to be forced to do a thing, by a fine fellow—such as this," K smirked of Lycius (so Woodhouse told his publisher in Sept. 1819).

My parents' bones are in their dusty urns
Sepulchred, where no kindled incense burns,   95
Seeing all their luckless race are dead, save me,
And I neglect the holy rite for thee.
Even as you list invite your many guests;
But if, as now it seems, your vision rests
With any pleasure on me, do not bid   100
Old Apollonius—from him keep me hid."
Lycius, perplex'd at words so blind and blank,
Made close inquiry; from whose touch she shrank,
Feigning a sleep; and he to the dull shade
Of deep sleep in a moment was betray'd.   105

   It was the custom then to bring away
The bride from home at blushing shut of day,
Veil'd, in a chariot, heralded along
By strewn flowers, torches, and a marriage song,
With other pageants: but this fair unknown   110
Had not a friend. So being left alone,
(Lycius was gone to summon all his kin)
And knowing surely she could never win
His foolish heart from its mad pompousness,
She set herself, high-thoughted, how to dress   115
The misery in fit magnificence.
She did so, but 'tis doubtful how and whence
Came, and who were her subtle servitors.
About the halls, and to and from the doors,
There was a noise of wings, till in short space   120
The glowing banquet-room shone with wide-arched grace.
A haunting music, sole perhaps and lone
Supportress of the faery-roof, made moan
Throughout, as fearful the whole charm might fade.
Fresh carved cedar, mimicking a glade   125
Of palm and plantain, met from either side,
High in the midst, in honour of the bride:
Two palms and then two plantains, and so on,
From either side their stems branch'd one to one
All down the aisled place; and beneath all   130
There ran a stream of lamps straight on from wall to wall.

So canopied, lay an untasted feast
Teeming with odours. Lamia, regal drest,
Silently paced about, and as she went,
In pale contented sort of discontent,   135
Mission'd her viewless° servants to enrich   *invisible*
The fretted[55] splendour of each nook and niche.
Between the tree-stems, marbled plain at first,
Came jasper pannels; then, anon, there burst
Forth creeping imagery of slighter trees,   140
And with the larger wove in small intricacies.
Approving all, she faded at self-will,
And shut the chamber up, close, hush'd and still,
Complete and ready for the revels rude,
When dreadful guests would come to spoil her solitude.   145

    The day appear'd, and all the gossip rout.
O senseless Lycius! Madman! wherefore flout
The silent-blessing fate, warm cloister'd hours,
And show to common eyes these secret bowers?
The herd approach'd; each guest, with busy brain,   150
Arriving at the portal, gaz'd amain,°   *fully, eagerly*
And enter'd marveling:[56] for they knew the street,
Remember'd it from childhood all complete
Without a gap, yet ne'er before had seen
That royal porch, that high-built fair demesne;°   *domain*
So in they hurried all, maz'd, curious and keen:
Save one, who look'd thereon with eye severe,   157
And with calm-planted steps walk'd in austere;
'Twas Apollonius: something too he laugh'd,
As though some knotty problem, that had daft°   *teased*
His patient thought, had now begun to thaw,
And solve and melt:[57]——'twas just as he foresaw.

[55]intricately carved

[56]Cf. the awe at Mulciber's creation of the splendid city in Hell (also as if by "magic"): "The hasty multitude / Admiring entered" (*PL* 1.730–31); K underlined all of 1.702–30.

[57]The language of Hamlet's wish for death (that his flesh "would melt, / Thaw, and resolve itself into a dew" [1.2.129–30]) echoes here, reinforced by Lycius's question to Lamia when she first sees Apollonius: "Why does your tender palm dissolve in dew?" (1.370). The substitution of *solve* for *resolve / dissolve* equates Apollonius's powers of solving with the dissolution of the body.

He met within the murmurous vestibule°   *lobby*
His young disciple. "'Tis no common rule,
 Lycius," said he, "for uninvited guest   165
 To force himself upon you, and infest
 With an unbidden presence the bright throng
 Of younger friends; yet must I do this wrong,
 And you forgive me." Lycius blush'd, and led
The old man through the inner doors broad-spread;   170
 With reconciling words and courteous mien
Turning into sweet milk the sophist's spleen.

   Of wealthy lustre was the banquet-room,
Fill'd with pervading brilliance and perfume:
 Before each lucid pannel fuming stood   175
A censer° fed with myrrh and spiced wood,   *incense-burner*
 Each by a sacred tripod held aloft,
 Whose slender feet wide-swerv'd upon the soft
Wool-woofed carpets: fifty wreaths of smoke
 From fifty censers their light voyage took   180
To the high roof, still mimick'd as they rose
 Along the mirror'd walls by twin-clouds odorous.
 Twelve sphered tables, by silk seats insphered,
High as the level of a man's breast rear'd
 On libbard's° paws, upheld the heavy gold   *leopard's*
Of cups and goblets, and the store thrice told
 Of Ceres' horn,[58] and, in huge vessels, wine
Come from the gloomy tun° with merry shine.   *cask*
 Thus loaded with a feast the tables stood,
 Each shrining in the midst the image of a God.   190

   When in an antichamber° every guest   *front room*
Had felt the cold full sponge to pleasure press'd,
 By minist'ring slaves, upon his hands and feet,
 And fragrant oils with ceremony meet
Pour'd on his hair, they all mov'd to the feast   195
 In white robes, and themselves in order placed
Around the silken couches, wondering
 Whence all this mighty cost and blaze of wealth could spring.

---

[58]Cornucopia (horn of plenty)—a bountiful harvest; "insphered" (183) is a word K made up.

Soft went the music the soft air along,
While fluent Greek a vowel'd undersong   200
Kept up among the guests, discoursing low
At first, for scarcely was the wine at flow;
But when the happy vintage touch'd their brains,
Louder they talk, and louder come the strains
Of powerful instruments:——the gorgeous dyes,   205
The space, the splendour of the draperies,
The roof of awful richness, nectarous cheer,
Beautiful slaves,[59] and Lamia's self, appear,
Now, when the wine has done its rosy deed,
And every soul from human trammels freed,   210
No more so strange; for merry wine, sweet wine,
Will make Elysian shades not too fair, too divine.
Soon was God Bacchus at meridian° height;   *highest*
Flush'd were their cheeks, and bright eyes double bright:
Garlands of every green, and every scent   215
From vales deflower'd, or forest-trees branch-rent,
In baskets of bright osier'd[60] gold were brought
High as the handles heap'd, to suit the thought
Of every guest; that each, as he did please,
Might fancy-fit[61] his brows, silk-pillow'd at his ease.   220

What wreath for Lamia? What for Lycius?
What for the sage, old Apollonius?
Upon her aching forehead be there hung
The leaves of willow and of adder's tongue;[62]
And for the youth, quick, let us strip for him   225
The thyrsus,[63] that his watching eyes may swim
Into forgetfulness; and, for the sage,
Let spear-grass and the spiteful thistle wage

---

[59]The slaves are ornaments as well as servants. The suspense of syntax allows Lamia
and her spectacle to "appear" as a fantasy of inebriation, but its completion, "appear, / . . . No more so strange," confirms the opposite: the splendor seem probable
because of inebriation (G. Stewart, 28–29).

[60]woven of willow

[61]make a wreath for

[62]fern with leaves that look like snakes' tongues, supposed to be medicinally soothing; the willow is a standard emblem of grief.

[63]Bacchus's vine-entwined staff, an emblem of inebriation.

War on his temples. Do not all charms fly
At the mere touch of cold philosophy?°   *science*
There was an awful° rainbow once in heaven: *awesome*
We know her woof, her texture; she is given
In the dull catalogue of common things.
Philosophy will clip an Angel's wings,
Conquer all mysteries by rule and line,   235
Empty the haunted air, and gnomed mine—
Unweave a rainbow, as it erewhile made
The tender-person'd Lamia melt into a shade.[64]

    By her glad Lycius sitting, in chief place,
Scarce saw in all the room another face,   240
Till, checking his love trance, a cup he took
Full brimm'd, and opposite sent forth a look
'Cross the broad table, to beseech a glance
From his old teacher's wrinkled countenance,
And pledge[65] him. The bald-head philosopher   245
Had fix'd his eye, without a twinkle or stir
Full on the alarmed beauty of the bride,
Brow-beating her fair form, and troubling her sweet pride.
Lycius then press'd her hand, with devout touch,
As pale it lay upon the rosy couch: 250
'Twas icy, and the cold ran through his veins;
Then sudden it grew hot, and all the pains
Of an unnatural heat shot to his heart.
"Lamia,[66] what means this? Wherefore dost thou start?[67]
Know'st thou that man?" Poor Lamia answer'd not.   255

---

[64]Haydon's *Autobiography* reports an inebriated K and Lamb agreeing that Isaac Newton's science of optics "had destroyed all the poetry of the rainbow by reducing it to the prismatic colours." In his lecture, "On Poetry in General" (1818), Hazlitt remarked that "the progress of knowledge" has a tendency to limit "the imagination, and to clip the wings of poetry"; scientific empiricism "strips" the "imagination" of its "visionary" and "fanciful" claims. The gnomes of folklore guarded the precious ore of their underground world. See also K's *Mr. Kean* (p. 76).

[65]drink a toast to

[66]The first time her name is voiced by anyone in the poem; said three times, it is also a ghostly reference to the Hermes Trismegistus ("thrice greatest") of Neo-Platonist religion (and kin to the classical Hermes, the nymph-chasing god of Part I, in magical powers).

[67](Why are you startled?)

He gaz'd into her eyes, and not a jot
Own'd° they the lovelorn piteous appeal: *recognized*
More, more he gaz'd: his human senses reel:
Some hungry spell that loveliness absorbs;
There was no recognition in those orbs.   260
"Lamia!" he cried——and no soft-toned reply.
The many heard, and the loud revelry
Grew hush; the stately music no more breathes;
The myrtle[68] sicken'd in a thousand wreaths.
By faint degrees, voice, lute, and pleasure ceased;   265
A deadly silence step by step increased,
Until it seem'd a horrid presence there,
And not a man but felt the terror in his hair.[69]
"Lamia!" he shriek'd; and nothing but the shriek
With its sad echo did the silence break.   270
"Begone, foul dream!" he cried, gazing again
In the bride's face, where now no azure vein
Wander'd on fair-spaced temples; no soft bloom
Misted the cheek; no passion to illume
The deep-recessed vision:——all was blight;   275
Lamia, no longer fair, there sat a deadly white.
"Shut, shut those juggling[70] eyes, thou ruthless man!
   Turn them aside, wretch! or the righteous ban
   Of all the Gods, whose dreadful images
   Here represent their shadowy presences,   280
   May pierce them on the sudden with the thorn
   Of painful blindness; leaving thee forlorn,
   In trembling dotage to the feeblest fright
   Of conscience, for their long offended might,
   For all thine impious proud-heart sophistries,°   *learnedness*
   Unlawful magic, and enticing lies.
   Corinthians! look upon that gray-beard wretch!
   Mark how, possess'd, his lashless eyelids stretch
   Around his demon eyes! Corinthians, see!
   My sweet bride withers at their potency."   290
   "Fool!" said the sophist, in an under-tone

[68]plant sacred to Venus, an emblem of love-constancy
[69]*horrid* literally means "hair standing on end."
[70]magic-working

Gruff with contempt; which a death-nighing moan
From Lycius answer'd, as heart-struck and lost,
He sank supine[71] beside the aching ghost.
"Fool! Fool!" repeated he, while his eyes still   295
Relented not, nor mov'd; "from every ill
   Of life have I preserv'd thee to this day,
   And shall I see thee made a serpent's prey?"
Then Lamia breath'd death breath; the sophist's eye,
Like a sharp spear, went through her utterly,   300
Keen, cruel, perceant,[72] stinging: she, as well
As her weak hand could any meaning tell,
Motion'd him to be silent; vainly so,
He look'd and look'd again a level——No!
"A Serpent!" echoed he; no sooner said,   305
Than with a frightful scream she vanished:
And Lycius' arms were empty of delight,
As were his limbs of life, from that same night.
On the high couch he lay!——his friends came round——
Supported him——no pulse, or breath they found,   310
And, in its marriage robe, the heavy body wound.*[73]

   *"Philostratus, in his fourth book *de Vita Apollonii*,[74] hath a
memorable instance in this kind, which I may not omit, of one
Menippus Lycius, a young man twenty-five years of age, that going betwixt Cenchreas and Corinth, met such a phantasm in the
habit of a fair gentlewoman, which taking him by the hand, carried him home to her house, in the suburbs of Corinth, and told
him she was a Phoenician by birth, and if he would tarry with her,
he should hear her sing and play, and drink such wine as never any
drank, and no man should molest him; but she, being fair and

[71]prone in stupor

[72]piercing (archaism)

[73]The asterisk is in *1820*. The last 3 lines may be a triplet. If so, the grammar is still
slippery: Was the body *wound* by Lycius's friends in the robe-shroud? Or have these
friends *found* the body thus *wound*? Or did they find a body with a death-*wound*
(injury), denied a poetic completion?

[74]Greek philosopher Flavius Philostratus (c. 170–244) wrote the life of Apollonius of
Tyana (in Asia Minor), 1st-c. Pythagorean philosopher known for moral and religious probity but was also "well skilled in magic, and thoroughly acquainted with
those arts which can captivate and astonish the vulgar" (from *Lemprière's Classical
Dictionary*, used by K).

lovely, would live and die with him, that was fair and lovely to behold. The young man, a philosopher, otherwise staid and discreet, able to moderate his passions, though not this of love, tarried with her a while to his great content, and at last married her, to whose wedding, amongst other guests, came Apollonius; who, by some probable conjectures, found her out to be a serpent, a lamia; and that all her furniture was, like Tantalus' gold, described by Homer, no substance but mere illusions. When she saw herself descried, she wept, and desired Apollonius to be silent, but he would not be moved, and thereupon she, plate, house, and all that was in it, vanished in an instant: many thousands took notice of this fact, for it was done in the midst of Greece."

> Burton's 'Anatomy of Melancholy.'
> *Part 3. Sect. 2. Memb. 1. Subs. 1.*

ISABELLA;
OR,
THE POT OF BASIL.
A STORY FROM BOCCACCIO

Keats and Reynolds had planned a volume of verse-tales based on Giovanni Boccaccio's Decameron, *a set of tales framed by and composed after the plague that ravaged Florence in the mid-fourteenth century.* Isabella *is the "new romance" to which Keats refers at the end of his March 1818 verse-epistle to Reynolds. He drafted the first six stanzas in February (while in Hampstead), then worked on it over the next two months in Teignmouth while caring for Tom, completing it by the end of April. It is a "new" romance in several ways: a fresh composition; a new focus on the genre's conventions and aesthetic ideology; a new genre of critical meta-romance. Not only is there no happy ending (there are shades of Shakespeare's* Romeo and Juliet*), no possibility of escaping the pains of existence, but the economic base that sustains "old romance" comes in for such a sharp review that G. B. Shaw commented that if Marx had sat in the British Library "writing a poem instead of a treatise on* Capital, *he would have written* Isabella" (The John Keats Memorial Volume, *ed. George C. Williamson [London: John Lane, 1921], p. 175). Every thing and every person is reduced to commodity, and the luxury of romance (as genre and as human desire) is exposed as implicated in heartless oppression. Keats shifts the locale* *from Boccaccio's Messina to Florence: home of the powerful Medici family and a major financial capital in Europe, the plague-ravaged world from which Boccaccio himself and the young aristocrat tale-tellers of* The Decameron *take pastoral refuge. Keats uses a new verse form—the brisk* ottava rima *from Italian epic and comic romance, and more recently, Byron's satires on romance,* Beppo *(published the month Keats started writing* Isabella*). The rhyme of* ababc *can sustain expansions of narrative or imagery; the couplet, as in a Shakespearean sonnet, is tunable to epigrammatic intensity, sudden reversal, or comic subversion; and the whole stanza can shape discrete inset poems. Keats uses all these resources. Reynolds (Keats reported to George and Georgiana in October 1818; see p. 208) thought* Isabella *a good "answer to the attacks made on me in Blackwood's Magazine and the Quarterly Review." Although Keats confessed to Reynolds (22 September 1819) that he thought the poem was still too "smokeable," it is clear that "the gentleness of old Romance" (XLIX) comes in for a rough ride.*

I.

FAIR Isabel, poor simple Isabel!
    Lorenzo, a young palmer[1] in Love's eye!
They could not in the self-same mansion dwell
    Without some stir of heart, some malady;
They could not sit at meals but feel how well
    It soothed each to be the other by;
They could not, sure, beneath the same roof sleep
But to each other dream, and nightly weep.

II.

With every morn their love grew tenderer,
    With every eve deeper and tenderer still;
He might not in house, field, or garden stir,
    But her full shape would all his seeing fill;
And his continual voice was pleasanter
    To her, than noise of trees or hidden rill;
Her lute-string gave an echo of his name,
She spoilt her half-done broidery with the same.[2]

          10

[1] religious quester. Shakespeare's Romeo uses this term in self-description.

[2] This kind of comedy, sharpened by the snap of the couplet rhyme, is one of the resources of *ottava rima*, and softly satirical. *broidery*: embroidery.

III.

He knew whose gentle hand was at the latch,
    Before the door had given her to his eyes;
And from her chamber-window he would catch
    Her beauty farther than the falcon spies;   20
And constant as her vespers[3] would he watch,
    Because her face was turn'd to the same skies;
And with sick longing all the night outwear,
To hear her morning-step upon the stair.

IV.

A whole long month of May in this sad plight
    Made their cheeks paler by the break of June:
"To-morrow will I bow to my delight,
    To-morrow will I ask my lady's boon."——
"O may I never see another night,
    Lorenzo, if thy lips breathe not love's tune."——   30
So spake they to their pillows; but, alas,
Honeyless days and days did he let pass;

V.

Until sweet Isabella's untouch'd cheek
    Fell sick within the rose's just domain,
Fell thin as a young mother's, who doth seek
    By every lull to cool her infant's pain:
"How ill she is," said he, "I may not speak,
    And yet I will, and tell my love all plain:
If looks speak love-laws, I will drink her tears,
And at the least 'twill startle off her cares."   40

VI.

So said he one fair morning, and all day
    His heart beat awfully against his side;
And to his heart he inwardly did pray
    For power to speak; but still the ruddy tide
Stifled his voice, and puls'd resolve away——
    Fever'd his high conceit° of such a bride,   *idea, image*

[3]evening prayers

Yet brought him to the meekness of a child:
Alas! when passion is both meek and wild!

VII.

So once more he had wak'd and anguished
    A dreary night of love and misery,   50
If Isabel's quick eye had not been wed
    To every symbol on his forehead high;
She saw it waxing[4] very pale and dead,
    And straight all flush'd; so, lisped tenderly,
"Lorenzo!"——here she ceas'd her timid quest,
But in her tone and look he read the rest.

VIII.

"O Isabella, I can half perceive
    That I may speak my grief into thine ear;
If thou didst ever any thing believe,
    Believe how I love thee, believe how near   60
My soul is to its doom: I would not grieve
    Thy hand by unwelcome pressing, would not fear[5]
Thine eyes by gazing; but I cannot live
Another night, and not my passion shrive.[6]

IX.

Love! thou art leading me from wintry cold,
    Lady! thou leadest me to summer clime,
And I must taste the blossoms that unfold
    In its ripe warmth this gracious morning time."
So said, his erewhile timid lips grew bold,
    And poesied[7] with hers in dewy rhyme: 70

[4]growing; becoming waxy

[5]put fear into

[6]The sense of *shrive* as "make religious confession" gathers into it the sense of "passion" as suffering for a spiritual principle.

[7]Writing as a poet (literally, *maker*), K makes *poesy* a rich verb, *poesied*: made a poem (rhymed) with; made a bouquet with. *OED* cites only K for such usage, an event warmly admired by E. S. Dallas in *Poetics: An Essay on Poetry* (1852): "We speak of [. . .] the poetry of life in general: thus also Keats, making mention of what is in plain English the rapture of a kiss, says that the lips *poesied* with each other" (9).

Great bliss was with them, and great happiness
Grew, like a lusty° flower in June's caress.   *vigorous*

X.

Parting they seem'd to tread upon the air,
    Twin roses by the zephyr[8] blown apart
Only to meet again more close, and share
    The inward fragrance of each other's heart.
She, to her chamber gone, a ditty fair
    Sang, of delicious love and honey'd dart;[9]
He with light steps went up a western hill,
And bade the sun farewell, and joy'd his fill.   80

XI.

All close[10] they met again, before the dusk
    Had taken from the stars its pleasant veil,
All close they met, all eves, before the dusk
    Had taken from the stars its pleasant veil,
Close in a bower of hyacinth and musk,
    Unknown of any, free from whispering tale.
Ah! better had it been for ever so,
Than idle ears should pleasure in their woe.[11]

XII.

Were they unhappy then?——It cannot be——
    Too many tears for lovers have been shed,   90
Too many sighs give we to them in fee,°   *(as obligation)*
    Too much of pity after they are dead,
Too many doleful stories do we see,

---

[8]light breeze, but with a faint reference to jealous, death-dealing Zephyrus (a mythological tale also involving the hyacinth flower in the next stanza).

[9]Cupid's arrow; the two words murmur "honeyed art" (sweet, painfully sweet).

[10]in secret, intimately

[11]In Isabella's world, any local spies or gossipers; K also points to the strange aesthetics of romance, which entertain with stories of others' woe. This aesthetic economy prepares for the next two stanzas, which comment on romance poetics and aesthetic pleasures: the language of enjoying riches at the expense of others' woe unfolds into the commodity critique that sparked Shaw's attention.

Whose matter in bright gold[12] were best be read;
Except in such a page where Theseus' spouse[13]
Over the pathless waves towards him bows.

XIII.

But, for the general award of love,
    The little sweet doth kill much bitterness;
Though Dido silent is in under-grove,[14]
    And Isabella's was a great distress,   100
Though young Lorenzo in warm Indian clove
    Was not embalm'd, this truth is not the less—
Even bees, the little almsmen[15] of spring-bowers,
Know there is richest juice in poison-flowers.

XIV.[16]

With her two brothers this fair lady dwelt,
    Enriched from ancestral merchandize,
And for them[17] many a weary hand did swelt[18]
    In torched mines and noisy factories,
And many once proud-quiver'd loins[19] did melt
    In blood from stinging whip;—with hollow eyes   110

---

[12]cf. "golden-tongued Romance" in the sonnet on *King Lear* (p. 92).

[13]Ariadne. There is a world of pathos in *pathless*, for Theseus abandoned his bride on the Isle of Naxos.

[14]underworld forest

[15]men hired to say prayers for their patrons

[16]In an unsigned review in Baldwin's *London Magazine* (Sept. 1820), John Scott meant to do K a favor, de-Hunting him, and insisting that what may seem "political" in his writing is really just "boyish petulance"; stanzas XIV–XVII were mere "schoolboy vituperation of trade and traders." Scott preferred the motive given in Boccaccio's tale: the brothers' horror at their sister's sexual license, especially with an employee of a lower social class. Against this 19th-c. trend, Shaw read the stanzas as virtual "Factory Commission Reports," an "immense indictment of the profiteers and exploiters with which Marx has shaken capitalistic civilization to its foundations" (*op. cit.* 175).

[17]The referent may be the brothers, or all 3, with Isabella innocent of the economy of her luxurious life (and her brothers' regard of her as a commodity).

[18]swelter, the reduction of humans to the laboring hand; *OED* cites K here. There is also an echo of Milton's hell (a passage K annotated): as Satan scans the fiery darkness, he discovers his comrade Beelzebub "weltring by his side" (*PL* 1.78).

[19]The adjective compresses a history: men from a hunting society (the quivers full of arrows hung from belts rested against their loins), sold into slavery.

Many all day in dazzling[20] river stood,
To take the rich-ored driftings of the flood.

XV.

For them the Ceylon[21] diver° held his breath,   *pearl-diver*
    And went all naked to the hungry shark;
For them his ears gush'd blood; for them in death
    The seal on the cold ice with piteous bark
Lay full of darts;[22] for them alone did seethe
    A thousand men in troubles wide and dark:
Half-ignorant, they° turn'd an easy wheel,   *the brothers*
That set sharp racks at work, to pinch and peel.   120

XVI.

Why were they proud? Because their marble founts
    Gush'd with more pride than do a wretch's tears?——
Why were they proud? Because fair orange-mounts
    Were of more soft ascent than lazar stairs?[23]——
Why were they proud? Because red-lin'd accounts[24]
    Were richer than the songs of Grecian years?—
Why were they proud? again we ask aloud,
Why in the name of Glory were they proud?

XVII.

Yet were these Florentines as self-retired
    In hungry pride and gainful cowardice,   130
As two close[25] Hebrews in that land inspired,°   *Palastine*
    Paled in° and vineyarded from beggar-spies,   *walled*

[20]This word, so involved with the enchantments of K's earlier poetry, is now situated in two competing registers: the beauty of a river to an aesthete's eyes, and the infliction of pain from the glare on workers' eyes. "Their eyes were so fatigued with the eternal dazzle and whiteness that they lay down on their backs upon deck to relieve their sight on the blue Sky," K told G&GK about an account of a polar expedition (Dec. 1818).

[21]The British accent is on the first syllable, a homophone with "seal on" (116).

[22]cf. love's "honey'd dart" (X).

[23]stairs to a lazar-house, for the miserably diseased poor ("leper" is a cognate).

[24]luxurious account books (here *red* does not signify debts).

[25]conspiring. *OED* cites 132 as the first adjective-forming of "vineyarded."

The hawks of ship-mast forests——the untired
    And pannier'd mules for ducats and old lies——
Quick cat's-paw on the generous stray-away,——
Great wits in Spanish, Tuscan, and Malay.[26]

XVIII.

How was it these same ledger-men[27] could spy
    Fair Isabella in her downy nest?
How could they find out in Lorenzo's eye
    A straying from his toil? Hot Egypt's pest   140
Into their vision covetous and sly![28]
    How could these money-bags see east and west?——
Yet so they did——and every dealer fair
Must see behind, as doth the hunted hare.

XIX.

O eloquent and famed Boccaccio!
    Of thee we now should ask forgiving boon,°   *bounty*
And of thy spicy myrtles as they blow,
    And of thy roses amorous of the moon,
And of thy lilies, that do paler grow
    Now they can no more hear thy ghittern's° tune,   *guitar's*
For venturing syllables that ill beseem
The quiet glooms of such a piteous theme.

XX.

Grant thou a pardon here, and then the tale
    Shall move on soberly, as it is meet;
There is no other crime, no mad assail   155
    To make old prose in modern rhyme more sweet:
But it is done——succeed the verse or fail——
    To honour thee, and thy gone spirit greet;

---

[26]They swoop down like hawks on trading fleets; they are tireless mules bearing large baskets filled with gold coins; they swiftly attack gullible spendthrifts; they schmooze with everyone.

[27]Shaw cheered this register of "a very full-blooded modern revolutionist," noting that even "Marx is more euphuistic in calling the profiteers *bourgeoisie* than Keats with his 'these same ledger-men'" (*Memorial Volume*, p. 176).

[28]The 3-day plague of darkness called down by Moses on Egypt (Exodus 10.21–23).

To stead° thee as a verse in English tongue,   *serve*
An echo of thee in the north-wind sung.   160

XXI.

These brethren having found by many signs
    What love Lorenzo for their sister had,
And how she lov'd him too, each unconfines
    His bitter thoughts to other, well nigh mad
That he, the servant of their trade designs,
    Should in their sister's love be blithe and glad,
When 'twas their plan to coax her by degrees
To some high noble and his olive-trees.²⁹

XXII.

And many a jealous conference had they,
    And many times they bit their lips alone,   170
Before they fix'd upon a surest way
    To make the youngster for his crime atone;
And at the last, these men of cruel clay°   *heartless flesh*
    Cut Mercy with a sharp knife to the bone;³⁰
For they resolved in some forest dim
To kill Lorenzo, and there bury him.

XXIII.

So on a pleasant morning, as he leant
    Into the sun-rise, o'er the balustrade³¹
Of the garden-terrace, towards him they bent
    Their footing through the dews; and to him said,   180
"You seem there in the quiet of content,³²
    Lorenzo, and we are most loth to invade

²⁹a source of economic wealth (olive oil)

³⁰acted pitilessly, like Shakespeare's Shylock seeking (with no "quality of Mercy") his pound of flesh from Antonio, for his default on a loan. K shades the comparison of the brothers to conspiring Hebrews (XVII).

³¹stone railing, with vases for the vertical supports

³²an adjective used as a noun, as if a mood were an atmosphere

Calm speculation;[33] but if you are wise,
Bestride your steed while cold is in the skies.

XXIV.

To-day we purpose, ay, this hour we mount
    To spur three leagues[34] towards the Apennine;
Come down, we pray thee, ere the hot sun count
    His dewy rosary on the eglantine."[35]
Lorenzo, courteously as he was wont,
    Bow'd a fair greeting to these serpents' whine;[36]   190
And went in haste, to get in readiness,
With belt, and spur, and bracing huntsman's dress.[37]

XXV.

And as he to the court-yard pass'd along,
    Each third step did he pause, and listen'd oft
If he could hear his lady's matin°-song,   *morning*
    Or the light whisper of her footstep soft;
And as he thus over his passion hung,
    He heard a laugh full musical aloft;
When, looking up, he saw her features bright
Smile through an in-door lattice, all delight.   200

XXVI.

"Love, Isabel!" said he, "I was in pain
    Lest I should miss to bid thee a good morrow:
Ah! what if I should lose thee, when so fain°   *willing*
    I am to stifle all the heavy sorrow
Of a poor three hours' absence? but we'll gain
    Out of the amorous dark what day doth borrow.
Good bye! I'll soon be back."——"Good bye!" said she:——
And as he went she chanted merrily.

[33]musings; but K lets the word suggest the brothers' business interests.

[34]A league is a variable measure, about 3 miles; the Apennines are a mountain-chain.

[35]Catholics say their prayers with rosary beads.

[36]Another brilliant phonic slide, this sending their oily greeting into "serpent swine."

[37]a cruel irony, since Lorenzo is the prey.

XXVII.

So the two brothers and their murder'd man[38]
    Rode past fair Florence, to where Arno's stream[39]   210
Gurgles through straiten'd banks, and still doth fan
    Itself with dancing bulrush, and the bream
Keeps head against the freshets. Sick and wan
    The brothers' faces in the ford did seem,
Lorenzo's flush with love.——They pass'd the water
Into a forest quiet for the slaughter.

XXVIII.

There was Lorenzo slain and buried in,
    There in that forest did his great love cease;
Ah! when a soul doth thus its freedom win,[40]
    It aches in loneliness—is ill at peace   220
As the break-covert blood-hounds[41] of such sin:
    They dipp'd their swords in the water, and did tease
Their horses homeward, with convulsed spur,
Each richer by his being a murderer.

XXIX.

They told their sister how, with sudden speed,
    Lorenzo had ta'en ship for foreign lands,
Because of some great urgency and need
    In their affairs, requiring trusty hands.
Poor Girl! put on thy stifling widow's weed,
    And 'scape at once from Hope's accursed bands;   230
To-day thou wilt not see him, nor to-morrow,
And the next day will be a day of sorrow.

---

[38]"The anticipation of the assassination is wonderfully conceived in one epithet," wrote Charles Lamb, in an unsigned review *(New Times,* 19 July 1820); Leigh Hunt agreed *(Indicator,* 2 Aug. 1820, p. 342). Lamb thought *Isabella* "the finest thing in the volume," and it was also admired by Matthew Arnold and Pre-Raphaelite painters.

[39]Florence's river.

[40]In Christian salvation, the eternal soul is prisoned in the mortal body and released at death. In Roman Catholicism, if one dies without last rites, the soul may linger in limbo or purgatory.

[41]breaking from cover in pursuit of prey.

XXX.

She weeps alone for pleasures not to be;
    Sorely she wept until the night came on,
And then, instead of love, O misery!
    She brooded o'er the luxury° alone: *self-indulgence*
His image in the dusk she seem'd to see,
    And to the silence made a gentle moan,
Spreading her perfect arms upon the air,
And on her couch low murmuring, "Where? O where?"[42]   240

XXXI.

But Selfishness,° Love's cousin, held not long   *self-concern*
    Its fiery vigil in her single breast;
She fretted for the golden hour, and hung
    Upon the time with feverish unrest——
Not long——for soon into her heart a throng
    Of higher occupants, a richer zest,
Came tragic; passion not to be subdued,
And sorrow for her love in travels rude.[43]

XXXII.

In the mid days of autumn, on their eves
    The breath of Winter comes from far away,   250
And the sick west continually bereaves
    Of some gold tinge, and plays a roundelay
Of death among the bushes and the leaves,
    To make all bare before he dares to stray
From his north cavern. So sweet Isabel
By gradual decay from beauty fell,[44]

XXXIII.

Because Lorenzo came not. Oftentimes
    She ask'd her brothers, with an eye all pale,
Striving to be itself, what dungeon climes

---

[42]Here, as in *Endymion*, the *ubi sunt (where are . . . ?)* trope is given to love-longing.
[43]beyond civilization
[44]K lets the syntax itself fall into the next stanza.

Could keep him off so long? They spake a tale   260
Time after time, to quiet her. Their crimes
    Came on them, like a smoke from Hinnom's vale;[45]
And every night in dreams they groan'd aloud,
To see their sister in her snowy shroud.

XXXIV.

And she had died in drowsy ignorance,
    But for a thing more deadly dark than all;
It came like a fierce potion, drunk by chance,
    Which saves a sick man from the feather'd pall
For some few gasping moments; like a lance,
    Waking an Indian from his cloudy hall   270
With cruel pierce,[46] and bringing him again
Sense of the gnawing fire at heart and brain.

XXXV.

It was a vision.——In the drowsy gloom,
    The dull of midnight, at her couch's foot
Lorenzo stood, and wept: the forest tomb
    Had marr'd his glossy hair which once could shoot
Lustre into the sun, and put cold doom
    Upon his lips, and taken the soft lute
From his lorn voice, and past his loamed ears
Had made a miry channel for his tears.   280

XXXVI.

Strange sound it was, when the pale shadow spake;
    For there was striving, in its piteous tongue,
To speak as when on earth it was awake,
    And Isabella on its music hung:
Languor there was in it, and tremulous shake,

---

[45]At this place King David's son Ahaz indulged human sacrifice, even "burnt his children in the fire, after the abomination of the heathen whom the LORD had cast out" (2 Chronicles 28.3). See also *PL* 1.403–4, marked by K.

[46]A verb K makes a noun; he is thinking of accounts of Native-American tortures about which he had been reading in William Robertson's *History of America*.

As in a palsied Druid's[47] harp unstrung;
And through it moan'd a ghostly under-song,
Like hoarse night-gusts sepulchral briars among.

XXXVII.

Its eyes, though wild, were still all dewy bright
    With love, and kept all phantom fear aloof   290
From the poor girl by magic of their light,
    The while it did unthread the horrid woof°   *weaving*
Of the late darken'd time,——the murderous spite
    Of pride and avarice,——the dark pine roof
In the forest,——and the sodden turfed dell,
Where, without any word, from stabs he fell.

XXXVIII.

Saying moreover, "Isabel,[48] my sweet!
    Red whortle-berries droop above my head,
And a large flint-stone weighs upon my feet;
    Around me beeches and high chestnuts shed   300
Their leaves and prickly nuts; a sheep-fold bleat
    Comes from beyond the river to my bed:
Go, shed one tear upon my heather-bloom,
And it shall comfort me within the tomb.

XXXIX.

I am a shadow now, alas! alas!
    Upon the skirts of human-nature dwelling
Alone: I chant alone the holy mass,
    While little sounds of life are round me knelling,
And glossy bees at noon do fieldward pass,
    And many a chapel bell the hour is telling,   310
Paining me through: those sounds grow strange to me,
And thou art distant in Humanity.

---

[47]The Druids were the poet-priests of ancient Britain.
[48]The name now sounds a chime with the *dell / fell* couplet of XXXVII.

XL.

I know what was, I feel full well what is,
    And I should rage, if spirits could go mad;
Though I forget the taste of earthly bliss,
    That paleness warms my grave, as though I had
A Seraph° chosen from the bright abyss   *major angel*
    To be my spouse: thy paleness makes me glad;
Thy beauty grows upon me, and I feel
A greater love through all my essence steal."[49]   320

XLI.

The Spirit mourn'd "Adieu!"—dissolv'd, and left
    The atom darkness in a slow turmoil;
As when of healthful midnight sleep bereft,
    Thinking on rugged hours and fruitless toil,
We put our eyes into a pillowy cleft,
    And see the spangly gloom froth up and boil:
It made sad Isabella's eyelids ache,
And in the dawn she started up awake;

XLII.

"Ha! ha!" said she, "I knew not this hard life,
    I thought the worst was simple misery;   330
I thought some Fate with pleasure or with strife
    Portion'd° us——happy days, or else to die;   *endowed*
But there is crime—a brother's bloody knife![50]
    Sweet Spirit, thou hast school'd my infancy:
I'll visit thee for this, and kiss thine eyes,
And greet thee morn and even in the skies."

---

[49]The faint punning of *steal* into *steel* (as if a knife) glints in a letter to Fanny Brawne: "Even when I am not thinking of you I receive your influence and a tenderer nature steeling upon me" (8 July 1819; see p. 259). In Feb. 1820 K recalls these lines to her after his dire hemorrhage: "I feel too much separated from you and could almost speak to you in the words of Lorenzo's Ghost to Isabella."

[50]The image, though it pertains to Lorenzo, evokes the fratricides of Genesis and *Hamlet*.

XLIII.

When the full morning came, she had devised
    How she might secret to the forest hie;
How she might find the clay, so dearly prized,
    And sing to it one latest lullaby;   340
How her short absence might be unsurmised,
    While she the inmost of the dream would try.
Resolv'd, she took with her an aged nurse,
And went into that dismal forest-hearse.

XLIV.

See, as they creep along the river side,
    How she doth whisper to that aged Dame,
And, after looking round the champaign wide,[51]
    Shows her a knife.——"What feverous hectic flame
Burns in thee, child?——What good can thee betide,
    That thou should'st smile again?"——The evening came,   350
And they had found Lorenzo's earthy bed;
The flint was there, the berries at his head.

XLV.

Who hath not loiter'd in a green church-yard,
    And let his spirit, like a demon-mole,
Work through the clayey soil and gravel hard,
    To see skull, coffin'd bones, and funeral stole;
Pitying each form that hungry Death hath marr'd,
    And filling it once more with human soul?
Ah! this is holiday to what was felt
When Isabella by Lorenzo knelt.   360

XLVI.

She gaz'd into the fresh-thrown mould, as though
    One glance did fully all its secrets tell;
Clearly she saw, as other eyes would know
    Pale limbs at bottom of a crystal well;[52]

[51]exurban fields
[52]Pushing someone into a deep well was another popular mode of murder.

Upon the murderous spot she seem'd to grow,   365
    Like to a native lily of the dell:
Then with her knife, all sudden, she began
To dig more fervently than misers can.[53]

XLVII.

Soon she turn'd up a soiled glove, whereon
    Her silk had play'd in purple phantasies,°   *(embroidery)*
She kiss'd it with a lip more chill than stone,
    And put it in her bosom, where it dries
And freezes utterly unto the bone
    Those dainties made to still an infant's cries:[54]
Then 'gan she work again; nor stay'd her care,
But to throw back at times her veiling hair.

XLVIII.

That old nurse stood beside her wondering,
    Until her heart felt pity to the core
At sight of such a dismal labouring,
    And so she kneeled, with her locks all hoar,°   *gray hair* 380
And put her lean hands to the horrid[55] thing:
    Three hours they labour'd at this travail sore;
At last they felt the kernel of the grave,
And Isabella did not stamp and rave.

XLIX.

Ah! wherefore all this wormy circumstance?
    Why linger at the yawning tomb so long?
O for the gentleness of old Romance,
    The simple plaining[56] of a minstrel's song!
Fair reader, at the old tale° take a glance,   *Boccaccio's*
    For here, in truth, it doth not well belong   390

---

[53]for stashed money

[54]A gothic undoing of both infant nurture by breast-feeding and erotic fixation.

[55]*horrid* means literally *causing hair to stand on end*. K plays the sound of this word from *hoar* and into *hours*.

[56]complaining, lament

To speak:——O turn thee to the very tale,
And taste the music of that vision pale.

L.

With duller steel than the Perséan sword
    They cut away no formless monster's head,[57]
But one, whose gentleness did well accord
    With death, as life. The ancient harps have said,
Love never dies, but lives, immortal Lord:
    If Love impersonate was ever dead,
Pale Isabella kiss'd it, and low° moan'd.   *softly*
'Twas love; cold,——dead indeed, but not dethroned.   400

LI.

In anxious secrecy they took it home,
    And then the prize was all for Isabel:
She calm'd its wild hair with a golden comb,
    And all around each eye's sepulchral cell
Pointed each fringed lash; the smeared loam
    With tears, as chilly as a dripping well,
She drench'd away:——and still she comb'd, and kept
Sighing all day——and still she kiss'd, and wept.

LII.

Then in a silken scarf,——sweet with the dews
    Of precious flowers pluck'd in Araby,   410
And divine liquids come with odorous ooze
    Through the cold serpent pipe[58] refreshfully,——
She wrapp'd it up; and for its tomb did choose
    A garden-pot, wherein she laid it by,
And cover'd it with mould, and o'er it set
Sweet Basil, which her tears kept ever wet.

[57]With a sword given to him by Mercury, Perseus cut off the Gorgon Medusa's head (she whose gaze turned men to stone, literally astonishing them).
[58]the perfumery

LIII.

And she forgot the stars, the moon, and sun,
　　And she forgot the blue above the trees,
And she forgot the dells where waters run,
　　And she forgot the chilly autumn breeze;　　　　420
She had no knowledge when the day was done,
　　And the new morn she saw not: but in peace
Hung over her sweet Basil evermore,
And moisten'd it with tears unto the core.

LIV.

And so she ever fed it with thin tears,
　　Whence thick, and green, and beautiful it grew,
So that it smelt more balmy than its peers
　　Of Basil-tufts in Florence; for it drew
Nurture besides, and life, from human fears,
　　From the fast mouldering head there shut from view:　　　430
So that the jewel, safely casketed,
Came forth, and in perfumed leafits spread.

LV.

O Melancholy, linger here awhile!
　　O Music, Music, breathe despondingly!
O Echo, Echo,[59] from some sombre isle,
　　Unknown, Lethean, sigh to us—O sigh!
Spirits in grief, lift up your heads, and smile;
　　Lift up your heads, sweet Spirits, heavily,
And make a pale light in your cypress glooms,
Tinting with silver wan your marble tombs.　　　440

LVI.

Moan hither, all ye syllables of woe,
　　From the deep throat of sad Melpomene![60]
Through bronzed lyre in tragic order go,
　　And touch the strings into a mystery;

[59]K nicely has the word enact its meaning.
[60]Greek muse of tragedy

Sound mournfully upon the winds and low;
    For simple Isabel[61] is soon to be
Among the dead: She withers, like a palm
Cut by an Indian for its juicy balm.

LVII.

O leave the palm to wither by itself;
    Let not quick Winter chill its dying hour!—   450
It may not be——those Baälites of pelf,[62]
    Her brethren, noted the continual shower
From her dead eyes; and many a curious elf,
    Among her kindred, wonder'd that such dower
Of youth and beauty should be thrown aside
By one mark'd out to be a Noble's bride.

LVIII.

And, furthermore, her brethren wonder'd much
    Why she sat drooping by the Basil green,
And why it flourish'd, as by magic touch;
    Greatly they wonder'd what the thing might mean: 460
They could not surely give belief, that such
    A very nothing would have power to wean
Her from her own fair youth, and pleasures gay,
And even remembrance of her love's delay.

LIX.

Therefore they watch'd a time when they might sift   465
    This hidden whim; and long they watch'd in vain;
For seldom did she go to chapel-shrift,°   *confession*
    And seldom felt she any hunger-pain;
And when she left, she hurried back, as swift
    As bird on wing to breast° its eggs again;   *brood over*
And, patient as a hen-bird, sat her there
Beside her Basil, weeping through her hair.

---

[61]A calculated echo, with a difference, of the poem's first line.
[62]The Philistine sun-god Baal is regarded by rival religions as a false god (here, of wealth).

LX.

Yet they contriv'd to steal the Basil-pot,
    And to examine it in secret place:
The thing was vile with green and livid spot,
    And yet they knew it was Lorenzo's face:
The guerdon° of their murder they had got,   *reward*
    And so left Florence in a moment's space,
Never to turn again.——Away they went,
With blood upon their heads, to banishment.   480

LXI.

O Melancholy, turn thine eyes away!
    O Music, Music, breathe despondingly!
O Echo, Echo, on some other day,
    From isles Lethean,° sigh to us—O sigh!   *forgetfulness*
Spirits of grief, sing not your "Well-a-way!"
    For Isabel, sweet Isabel, will die;
Will die a death too lone and incomplete,
Now they have ta'en away her Basil sweet.

LXII.

Piteous she look'd on dead and senseless things,
    Asking for her lost Basil amorously: 490
And with melodious chuckle in the strings
    Of her lorn voice, she oftentimes would cry
After the Pilgrim in his wanderings,
    To ask him where her Basil was; and why
'Twas hid from her: "For cruel 'tis," said she,
"To steal my Basil-pot away from me."

LXIII.

And so she pined, and so she died forlorn,
    Imploring for her Basil to the last.
No heart was there in Florence but did mourn
    In pity of her love, so overcast.   500
And a sad ditty of this story born
    From mouth to mouth through all the country pass'd:
Still is the burthen° sung——"O cruelty,   *refrain*
To steal my Basil-pot away from me!"

§ Isabella in *The Decameron*

Giovanni Boccaccio (1313–75) escaped the Black Death, which ravaged Florence 1348–49, killing his father, stepmother, and many friends. The frame-tale of The Decameron, *written 1349–51, is this plague, from which a group of young artistocrats flee to a country estate. There, with servants aplenty to take care of their material needs, they amuse themselves with music, feasting, dancing, and storytelling. Keats read the first English translation of* The Decameron, *by John Florio (London: 1620), in the fifth edition of 1684. Author of the first Italian-English dictionary, Florio also translated Montaigne and may have known Shakespeare.*

> *The Fourth Day, The Fift Novell. Wherein Is Plainly Proved, That Love Cannot Be Rooted Uppe, By Any Humane Power Or Providence; Especially In Such Soule, Where It Hath Bene Really Apprehended.*
>
> *The three Brethren to Isabella, slew a Gentleman that secretly loved her. His ghost appeared to her in her sleepe, and shewed her in what place they had buried his body. She (in silent manner) brought away his head, and putting it into a pot of earth, such as Flowers, Basile, or other sweete hearbes are usually set in; she watered it (a long while) with her teares. Wherefore her Brethren having intelligence; soone after she dyed, with meere conceite of sorrow.*

The Novell of Madame Eliza being finished, and some-what commended by the King, in regard of the Tragicall conclusion; Philomena was enjoyned to proceede next with her discourse. She being overcome with much compassion, for the hard Fortunes of Noble Gerbino, and his beautifull Princesse, after an extreame and vehement sighe, thus she spake. My Tale (worthy Ladies) extendeth not to persons of so high birth or quality, as they were of whom Madame Eliza gave you relation: yet (peradventure) it may prove to be no lesse pittifull. And now I remember my selfe, Messina so lately spoken of, is the place where this accident also happened.

In Messina there dwelt three young men, Brethren, and Merchants by their common profession, who becomming very rich by the death of their Father, lived in very good fame and repute.[1] Their

[1]K changes the family from 3 brothers (like the Keatses) to 2.

Father was of San Gemignano, and they had a Sister named Isabella, young, beautifull, and well conditioned; who upon some occasion, as yet remained unmarried. A proper youth, being a Gentleman borne in Pisa, and named Lorenzo, as a trusty factor or servant, had the managing of the brethrens businesse and affaires. This Lorenzo being of comely personage, affable, and excellent in his behaviour, grew so gracious in the eyes of Isabella, that she affoorded him many very respective lookes, yea, kindnesses of no common quality. Which Lorenzo taking notice of, and observing by degrees from time to time, gave over all other beauties in the City, which might allure any affection from him, and onely fixed his heart on her, so that their love grew to a mutuall embracing, both equally respecting one another, and entertaining kindnesses, as occasion gave leave.

Long time continued this amorous league of love, yet not so cunningly concealed, but at the length, the secret meeting of Lorenzo and Isabella, to ease their poore soul of Loves oppressions, was discovered by the eldest of the Brethren, unknowne to them who were thus betrayed. He being a man of great discretion, although this sight was highly displeasing to him: yet notwithstanding, he kept it to himselfe till the next morning, labouring his braine what might best be done in so urgent a case. When day was come, he resorted to his other Brethren, and told them what he had seene in the time past, betweene their sister and Lorenzo.

Many deliberations passed on this case; but after all, thus they concluded together, to let it proceede on with patient supportance, that no scandall might ensue to them, or their Sister, no evill acte being (as yet) committed. And seeming, as if they knew not of their love, had a wary eye still upon her secret walkes, awaiting for some convenient time, when without their owne prejudice, or Isabellaes knowledge, they might safely breake off this their stolne love, which was altogether against their liking. So, shewing no worse countenance to Lorenzo, then formerly they had done, but imploying and conversing with him in kinde manner; it fortuned, that riding (all three) to recreate themselves out of the City, they tooke Lorenzo in their company, and when they were come to a solitarie place, such as best suited with their vile purpose: they ran sodainly upon Lorenzo, slew him, and afterward enterred his body, where hardly it could be discovered by any one. Then they returned backe to Messina, and gave it forth (as a credible report) that they had sent him abroad about their affaires, as formerly they were wont to do: which every one verily beleeved, because they knew no reason why they should conceite any otherwise.

Isabella, living in expectation of his returne, and perceiving his stay to her was so offensive long: made many demands to her Brethren, into what parts they had sent him, that his tarrying was so quite from all wonted course. Such was her importunate speeches to them, that they taking it very discontentedly, one of them returned her this frowning answer. What is your meaning Sister, by so many questionings after Lorenzo? What urgent affaires have you with him, that makes you so impatient upon his absence? If hereafter you make any more demands for him, we shall shape you such a reply, as will be but little to your liking. At these harsh words, Isabella fell into abundance of teares, where-among she mingled many sighes and groanes, such as were able to overthrow a farre stronger constitution: so that, being full of feare and dismay, yet no way distrusting her brethrens cruell deede; she durst not question any more after him.

In the silence of darke night, as she lay afflicted in her bed, oftentimes would she call for Lorenzo, entreating his speedy returning to her: And then againe, as if he had bene present with her, she checkt and reproved him for his so long absence. One night amongst the rest, she being growen almost hopelesse, of ever seeing him againe, having a long while wept and greevously lamented; her senses and faculties utterly spent and tired, that she could not utter any more complaints, she fell into a trance or sleepe; and dreamed, that the ghost of Lorenzo appeared unto her, in torne and unbefitting garments, his lookes pale, meager, & staring: & (as she thought) thus spake to her. 'My deere love Isabella, thou dost nothing but torment thy selfe, with calling on me, accusing me for overlong tarrying from thee: I am come therefore to let thee know, that thou canst not enjoy my company any more, because the very same day when last thou sawest me, thy brethren most bloodily murthered me.' And acquainting her with the place where they had buried his mangled body: hee strictly charged her, not to call him at any time afterward, and so vanished away.

The young Damosell awaking, and giving some credite to her Vision, sighed and wept exceedingly; and after she was risen in the morning, not daring to say any thing to her brethren, she resolutely determined, to go see the place formerly appointed her, onely to make triall, if that which she seemed to see in her sleepe, should carry any likely-hood of truth. Having obtained favour of her brethren, to ride a dayes journey from the City, in company of her trusty Nurse, who long time had attended on her in the house, and knew the secret passages of her love: they rode directly to the designed place, which being covered with some store of dried leaves, & more deeply sunke then any other part of the ground therabout, they digged not farre, but they found the body of murthered Lorenzo, as yet very little corrupted or impaired, and then perceived the truth of her vision.

Wisedome and government so much prevailed with her, as to instruct her soule, that her teares spent there, were meerley fruitelesse and in vaine, neither did the time require any long tarrying there. Gladly would she have carried the whole body with her, secretly to bestow honourable enterment on it, but it exceeded the compasse of her ability. Wherefore, in regard she could not have all, yet she would be possessed of a part, and having brought a keene razor with her, by helpe of the Nurse, she divided the head from the body, and wrapped it up in a Napkin, which the Nurse conveyed into her lap, & then laide the body in the ground againe. Thus being undiscovered by any, they departed thence, and arrived at home in convenient time, where being alone by themselves in the Chamber: she washed the head over and over with her teares, and bestowed infinite kisses thereon.

Not long after, the Nurse having brought her a large earthen pot, such as we use to set Basile, Marjerom, Flowers, or other sweet hearbes in, and shrowding the head in a silken Scarfe, put it into the pot, covering it with earth, and planting divers rootes of excellent Basile therein, which she never watered, but either with her teares, Rose water, or water distilled from the Flowers of Oranges. This pot she used continually to sitte by, either in her chamber, or any where else: for she carried it alwaies with her, sighing and breathing foorth sad complaints thereto, even as if they had beene uttered to her Lorenzo, and day by day this was her continuall exercise, to the no meane admiration of her bretheren, and many other friends that beheld her.

So long she held on in this mourning manner, that, what by the continuall watering of the Basile, and putrifaction of the head, so buried in the pot of earth; it grew very flourishing, and most odoriferous to such as scented it, that as no other Basile could possibly yeeld so sweete a savour. The neighbours noting this behaviour in her, observing the long continuance thereof, how much her bright beauty was defaced, and the eyes sunke into her head by incessant weeping, made many kinde and friendly motions, to understand the reason of her so violent oppressions; but could not by any meanes prevaile with her, or win any discovery by her Nurse, so faithfull was she in secrecie to her. Her brethren also waxed wearie of this carriage in her; and having very often reproved her for it, without any other alteration in her: at length, they closely stole away the potte of Basile from her, for which she made infinite wofull lamentations, earnestly entreating to have it restored againe, avouching that she could not live without it.

Perceiving that she could not have the pot againe, she fell into an extreame sicknesse, occasioned onely by her ceaselesse weeping: and never urged she to have any thing, but the restoring of her Basile pot. Her brethren grew greatly amazed thereat, because she never called for ought else beside; and thereupon were very desirous to ransacke the pot to the very bottome. Having emptied out all the earth, they found the Scarfe of silke, wherein the head of Lorenzo was wrapped; which was (as yet) not so much consumed, but by the lockes of haire, they knew it to be Lorenzoes head, whereat they became confounded with amazement.

Fearing least their offence might come to open publication, they buried it very secretly; and, before any could take notice thereof, they departed from Messina, and went to dwell in Naples, Isabella crying and calling still for her pot of Basile, being unable to give over mourning, dyed within a few dayes after. Thus have you heard the hard fate of poore Lorenzo and his Isabella. Within no long while after, when this accident came to be publikely knowne, an excellent ditty was composed thereof beginning thus.

> Cruell and unkinde was the Christian?
> That robd me of my Basiles blisse, etc.

———

The Fourth Day, The Sixt Novell

The Novell which Madam Philomena had so graciously related, was highly pleasing unto the other Ladies; because they had oftentimes heard the Song, without knowing who made it or upon what occasion it was composed.

The Eve of St. Agnes

Keats began this poem in early winter 1819. According to legend, a young virgin who performs certain rituals on this eve will dream of her future husband. Agnes, patron saint of virgins, was a thirteen-year-old Christian martyr in early fourth-century Rome, condemned to a night of gang-rape in the brothels before her execution. This first torture was prevented by a miraculous storm of thunder and lightning, a climate that appears at the end of Keats's poem. In the artistry of his Spenserian stanzas (his first return to the form after his very first poem), Keats spins an ironic romance—indulging the pleasures of the genre (love, imagination, gorgeous sensuality with a spiritual aura) while applying a playful, sometimes satiric, sometimes darkly shaded perspective to its illusions. With Romeo and Juliet in mind, Keats wanted to indicate the sexual heat of his lovers, but publisher Taylor, worried about indecency and offense to female readers, forced some alterations (September 1819). Though Keats complied with angry reluctance ("he says he does not want ladies to read his poetry:—that he writes for men," Woodhouse sighed to Taylor), the imagery of stars and flowers in XXXVI does the job. I give some of the canceled text in my footnotes, using a single slash (/) to indicate different wordings within one verse line and two slashes (//) to indicate another verse line. I also append two deleted stanzas, preserved in George Keats's copy.

I

St. Agnes' Eve—Ah, bitter chill it was!
The owl, for all his feathers, was a-cold;
The hare limp'd trembling through the frozen grass,
And silent was the flock in woolly fold:
Numb were the Beadsman's fingers,[1] while he told
His rosary, and while his frosted breath,
Like pious incense from a censer old,
Seem'd taking flight for heaven, without a death,
Past the sweet Virgin's picture, while his prayer he saith.

II

His prayer he saith, this patient, holy man;   10
Then takes his lamp, and riseth from his knees,

[1]A pensioner paid to say prayers, the beadsman is outside in the estate's freezing cold chapel saying a rosary for the salvation of the aristocrats (descendants of "the sculptur'd dead") partying indoors.

And back returneth, meagre, barefoot, wan,
Along the chapel aisle by slow degrees:
The sculptur'd dead, on each side, seem to freeze,
Emprison'd in black, purgatorial rails:
Knights, ladies, praying in dumb orat'ries,°   *chapels*
He passeth by; and his weak spirit fails
To think how they may ache in icy hoods and mails.°   *armor*

III

Northward he turneth through a little door,
And scarce three steps, ere Music's golden tongue   20
Flatter'd to tears this aged man and poor;
But no—already had his deathbell rung;
The joys of all his life were said and sung:
His was harsh penance on St. Agnes' Eve:
Another way he went, and soon among
Rough ashes sat he for his soul's reprieve,
And all night kept awake, for sinners' sake to grieve.

IV

That ancient Beadsman heard the prelude soft;
And so it chanc'd, for many a door was wide,
From hurry to and fro. Soon, up aloft,   30
The silver, snarling trumpets 'gan to chide:
The level chambers, ready with their pride,
Were glowing to receive a thousand guests:
The carved angels, ever eager-eyed,
Star'd, where upon their heads the cornice rests,
With hair blown back, and wings put cross-wise on their breasts.

V

At length burst in the argent revelry,
With plume, tiara, and all rich array,
Numerous as shadows haunting fairily
The brain, new stuff'd, in youth, with triumphs gay   40
Of old romance.² These let us wish away,
And turn, sole-thoughted, to one Lady there,

²the literary genre

Whose heart had brooded, all that wintry day,
On love, and wing'd St. Agnes' saintly care,
As she had heard old dames full many times declare.

VI

They told her how, upon St. Agnes' Eve,
Young virgins might have visions of delight,
And soft adorings from their loves receive
Upon the honey'd middle of the night,
If ceremonies due they did aright;   50
As, supperless to bed they must retire,
And couch supine their beauties, lily white;
Nor look behind, nor sideways, but require
Of Heaven with upward eyes for all that they desire.[3]

VII

Full of this whim was thoughtful Madeline:
The music, yearning like a God in pain,
She scarcely heard: her maiden eyes divine,
Fix'd on the floor, saw many a sweeping train°   *skirt*
Pass by—she heeded not at all: in vain
Came many a tiptoe, amorous cavalier,   60
And back retir'd; not cool'd by high disdain,
But she saw not: her heart was otherwhere:
She sigh'd for Agnes' dreams, the sweetest of the year.

VIII

She danc'd along with vague, regardless eyes,
Anxious her lips, her breathing quick and short:[4]
The hallow'd hour was near at hand: she sighs
Amid the timbrels,° and the throng'd resort   *tambourines*
Of whisperers in anger, or in sport;
'Mid looks of love, defiance, hate, and scorn,
Hoodwink'd[5] with faery fancy; all amort,°   *dead* 70

---

[3]See the supplement (p. 352) for the stanza canceled here, at Taylor's insistence.
[4]canceled] Her anxious lips mouth full pulp'd with rosy thoughts
[5]A term in falconry: the bird before being released is hooded, hence unable to see.

Save to St. Agnes and her lambs unshorn,
And all the bliss to be before to-morrow morn.[6]

IX

So, purposing each moment to retire,
She linger'd still. Meantime, across the moors,
Had come young Porphyro,[7] with heart on fire
For Madeline. Beside the portal doors,
Buttress'd from moonlight,[8] stands he, and implores
All saints to give him sight of Madeline,
But for one moment in the tedious hours,
That he might gaze and worship all unseen;   80
Perchance speak, kneel, touch, kiss—in sooth such things have been.

X

He ventures in: let no buzz'd whisper tell:[9]
All eyes be muffled, or a hundred swords
Will storm his heart, Love's fev'rous citadel:
For him, those chambers held barbarian hordes,
Hyena foemen, and hot-blooded lords,
Whose very dogs would execrations howl
Against his lineage:[10] not one breast affords
Him any mercy, in that mansion foul,
Save one old beldame,[11] weak in body and in soul.   90

---

[6]It was a custom during the singing of *Agnus Dei* (Lamb of God) at St. Agnes' Day mass, to bless two white unshorn lambs, whose wool nuns then spun and wove.

[7]The name evokes *porphyra*, "purple," a precious dye for garments of the nobility; "purple blood" signifies royalty and nobility; *porphyre* is a purple serpent. On another level of information, Porphyry (3d c.), a famous antagonist of Christianity, instituted Neo-Platonism throughout the Roman Empire a few decades before the martyrdom of Christian St. Agnes.

[8]Shadowed by a buttress (a castle-wall's external support-arch).

[9]canceled] He ventures in wrapped / cloak'd up / in a dark disguise // In ventures he—let no damn'd whisper tell

[10]As in *Romeo and Juliet*, the families are at war.

[11]grandmother, old nurse; cf. Juliet's nurse Angelica in *Romeo and Juliet*, also a go-between for the lovers. Both names, like Angel, derive from the Greek *angelos* (messenger).

XI

Ah, happy chance! the aged creature came,
Shuffling along with ivory-headed wand,°   cane
To where he stood, hid from the torch's flame,
Behind a broad hall-pillar, far beyond
The sound of merriment and chorus bland:°   soft
He startled her; but soon she knew his face,
And grasp'd his fingers in her palsied hand,
Saying, "Mercy, Porphyro! hie thee from this place;
They are all here to-night, the whole blood-thirsty race!

XII

Get hence! get hence! there's dwarfish Hildebrand;   100
He had a fever late, and in the fit
He cursed thee and thine, both house and land:
Then there's that old Lord Maurice, not a whit
More tame for his grey hairs—Alas me! flit!
Flit like a ghost away."—"Ah, Gossip° dear,   confidant
We're safe enough; here in this arm-chair sit,
And tell me how"—"Good Saints! not here, not here;
Follow me, child, or else these stones will be thy bier."[12]

XIII

He follow'd through a lowly arched way,
Brushing the cobwebs with his lofty plume,   110
And as she mutter'd "Well-a——well-a-day!"
He found him in a little moonlight room,
Pale, lattic'd, chill, and silent as a tomb.
"Now tell me where is Madeline," said he,
"O tell me, Angela, by the holy loom
Which none but secret sisterhood may see,
When they St. Agnes' wool are weaving piously."

XIV

"St. Agnes! Ah! it is St. Agnes' Eve—
Yet men will murder upon holy days:
Thou must hold water in a witch's sieve,   120

---

[12]coffin-stand

And be liege-lord of all the Elves and Fays,°   *sprites*
To venture so: it fills me with amaze[13]
To see thee, Porphyro!—St. Agnes' Eve!
God's help! my lady fair the conjuror plays
This very night: good angels her deceive!
But let me laugh awhile, I've mickle° time to grieve."   *much*

XV

Feebly she laugheth in the languid moon,
While Porphyro upon her face doth look,
Like puzzled urchin on an aged crone
Who keepeth clos'd a wond'rous riddle-book,   130
As spectacled she sits in chimney nook.
But soon his eyes grew brilliant, when she told
His lady's purpose; and he scarce could brook°   *restrain*
Tears, at the thought of those enchantments cold,
And Madeline asleep in lap of legends old.

XVI

Sudden a thought came like a full-blown rose,
Flushing his brow, and in his pained heart
Made purple riot:[14] then doth he propose
A stratagem, that makes the beldame start:°   *(startles her)*
"A cruel man and impious thou art: 140
Sweet lady, let her pray, and sleep, and dream
Alone with her good angels, far apart
From wicked men like thee. Go, go!—I deem
Thou canst not surely be the same that thou didst seem."

XVII

"I will not harm her, by all saints I swear,"
Quoth Porphyro: "O may I ne'er find grace
When my weak voice shall whisper its last prayer,
If one of her soft ringlets I displace,
Or look with ruffian passion in her face:

---

[13]K-coined noun; cf *Lamia* 1.322.

[14]canceled] Sudden a thought more rosy than the rose // Heated his Brow / Flushed his young Cheek // Made riot fierce / Made purple riot.

Good Angela, believe me by these tears;　　　　　　　　150
Or I will, even in a moment's space,
Awake, with horrid shout, my foemen's ears,
And beard[15] them, though they be more fang'd than wolves and bears."

XVIII

"Ah! why wilt thou affright a feeble soul?
A poor, weak, palsy-stricken, churchyard thing,
Whose passing-bell° may ere the midnight toll;　　　*death-knell*
Whose prayers for thee, each morn and evening,
Were never miss'd."—Thus plaining,[16] doth she bring
A gentler speech from burning Porphyro;
So woful, and of such deep sorrowing,　　　　　　　160
That Angela gives promise she will do
Whatever he shall wish, betide her weal or woe.

XIX

Which was, to lead him, in close secrecy,
Even to Madeline's chamber,[17] and there hide
Him in a closet,° of such privacy　　　　　　　　*small room*
That he might see her beauty unespied,
And win perhaps that night a peerless bride,
While legion'd fairies pac'd the coverlet,
And pale enchantment held her sleepy-eyed.
Never on such a night have lovers met,　　　　　　170
Since Merlin paid his Demon all the monstrous debt.[18]

XX

"It shall be as thou wishest," said the Dame:
"All cates[19] and dainties shall be stored there
Quickly on this feast-night: by the tambour frame[20]

[15]confront, dare to combat
[16]lamenting
[17]cancelled] Bedchamber
[18]In Arthurian legend, magician Merlin found his powers turned against him by enchantress Vivien, who repaid his love by imprisoning him in a cave, where he died.
[19]exquisite food (*cater* is a cognate, as is *delicate*; see 271).
[20]tambourine-shaped frame for needlework

Her own lute thou wilt see: no time to spare,
For I am slow and feeble, and scarce dare
On such a catering trust my dizzy head.
Wait here, my child, with patience; kneel in prayer
The while: Ah! thou must needs the lady wed,
Or may I never leave my grave among the dead."   180

XXI

So saying, she hobbled off with busy fear.
The lover's endless minutes slowly pass'd;
The dame return'd, and whisper'd in his ear
To follow her; with aged eyes aghast
From fright of dim espial. Safe at last,
Through many a dusky gallery, they gain
The maiden's chamber, silken, hush'd, and chaste;
Where Porphyro took covert,[21] pleas'd amain.°   *fully*
His poor guide hurried back with agues° in her brain.[22]   *flutters*

XXII

Her falt'ring hand upon the balustrade,°   *bannister*
Old Angela was feeling for the stair,
When Madeline, St. Agnes' charmed maid,
Rose, like a mission'd° spirit, unaware: *commissioned*
With silver taper's° light, and pious care,   *(candle)*
She turn'd, and down the aged gossip led
To a safe level matting. Now prepare,
Young Porphyro, for gazing on that bed;
She comes, she comes again, like ring-dove fray'd and fled.[23]

XXIII

Out went the taper as she hurried in;
Its little smoke, in pallid moonshine, died: 200
She clos'd the door, she panted, all akin
To spirits of the air, and visions wide:

[21]canceled] He in a panting covert will remain
[22]canceled] From purgatory sweet to view love's own domain / or what may he attain
[23]In fearful flight from a predator ("like doves, whom the Eagle doth affray" [*FQ* V.XII.v]).

No utter'd syllable, or, woe betide!
But to her heart, her heart was voluble,°   *beating audibly*
Paining with eloquence her balmy side;
As though a tongueless nightingale should swell
Her throat in vain, and die, heart-stifled, in her dell.[24]

XXIV

A casement° high and triple-arch'd there was,   *window*
All garlanded with carven imag'ries
Of fruits, and flowers, and bunches of knot-grass,   210
And diamonded with panes of quaint device,
Innumerable of stains and splendid dyes,
As are the tiger-moth's deep-damask'd wings;
And in the midst, 'mong thousand heraldries,
And twilight saints, and dim emblazonings,
A shielded scutcheon blush'd with blood of queens and kings.[25]

XXV

Full on this casement shone the wintry moon,
And threw warm gules[26] on Madeline's fair breast,
As down she knelt for heaven's grace and boon;°   *favor*
Rose-bloom fell on her hands, together prest,   220
And on her silver cross soft amethyst,
And on her hair a glory,° like a saint: *halo*
She seem'd a splendid angel, newly drest,
Save wings, for heaven:—Porphyro grew faint:
She knelt, so pure a thing, so free from mortal taint.

XXVI

Anon his heart revives: her vespers[27] done,
Of all its wreathed pearls her hair she frees;
Unclasps her warmed jewels one by one;

---

[24]Referring to Philomel, the maiden whose rapist cut her tongue out to prevent a report; she was turned into a nightingale.

[25]*heraldries*: family coats of arms (*scutcheons*); *blood*: bloodline, Madeline's family lineage.

[26]heraldric red

[27]evening prayers; Vesper is also the name of Venus as evening star.

Loosens her fragrant bodice;[28] by degrees
Her rich attire creeps rustling to her knees: 230
Half-hidden, like a mermaid in sea-weed,[29]
Pensive awhile she dreams awake, and sees,
In fancy, fair St. Agnes in her bed,
But dares not look behind, or all the charm is fled.[30]

XXVII

Soon, trembling in her soft and chilly nest,
In sort of wakeful swoon, perplex'd she lay,
Until the poppied[31] warmth of sleep oppress'd
Her soothed limbs, and soul fatigued away;
Flown, like a thought, until the morrow-day;
Blissfully haven'd both from joy and pain;[32]   240
Clasp'd like a missal where swart Paynims pray;[33]
Blinded alike from sunshine and from rain,
As though a rose should shut, and be a bud again.

XXVIII

Stol'n to this paradise,[34] and so entranced,
Porphyro gazed upon her empty dress,
And listen'd to her breathing, if it chanced
To wake into a slumberous tenderness;
Which when he heard, that minute did he bless,
And breath'd himself: then from the closet crept,
Noiseless as fear in a wide wilderness,   250
And over the hush'd carpet, silent, stept,
And 'tween the curtains peep'd, where, lo!—how fast she slept.

---

[28]canceled] her bosom jewels / loosens her bursting bodice / her bodice lace string / her Boddice and her bosom bar / Loosens her fragrant bodice and bare Her /

[29]canceled] Syren of the Sea

[30]Evoking Orpheus's constraint in leading his beloved Eurydice out of hell.

[31]Fragrant and narcotic (opium, in common use as a sleep-drug, is made from poppies).

[32]Contrasting the sensibility of *Ode on Melancholy*, enhanced by this intertext.

[33]Clasped shut and held like a prayer-book concealed from the sight of hostile, dark-skinned non-Christians (pagan or "paynim" Muslims); *clasped* also suggests "arrested," with *pray* punning as *prey* (on), or persecute.

[34]Evoking Satan's entry into the Garden of Eden to corrupt Eve (*PL* 4 and 9).

XXIX

Then by the bed-side, where the faded moon
Made a dim, silver twilight, soft he set
A table, and, half anguish'd, threw thereon   255
A cloth of woven crimson, gold, and jet:—
O for some drowsy Morphean amulet!°   *sleep charm*
The boisterous, midnight, festive clarion,
The kettle-drum, and far-heard clarionet,
Affray° his ears, though but in dying tone:—   *alarm*
The hall door shuts again, and all the noise is gone.

XXX

And still she slept an azure-lidded sleep,
In blanched linen, smooth, and lavender'd,
While he from forth the closet brought a heap
Of candied apple, quince, and plum, and gourd;°   *melon*
With jellies soother[35] than the creamy curd,
And lucent syrops, tinct with cinnamon;
Manna[36] and dates, in argosy transferr'd
From Fez; and spiced dainties, every one,
From silken Samarcand to cedar'd Lebanon.[37]   270

XXXI

These delicates he heap'd with glowing hand
On golden dishes and in baskets bright
Of wreathed silver: sumptuous they stand
In the retired quiet of the night,
Filling the chilly room with perfume light.——
"And now, my love, my seraph° fair, awake!   *angel*
Thou art my heaven, and I thine eremite:°   *worshipper*
Open thine eyes, for meek St. Agnes' sake,
Or I shall drowse beside thee, so my soul doth ache."

[35]K-coinage: smoother and more soothing.

[36]Food so rare it seems divine. See *Endymion* 1.766, *La belle dame* (p. 248), and Exodus 16.14ff.

[37]*argosy*: merchant ship. The regions named supply the exotic luxuries enjoyed by the feudal aristocracy: Fez in northern Morocco for sugar, the ancient Persian city of Samarkand (Damascus) for silk goods, and Lebanon for fine cedar.

XXXII

Thus whispering, his warm, unnerved arm   280
Sank in her pillow. Shaded was her dream
By the dusk curtains:—'twas a midnight charm
Impossible to melt as iced stream:
The lustrous salvers° in the moonlight gleam;   *trays*
Broad golden fringe upon the carpet lies:
It seem'd he never, never could redeem
From such a stedfast spell his lady's eyes;
So mus'd awhile, entoil'd in woofed° phantasies.   *woven*

XXXIII

Awakening up, he took her hollow lute,—
Tumultuous,—and, in chords that tenderest be,   290
He play'd an ancient ditty, long since mute,
In Provence call'd, "La belle dame sans mercy":[38]
Close to her ear touching the melody;—
Wherewith disturb'd, she utter'd a soft moan:
He ceased—she panted quick—and suddenly
Her blue affrayed[39] eyes wide open shone:
Upon his knees he sank, pale as smooth-sculptured stone.

XXXIV

Her eyes were open, but she still beheld,
Now wide awake, the vision of her sleep:
There was a painful change, that nigh expell'd   300
The blisses of her dream so pure and deep
At which fair Madeline began to weep,
And moan forth witless° words with many a sigh;   *baffled*
While still her gaze on Porphyro would keep;
Who knelt, with joined hands and piteous eye,
Fearing to move or speak, she look'd so dreamingly.

[38]The Provencal region of southern France is famed for its medieval troubadours; in the poem by Alain Chartier (1424), a lady earns this title for refusing a suitor. In April 1819 K writes his own ballad of a "Belle Dame" who seduces, then abandons "sans mercy" or "merci."

[39]alarmed; but also with the archaic sense of "disturbed, or startled, from sleep or quiet, as from a sudden noise does; alarmed from such startling" (*OED*, citing *Eve of St. Agnes* twice).

XXXV

"Ah, Porphyro!" said she, "but even now
Thy voice was at sweet tremble in mine ear,
Made tuneable with every sweetest vow;
And those sad eyes were spiritual and clear: 310
How chang'd thou art! how pallid, chill, and drear!
Give me that voice again, my Porphyro,
Those looks immortal, those complainings° dear!   *laments*
Oh leave me not in this eternal woe,
For if thou diest, my Love, I know not where to go."

XXXVI

Beyond a mortal man impassion'd far
At these voluptuous accents, he arose,
Ethereal, flush'd, and like a throbbing star
Seen mid the sapphire heaven's deep repose;
Into her dream he melted, as the rose   320
Blendeth its odour with the violet,—⁴⁰
Solution° sweet: meantime the frost-wind blows   *fusion*
Like Love's alarum,⁴¹ pattering the sharp sleet
Against the window-panes; St. Agnes' moon hath set.

XXXVII

'Tis dark: quick pattereth the flaw°-blown sleet: *storm*
"This is no dream, my bride, my Madeline!"
'Tis dark: the iced gusts still rave and beat:⁴²
"No dream, alas! alas! and woe is mine!
Porphyro will leave me here to fade and pine.—
Cruel! what traitor could thee hither bring?   330
I curse not, for my heart is lost in thine,
Though thou forsakest a deceived thing;—
A dove forlorn and lost with sick unpruned° wing."   *bedraggled*

---

⁴⁰For the text replaced by 314–22, see the supplement (p. 353).

⁴¹Cupid's warning

⁴²K underscored Milton's imagination of the environs of Hell: "a frozen continent / Lies dark and wild, beat with perpetual storms / Of whirlwind and dire hail" (*PL* 2.587–89); and also the hellish climate visited on earth after the fall: "snow and hail and stormy gust and flaw" (10.698).

XXXVIII

"My Madeline! sweet dreamer! lovely bride!
Say, may I be for aye° thy vassal blest?[43]   *ever*
Thy beauty's shield, heart-shaped and vermeil dyed?
Ah, silver shrine, here will I take my rest
After so many hours of toil and quest,
A famish'd pilgrim,—saved by miracle.
Though I have found, I will not rob thy nest   340
Saving of thy sweet self; if thou think'st well
To trust, fair Madeline, to no rude infidel.°   *unbeliever*

XXXIX

Hark! 'tis an elfin-storm from faery land,
Of haggard[44] seeming, but a boon indeed:
Arise—arise! the morning is at hand;——
The bloated wassaillers will never heed:——
Let us away, my love, with happy speed;
There are no ears to hear, or eyes to see,——
Drown'd all in Rhenish and the sleepy mead:[45]
Awake! arise! my love, and fearless be,   350
For o'er the southern moors I have a home for thee."

XL

She hurried at his words, beset with fears,
For there were sleeping dragons[46] all around,
At glaring watch, perhaps, with ready spears——
Down the wide stairs a darkling way they found.—
In all the house was heard no human sound.
A chain-droop'd lamp was flickering by each door;
The arras,° rich with horseman, hawk, and hound,   *tapestry*
Flutter'd in the besieging wind's uproar;
And the long carpets rose along the gusty floor.   360

[43]K would tell Fanny Brawne (25 July 1819): "the very first week I knew you I wrote myself your vassal" (devoted slave).

[44]bewitched, wild.

[45]wine and rum

[46]Dragoons, or guards, imagined as mythical beasts of "romance."

XLI

They glide, like phantoms, into the wide hall;
Like phantoms to the iron porch they glide;
Where lay the Porter,° in uneasy sprawl,   *gatekeeper*
With a huge empty flaggon by his side:
The wakeful bloodhound rose, and shook his hide,
But his sagacious eye an inmate owns:[47]
By one, and one, the bolts full easy slide:——
The chains lie silent on the footworn stones;——
The key turns, and the door upon its hinges groans.

XLII

And they are gone: ay, ages long ago   370
These lovers fled away into the storm.
That night the Baron dreamt of many a woe,
And all his warrior-guests, with shade and form
Of witch, and demon, and large coffin-worm,
Were long be-nightmar'd. Angela the old
Died palsy-twitch'd, with meagre face deform;
The Beadsman, after thousand aves told,[48]
For aye unsought for slept among his ashes cold.

§ Canceled Stanzas

(from George Keats's transcript of Keats's original fair copy)

(intended stanza after VI)

'Twas said her future lord would there appear
Offering as sacrifice—all in the dream—
Delicious food even to her sips brought near;
Viands and wine and fruit and sugar'd cream,
To touch her palate with the fine extreme
Of relish: then soft music heard; and then
More pleasures followed in a dizzy stream

---

[47]recognizes a resident (Madeline).
[48]"Ave Maria" ("Hail Mary") prayers, part of the rosary.

Palpable almost: then to wake again
Warm in the virgin morn, no weeping Magdalen.[1]

(intended text for 314–22)
So while she speaks his arms encroaching slow
Have zon'd her, heart to heart—loud, loud the dark winds blow:

For on the midnight came a tempest fell.°   dire
More sooth for that his close rejoinder flows
Into her burning ear: and still the spell
Unbroken guards her in serene repose.
With her wild dream he mingled as a rose
Marryeth its odour to a violet.
Still, still she dreams . . .

The Odes of 1819

In 1820, these are dispersed in a subsection of "Poems," along with tetrameter songs, rondeaus, and other odes, among these Fancy *(p. 364) and* Robin Hood *(p. 100–101). The order here follows 1820. Keats wrote odes early and late, from* Ode to Apollo *(1814) to* Ode to Fanny *(1820). The most famous group, a virtual macrotext, was this run of odes, composed in a burst of inspiration between April and September 1819. Except for* Ode on Indolence, *first published in 1848, all were in 1820. How surprising, in light of their achieved fame, that these Odes were commented on only in passing by the first reviews! The Odes didn't draw intense interest until their publication in 1848, in the context of Keats's life and letters, and in an age when poets and their readers preferred lyrics to endeavors after a long poem.* Ode to Psyche *was written in April, others soon after, and* To Autumn *in September. Using sonnet resources (quatrains, sestets, an occasional couplet), in varying meters and stanzas (often a 10-line stanza, with its rhymes in sonnetlike units of 4 and 6), Keats finds a new flexibility of form, played across a stanza-paced dramatic arc of thought. The Odes of 1819 involve not only personal but also cultural and political contexts: the Elgin Marbles, the pervasive use of opium as a painkiller, news of social misery and political unrest, the loss of Tom to death and George to America, and the poet's nagging*

[1] Prostitute Mary Magdalen (and icon of a "fallen" woman); in K's day hospitals for unwed mothers were called Magdalens. *Madeline* is a name derived from *Magdalen*.

sensation that he would die young. The language is enriched by literary allusion, as dense as it is casual, ranging through the Bible, Keats's earlier poetry and its hostile reviews, and favorite poets: Spenser, Shakespeare, Milton, Thomson, Collins, Chatterton, Coleridge, and Wordsworth.

Yet for all these contexts, the Odes weave their own fields of verbal nuance, reverberation, and imagery across a flux and reflux of desire, thought, internal argument, self-correction. Nineteenth-century readers admired the beauties of the language and its sensuous intensity—the tactile, auditory, visual qualities, even sensations of smell and taste. Later readers have praised the intellectual drama, variously called a poetry of "internal debate," of "paradox" and "contradiction," a "rhetoric of irony," a poetics of "indeterminacy." Convinced that "a question is the best beacon toward a little speculation," and that knowledge was less a matter of "resting places and seeming sure points of Reasoning" than of "question and answer—a little pro and con," Keats threads these odes on key questions—"Was it a vision, or a waking dream?"; "What leaf-fringed legend haunts about thy shape . . . ?"; "Where are the songs of spring?"—which the poetry answers with a pro and con: a poet's mind as a "rosy sanctuary" and a place of mere "shadowy thought"; a bird-song that evokes "full-throated ease" and "easeful death"; visual art that seems both "for ever young" and a "cold pastoral"; an intensity of "Beauty" that is always a "Beauty that must die"; a sensuous "indolence" that cannot stay "sheltered from annoy" of busy thoughts; an autumnal season of ripe fruition and coming death.

ODE TO A NIGHTINGALE.[1]

1.

My heart aches, and a drowsy numbness pains
   My sense, as though of hemlock I had drunk,
Or emptied some dull opiate[2] to the drains
   One minute past, and Lethe-wards had sunk:
'Tis not through envy of thy happy lot,

---

[1]To make money, K published this ode first in *Annals of the Fine Arts*, vol. 4 (July 1819): 107–12. The nightingale is often associated with Ovid's horrific story of Philomela (see p. 346, n. 24); in another tradition, the nightingale sings with a thorn pierced into its heart (the pain of love). As K is aware, Milton, Wordsworth, and Coleridge all had nightingale poems, consciously engaged with the tradition; so did sonnet-writer Charlotte Smith. Charles Brown reports K's inspiration by a nightingale in a tree at Wentworth Place.

[2]In small doses, hemlock is a sedative; in large doses, it is a poison (Socrates used it for suicide). Opium dissolved in alcohol was a common painkiller, which K himself used in his last days.

But being too happy in thine happiness,—
    That thou, light-winged Dryad of the trees,
        In some melodious plot
Of beechen green, and shadows numberless,
    Singest of summer in full-throated ease.   10

2.

O, for a draught of vintage!° that hath been   *aged wine*
    Cool'd a long age in the deep-delved earth,[3]
Tasting of Flora and the country green,
    Dance, and Provençal[4] song, and sunburnt mirth!
O for a beaker full of the warm South,
    Full of the true, the blushful Hippocrene,
        With beaded bubbles winking at the brim,
            And purple-stained mouth;
    That I might drink, and leave the world unseen,[5]
    And with thee fade away into the forest dim: 20

3.

Fade far away, dissolve, and quite forget
    What thou among the leaves hast never known,
The weariness, the fever, and the fret
    Here, where men sit and hear each other groan;
Where palsy shakes a few, sad, last gray hairs,
    Where youth grows pale, and spectre-thin, and dies;[6]
        Where but to think is to be full of sorrow
            And leaden-eyed despairs,
    Where Beauty cannot keep her lustrous eyes,
    Or new Love pine at them beyond to-morrow.   30

[3]Arthurian magician Merlin dwells "in a deep delve, farre from the view of day, / That no living wight he mote be found" (*FQ* III.iii.vii).

[4]Region of southern France, famed in the middle ages for its troubadours.

[5]The adjective may modify both *I* and *world*.

[6]An echo of Wordsworth's memory of himself in moods of "darkness, and amid the many shapes / Of joyless day-light; when the fretful stir / Unprofitable, and the fever of the world, / Have hung upon the beatings of my heart" (*Tintern Abbey* 52–55); see K on *Tintern Abbey* in the letter of 3 May 1818 (p. 130). Both poets recall Macbeth's envy of Duncan "in his grave; / After life's fitful fever he sleeps well" (3.322–23). K also echoes Wordsworth's image of an ideal life "from diminution safe and weakening age; / While man grows old, and dwindles, and decays" (*Excursion* 4.759–60).

4.

Away! away! for I will fly to thee,
    Not charioted by Bacchus and his pards,°   *leopards*
But on the viewless wings of Poesy,
    Though the dull brain perplexes and retards:
Already with thee! tender is the night,
    And haply[7] the Queen-Moon is on her throne,
        Cluster'd around by all her starry Fays;°   *fairies*
           But here there is no light,
    Save what from heaven is with the breezes blown
        Through verdurous glooms and winding mossy ways.   40

5.

I cannot see what flowers are at my feet,
    Nor what soft incense hangs upon the boughs,
But, in embalmed darkness, guess each sweet
    Wherewith the seasonable month endows
The grass, the thicket, and the fruit-tree wild;
    White hawthorn, and the pastoral eglantine;
        Fast fading violets cover'd up in leaves;
           And mid-May's eldest child,
    The coming musk-rose, full of dewy wine,[8]
        The murmurous haunt of flies on summer eves.   50

6.

Darkling[9] I listen; and, for many a time
    I have been half in love with easeful Death,
Call'd him soft names in many a mused rhyme,
    To take into the air my quiet breath;
        Now more than ever seems it rich to die,
    To cease upon the midnight with no pain,
        While thou art pouring forth thy soul abroad
           In such an ecstasy!

[7]happily; perhaps

[8]The guessing echoes Fairy-king Oberon's description of a verdant bank where abides a snakeskin, the juices of which make a sleeper fall in love with whatever is first seen on waking (*Midsummer Night's Dream* 2.1.249–58)—and thus the potential for the cheat of fancy.

[9]in the dark (modifying *I*); a little creature of darkness, a little muse of death.

Still wouldst thou sing, and I have ears in vain—
  To thy high requiem° become a sod.   *funeral mass* 60

7.

Thou wast not born for death, immortal Bird!
  No hungry generations tread thee down;
The voice I hear this passing night was heard
  In ancient days by emperor and clown:°   *rustic, peasant*
Perhaps the self-same song that found a path
    Through the sad heart of Ruth, when, sick for home,
      She stood in tears amid the alien corn;[10]
        The same that oft-times hath
  Charm'd magic casements, opening on the foam
  Of perilous seas,[11] in faery lands forlorn.   70

8.

Forlorn! the very word is like a bell
  To toll me back from thee to my sole self!
Adieu! the fancy cannot cheat so well
  As she is fam'd to do, deceiving elf.
Adieu! adieu! thy plaintive anthem fades
    Past the near meadows, over the still stream,
      Up the hill-side; and now 'tis buried deep
        In the next valley-glades:
  Was it a vision, or a waking dream?[12]
    Fled is that music:—Do I wake or sleep?   80

[10]Compelled by famine, Ruth eked out a living as a gleaner in far-away foreign fields (Ruth 1–2).

[11]A reflexive punning into *perilous ease* (thus revising *easeful* and *ease*).

[12]The close involves the music of other poets: Charlotte Smith's *On the Departure of the Nightingale* (1784), "Sweet poet of the woods!—a long adieu!"; the opening of Spenser's *Amoretti* 77: "Was it a dreame, or did I see it playne?"; a spellbound lover in *Midsummer Night's Dream*: "Are you sure / That we are awake? It seems to me / That yet we sleep, we dream" (4.1.194–96); Wordsworth's lament in the "Intimations" *Ode*, "Whither is fled the visionary gleam? / Where is it now, the glory and the dream?" (56–57), and his phrase "waking dream" in *Yarrow Visited* (1815). Also in play are K's self-listening (*Ode to Psyche* 5–6) and Hazlitt's remark that "Spenser was the poet of our waking dreams," his "music . . . lulling the senses into a deep oblivion of the jarring noises of the world from which we have no wish ever to be recalled" (*On Chaucer and Spenser*, 1818).

ODE ON A GRECIAN URN[1]

1.

THOU still[2] unravish'd bride of quietness,
    Thou foster-child of silence and slow time,
Sylvan° historian, who canst thus express   *woodland*
    A flowery tale more sweetly than our rhyme:
What leaf-fring'd legend haunts about thy shape
    Of deities or mortals, or of both,
        In Tempe or the dales of Arcady?[3]
    What men or gods are these? What maidens loth?
What mad pursuit? What struggle to escape?
        What pipes and timbrels?[4] What wild ecstasy?   10

2.

Heard melodies are sweet, but those unheard
    Are sweeter; therefore, ye soft pipes, play on;
Not to the sensual ear, but, more endear'd,
    Pipe to the spirit ditties of no tone:
Fair youth, beneath the trees, thou canst not leave
    Thy song, nor ever can those trees be bare;
        Bold Lover, never, never canst thou kiss,
Though winning near the goal—yet, do not grieve;
    She cannot fade, though thou hast not thy bliss,
        For ever wilt thou love, and she be fair!   20

3.

Ah, happy, happy[5] boughs! that cannot shed
    Your leaves, nor ever bid the Spring adieu;

[1]First published in *Annals of the Fine Arts*, Jan. 1820, pp. 638–39, this ode is an ekphrasis (word-picture) of three scenes on an imaginary urn (K had seen several at the British Museum): a scene of sexual revelry and pursuit of reluctant maidens; a piper beneath the trees and a male lover in pursuit of a maiden; a ritual sacrifice, perhaps inspired by an Elgin-Marble frieze.

[2]A punningly packed word: as yet; unmoving and unchanging; static; quiet.

[3]A design of leaves that sometimes frames a legend (caption). The ancient Greek districts of Tempe and Arcady, famed for beauty and serenity, were frequented by the gods, often in erotic heat.

[4]tambourines

[5]joyous, fortunate

And, happy melodist, unwearied,
    For ever piping songs for ever new;
More happy love! more happy, happy love!
    For ever warm and still to be enjoy'd,
        For ever panting, and for ever young;
All breathing human passion far above,[6]
    That leaves a heart high-sorrowful and cloy'd,
        A burning forehead, and a parching tongue.   30

4.

Who are these coming to the sacrifice?
    To what green altar, O mysterious[7] priest,
Lead'st thou that heifer lowing at the skies,
    And all her silken flanks with garlands drest?
What little town by river or sea shore,
    Or mountain-built with peaceful citadel,°   *fortress*
        Is emptied of this folk, this pious morn?
And, little town, thy streets for evermore
    Will silent be; and not a soul to tell
        Why thou art desolate, can e'er return.   40

5.

O Attic shape! Fair attitude! with brede
    Of marble men and maidens overwrought,[8]
With forest branches and the trodden weed;
    Thou, silent form, dost tease us out of thought
As doth eternity: Cold Pastoral!
    When old age shall this generation waste,
        Thou shalt remain, in midst of other woe

---

[6]The syntax of this line is richly ambiguous, with a fleeting suggestion that the urn's figures of art breathe human passion in a realm far above. Even in the next line's differentiation of human passion, there is a division: Is the passion of the urn's figures superior to (above) human passion? Or is it disengaged from, unaware of it (above it all)?

[7]unknown; also religious "mysteries" (occult rites and lore).

[8]The urn, from Attica (Athens's district), is overwrought (overlaid) in design, with a punning hint of beings agonized in arrest (*brede* puns in sympathy on what cannot happen, *breed*); *attitude* involves a range of suggestion: in the object, a composition of elements, a theatrical pose; in the beholding subject, a disposition; and for both viewer and object, a setting in a frame of reference.

Than ours, a friend to man, to whom thou say'st,
"Beauty is truth, truth beauty,"—that is all
Ye know on earth, and all ye need to know.[9]   50

ODE TO PSYCHE

In the pages of 30 April 1819 from his long letter to George and Georgiana, Keats gives this prologue to a transcription of Ode to Psyche:

The following Poem – the last I have written is the first and the only one with which I have taken even moderate pains – I have for the most part dash'd of my lines in a hurry – This I have done leisurely – I think it reads the more richly for it and will I hope encourage me to write other thing in even a more peacable and healthy spirit. You must recollect that Psyche was not embodied as a goddess before the time of Apulieus the Platonist who lived afterr the Agustan age, and consequently the Goddess was never worshipped or sacrificed to with any of the ancient fervour – and perhaps never thought of in the old religion – I am more orthodox that to let a hethen Goddess be so neglected—

Keats owned Lemprière's Classical Dictionary, *in which the listing for Psyche reads: "The word signifies the soul, and this personification of Psyche first mentioned by Apuleius is thus posterior to the Augustan age, though it is connected with ancient mythology." The legend of Cupid and Psyche is in chapter 22 of* The Golden Ass, *a second-century satire by the African Apuleius, translated in 1566. For sneaking a peek at her mysterious nocturnal lover, Psyche had to undergo a long term of expiation before gaining immortality and a reunion with Cupid. The latest addition to the pantheon, she is deified just as Christianity was emerging, during the reign of Emperor Caesar Augustus. Mary Tighe's* Psyche (1805), *a romance in Spenserian stanzas also based on Apuleius, which Keats read in his schooldays, is echoed in several places. He was reflecting at this time on the development of the soul through suffering (see the part of his journal letter written 21 April 1819 [p. 250], part of the same long letter that contains a draft of the* Ode).

[9]The quotation marks in line 49, not in any ms nor in *Annals*, may have been placed by Taylor or Woodhouse, with or without K's approval. Without these, it is unclear how much the urn is imagined to say (5 words? the last 2 lines?), or what the referent of *ye* is in the final line. For K's comments on poetic truth and poetic beauty, see the opening of *Endymion* and several letters: 22 Nov. 1817 to Bailey, Dec. 1817 to his brothers, and 19 March 1819 to G&GK.

O GODDESS! hear these tuneless numbers,° wrung   *meters*
   By sweet enforcement and remembrance dear,
And pardon that thy secrets should be sung
   Even into thine own soft-conched° ear: *shell-shaped*
Surely I dreamt to-day, or did I see
   The winged Psyche with awaken'd eyes?[1]
I wander'd in a forest thoughtlessly,[2]
   And, on the sudden, fainting with surprise,
Saw two fair creatures, couched side by side
   In deepest grass, beneath the whisp'ring roof   10
   Of leaves and trembled blossoms, where there ran
      A brooklet, scare espied:[3]

'Mid hush'd, cool-rooted flowers, fragrant-eyed,
   Blue, silver-white, and budded Tyrian,°   *deep purple*
They lay calm-breathing on the bedded grass;
   Their arms embraced, and their pinions° too;   *wings*
   Their lips touch'd not, but had not bade adieu
As if disjoined by soft-handed slumber,
And ready still past kisses to outnumber
   At tender eye-dawn of aurorean° love: *dawning* 20
      The winged boy° I knew;   *Cupid*
   But who wast thou, O happy, happy dove?
      His Psyche true!

---

[1]A standard rhetoric of dream vision, e.g., Spenser's *Amoretti* 76: "Was it a dreame, or did I see it playne . . . ?"

[2]Another conventional situation, usually a prelude to adventure, sometimes peril; *thoughtlessly* plays against the advent of "thought" in the form of "psyche" whose name implies this as well.

[3]The scene recasts Satan's spying of Adam and Eve: "the loveliest pair . . . Under a tuft of shade that on a green / Stood whispering soft, by a fresh Fountain side / They sat them down" (*PL* 4.321–27); and later, the epic narrator's account of the pair "side by side" in "thir inmost bower" making "connubial Love" (4.742–43), then as "two fair Creatures . . . asleep secure of harm" (4.790–91).

O latest born and loveliest vision far
    Of all Olympus' faded hierarchy![4]
Fairer than Phœbe's sapphire-region'd star,
    Or Vesper, amorous glow-worm of the sky;[5]
Fairer than these, though temple thou hast none,
    Nor altar heap'd with flowers;
Nor virgin-choir to make delicious moan   30
        Upon the midnight hours;
No voice, no lute, no pipe, no incense sweet
    From chain-swung censer teeming;
No shrine, no grove, no oracle, no heat
    Of pale-mouth'd prophet dreaming.[6]

O brightest! though too late for antique[7] vows,
    Too, too late for the fond believing lyre,[8]
When holy were the haunted forest boughs,
    Holy the air, the water, and the fire;
Yet even in these days so far retir'd   40
    From happy pieties, thy lucent fans,[9]
    Fluttering among the faint Olympians,
I see, and sing, by my own eyes inspired.
So let me be thy choir, and make a moan
        Upon the midnight hours;
Thy voice, thy lute, thy pipe, thy incense sweet
    From swinged censer teeming;
Thy shrine, thy grove, thy oracle, thy heat
    Of pale-mouth'd prophet dreaming.

---

[4]The classical gods eclipsed by Christianity.

[5]Goddess Phœbe's "star" is the moon; Vesper evokes Venus, Cupid's jealous mother.

[6]Alluding to the rout by Christianity of the pagan Greek deities in Milton's *On the Morning of Christ's Nativity* (1629): "The Oracles are dumb, / No voice . . . No nightly trance, or breathed spell, / Inspires the pale-ey'd priest from the prophetic cell" (xix).

[7]British-pronounced on the first syllable, a pun on *antic*.

[8]ancient odes of religious veneration; *fond*: devoted, foolish.

[9]wings; "Psyche is generally represented with the wings of a butterfly, to intimate the lightness of the soul, of which the butterfly is a symbol" (*Lemprière*).

Yes, I will be thy priest, and build a fane°   *temple*   50
 In some untrodden region of my mind,[10]
Where branched thoughts, new grown with pleasant pain,
 Instead of pines shall murmur in the wind:
Far, far around shall those dark-cluster'd trees
 Fledge° the wild-ridged mountains steep by steep;   *feather*
And there by zephyrs,° streams, and birds, and bees,   *breezes*
 The moss-lain Dryads shall be lull'd to sleep;
And in the midst of this wide quietness
A rosy sanctuary will I dress
With the wreath'd trellis of a working brain,   60
 With buds, and bells, and stars without a name,
With all the gardener Fancy[11] e'er could feign,
 Who breeding flowers, will never breed the same:
And there shall be for thee all soft delight
 That shadowy thought can win,
A bright torch, and a casement ope at night,
 To let the warm Love in!

FANCY

*In aesthetic theory, "Fancy" is often regarded as inferior to "Imagination": frivolous, shaped on accidents and contingencies of sensation rather than a force of visionary imagination. "Fancy" is also (as Keats makes clear) prone to she-gendering—a charming sprite, a "deceiving elf" (*Ode to a Nightingale*). Composed in late 1818, in the octosyllabic couplets of seventeenth-century song (Milton's L'Allegro), Fancy pleased Keats as "a sort of rondeau which I think I shall become partial to – because you have one idea amplified with greater ease and more delight and freedom than in the sonnet" (so he told George and Georgiana when he wrote the poem out for them); he hoped to make a volume of such "minor poems," which "people will realish who cannot bear the burthen*

[10]Echoing Spenser's *Amoretti* 22: "Her temple fayre is built within my mind, / In which her glorious ymage placèd is, / On which my thoughts doo day and night attend / Like sacred priests" (5–8). See letter of 3 May 1818 on the Chamber of Maiden-Thought (p. 130).

[11]This inventive faculty is often imaged as a gardener who improves nature; *feign* means invent or dissemble, with Shakespearean punning on *fain* (wish) and *fane* (temple; cf. l. 50); the word and its syntax are embedded in Spenser's *Hymne in Honour of Love* (1596), about a jealous lover whose fears "to his fayning fansie represent / Sights never seene, and thousand shadowes vaine, / To break his sleepe, and waste his ydle braine" (254–56).

of a long poem" (2–3 January 1819)—the work of Endymion *implicit in the punning "relish"/ "real" and* burthen *(load; refrain). Part of the fun of poetic "fancy" is the opportunity for playful rhyme-pairings.*

EVER let the Fancy roam,
Pleasure never is at home:
At a touch sweet Pleasure melteth,
Like to bubbles when rain pelteth;
Then let winged Fancy[1] wander
Through the thought still spread beyond her:[2]
Open wide the mind's cage-door,
She'll dart forth, and cloudward soar.
O sweet Fancy! let her loose;
Summer's joys are spoilt by use,   10
And the enjoying of the Spring
Fades as does its blossoming;
Autumn's red-lipp'd fruitage too,
Blushing through the mist and dew,
Cloys with tasting: What do then?
Sit thee by the ingle,° when   *hearth*
The sear faggot° blazes bright,   *bundle of branches*
Spirit of a winter's night;
When the soundless earth is muffled,
And the caked snow is shuffled   20
From the ploughboy's heavy shoon;°   *shoes*
When the Night doth meet the Noon
In a dark conspiracy
To banish Even from her sky.
Sit thee there, and send abroad,
With a mind self-overaw'd,
Fancy, high-commission'd:——send her!
She has vassals to attend her:
She will bring, in spite of frost,
Beauties that the earth hath lost;   30
She will bring thee, all together,
All delights of summer weather;

[1]Like an angel or fairy, or like partner to winged Pegasus.
[2]A cheeky "Cockney" rhyme (like so many others in this verse).

All the buds and bells of May,
From dewy sward or thorny spray;
All the heaped Autumn's wealth,
With a still, mysterious stealth:
She will mix these pleasures up
Like three fit wines in a cup,
And thou shalt quaff it:—thou shalt hear
Distant harvest-carols clear;   40
Rustle of the reaped corn;
Sweet birds antheming the morn:
And, in the same moment——hark!
'Tis the early April lark,
Or the rooks, with busy caw,
Foraging for sticks and straw.
Thou shalt, at one glance, behold
The daisy and the marigold;
White-plum'd lilies, and the first
Hedge-grown primrose that hath burst;   50
Shaded hyacinth, alway
Sapphire queen of the mid-May;
And every leaf, and every flower
Pearled with the self-same shower.
Thou shalt see the field-mouse peep
Meagre from its celled sleep;
And the snake all winter-thin
Cast on sunny bank its skin;
Freckled nest-eggs thou shalt see
Hatching in the hawthorn-tree,   60
When the hen-bird's wing doth rest
Quiet on her mossy nest;
Then the hurry and alarm
When the bee-hive casts its swarm;
Acorns ripe down-pattering,
While the autumn breezes sing.

    Oh, sweet Fancy! let her loose;
Every thing is spoilt by use:
Where's the cheek that doth not fade,
Too much gaz'd at? Where's the maid   70

Whose lip mature is ever new?
Where's the eye, however blue,
Doth not weary? Where's the face
One would meet in every place?
Where's the voice, however soft,
One would hear so very oft?
At a touch sweet Pleasure melteth
Like to bubbles when rain pelteth.
Let, then, winged Fancy find
Thee a mistress to thy mind:[3]   80
Dulcet-eyed as Ceres' daughter,°   *Prosephine*
Ere the God of Torment° taught her   *Pluto*
How to frown and how to chide;
With a waist and with a side
White as Hebe's, when her zone
Slipt its golden clasp, and down
Fell her kirtle° to her feet,   *garment*
While she held the goblet sweet,
And Jove grew languid.[4]—Break the mesh
Of the Fancy's silken leash;   90
Quickly break her prison-string
And such joys as these she'll bring.–
Let the winged Fancy roam,
Pleasure never is at home.

§ "Fancy" in *Paradise Lost*

Adam is helping Eve understand a disturbing dream she had the night before (5.103–13, underlined by Keats). The "She" is "Fancy."

                    Of all external things,
Which the five watchful senses represent,
She forms imaginations, airy shapes,
Which Reason, joining, or disjoining, frames
All what we affirm or what deny, and call

---

[3]A piece of rhyming wit: *find* finds its partner in *mind*.

[4]Hebe, Jupiter and Juno's young virginal daughter, was cup-bearer to the gods until an accident loosened her belt (zone) and exposed her. Displeased, Jupiter gave the boy Ganymede the office of honor.

Our knowledge or opinion; then retires
Into her private cell when nature rests.
Oft in her absence mimic Fancy wakes
To imitate her; but misjoining shapes,[1]
Wild work produces oft, and most in dreams;
Ill matching words and deeds long past or late.

TO AUTUMN[1]

1.

SEASON of mists and mellow fruitfulness,
  Close bosom-friend of the maturing sun;
Conspiring with him how to load and bless
  With fruit the vines that round the thatch-eves[2] run;
To bend with apples the moss'd cottage-trees,
  And fill all fruit with ripeness to the core;
    To swell the gourd, and plump the hazel shells
With a sweet kernel; to set budding more,
  And still more, later flowers for the bees,
  Until they think warm days will never cease,
    For Summer has o'er-brimm'd their clammy cells.

10

2.

Who hath not seen thee oft amid thy store?
  Sometimes whoever seeks abroad may find
Thee sitting careless on a granary floor,
  Thy hair soft-lifted by the winnowing wind;
Or on a half-reap'd furrow sound asleep,
  Drows'd with the fume of poppies,[3] while thy hook
    Spares the next swath and all its twined flowers:

---

[1]The last two words may be verb-noun or adjective-verb.

---

[1]Composed 19–21 Sept. 1819 in Winchester, a tranquil village in southern England; see K's letter to Reynolds, 21 Sept. (p. 266). "Autumn" involves harvest bounty with impending death—the reaper as grim reaper, autumn as the prelude to winter (see Shakespeare's sonnet, "That time of year thou may'st in me behold"). Among other poems echoed are Thomson's *Autumn* in *The Seasons* (1740) and the last stanza of Coleridge's *Frost at Midnight*.

[2]The eaves of thatched cottage roofs.

[3]Opium is manufactured from poppies.

And sometimes like a gleaner thou dost keep
    Steady thy laden head across a brook;   20
Or by a cyder-press, with patient look,
    Thou watchest the last oozings hours by hours.

3.

Where are the songs of Spring? Ay, where are they?[4]
    Think not of them, thou hast thy music too,—
While barred clouds bloom the soft-dying day,
    And touch the stubble-plains with rosy hue;
Then in a wailful choir the small gnats mourn
    Among the river sallows,[5] borne aloft
        Or sinking as the light wind lives or dies;
And full-grown lambs loud bleat from hilly bourn;[6]   30
    Hedge-crickets sing; and now with treble soft
    The red-breast whistles from a garden-croft;
        And gathering swallows twitter in the skies.

ODE ON MELANCHOLY

In May 1819 Keats paraphrased a couplet from Wordsworth's "Intimations" Ode: "Nothing can bring back the hour / Of splendour in the grass and glory in the flower" (181–82), commenting, "I once thought this a Melancholist's dream" (see p. 256). "Melancholy" denotes "black" moods; Hamlet is famously "The Melancholy Dane." Burton's Anatomy of Melancholy *(1621), which Keats relished, offers an elaborate analysis as well as an anthology of notable remarks. Taking a stock eighteenth-century subject (Charlotte Smith has a sonnet* To Melancholy*), Keats revises the convention of mourning into a sensibility tuned to the exquisite evanescence of joy, pleasure, and beauty. He originally had a macabre, mock-heroic first stanza about the quest for the goddess Melancholy (see p. 371).*

---

[4]The *Ubi sunt* trope ("Where are they now?") that traditionally cues nostalgia for lost worlds, the implied answer being "gone"; cf. stanza IV of Wordsworth's "Intimations" *Ode* (p. 357, n. 12).

[5]willows (an emblem of death).

[6]boundary, region.

Manuscript of stanzas 1 and 2 of *Ode on Melancholy*, 1819.

1.

No, no, go not to Lethe, neither twist
    Wolf's-bane, tight-rooted, for its poisonous wine;
Nor suffer thy pale forehead to be kiss'd
    By nightshade, ruby grape of Proserpine;[1]
Make not your rosary of yew-berries,[2]
    Nor let the beetle, nor the death-moth be
        Your mournful Psyche,[3] nor the downy owl
A partner in your sorrow's mysteries;°   *religious rites*
    For shade to shade will come too drowsily,
        And drown the wakeful anguish of the soul.   10

2.

But when the melancholy fit shall fall
    Sudden from heaven like a weeping cloud,
That fosters the droop-headed flowers all,
    And hides the green hill in an April shroud;
Then glut thy sorrow on a morning rose,
    Or on the rainbow of the salt sand-wave,
        Or on the wealth of globed[4] peonies;
Or if thy mistress some rich anger shows,
    Emprison her soft hand, and let her rave,
        And feed deep, deep upon her peerless eyes.   20

3.

She[5] dwells with Beauty—Beauty that must die;
    And Joy, whose hand is ever at his lips
Bidding adieu; and aching Pleasure nigh,
    Turning to poison while the bee-mouth sips:[6]
Ay, in the very temple of Delight

---

[1] Both are poisons. Proserpine's seasonal returns and departures are relevant to the fluxes of melancholy aesthetics.

[2] Yew is associated with death; a rosary is a string of prayer-beads.

[3] Scarab beetles (jewel-bugs) were placed in Egyptian tombs as portents of resurrection; the markings on a death's-head moth resemble a skull; the hoot of an owl is an omen of death.

[4] *OED* credits this as the first instance of the noun transferred into a verbal adjective.

[5] The referent pivots from the mistress to Melancholy.

[6] See the 21 April 1819 section of Keats's long letter (p. 250) on this relentless transformation.

Veil'd Melancholy has her sovran shrine,
    Though seen of none save him whose strenuous tongue
Can burst Joy's grape against his palate fine;[7]
    His soul shall taste the sadness of her might,
    And be among her cloudy trophies hung.   30

§ Canceled First Stanza[1]

Though you should build a bark of dead men's bones,
    And rear a phantom gibbet° for a mast,   *gallows*
Stitch creeds together for a sail, with groans
    To fill it out, bloodstained and aghast;
Although your rudder be a Dragon's tail,
    Long sever'd, yet still hard with agony,
        Your cordage large uprootings from the skull
Of bald Medusa;[2] certes° you would fail   *certainly*
    To find the Melancholy, whether she
        Dreameth in any isle of Lethe dull.

Hyperion. A Fragment

This fragment follows Ode on Melancholy *to close the 1820 volume. "Titan Heav'n's first-born, / With his enormous brood, and birth-right seized / By younger Saturn; he from mightier Jove / His own and Rhea's son like measure found: / So Jove usurping reign'd": so Milton gives the kernel (*PL *1.510–15), drawing on the Hesiod's* Theogony *(8th c.* BCE*). Keats underscored these lines. He conceived* Hyperion *as a* Lear-*like antidote to* Endymion. *Where the Romance has a human shepherd "led on . . . by circumstance" and finally immortalized by divine love,* Hyperion *opens with the old generation of Titan gods fallen into mortality and the new generation, the Olympian gods, ascendant. Keats's designated hero was to be Hyperion's successor, the new Sun God Apollo, "a fore-seeing God" able to " shape his actions like one" (Keats explained to Haydon). That Apollo was also the god of metaphorical light, of medicine and poetry together, mattered intensely*

---

[7]refined, sensitive.

---

[1]On Brown's ms (Harvard) this is crossed out in pencil. It spoofs a heroic quest for the Goddess Melancholy, calculated on a vehicle formed from relics and trophies of knightly victories. The next stanza begins "No, no, go not to Lethe. . . ."
[2]The Gorgon, a snake-haired monster whose gaze turns beholders to stone; finally slain by Perseus, using his shield as a mirror to gauge the thrust of his sword.

to Keats, too; and the idiom of classical mythology was liberating. Though Keats wielded the epic signal of Miltonic blank verse and modeled his opening books on the opening books of Paradise Lost, *he rejected Milton's "ballance of good and evil" (so he lays it out to Reynolds, 3 May 1818). He wanted a sublimity not underpinned by Christian theology's "certain points and resting places in reasoning," on which Milton seemed too easily to rest. The pulse of his epic would be a Wordsworthian "burden of the Mystery," and its poetry would course with "dark Passages": the knowledge "that the World is full of Misery and Heartbreak, Pain, Sickness, and oppression."*

Keats coined words to do justice to his vision: Saturn's "realmless" eyes (1.19), an iron-"stubborn'd" world (2.17), Apollo's "gloomless" eyes (3.80) and the "liegeless" air that awaits his command (3.92). In all this, Keats's ideal of Apollo, that "fore-seeing" benefactor of humanity, contended with compassion for the doomed god Hyperion, tortured by the mortal fate of his brother-gods, and sensing his own fall. Keats wrote the first two books of this new bid for poetic fame from late September to early December, with his own brother failing in the next room (Tom died on 1 December). Returning intermittently to the project across the early months of 1819, he gave up after 136 lines into Book III, handing Woodhouse the manuscript for review. Widely admired by Keats's contemporaries (including Shelley and Byron), Hyperion *now counts as one of the greatest reinterpretations of Milton's theme of "paradise lost," and one of the finest, most skilled renditions of Miltonic blank verse.*

BOOK I.

DEEP in the shady sadness of a vale
Far sunken from the healthy breath of morn,[1]
Far from the fiery noon, and eve's one star,
Sat gray-hair'd Saturn,[2] quiet as a stone,
Still as the silence round about his lair;
Forest on forest hung about his head
Like cloud on cloud. No stir of air was there,

[1]"Sweet is the breath of morn," says Eve to Adam, in unfallen Eden (*PL* 4.641); see K's note on the word "vale" in a comparison to hell, *PL* 1.321 (p. 227), and the emotional saturation of hell's "Regions of sorrow, doleful shades" (1.65), lines he underlined. This opening sonnet-stanza is tuned with spondees, repetitions, and nonce rhymes that reinforce a sensation of stasis.

[2]The poignant echo of *Sat* in *Saturn* at once echoes and revises the pun at the opening of *PL* 2, where, in the council in Pandemonium, "Satan exalted sat, by merit raised" (5). Editor Miriam Allott notes an echo of Chapman's Zeus (Jove) imagining his "dejected Sire" and his allies, "who sit so far beneath / They never see the flying Sunne, nor hear the winds that breathe" (Homer's *Iliad* 8.422–24).

Not so much life as on a summer's day
Robs not one light seed from the feather'd grass,
But where the dead leaf fell, there did it rest.   10
A stream went voiceless by, still deadened more
By reason of his fallen divinity
Spreading a shade: the Naiad 'mid her reeds
Press'd her cold finger closer to her lips.

    Along the margin-sand large foot-marks went,
No further than to where his feet had stray'd,
And slept there since. Upon the sodden ground
His old right hand lay nerveless, listless, dead,
Unsceptred; and his realmless eyes were closed;
While his bow'd head seem'd list'ning to the Earth,   20
His ancient mother, for some comfort yet.

    It seem'd no force could wake him from his place;
But there came one,° who with a kindred hand   *Thea*
Touch'd his wide shoulders, after bending low
With reverence, though to one who knew it not.
She was a Goddess of the infant world;
By her in stature the tall Amazon
Had stood a pigmy's height: she would have ta'en
Achilles by the hair and bent his neck;
Or with a finger stay'd Ixion's wheel.³   30
Her face was large as that of Memphian sphinx,⁴
Pedestal'd haply in a palace court,
When sages look'd to Egypt for their lore.
But oh! how unlike marble was that face:
How beautiful, if sorrow had not made
Sorrow more beautiful than Beauty's self.
There was a listening fear in her regard,
As if calamity had but begun;

³For offending Jove with insolence, Ixion was bound eternally to a wheel of torture in Hades.

⁴Memphis was a major city in ancient Egypt. Egyptian ruins were of intense interest after Napoleon invaded Egypt in 1798, with archeologists and artists in tow. K had seen some of these in the British Museum and (editor Douglas Bush suggests) may have read the review of Light's *Travels in Egypt* in the *Quarterly* (vol. 19), immediately preceding the review of *Endymion*.

As if the vanward° clouds of evil days[5]   *battle front-line*
Had spent their malice, and the sullen rear   40
Was with its stored thunder labouring up.
One hand she press'd upon that aching spot
Where beats the human heart, as if just there,
Though an immortal, she felt cruel pain:
The other upon Saturn's bended neck
She laid, and to the level of his ear
Leaning with parted lips, some words she spake
In solemn tenour and deep organ tone:
Some mourning words, which in our feeble tongue
Would come in these like accents; O how frail   50
To that large utterance of the early Gods!
"Saturn, look up! – though wherefore, poor old King?[6]
I have no comfort for thee, no not one:
I cannot say, 'O wherefore sleepest thou?'
For heaven is parted from thee, and the earth
Knows thee not, thus afflicted, for a God;
And ocean too, with all its solemn noise,
Has from thy sceptre pass'd; and all the air
Is emptied of thine hoary majesty.
Thy thunder, conscious of the new command,   60
Rumbles reluctant[7] o'er our fallen house;°   *dynasty*
And thy sharp lightning in unpractised hands
Scorches and burns our once serene domain.
O aching time! O moments big as years!
All as ye pass swell out the monstrous truth,
And press it so upon our weary griefs
That unbelief has not a space to breathe.
Saturn, sleep on:——O thoughtless, why did I
Thus violate thy slumbrous solitude?
Why should I ope thy melancholy eyes?   70
Saturn, sleep on! while at thy feet I weep."

[5]Echoing Milton's description of his own circumstances, after the restoration of the monarchy: "fall'n on evil days" (*PL* 7.25); Milton was part of the regicidal parliamentary interregnum. See K's comment on this plight in his note to *PL* 1.598–99 (p. 230).

[6]The phrase evokes both Shakespeare's exiled Lear and mad King George III (still alive, but stripped of power, when K wrote this poem).

[7]literally, "struggling against"; see K's note on this word in *PL* (p. 235).

As when, upon a tranced summer-night,
Those green-rob'd senators of mighty woods,
Tall oaks, branch-charmed by the earnest stars,
Dream, and so dream all night without a stir,
Save from one gradual solitary gust
Which comes upon the silence, and dies off,
As if the ebbing air had but one wave;
So came these words and went;[8] the while in tears
She touch'd her fair large forehead to the ground,   80
Just where her falling hair might be outspread
A soft and silken mat for Saturn's feet.
One moon, with alteration slow, had shed
Her silver seasons four upon the night,
And still these two were postured motionless,
Like natural sculpture in cathedral cavern;
The frozen God still couchant° on the earth,   *prone (heraldic term)*
And the sad Goddess weeping at his feet:
Until at length old Saturn lifted up
His faded eyes, and saw his kingdom gone,   90
And all the gloom and sorrow of the place,
And that fair kneeling Goddess; and then spake,
As with a palsied tongue, and while his beard
Shook horrid[9] with such aspen-malady:
"O tender spouse° of gold Hyperion,   *(also sister)*
  Thea, I feel thee ere I see thy face;
  Look up, and let me see our doom in it;
  Look up, and tell me if this feeble shape
  Is Saturn's; tell me, if thou hear'st the voice
  Of Saturn; tell me, if this wrinkling brow,   100
  Naked and bare of its great diadem,
  Peers like the front° of Saturn. Who had power   *brow*
  To make me desolate? whence came the strength?
  How was it nurtur'd to such bursting forth,
  While Fate seem'd strangled in my nervous° grasp?   *vigorous*
  But it is so; and I am smother'd up,
  And buried from all godlike exercise

---

[8]The poem's first epic simile is about the impotence of speech in the aftermath of catastrophe.

[9]K evokes the literal meaning, "hair standing on end." Cf. *Isabella*, l. 381.

Of influence benign on planets pale,
Of admonitions to the winds and seas,
Of peaceful sway above man's harvesting,   110
And all those acts which Deity supreme
Doth ease its heart of love in.——I am gone
Away from my own bosom: I have left
My strong identity, my real self,
Somewhere between the throne, and where I sit
Here on this spot of earth. Search, Thea, search!
Open thine eyes eterne, and sphere them round
Upon all space: space starr'd, and lorn of light;
Space region'd with life-air; and barren void;
Spaces of fire, and all the yawn of hell.——   120
Search, Thea, search! and tell me, if thou seest
A certain shape or shadow, making way
With wings or chariot fierce to repossess
A heaven he lost erewhile: it must——it must
Be of ripe progress——Saturn must be King.
Yes, there must be a golden victory;[10]
There must be Gods thrown down, and trumpets blown
Of triumph calm, and hymns of festival
Upon the gold clouds metropolitan,
Voices of soft proclaim, and silver stir   130
Of strings in hollow shells; and there shall be
Beautiful things made new, for the surprise
Of the sky-children; I will give command:
Thea! Thea! Thea! where is Saturn?"

This passion lifted him upon his feet,
And made his hands to struggle in the air,
His Druid[11] locks to shake and ooze with sweat,
His eyes to fever out, his voice to cease.
He stood, and heard not Thea's sobbing deep;

---

[10]K evokes but does not put into play the Roman mythologies in which defeated Saturn flees to Italy, where he reigned over a "Golden Age" of serenity and peace. K also suppresses the lore of Saturn's hostility to his sons, enacted as cannibalism.

[11]Editor Ernest de Selincourt notes that K owned Edward Davies' *Celtic Researches* (1804), which argued the affinity of the Titans and the pre-Christian celts (the Druids).

A little time, and then again he snatch'd   140
Utterance thus.——"But cannot I create?
  Cannot I form? Cannot I fashion forth
  Another world, another universe,
  To overbear and crumble this to nought?
  Where is another chaos? Where?"——That word
Found way unto Olympus, and made quake
The rebel three.[12]——Thea was startled up,
And in her bearing was a sort of hope,
As thus she quick-voic'd spake, yet full of awe.

"This cheers our fallen house: come to our friends,   150
  O Saturn! come away, and give them heart;
  I know the covert, for thence came I hither."
Thus brief; then with beseeching eyes she went
With backward footing[13] through the shade a space:
He follow'd, and she turn'd to lead the way
Through aged boughs, that yielded like the mist
Which eagles cleave upmounting from their nest.

    Meanwhile in other realms big tears were shed,[14]
More sorrow like to this, and such like woe,
Too huge for mortal tongue or pen of scribe: 160
The Titans fierce, self-hid, or prison-bound,
Groan'd for the old allegiance once more,
And listen'd in sharp pain for Saturn's voice.
But one of the whole mammoth-brood still kept
His sov'reignty, and rule, and majesty;——
Blazing Hyperion on his orbed fire
Still sat,[15] still snuff'd the incense, teeming up
From man to the sun's God; yet unsecure:
For as among us mortals omens drear

---

[12]The revolt fraternity, now reigning from Mt. Olympus: Jupiter (replacing Saturn), Neptune (replacing Oceanus), and their brother Pluto inheriting the underworld.

[13]This is respect for a king, not turning her back on, but facing him always.

[14]Maybe the flattest line K ever wrote; I thought it was a place-holder until I saw that he retained it in *The Fall of Hyperion*!

[15]Hyperion's fate impends in this repetition from Saturn, l. 4.

Fright and perplex, so also shuddered he[16]—— 170
Not at dog's howl, or gloom-bird's hated screech,
Or the familiar visiting of one
Upon the first toll of his passing-bell,° *death-knell*
Or prophesyings of the midnight lamp;
But horrors, portion'd to a giant nerve,
Oft made Hyperion ache. His palace bright
Bastion'd with pyramids of glowing gold,
And touch'd with shade of bronzed obelisks,
Glar'd a blood-red through all its thousand courts,
Arches, and domes, and fiery galleries; 180
And all its curtains of Aurorian[17] clouds
Flush'd angerly: while sometimes eagle's wings,
Unseen before by Gods or wondering men,
Darken'd the place; and neighing steeds were heard,
Not heard before by Gods or wondering men.[18]
Also, when he would taste the spicy wreaths
Of incense, breath'd aloft from sacred hills,
Instead of sweets, his ample palate took
Savour of poisonous brass and metal sick:[19]
And so, when harbour'd in the sleepy west, 190
After the full completion of fair day,——
For rest divine upon exalted couch
And slumber in the arms of melody,
He pac'd away the pleasant hours of ease
With stride colossal,[20] on from hall to hall;

[16]Critic Stuart Ende comments that this and many ensuing comparisons, with their vehicles of description in mortal registers, already have Hyperion in the fallen world. This analogy echoes Milton's description of a lunar eclipse that "with fear of change / Perplexes monarchs" (*PL* 1.598–99)—underlined by K and annotated with a cheer for Milton's republicanism (see p. 229).

[17]Aurora parts the curtains of the dawn when she rises from the bed of her husband Night.

[18]These qualifiers place Hyperion in equivalence with mortal men.

[19]"The last two years taste like brass upon my Palate," K wrote to Fanny Brawne in August 1820, as he was preparing to leave England and her (forever, he feared).

[20]In *Ozymandias* (published in *The Examiner*, 1818), Shelley ironizes a vainglorious king who survives in the modern age only in the "colossal Wreck" of his statue. Both he and K evoke about-to-be assassinated Julius Caesar: "he doth bestride the narrow world / Like a Colossus" (*Julius Caesar* 1.2.135–36)—and behind the word is the Colossus of Rhodes, a 100-ft. statue of sun-god Helios, one of the seven wonders, destroyed in antiquity.

While far within each aisle and deep recess,
His winged minions in close clusters stood,
Amaz'd and full of fear; like anxious men
Who on wide plains gather in panting troops,
When earthquakes jar their battlements and towers.   200
Even now, while Saturn, rous'd from icy trance,
Went step for step with Thea through the woods,
Hyperion, leaving twilight in the rear,
Came slope upon the threshold of the west;[21]
Then, as was wont,° his palace-door flew open   *usual*
In smoothest silence, save what solemn tubes,
Blown by the serious Zephyrs, gave of sweet
And wandering sounds, slow-breathed melodies;
And like a rose in vermeil tint and shape,
In fragrance soft, and coolness to the eye,   210
That inlet to severe magnificence
Stood full blown, for the God to enter in.

     He enter'd, but he enter'd full of wrath;
His flaming robes stream'd out beyond his heels,
And gave a roar, as if of earthly fire,
That scar'd away the meek ethereal Hours°   *sun nymphs*
And made their dove-wings tremble. On he flared,[22]
From stately nave to nave, from vault to vault,
Through bowers of fragrant and enwreathed light,
And diamond-paved lustrous long arcades,   220
Until he reach'd the great main cupola;
There standing fierce beneath, he stampt his foot,
And from the basements deep to the high towers
Jarr'd his own golden region; and before
The quavering thunder thereupon had ceas'd,
His voice leapt out, despite of godlike curb,
To this result: "O dreams of day and night!
  O monstrous forms! O effigies of pain!
  O spectres busy in a cold, cold gloom!
  O lank-ear'd Phantoms of black-weeded pools!   230

---

[21]where the sun has set.

[22]In the revised fragment, *The Fall of Hyperion: A Dream*, K stopped here (see p. 415).

Why do I know ye? why have I seen ye? why
Is my eternal essence thus distraught
To see and to behold these horrors new?
Saturn is fallen, am I too to fall?
Am I to leave this haven of my rest,
This cradle of my glory, this soft clime,
This calm luxuriance of blissful light,
These crystalline pavilions, and pure fanes,°   *temples*
Of all my lucent empire?[23] It is left
Deserted, void, nor any haunt of mine.   240
The blaze, the splendor, and the symmetry,
I cannot see—but darkness, death and darkness.
Even here, into my centre of repose,
The shady visions[24] come to domineer,
Insult, and blind, and stifle up my pomp.—
Fall!—No, by Tellus° and her briny robes!   *(his mother)*
Over the fiery frontier of my realms
I will advance a terrible right arm
Shall scare that infant thunderer, rebel Jove,
And bid old Saturn take his throne again."—   250
He spake, and ceas'd, the while a heavier threat
Held struggle with his throat but came not forth;
For as in theatres of crowded men
Hubbub increases more they call out "Hush!"
So at Hyperion's words the Phantoms pale
Bestirr'd themselves, thrice horrible and cold;
And from the mirror'd level where he stood
A mist arose, as from a scummy marsh.
At this, through all his bulk an agony
Crept gradual, from the feet unto the crown,   260
Like a lithe serpent vast and muscular

[23]Echoing defeated Satan's stunned survey of hell: "Is this the Region, this the Soil, the Clime, / Said then the lost Arch-Angel, this the seat / That we must change for Heav'n, this mournful gloom / For that celestial light?" (*PL* 1.242–45); Milton himself is echoing (as K knows) the great lament of dying John of Gaunt (whose son deposes, then has murdered, his cousin Richard II) for the end of England as he knew and loved it: "this sceptered isle, / This earth of majesty, this seat of Mars, / This other Eden, demi-paradise, / . . . / Is now leased out—" (*Richard II* 2.1.40ff).

[24]The syntax makes "shady visions" seem independent agents, while the terms also suggest this as an effect of Hyperion's darkening vision, his apprehension of dark passages.

Making slow way, with head and neck convuls'd
From over-strained might.[25] Releas'd, he fled
To the eastern gates, and full six dewy hours
Before the dawn in season due should blush,
He breath'd fierce breath against the sleepy portals,
Clear'd them of heavy vapours, burst them wide
Suddenly on the ocean's chilly streams.
The planet orb of fire, whereon he rode
Each day from east to west the heavens through,   270
Spun round in sable curtaining of clouds;
Not therefore veiled quite, blindfold, and hid,
But ever and anon the glancing spheres,
Circles, and arcs, and broad-belting colure,[26]
Glow'd through, and wrought upon the muffling dark
Sweet-shaped lightnings from the nadir deep
Up to the zenith,——hieroglyphics old,
Which sages and keen-eyed astrologers
Then living on the earth, with labouring thought
Won from the gaze of many centuries:[27]   280
Now lost, save what we find on remnants huge
Of stone, or marble swart; their import gone,
Their wisdom long since fled.——Two wings this orb
Possess'd for glory, two fair argent wings,
Ever exalted at the God's approach:
And now, from forth the gloom their plumes immense
Rose, one by one, till all outspreaded were;
While still the dazzling globe maintain'd eclipse,
Awaiting for Hyperion's command.
Fain would he have commanded, fain took throne   290
And bid the day begin, if but for change.
He might not:——No, though a primeval God:

[25]Evoking both the plague of Moses on his Egyptian masters (Exodus) and Satan's insinuation into the Garden of Eden and possession of the serpent's body (*PL* 9.180–90, underlined and commented on by K; see p. 236–37), as well as K's sensation of "dark passages": "We are in a Mist . . . We feel the 'burden of the Mystery'" (3 May 1818; see p. 130).

[26]K underlined Satan's space-journeying around earth, "traversing each Colure" (*PL* 9.66)—the two great circles intersecting at right angles at the poles, dividing earth into quarters.

[27]Like the Egyptian monoliths; the Rosetta stone, discovered in 1799, had yet to be deciphered.

The sacred seasons might not be disturb'd.
Therefore the operations of the dawn
Stay'd in their birth, even as here 'tis told.
Those silver wings expanded sisterly,
Eager to sail their orb; the porches wide
Open'd upon the dusk demesnes° of night;   *domains*
And the bright Titan, phrenzied with new woes,
Unus'd to bend, by hard compulsion bent   300
His spirit to the sorrow of the time;
And all along a dismal rack of clouds,
Upon the boundaries of day and night,
He stretch'd himself in grief and radiance faint.
There as he lay, the Heaven with its stars
Look'd down on him with pity, and the voice
Of Cœlus, from the universal space,
Thus whisper'd low and solemn in his ear.
"O brightest of my children dear, earth-born
  And sky-engendered, Son of Mysteries   310
  All unrevealed even to the powers
  Which met at thy creating; at whose joys
  And palpitations sweet, and pleasures soft,
  I, Cœlus, wonder, how they came and whence;
  And at the fruits thereof what shapes they be,
  Distinct, and visible; symbols divine,
  Manifestations of that beauteous life
  Diffus'd unseen throughout eternal space:
  Of these new-form'd art thou, oh brightest child!
  Of these, thy brethren and the Goddesses!   320
  There is sad feud among ye, and rebellion
  Of son against his sire. I saw him fall,
  I saw my first-born° tumbled from his throne!   *Saturn*
  To me his arms were spread, to me his voice
  Found way from forth the thunders round his head!
  Pale wox° I, and in vapours hid my face.   *waxed*
  Art thou, too, near such doom? vague fear there is:
  For I have seen my sons most unlike Gods.
  Divine ye were created, and divine
  In sad demeanour, solemn, undisturb'd,   330
  Unruffled, like high Gods, ye liv'd and ruled:

Now I behold in you fear, hope, and wrath;
Actions of rage and passion; even as
I see them, on the mortal world beneath,
In men who die.——This is the grief, O Son!
Sad sign of ruin, sudden dismay, and fall!
Yet do thou strive; as thou art capable,
As thou canst move about, an evident God;[28]
And canst oppose to each malignant hour
Ethereal presence:——I am but a voice;   340
My life is but the life of winds and tides,
No more than winds and tides can I avail:——
But thou canst.——Be thou therefore in the van°   *forefront*
Of circumstance; yea, seize the arrow's barb
Before the tense string° murmur.——To the earth! *(of your enemy)*
For there thou wilt find Saturn, and his woes.
Meantime I will keep watch on thy bright sun,
And of thy seasons be a careful nurse."——
Ere half this region-whisper had come down,
Hyperion arose, and on the stars   350
Lifted his curved lids, and kept them wide
Until it ceas'd; and still he kept them wide:
And still they were the same bright, patient stars.
Then with a slow incline of his broad breast,
Like to a diver in the pearly seas,
Forward he stoop'd over the airy shore,
And plung'd all noiseless into the deep night.

BOOK II.

JUST at the self-same beat of Time's wide wings
Hyperion slid into the rustled air,
And Saturn gain'd with Thea that sad place
Where Cybele[1] and the bruised Titans mourn'd.
It was a den where no insulting light

---

[28]Coelus is the sky, not an embodied (evident) God.

---

[1]Saturn's wife, mother of the rebel gods. The Titan names were available to K in such contemporary guides as "Edward Baldwin" (William Godwin), *The Pantheon: or Ancient History of the Gods of Greece and Rome*, and *Lemprière's Classical Dictionary*.

Could glimmer on their tears; where their own groans
They felt, but heard not, for the solid roar
Of thunderous waterfalls and torrents hoarse,
Pouring a constant bulk, uncertain where.[2]
Crag jutting forth to crag, and rocks that seem'd   10
Ever as if just rising from a sleep,
Forehead to forehead held their monstrous horns;
And thus in thousand hugest phantasies
Made a fit roofing to this nest of woe.
Instead of thrones, hard flint they sat upon,
Couches of rugged stone, and slaty ridge
Stubborn'd with iron. All were not assembled:
Some chain'd in torture, and some wandering.
Cœus, and Gyges, and Briareüs,
Typhon, and Dolor, and Porphyrion,   20
With many more, the brawniest in assault,
Were pent in regions of laborious breath;[3]
Dungeon'd in opaque element, to keep
Their clenched teeth still clench'd, and all their limbs
Lock'd up like veins of metal, crampt and screw'd;
Without a motion, save of their big hearts
Heaving in pain, and horribly convuls'd
With sanguine feverous boiling gurge[4] of pulse.
Mnemosyne was straying in the world;°   *(seeking Apollo)*
Far from her moon had Phœbe wandered;   30
And many else were free to roam abroad,
But for the main, here found they covert drear.
Scarce images of life, one here, one there,
Lay vast and edgeways; like a dismal cirque
Of Druid stones,[5] upon a forlorn moor,
When the chill rain begins at shut of eve,[6]

---

[2]K pours the sound of *roar* through "torrents hoarse, / Pouring." In a world of pain, K's poetry throughout this book creates a hell of pained sounds.

[3]Volcanoes were thought to be the effect of this pent-up rage.

[4]whirlpool; K underlined this word in *PL* 12.41.

[5]K had seen such a configuration near Keswick (in the Lake District) on his tour with Brown.

[6]Eve recalls returning to Adam "at shut of evening flowers" (*PL* 9.278, underlined by K).

In dull November, and their chancel vault,
The Heaven itself, is blinded throughout night.
Each one kept shroud, nor to his neighbour gave
Or word, or look, or action of despair.   40
Creüs was one; his ponderous iron mace
Lay by him, and a shatter'd rib of rock
Told of his rage, ere he thus sank and pined.
Iäpetus another; in his grasp,
A serpent's plashy[7] neck; its barbed tongue
Squeez'd from the gorge, and all its uncurl'd length
Dead; and because the creature could not spit
Its poison in the eyes of conquering Jove.
Next Cottus: prone he lay, chin uppermost,
As though in pain; for still upon the flint   50
He ground severe his skull, with open mouth
And eyes at horrid working. Nearest him
Asia, born of most enormous Caf,
Who cost her mother Tellus keener pangs,[8]
Though feminine, than any of her sons:
More thought than woe was in her dusky face,
For she was prophesying of her glory;
And in her wide imagination stood
Palm-shaded temples, and high rival fanes,
By Oxus or in Ganges' sacred isles.   60
Even as Hope upon her anchor leans,
So leant she, not so fair, upon a tusk
Shed from the broadest of her elephants.
Above her, on a crag's uneasy shelve,
Upon his elbow rais'd, all prostrate else,
Shadow'd Enceladus; once tame and mild
As grazing ox unworried in the meads;
Now tiger-passion'd, lion-thoughted, wroth,
He meditated, plotted, and even now
Was hurling mountains in that second war,   70
Not long delay'd, that scar'd the younger Gods
To hide themselves in forms of beast and bird.

[7]color-splashed (*OED* cites this passage).
[8]The language recalls Milton's: Proserpine's abduction by Pluto "cost Ceres all that pain" (*PL* 4.271), a line that struck K with particular power.

Not far hence Atlas; and beside him prone
Phorcus, the sire of Gorgons. Neighbour'd close
Oceanus, and Tethys, in whose lap
Sobb'd Clymene among her tangled hair.
In midst of all lay Themis, at the feet
Of Ops° the queen all clouded round from sight;   *(Cybele)*
No shape distinguishable,[9] more than when
Thick night confounds the pine-tops with the clouds: 80
And many else whose names may not be told.
For when the Muse's wings are air-ward spread,
Who shall delay her flight? And she must chaunt
Of Saturn, and his guide, who now had climb'd
With damp and slippery footing from a depth
More horrid still. Above a sombre cliff
Their heads appear'd, and up their stature grew
Till on the level height their steps found ease:
Then Thea spread abroad her trembling arms
Upon the precincts of this nest of pain,   90
And sidelong fix'd her eye on Saturn's face:
There saw she direst strife; the supreme God
At war with all the frailty of grief,
Of rage, of fear, anxiety, revenge,
Remorse, spleen, hope, but most of all despair.
Against these plagues he strove in vain; for Fate
Had pour'd a mortal oil upon his head,
A disanointing° poison: so that Thea,   *(Keats coinage)*
Affrighted, kept her still, and let him pass
First onwards in, among the fallen tribe.   100

    As with us mortal men, the laden heart
Is persecuted more, and fever'd more,
When it is nighing to the mournful house
Where other hearts are sick of the same bruise;
So Saturn, as he walk'd into the midst,
Felt faint, and would have sunk among the rest,
But that he met Enceladus's eye,
Whose mightiness, and awe of him, at once

[9] Milton's similar description of death (*PL* 2.667–78)—lines K double-underlined.

Came like an inspiration; and he shouted,
"Titans, behold your God!" at which some groan'd;   110
Some started on their feet; some also shouted;
Some wept, some wail'd, all bow'd with reverence;
And Ops, uplifting her black folded veil,
Show'd her pale cheeks, and all her forehead wan,
Her eye-brows thin and jet, and hollow eyes.
There is a roaring in the bleak-grown pines
When Winter lifts his voice; there is a noise
Among immortals when a God gives sign,
With hushing finger, how he means to load
His tongue with the full weight of utterless thought,   120
With thunder, and with music, and with pomp:
Such noise is like the roar of bleak-grown pines;
Which, when it ceases in this mountain'd world,
No other sound succeeds; but ceasing here,
Among these fallen, Saturn's voice therefrom
Grew up like organ, that begins anew
Its strain, when other harmonies, stopt short,
Leave the dinn'd air vibrating silverly.
Thus grew it up——"Not in my own sad breast,
  Which is its own great judge and searcher out,   130
  Can I find reason why ye should be thus:
  Not in the legends of the first of days,
  Studied from that old spirit-leaved book
  Which starry Uranus with finger bright
  Sav'd from the shores of darkness, when the waves
  Low-ebb'd still hid it up in shallow gloom;——
  And the which book ye know I ever kept
  For my firm-based footstool:——Ah, infirm!
  Not there, nor in sign, symbol, or portent
  Of element, earth, water, air, and fire,——   140
  At war, at peace, or inter-quarreling
  One against one, or two, or three, or all
  Each several one against the other three,
  As fire with air loud warring when rain-floods
  Drown both, and press them both against earth's face,
  Where, finding sulphur, a quadruple wrath
  Unhinges the poor world;——not in that strife,

Wherefrom I take strange lore, and read it deep,
Can I find reason why ye should be thus:
No, no-where can unriddle, though I search,   150
And pore on Nature's universal scroll
Even to swooning, why ye, Divinities,
The first-born of all shap'd and palpable Gods,
Should cower beneath what, in comparison,
Is untremendous° might. Yet ye are here, *(Keats coinage)*
O'erwhelm'd, and spurn'd, and batter'd, ye are here!
O Titans, shall I say 'Arise!'——Ye groan:
Shall I say 'Crouch!'——Ye groan. What can I then?
O Heaven wide! O unseen parent dear!
What can I? Tell me, all ye brethren Gods,   160
How we can war, how engine our great wrath!
O speak your counsel now, for Saturn's ear
Is all a-hunger'd. Thou, Oceanus,
Ponderest high and deep; and in thy face
I see, astonied,° that severe content   *stunned*
Which comes of thought and musing: give us help!"

 So ended Saturn; and the God of the Sea,
Sophist and sage, from no Athenian grove,° *(formal education)*
But cogitation° in his watery shades,   *(self education)*
Arose, with locks not oozy, and began,   170
In murmurs, which his first-endeavouring tongue
Caught infant-like from the far-foamed sands.
"O ye, whom wrath consumes! who, passion-stung,
 Writhe at defeat, and nurse your agonies!
Shut up your senses, stifle up your ears,
My voice is not a bellows unto ire.
Yet listen, ye who will, whilst I bring proof
How ye, perforce, must be content to stoop:
And in the proof much comfort will I give,
If ye will take that comfort in its truth.   180
We fall by course of Nature's law, not force
Of thunder, or of Jove. Great Saturn, thou
Hast sifted well the atom-universe;
But for this reason, that thou art the King,
And only blind from sheer supremacy,

One avenue was shaded from thine eyes,
Through which I wandered to eternal truth.
And first, as thou wast not the first of powers,
So art thou not the last; it cannot be:
Thou art not the beginning nor the end.[10]   190
From chaos and parental darkness came
Light, the first fruits of that intestine broil,
That sullen ferment, which for wondrous ends
Was ripening in itself. The ripe hour came,
And with it light, and light, engendering
Upon its own producer, forthwith touch'd
The whole enormous matter into life.
Upon that very hour, our parentage,
The Heavens and the Earth, were manifest:
Then thou first-born, and we the giant-race,   200
Found ourselves ruling new and beauteous realms.
Now comes the pain of truth, to whom 'tis pain;
O folly! for to bear all naked truths,
And to envisage circumstance, all calm,
That is the top of sovereignty. Mark well!
As Heaven and Earth are fairer, fairer far
Than Chaos and blank Darkness, though once chiefs;
And as we show beyond that Heaven and Earth
In form and shape compact and beautiful,
In will, in action free, companionship,   210
And thousand other signs of purer life;
So on our heels a fresh perfection treads,
A power more strong in beauty, born of us
And fated to excel us, as we pass
In glory that old Darkness: nor are we
Thereby more conquer'd, than by us the rule
Of shapeless Chaos. Say, doth the dull soil
Quarrel with the proud forests it hath fed,
And feedeth still, more comely than itself?
Can it deny the chiefdom of green groves?   220
Or shall the tree be envious of the dove

[10]The classical orders would be superseded by the theology of the Judeo-Christian God: "I am the Alpha and Omega, the beginning and the ending" (Revelation 1.8).

Because it cooeth, and hath snowy wings
To wander wherewithal and find its joys?
We are such forest-trees, and our fair boughs
Have bred forth, not pale solitary doves,
But eagles golden-feather'd, who do tower
Above us in their beauty, and must reign
In right thereof; for 'tis the eternal law
That first in beauty should be first in might:
Yea, by that law, another race may drive   230
Our conquerors to mourn as we do now.
Have ye beheld the young God of the Seas,°   *Neptune*
My dispossessor? Have ye seen his face?
Have ye beheld his chariot, foam'd along
By noble winged creatures he hath made?
I saw him on the calmed waters scud,
With such a glow of beauty in his eyes,
That it enforc'd me to bid sad farewell
To all my empire: farewell sad I took,
And hither came, to see how dolorous fate   240
Had wrought upon ye; and how I might best
Give consolation in this woe extreme.
Receive the truth, and let it be your balm."[11]

Whether through poz'd° conviction, or disdain,   *posed*
They guarded silence, when Oceanus
Left murmuring, what deepest thought can tell?
But so it was, none answer'd for a space,
Save one whom none regarded, Clymene;
And yet she answer'd not, only complain'd,
With hectic lips, and eyes up-looking mild,   250
Thus wording timidly among the fierce:
"O Father, I am here the simplest voice,
    And all my knowledge is that joy is gone,
    And this thing woe crept in among our hearts,
    There to remain for ever, as I fear:
    I would not bode of evil, if I thought

---

[11]While there is a long critical tradition of citing Oceanus's calm philosophy as representing K's own view, K places it in a character in a "dramatic" debate, a possible but not absolute resting place in reasoning.

So weak a creature could turn off the help
Which by just right should come of mighty Gods;
Yet let me tell my sorrow, let me tell
Of what I heard, and how it made me weep,   260
And know that we had parted from all hope.
I stood upon a shore, a pleasant shore,
Where a sweet clime was breathed from a land
Of fragrance, quietness, and trees, and flowers.
Full of calm joy it was, as I of grief;
Too full of joy and soft delicious warmth;
So that I felt a movement in my heart
To chide, and to reproach that solitude
With songs of misery, music of our woes;
And sat me down, and took a mouthed shell   270
And murmur'd into it, and made melody——
O melody no more! for while I sang,
And with poor skill let pass into the breeze
The dull shell's echo, from a bowery strand
Just opposite, an island of the sea,
There came enchantment with the shifting wind,
That did both drown and keep alive my ears.
I threw my shell away upon the sand,
And a wave fill'd it, as my sense was fill'd
With that new blissful golden melody.   280
A living death was in each gush of sounds,
Each family of rapturous hurried notes,
That fell, one after one, yet all at once,
Like pearl beads dropping sudden from their string:
And then another, then another strain,
Each like a dove leaving its olive perch,
With music wing'd instead of silent plumes,
To hover round my head, and make me sick
Of joy and grief at once. Grief overcame,
And I was stopping up my frantic ears,   290
When, past all hindrance of my trembling hands,
A voice came sweeter, sweeter than all tune,
And still it cried, 'Apollo! young Apollo!
The morning-bright Apollo! young Apollo!'
I fled, it follow'd me, and cried 'Apollo!'

O Father, and O Brethren, had ye felt
Those pains of mine; O Saturn, hadst thou felt,
Ye would not call this too indulged tongue
Presumptuous, in thus venturing to be heard."

So far her voice flow'd on, like timorous brook   300
That, lingering along a pebbled coast,
Doth fear to meet the sea: but sea it met,
And shudder'd; for the overwhelming voice
Of huge Enceladus swallow'd it in wrath:[12]
The ponderous syllables, like sullen waves
In the half-glutted hollows of reef-rocks,
Came booming thus, while still upon his arm
He lean'd; not rising, from supreme contempt.
"Or shall we listen to the over-wise,
Or to the over-foolish giant, Gods?   310
Not thunderbolt on thunderbolt, till all
That rebel Jove's whole armoury were spent,
Not world on world upon these shoulders piled,
Could agonize me more than baby-words
In midst of this dethronement horrible.[13]
Speak! roar! shout! yell! ye sleepy Titans all.
Do ye forget the blows, the buffets vile?
Are ye not smitten by a youngling arm?
Dost thou forget, sham Monarch of the Waves,
Thy scalding in the seas? What, have I rous'd   320
Your spleens with so few simple words as these?
O joy! for now I see ye are not lost:
O joy! for now I see a thousand eyes
Wide glaring for revenge!"——As this he said,
He lifted up his stature vast, and stood,
Still without intermission speaking thus:

[12]Enceladus recalls Moloch in *PL* (K underlined 2.73–81), the "fiercest spirit" of the fallen angels.

[13]Echoing Satan's defiance: "the unconquerable will, / And study of revenge, immortal hate, / And courage never to submit or yield, / And what is else not to be overcome; / That glory never shall his wrath or might / Extort from me"; "Fallen Cherub, to be weak is miserable, / Doing or suffering"; "Awake, arise, or be for ever fallen" (*PL* 1.106–11, 157–58, 330—all underlined by K).

"Now ye are flames, I'll tell you how to burn,
  And purge the ether of our enemies;
  How to feed fierce the crooked stings of fire,
  And singe away the swollen clouds of Jove,   330
Stifling that puny essence in its tent.
  O let him feel the evil he hath done;
For though I scorn Oceanus's lore,
Much pain have I for more than loss of realms:
The days of peace and slumberous calm are fled;
Those days, all innocent of scathing war,
When all the fair Existences of heaven
Came open-eyed to guess what we would speak:——
That was before our brows were taught to frown,
Before our lips knew else but solemn sounds;   340
That was before we knew the winged thing,
Victory, might be lost, or might be won.
And be ye mindful that Hyperion,
Our brightest brother, still is undisgraced——
Hyperion, lo! his radiance is here!"

  All eyes were on Enceladus's face,
And they beheld, while still Hyperion's name
Flew from his lips up to the vaulted rocks,
A pallid gleam across his features stern:
Not savage, for he saw full many a God   350
Wroth as himself. He look'd upon them all,
And in each face he saw a gleam of light,
But splendider in Saturn's, whose hoar locks
Shone like the bubbling foam about a keel
When the prow sweeps into a midnight cove.
In pale and silver silence they remain'd,
Till suddenly a splendour, like the morn,
Pervaded all the beetling gloomy steeps,
All the sad spaces of oblivion,
And every gulf, and every chasm old,   360
And every height, and every sullen depth,
Voiceless, or hoarse with loud tormented streams:
And all the everlasting cataracts,
And all the headlong torrents far and near,

Mantled before in darkness and huge shade,
Now saw the light and made it terrible.
It was Hyperion:——a granite peak
His bright feet touch'd, and there he stay'd to view
The misery his brilliance had betray'd
To the most hateful seeing of itself.   370
Golden his hair of short Numidian curl,
Regal his shape majestic, a vast shade
In midst of his own brightness,[14] like the bulk
Of Memnon's image at the set of sun
To one who travels from the dusking East:
Sighs, too, as mournful as that Memnon's harp
He utter'd, while his hands contemplative
He press'd together, and in silence stood.[15]
Despondence seiz'd again the fallen Gods
At sight of the dejected King of Day,   380
And many hid their faces from the light:
But fierce Enceladus sent forth his eyes
Among the brotherhood; and, at their glare,
Uprose Iäpetus, and Creüs too,
And Phorcus, sea-born, and together strode
To where he towered on his eminence.
There those four shouted forth old Saturn's name;
Hyperion from the peak loud answered, "Saturn!"
Saturn sat near the Mother of the Gods,
In whose face was no joy, though all the Gods   390
Gave from their hollow throats the name of "Saturn!"

BOOK III.

THUS in alternate uproar and sad peace,
Amazed were those Titans utterly.
O leave them, Muse! O leave them to their woes;
For thou art weak to sing such tumults dire:

[14]Evoking Satan's grandeur as "archangel ruined" (PL 1.591ff) and his blazing
rhetoric: "to confirm his words out flew / Millions of flaming swords . . . / . . . the
sudden blaze / Far round illumined Hell" (663ff), phrases underlined by K.

[15]Lemprière's Classical Dictionary reports the legend: Achilles slew Aurora's son
Memnon; his statue in the Egyptian city of Thebes was said in Baldwin's mythology
to issue melodious music at sunrise and mournful music at sunset.

A solitary sorrow best befits
Thy lips, and antheming a lonely grief.
Leave them, O Muse! for thou anon wilt find
Many a fallen old Divinity
Wandering in vain about bewildered shores.
Meantime touch piously the Delphic harp,   10
And not a wind of heaven but will breathe
In aid soft warble from the Dorian flute;[1]
For lo! 'tis for the Father of all verse.
Flush every thing that hath a vermeil hue,
Let the rose glow intense and warm the air,
And let the clouds of even and of morn
Float in voluptuous fleeces o'er the hills;
Let the red wine within the goblet boil,
Cold as a bubbling well; let faint-lipp'd shells,
On sands, or in great deeps, vermilion turn   20
Through all their labyrinths; and let the maid
Blush keenly, as with some warm kiss surpris'd.
Chief isle of the embowered Cyclades,
Rejoice, O Delos,° with thine olives green,   *(Apollo's birthplace)*
And poplars, and lawn-shading palms, and beech,
In which the Zephyr breathes the loudest song,
And hazels thick, dark-stemm'd beneath the shade:
Apollo is once more the golden theme!
Where was he, when the Giant of the Sun
Stood bright, amid the sorrow of his peers?   30
Together had he left his mother fair
And his twin-sister° sleeping in their bower,   *Diana*
And in the morning twilight wandered forth
Beside the osiers of a rivulet,
Full ankle-deep in lilies of the vale.
The nightingale had ceas'd, and a few stars
Were lingering in the heavens, while the thrush
Began calm-throated. Throughout all the isle
There was no covert, no retired cave
Unhaunted by the murmurous noise of waves,   40

---

[1]Apollo's oracle is at Delphi; Dorian music is stately. K underlined "the Dorian
mood / Of flutes and soft recorders" that cheer the fallen angels in their military for-
mation (*PL* 2.550–51).

Though scarcely heard in many a green recess.
He listen'd, and he wept, and his bright tears
Went trickling down the golden bow he held.
Thus with half-shut suffused eyes he stood,
While from beneath some cumbrous boughs hard by
With solemn step an awful° Goddess came,   *awesome*
And there was purport in her looks for him,
Which he with eager guess began to read
Perplex'd, the while melodiously he said:
"How cam'st thou over the unfooted sea?   50
  Or hath that antique mien and robed form
Mov'd in these vales invisible till now?
Sure I have heard those vestments sweeping o'er
The fallen leaves, when I have sat alone
In cool mid-forest. Surely I have traced
The rustle of those ample skirts about
These grassy solitudes, and seen the flowers
Lift up their heads, as still the whisper pass'd.
Goddess! I have beheld those eyes before,
And their eternal calm, and all that face,   60
Or I have dream'd."——"Yes," said the supreme shape,
"Thou hast dream'd of me; and awaking up
Didst find a lyre all golden by thy side,
Whose strings touch'd by thy fingers, all the vast
Unwearied ear of the whole universe
Listen'd in pain and pleasure at the birth
Of such new tuneful wonder. Is't not strange
That thou shouldst weep, so gifted? Tell me, youth,
What sorrow thou canst feel; for I am sad
When thou dost shed a tear: explain thy griefs   70
To one who in this lonely isle hath been
The watcher of thy sleep and hours of life,
From the young day when first thy infant hand
Pluck'd witless the weak flowers, till thine arm
Could bend that bow heroic to all times.
Show thy heart's secret to an ancient Power
Who hath forsaken old and sacred thrones
For prophecies of thee, and for the sake
Of loveliness new born."——Apollo then,

With sudden scrutiny and gloomless eyes,   80
Thus answer'd, while his white melodious throat
Throbb'd with the syllables.——"Mnemosyne!
  Thy name is on my tongue, I know not how;
  Why should I tell thee what thou so well seest?
  Why should I strive to show what from thy lips
  Would come no mystery? For me, dark, dark,
  And painful vile oblivion seals my eyes:[2]
  I strive to search wherefore I am so sad,
  Until a melancholy numbs my limbs;
  And then upon the grass I sit, and moan,   90
  Like one who once had wings.——O why should I
  Feel curs'd and thwarted, when the liegeless air
  Yields to my step aspirant? why should I
  Spurn the green turf as hateful to my feet?
  Goddess benign, point forth some unknown thing:
  Are there not other regions than this isle?
  What are the stars? There is the sun, the sun!
  And the most patient brilliance of the moon!
  And stars by thousands! Point me out the way
  To any one particular beauteous star,   100
  And I will flit into it with my lyre,
  And make its silvery splendour pant with bliss.
  I have heard the cloudy thunder: Where is power?
  Whose hand, whose essence, what divinity
  Makes this alarum in the elements,
  While I here idle listen on the shores
  In fearless yet in aching ignorance?
  O tell me, lonely Goddess, by thy harp,
  That waileth every morn and eventide,
  Tell me why thus I rave, about these groves!   110
  Mute thou remainest——Mute! yet I can read
  A wondrous lesson in thy silent face:
  Knowledge enormous makes a God of me.
  Names, deeds, gray legends, dire events, rebellions,
  Majesties, sovran voices, agonies,
  Creations and destroyings, all at once

[2]Echoing blind Samson in Milton's *Samson Agonistes* (80).

Pour into the wide hollows of my brain,
And deify me, as if some blithe wine
Or bright elixir[3] peerless I had drunk,
And so become immortal."——Thus the God,   120
While his enkindled eyes, with level glance
Beneath his white soft temples, stedfast kept
Trembling with light upon Mnemosyne.
Soon wild commotions shook him, and made flush
All the immortal fairness of his limbs;[4]
Most like the struggle at the gate of death;
Or liker still to one who should take leave
Of pale immortal death, and with a pang
As hot as death's is chill, with fierce convulse
Die into life: so young Apollo anguish'd;   130
His very hair, his golden tresses famed
Kept undulation round his eager neck.
During the pain Mnemosyne upheld
Her arms as one who prophesied.——At length
Apollo shriek'd;——and lo! from all his limbs
Celestial   *   *   *   *   *   *
*   *   *   *   *   *   *   * 5

THE END.

[3]In alchemy, the potion that confers immortality.

[4]K's draft shows his effort to wean Apollo from bower-romance: "~~Roseate and painted as a ravish'd nymph~~ / Into a hue more roseate than sweet-pain / Gives to a ravish'd Nymph ~~new r~~ when her warm tears / Gush luscious with no sob. ~~Or 'twas~~ Or more severe;—— /" But even Leigh Hunt was uneasy: "there is something too effeminate and human in the way in which Apollo receives the exaltation which his wisdom is giving him. He weeps and wonders somewhat too fondly; but his powers gather nobly on him as he proceeds" (*Indicator* 14, 9 Aug. 1820, p. 350); Apollo "suffers a little too exquisitely among the lilies" (*Lord Byron*, 1828, p. 219). Subsequent readers note a seeming relapse to *Endymion*-style diction and tropes.

[5]draft, beneath line 135]: ~~he was the God!~~ and ~~and godlike.~~

The fragment ends here, with asterisks and "The End" supplied by the publisher. In his copy of *Endymion*, Woodhouse notes that the plan was to show "the dethronement of Hyperion" by Apollo, "of Oceanus by Neptune, of Saturn by Jupiter &c and the war of the Giants for Saturn's reestablishment—with other events, of which we have but very dark hints in the Mythological poets of Greece & Rome. In fact, the incidents would have been pure creations of the Poet's brain."

The Fall of Hyperion: A Dream

In Hyperion *Keats lingered over the stunned agony of the fallen gods and the anxious apprehensions of the yet-to-fall Hyperion, brother to the already fallen Titan king, Saturn. Unable to go on with the project in the months after his own brother's death, he took it up late in 1819, recasting it as a Dantean dream vision: a poet's dream of his own wakening into a wide wasteland (with echoes of and allusions to* Purgatorio*), and experience of his own near death. He meets Moneta ("admonition"), sole remnant of the Titans and bearer of their world in her memory. There is no god of poetry, only a human poet whom she accuses of being no poet, just a uselessly fevered dreamer. To his protests, she offers him a test, taking him into the theater of her memory (and back to the text of* Hyperion*) to be immersed in the misery of the Titans. With the burden of her foreknowledge (and the fresh memory of his own near death), the poet witnesses Hyperion's anxiety. Keats abandoned this attempt, too, unable to differentiate a "false beauty proceeding from art" from "the true voice of feeling" (so he confessed to Reynolds, Sept. 1819). Even so, this art continued to generate new words for feeling:* faulture *(1.70), fault and failure; sooth (1.155), smooth, soothing, and sooth (truth); mourn as a noun (1.231); immortal sickness (1.258), a paradox wrung from the medical term, mortal sickness; Moneta's visionless eyes (1.267); adorant (1.283) for prayerful and adoring.*

The Fall of Hyperion first appeared in 1856 when R. M. Milnes published Another Version of Hyperion *in Miscellanies of the Philobiblion Society. It was thought then to be the original ms from which* Hyperion *was sprung (rather than a revision)—a prescient herald of emerging Victorian debates about the relevance of poets, poetic vision, and poetic idealism to the modern age. The text here was prepared with reference to Richard Woodhouse's ms. My footnotes do not repeat information in the annotations to* Hyperion.

The Fall of Hyperion: A Dream

Canto I

Fanatics° have their dreams, wherewith they weave   *cultists*
A paradise for a sect; the savage too
From forth the loftiest fashion° of his sleep   *invention*
Guesses at Heaven; pity these have not
Trac'd upon vellum° or wild Indian leaf   *parchment*

The shadows of melodious utterance.
But bare of laurel[1] they live, dream, and die;
For Poesy alone can tell her dreams,
With the fine spell of words alone can save
Imagination from the sable charm   10
And dumb° enchantment. Who alive can say,   *mute*
"Thou art no Poet; mayst not tell thy dreams?"
Since every man whose soul is not a clod
Hath visions and would speak, if he had lov'd,
And been well nurtured in his mother tongue.
Whether the dream now purposed to rehearse
Be poet's or Fanatic's will be known
When this warm scribe my hand is in the grave.[2]

    Methought I stood[3] where trees of every clime,
Palm, myrtle, oak, and sycamore, and beech,   20
With plantain and spice-blossoms, made a screen,
In neighbourhood of fountains, by the noise
Soft showering in mine ears, and, by the touch
Of scent, not far from roses. Turning round,
I saw an arbour with a drooping roof
Of trellis vines, and bells, and larger blooms,
Like floral-censers swinging light in air;
Before its wreathed doorway, on a mound
Of moss, was spread a feast of summer fruits,
Which nearer seen, seem'd refuse of a meal   30
By Angel tasted or our Mother Eve;[4]
For empty shells were scattered on the grass,
And grapestalks but half-bare, and remnants more

[1]The laurel wreath, bestowed as a public honor, is the emblem of poetic fame associated with Apollo. K echoes Thomas Gray's surmise in *Elegy Written in a Country Churchyard* (1751) that "some mute inglorious Milton here may rest" (59); he is also thinking of Wordsworth's reference in Book 1 of *The Excursion* (1814) to those "Poets" in sensibility who lack "the accomplishment of verse" (80).

[2]In a letter to Woodhouse, K referred to this verse-paragraph as "the induction" to the dream; for the last image, compare *This Living Hand*.

[3]The first dreamscape (19–46), cued as medieval dream allegory ("Methought"), evokes the realm of "Flora, and old Pan" in *Sleep and Poetry* (101–21) and the "Chamber of Infant Thought" in the letter of 3 May 1818.

[4]Alluding to the meal Eve served to Adam and the angel who visits Eden to tutor him (*PL* 5.303–7 and 326–28), lines K marked in his copy.

Sweet smelling, whose pure kinds I could not know.
Still was more plenty than the fabled horn[5]
Thrice emptied could pour forth at banqueting
For Proserpine return'd to her own fields,
Where the white heifers low. And appetite
More yearning than on earth I ever felt
Growing within, I ate deliciously;   40
And, after not long, thirsted, for thereby
Stood a cool vessel of transparent juice
Sipp'd by the wander'd bee, the which I took,
And, pledging all the Mortals of the World,
And all the dead whose names are in our lips,°   *still spoken of*
Drank. That full draught is parent of my theme.[6]
No Asian poppy,° nor Elixir fine°   *opium / subtle potion*
Of the soon-fading jealous Caliphat,
No poison gender'd in close Monkish cell
To thin the scarlet conclave of old Men,[7]   50
Could so have rapt unwilling life away.
Among the fragrant husks and berries crush'd,
Upon the grass, I struggled hard against
The domineering potion, but in vain:
The cloudy swoon came on, and down I sunk
Like a Silenus[8] on an antique vase.
How long I slumber'd 'tis a chance to guess.
When sense of life return'd, I started up,
As if with wings; but the fair trees were gone,
The mossy mound and arbour were no more;   60
I look'd around upon the carved sides
Of an old sanctuary with roof august,
Builded so high, it seem'd that filmed clouds
Might spread beneath as o'er the stars of heaven.
So old the place was, I remember'd none

---

[5]The cornucopia, emblem of Ceres.

[6]The drink engenders the dream-within-a-dream that constitutes the rest of the fragment.

[7]Stock figures of intrigue in the genre of gothic fiction: a caliph is a Muslim ruler, here poisoning a rival (that elixir) but doomed ("soon fading") himself; the scarlet conclave is the red-robed College of Cardinals in the Vatican, who convene on the Pope's death to elect a successor.

[8]A jolly old satyr (half god, half goat), companion of Bacchus.

The like upon the earth; what I had seen
Of gray Cathedrals, buttress'd walls, rent towers,
The superannuations° of sunk realms,   *remnants*
Or Nature's Rocks toil'd hard in waves and winds,
Seem'd but the faulture of decrepit things   70
To° that eternal domed monument.   *compared to*
Upon the marble at my feet there lay
Store of strange vessels, and large draperies
Which needs had been of dyed asbestus wove,
Or° in that place the moth could not corrupt,[9]   *or else*
So white the linen; so, in some, distinct
Ran imageries from a sombre loom.
All in a mingled heap confused there lay
Robes, golden tongs, censer and chafing-dish,
Girdles, and chains, and holy jewelries[10]—   80

    Turning from these with awe, once more I raised
My eyes to fathom the space every way;
The embossed roof, the silent massy range
Of columns north and South, ending in mist
Of nothing; then to Eastward, where black gates
Were shut against the sunrise evermore.
Then to the West I look'd, and saw far off
An image, huge of feature as a cloud,
At level of whose feet an altar slept,
To be approach'd on either side by steps,   90
And marble balustrade,° and patient travail   *railing*
To count with toil the innumerable degrees.
Towards the altar sober-pac'd I went,
Repressing haste, as too unholy there;
And, coming nearer, saw beside the shrine
One minist'ring; and there arose a flame.
When in mid-May[11] the sickening East Wind
Shifts sudden to the South, the small warm rain
Melts out the frozen incense from all flowers,

[9]Alluding to Jesus's instruction to "lay up for yourselves treasures in heaven, where neither moth nor rust doth corrupt" (Matthew 6.20).

[10]Remnants of Greek and Hebrew rituals.

[11]Woodhouse has "midway." Poet A. E. Housman proposed the correction to "mid-May" (*TLS: Times Literary Supplement*, 8 May 1924).

And fills the air with so much pleasant health   100
That even the dying man forgets his shroud;
Even so that lofty sacrificial fire,
Sending forth Maian incense,[12] spread around
Forgetfulness of everything but bliss,
And clouded all the altar with soft smoke,
From whose white fragrant curtains thus I heard
Language pronounc'd: "If thou canst not ascend
  These steps, die on that marble where thou art.
  Thy flesh, near cousin to the common dust,
  Will parch for lack of nutriment—thy bones   110
  Will wither in few years, and vanish so
  That not the quickest eye could find a grain
  Of what thou now art on that pavement cold.
  The sands of thy short life are spent this hour,
  And no hand in the Universe can turn
  Thy hourglass, if these gummed° leaves be burnt   *aromatic*
  Ere thou canst mount up these immortal steps."
I heard, I look'd: two senses both at once,
So fine, so subtle, felt the tyranny
Of that fierce threat and the hard task proposed.   120
Prodigious seem'd the toil; the leaves were yet
Burning, when suddenly a palsied chill
Struck from the paved level up my limbs,
And was ascending quick to put cold grasp
Upon those streams° that pulse beside the throat.[13]   *arteries*
I shriek'd; and the sharp anguish of my shriek
Stung my own ears—I strove hard to escape
The numbness, strove to gain the lowest step.
Slow, heavy, deadly was my pace: the cold
Grew stifling, suffocating, at the heart;   130
And when I clasp'd my hands I felt them not.
One minute before death, my iced foot touch'd
The lowest stair; and as it touch'd, life seem'd

[12]Maia is the Greek goddess of May. K borrows language from the end of Canto 24 of Dante's *Purgatorio*, about the enrichment and nourishment of the soul.

[13]K underlined Adam's realization of Eve's mortal fall: "Astonied stood and blank, while horror chill / Ran through his veins and all his joints relax'd" (*PL* 9.890–92); cf. *Hyperion* 2.165. K had seen both his mother and his brother die.

To pour in at the toes. I mounted up,
As once fair angels on a ladder flew
From the green turf to heaven.[14]—"Holy Power,"
Cried I, approaching near the horned shrine,[15]
"What am I that should so be saved from death?
What am I, that another death come not
To choak my utterance, sacrilegious, here?"   140
Then said the veiled shadow—"Thou hast felt
What 'tis to die and live again before
Thy fated hour. That thou hadst power to do so
Is thine own safety; thou hast dated on°   *postponed*
Thy doom."—"High Prophetess," said I, "purge off
Benign, if so it please thee, my mind's film."[16]—
"None can usurp this height," returned that shade,
"But those to whom the miseries of the world
Are misery, and will not let them rest.[17]
All else who find a haven in the world,   150
Where they may thoughtless sleep away their days,
If by a chance into this fane° they come,   *temple*
Rot on the pavement where thou rotted'st half."—
"Are there not thousands in the world," said I,
Encouraged by the sooth voice of the shade,
"Who love their fellows even to the death;

[14]Just before God promises Jacob that his descendants will claim the earth, Jacob dreams of a ladder from earth to heaven and "the angels of God ascending and descending on it" (Genesis 28.12); Milton alludes to this dream in describing Satan's view of the stairs to Heaven's Gate (*PL* 3.510–11), lines marked by K.

[15]Horns often embellish ancient altars, such as the one Moses is instructed to make (Exodus 27.2); the image may also involve a Keatsian symbolism, the "horn-book" of instruction in the "vale of Soul-making" (letter of 21 April 1819).

[16]Echoing blind Milton's plea for "Celestial Light" to "irradiate" his mind: "all mist from thence / Purge and disperse, that I may see and tell / Of things invisible to mortal sight" (*PL* 3.51–55).

[17]In this poetic representation of a dream, lines 147–210 unfold a set of distinctions across which the status of the "I" (erstwhile dreamer and present poet) is negotiated: visionary dreamers who feel "the miseries" of the world versus mere sleepers, and the poet "half" of each (147–53); those who feel miseries, humanitarian doers versus visionary dreamers (154–60); weak, fevered dreamers who cannot bear misery versus humanitarian benefactors (161–71); those who accept the alternation of joy and pain versus the self-poisoning dreamer (171–81); poets of wisdom and healing versus novice poets (187–92); healing poets versus merely impotent dreamers (188–202); true poets versus pretenders and braggarts (202–10).

Who feel the giant agony of the world;[18]
And more, like slaves to poor humanity,
Labour for mortal good? I sure should see
Other men here; but I am here alone."   160
"They whom thou spak'st of are no vision'ries,"
Rejoin'd that voice—"They are no dreamers weak,
They seek no wonder but the human face,
No music but a happy-noted voice—
They come not here, they have no thought to come—
And thou art here, for thou art less than they.
What benefit canst thou do, or all thy tribe,
To the great World? Thou art a dreaming thing,
A fever of thyself—think of the Earth:
What bliss even in hope is there for thee?   170
What haven? Every creature hath its home;
Every sole man hath days of joy and pain,
Whether his labours be sublime or low—
The pain alone, the joy alone, distinct:
Only the dreamer venoms all his days,
Bearing more woe than all his sins deserve.
Therefore, that happiness be somewhat shar'd,
Such things as thou art are admitted oft
Into like gardens thou didst pass erewhile,
And suffer'd° in these temples: for that cause   *allowed entry*
Thou standest safe beneath this statue's knees."
"That I am favoured for unworthiness,
By such propitious parley medicin'd
In sickness not ignoble, I rejoice,
Aye, and could weep for love of such award."   185
So answer'd I, continuing, "If it please,
Majestic shadow,[19] tell me: sure not all
Those melodies sung into the world's ear

---

[18]See the agenda declared in *Sleep and Poetry* 122–25.

[19]The epithets "shade" and "shadow" evoke Dante's *Purgatorio* and the veiled Beatrice of *Paradiso*, as well as the veiled goddess Isis of Egyptian mythology. In Woodhouse's ms, 187–210 are canceled, with a note that this was K's intention (187 is repeated at 211, and 194–98 at 216–20), and in 1856 *The Fall* appeared without them. Editorial tradition has restored them to document K's compositional process and pressing concerns; see the comparison of poetry and philosophy in the letter of 19 March 1819.

Are useless: sure a poet is a sage,
A humanist,° Physician to all Men.   *humanitarian* 190
That I am none I feel, as vultures feel
They are no birds when eagles are abroad.
What am I then? Thou spakest of my tribe:
What tribe?"—The tall shade veiled in drooping white
Then spake, so much more earnest, that the breath   195
Moved the thin linen folds that drooping hung
About a golden censer from the hand
Pendent—"Art thou not of the dreamer tribe?
  The poet and the dreamer are distinct,
  Diverse, sheer opposite, antipodes.°   *polar opposites*
  The one pours out a balm upon the world,
  The other vexes it." Then shouted I
Spite of myself, and with a Pythia's spleen:[20]
"Apollo! Faded, far-flown Apollo!
  Where is thy misty pestilence[21] to creep
  Into the dwellings, through the door crannies,
  Of all the mock lyrists, large self-worshippers,
  And careless hectorers° in proud bad verse?   *bullies, braggarts*
  Though I breathe death with them it will be life
  To see them sprawl before me into graves.   210
  Majestic shadow, tell me where I am:
  Whose altar this, for whom this incense curls:
  What image this whose face I cannot see
  For the broad marble knees; and who thou art,
  Of accent feminine, so courteous?"
Then the tall shade, in drooping linen veil'd,
Spoke out, so much more earnest, that her breath
Stirr'd the thin folds of gauze that drooping hung
About a golden censer from her hand
Pendent; and by her voice I knew she shed   220
Long-treasured tears. "This temple sad and lone
  Is all° spar'd from the thunder of a war   *all that is*
  Foughten long since by giant hierarchy

[20]The Pythia is the priestess at the temple of Delphi who delivered the oracles of Apollo.
[21]In the *Iliad*, Apollo is also the agent of plagues; the diatribe against modern poets is aimed, variously, at Byron, Wordsworth, and Hunt.

Against rebellion: this old image here,
Whose carved features wrinkled as he fell,
Is Saturn's; I, Moneta, left supreme,
Sole Priestess of his desolation."[22]—
I had no words to answer, for my tongue,
Useless, could find about its roofed home
No syllable of a fit Majesty   230
To make rejoinder to Moneta's mourn.
There was a silence while the altar's blaze
Was fainting for sweet food. I look'd thereon,
And on the paved floor, where nigh were piled
Faggots° of cinnamon, and many heaps   *bundles*
Of other crisped spice-wood—then again
I look'd upon the altar, and its horns
Whiten'd with ashes, and its lang'rous flame,
And then upon the offerings again;
And so by turns—till sad Moneta cried,   240
"The sacrifice is done, but not the less
  Will I be kind to thee for thy good will.
  My power, which to me is still a curse,
  Shall be to thee a wonder; for the scenes
  Still swooning vivid through my globed brain
  With an electral changing misery
  Thou shalt with those dull mortal eyes behold,
  Free from all pain, if wonder pain thee not."
As near as an immortal's sphered words
Could to a Mother's soften, were these last: 250
And yet I had a terror of her robes,
And chiefly of the veils, that from her brow
Hung pale, and curtain'd her in mysteries,
That made my heart too small to hold its blood.
This saw that Goddess, and with sacred hand
Parted the veils. Then saw I a wan face,
Not pin'd° by human sorrows, but bright-blanch'd   *wasted, pained*
By an immortal sickness which kills not;

---

[22]The shattered statue evokes Shelley's *Ozymandias*. Moneta is an alternative name for Mnemosyne, a Titan, then, by Jupiter, mother of the Muses, and in the first *Hyperion* the mentor to Apollo. In some myths Jupiter's wife Juno is called "Moneta" ("she who warns") after she warned the Romans of the invading Gauls.

It works a constant change, which happy death
Can put no end to; deathwards progressing   260
To no death was that visage; it had passed
The lily and the snow; and beyond these
I must not think now, though I saw that face—
But for her eyes I should have fled away.
They held me back with a benignant light,
Soft-mitigated by divinest lids
Half-closed, and visionless entire they seem'd
Of all external things—they saw me not,
But in blank splendour beam'd like the mild moon,
Who comforts those she sees not, who knows not   270
What eyes are upward cast. As I had found
A grain of gold upon a mountain's side,
And twing'd with avarice strain'd out my eyes
To search its sullen entrails rich with ore,
So at the view of sad Moneta's brow
I ached to see what things the hollow brain
Behind enwombed: what high tragedy
In the dark secret Chambers of her skull
Was acting, that could give so dread a stress
To her cold lips, and fill with such a light   280
Her planetary eyes, and touch her voice
With such a sorrow—"Shade of Memory!"[23]
Cried I, with act adorant at her feet,
"By all the gloom hung round thy fallen house,
  By this last Temple, by the golden age,[24]
  By great Apollo, thy dear foster child,
  And by thy self, forlorn divinity,
  The pale Omega[25] of a wither'd race,
  Let me behold, according as thou said'st,
  What in thy brain so ferments to and fro."—   290
No sooner had this conjuration passed
My devout lips, than side by side we stood
(Like a stunt bramble by a solemn pine)

[23]Moneta's alternative name means "Memory"; see lines 1.331 and 2.50.

[24]After his overthrow by Jupiter, Saturn fled to Italy, where he presided over a "Golden Age" of serenity and peace.

[25]Last letter of the Greek alphabet.

Deep in the shady sadness of a vale,[26]
Far sunken from the healthy breath of morn,
Far from the fiery noon and Eve's one star.
Onward I look'd beneath the gloomy boughs,
And saw what first I thought an Image huge,
Like to the Image pedestal'd so high
In Saturn's Temple. Then Moneta's voice   300
Came brief upon mine ear,—"So Saturn sat
  When he had lost his realms."—Whereon there grew
A power within me of enormous ken°   *range*
To see as a God sees, and take the depth
Of things as nimbly as the outward eye
Can size and shape pervade. The lofty theme
At those few words hung vast before my mind
With half-unravel'd web. I set myself
Upon an Eagle's watch, that I might see,
And seeing ne'er forget. No stir of life   310
Was in this shrouded vale, not so much air
As in the zoning[27] of a Summer's day
Robs not one light seed from the feather'd grass,
But where the dead leaf fell there did it rest.
A stream went noiseless by, still deaden'd more
By reason of the fallen Divinity
Spreading more shade; the Naiad mid her reeds
Press'd her cold finger closer to her lips.
Along the margin-sand large foot-marks went
No further than to where old Saturn's feet   320
Had rested, and there slept, how long a sleep!
Degraded, cold, upon the sodden ground
His old right hand lay nerveless, listless, dead,
Unsceptred; and his realmless eyes were closed,
While his bow'd head seem'd listening to the Earth,
His ancient mother, for some comfort yet.[28]

---

[26]The first line of *Hyperion;* from here on, K incorporates this first attempt, revising it to make the poet not just the epic narrator but a witness, suffering the burden of what he witnesses.

[27]*OED* credits K with coining this gerund: covering the zone of.

[28]Heaven and Earth are the parents of Saturn and the other Titans (cf. 357–58).

It seem'd no force could wake him from his place;
But there came one who, with a kindred hand
Touch'd his wide shoulders, after bending low
With reverence, though to one who knew it not.   330
Then came the griev'd voice of Mnemosyne,
And griev'd I hearken'd. "That divinity
Whom thou saw'st step from yon forlornest wood,
And with slow pace approach our fallen King,
Is Thea,[29] softest-natur'd of our Brood."
I mark'd the goddess in fair statuary
Surpassing wan Moneta by the head,°   *a head taller*
And in her sorrow nearer woman's tears.
There was a listening fear in her regard,
As if calamity had but begun;   340
As if the vanward clouds of evil days
Had spent their malice, and the sullen rear
Was with its stored thunder labouring up.
One hand she press'd upon that aching spot
Where beats the human heart, as if just there,
Though an immortal, she felt cruel pain;
The other upon Saturn's bended neck
She laid, and to the level of his hollow ear
Leaning, with parted lips some words she spoke
In solemn tenor and deep organ tune;   350
Some mourning words, which in our feeble tongue
Would come in this-like accenting; how frail
To that large utterance of the early Gods!—
"Saturn, look up—and for what, poor lost King?
  I have no comfort for thee, no—not one—
  I cannot cry, *Wherefore thus sleepest thou?*
  For heaven is parted from thee, and the earth
  Knows thee not, so afflicted, for a God.
  And Ocean, too, with all its solemn noise,
  Has from thy sceptre pass'd and all the air   360
  Is emptied of thy hoary Majesty.
  Thy thunder, captious° at the new command,   *quarrelsome*
  Rumbles reluctant o'er our fallen house;
  And thy sharp lightning in unpractised hands

---

[29]Hyperion's sister and wife.

Scourges and burns our once serene domain.
With such remorseless speed still come new woes
That unbelief has not a space to breathe.
Saturn, sleep on:—Me thoughtless, why should I
Thus violate thy slumbrous solitude?
Why should I ope thy melancholy eyes?   370
Saturn, sleep on, while at thy feet I weep."—

    As when upon a tranced Summer night,
Forests, branch-charmed by the earnest stars,
Dream, and so dream all night, without a noise,
Save from one gradual solitary gust
Swelling upon the silence, dying off,
As if the ebbing air had but one wave;
So came these words, and went; the while in tears
She press'd her fair large forehead to the earth,
Just where her fallen hair might spread in curls,   380
A soft and silken mat for Saturn's feet.
Long, long, those two were postured motionless,
Like sculpture builded up upon the grave
Of their own power. A long awful time
I look'd upon them; still they were the same,
The frozen God still bending to the Earth,
And the sad Goddess weeping at his feet.
Moneta silent. Without stay or prop
But my own weak mortality, I bore
The load of this eternal quietude,   390
The unchanging gloom and the three fixed shapes
Ponderous upon my senses a whole Moon.
For by my burning brain I measured sure
Her silver seasons shedded on the night,
And every day by day methought I grew
More gaunt and ghostly.—Oftentimes I pray'd
Intense, that Death would take me from the vale
And all its burthens—Gasping with despair
Of change, hour after hour I curs'd myself,
Until old Saturn raised his faded eyes,   400
And look'd around, and saw his Kingdom gone,
And all the gloom and sorrow of the place,
And that fair kneeling Goddess at his feet.

As the moist scent of flowers, and grass, and leaves
Fills forest dells with a pervading air
Known to the woodland nostril, so the words
Of Saturn fill'd the mossy glooms around,
Even to the hollows of time-eaten oaks,
And to the windings of the foxes' hole,
With sad, low tones, while thus he spake, and sent   410
Strange musings to the solitary Pan.[30]

"Moan, brethren, moan; for we are swallow'd up
And buried from all godlike exercise
Of influence benign on planets pale,
And peaceful sway upon man's harvesting,
And all those acts which Deity supreme
Doth ease its heart of love in. Moan and wail.
Moan, brethren, moan; for lo! the rebel spheres
Spin round; the stars their antient courses keep,
Clouds still with shadowy moisture haunt the earth,   420
Still suck their fill of light from Sun and Moon,
Still buds the tree, and still the sea-shores murmur.
There is no death in all the universe
No smell of Death—There shall be death—Moan, moan,
Moan, Cybele,[31] moan, for thy pernicious babes
Have changed a God into a shaking Palsy.
Moan, brethren, moan; for I have no strength left,
Weak as the reed—weak—feeble as my voice—
O, O, the pain, the pain of feebleness
Moan, moan; for still I thaw—or give me help: 430
Throw down those Imps,° and give me victory.   *rebel Titan sons*
Let me hear other groans, and trumpets blown
Of triumph calm, and hymns of festival
From the gold peaks of Heaven's high piled clouds;
Voices of soft proclaim, and silver stir
Of strings in hollow shells; and let there be
Beautiful things made new for the surprise
Of the sky children."—So he feebly ceas'd,

---

[30]"solitary" because of the general desolation now in the natural world, and more particularly, his loss of the nymph Syrinx.
[31]Saturn's wife, mother of the rebellious gods.

With such a poor and sickly sounding pause,
Methought I heard some old Man of the earth   440
Bewailing earthly loss; nor could my eyes
And ears act with that unison of sense
Which marries sweet sound with the grace of form,
And dolorous accent from a tragic harp
With large-limb'd visions—More I scrutinized:
Still fix'd he sat beneath the sable trees,
Whose arms spread straggling in wild serpent forms,
With leaves all hush'd: his awful presence there
(Now all was silent) gave a deadly lie
To what I erewhile heard: only his lips   450
Trembled amid the white curls of his beard.
They told the truth, though round the snowy locks
Hung nobly, as upon the face of heaven
A midday fleece of clouds. Thea arose,
And stretch'd her white arm through the hollow dark,
Pointing some whither: whereat he too rose
Like a vast giant seen by men at sea
To grow pale from the waves at dull midnight.
They melted from my sight into the woods:
Ere I could turn, Moneta cried—"These twain   460
  Are speeding to the families of grief,
   Where roof'd in by black rocks they waste in pain
   And darkness, for no hope."—And she spake on,
As ye may read who can unwearied pass
Onward from the Antichamber° of this dream,   *entry room*
Where, even at the open doors awhile
I must delay, and glean my memory
Of her high phrase—perhaps no further dare.—   468

Canto II

"Mortal, that thou may'st understand aright,
  I humanize my sayings to thine ear,
  Making comparisons of earthly things;[1]
  Or thou might'st better listen to the wind,

[1]The method Archangel Raphael uses—"lik'ning spiritual to corporal forms"—to relate to Adam the "exploits / Of warring Spirits" (the war in Heaven, fought between the legions of Satan and Christ; *PL* 5.565ff.).

Whose language is to thee a barren noise,
Though it blows legend-laden[2] through the trees—
In melancholy realms big tears are shed,
More sorrow like to this, and such-like woe,
Too huge for mortal tongue, or pen of scribe.
The Titans fierce, self-hid, or prison-bound,   10
Groan for the old allegiance once more,
Listening in their doom for Saturn's voice.
But one of our whole eagle-brood still keeps
His sov'reignty, and Rule, and Majesty;
Blazing Hyperion on his orbed fire   15
Still sits, still snuffs the incense teeming up
From man to the Sun's God—yet unsecure,
For as upon the Earth dire prodigies°   *ominous events*
Fright and perplex, so also shudders he:
Not at dog's howl or gloom-bird's Even° screech,   *Evening*
Or the familiar visiting of one
Upon the first toll of his passing bell;°   *death knell*
But horrors, portion'd to a giant nerve
Make great Hyperion ache. His palace bright,
Bastion'd with pyramids of glowing gold,
And touch'd with shade of bronzed obelisks,
Glares a blood red through all the thousand Courts,
Arches, and domes, and fiery galleries;
And all its curtains of Aurorian clouds
Flush angerly; when he would taste the wreaths   30
Of incense breath'd aloft from sacred hills,
Instead of sweets, his ample palate takes
Savour of poisonous brass and metals sick
Wherefore when harbour'd in the sleepy West,
After the full completion of fair day,
For rest divine upon exalted couch,
And slumber in the arms of melody,
He paces through the pleasant hours of ease
With strides colossal, on from Hall to Hall,

---

[2]In a letter of 21 Sept. 1819 to Woodhouse, K expressed his pleasure at the "fine sound" of this word (cf. "leaf-fringed legend" in *Ode on a Grecian Urn*).

While, far within each aisle and deep recess   40
His winged minions in close clusters stand
Amaz'd, and full of fear; like anxious men
Who on a wide plain gather in sad troops
When earthquakes jar their battlements and towers.
Even now, while Saturn, rous'd from icy trance
Goes, step for step, with Thea from yon woods,
Hyperion, leaving twilight in the rear,
Is sloping to the threshold of the west.—
Thither we tend."—Now in clear light I stood,
Reliev'd from the dusk vale. Mnemosyne   50
Was sitting on a square edg'd polish'd stone,
That in its lucid depth reflected pure
Her priestess-garments.[3] My quick eyes ran on
From stately nave to nave, from vault to vault,
Through bowers of fragrant and enwreathed light
And diamond paved lustrous long arcades.[4]
Anon rush'd by the bright Hyperion;
His flaming robes stream'd out beyond his heels,
And gave a roar, as if of earthy fire,
That scar'd away the meek ethereal hours   60
And made their dove-wings tremble: on he flared[5]—

[3]Alluding to the steep stairs up the side of the Mount of Purgatory in which poet-dreamer Dante sees himself reflected: "The lowest stair was marble white, so smooth / And polish'd, that therein my mirror'd form / Distinct I saw" (*Purgatorio* 9.94–96; H. F. Cary's trans.).

[4]In the first fragment, these actions were Hyperion's.

[5]The sentence recalls Satan's motions through Chaos, "on he fares" (*PL* 2.940) and nearing Eden's border (4.131). K's ms ends here, at this threshold of fierce anxiety.

Letter to Georgiana Augusta Keats, 13–28 January 1820[1]

While George is in London to raise money from Tom's estate, Keats writes to Georgiana of his weariness of society. After George's departure at the end of the month, Keats does not see nor write to him again.

My dear Sis., [. . .]

The worst of men are those whose self interests are their passions; the next those whose passions are their self-interest. Upon the whole I dislike mankind: whatever people on the other side of the question may advance, they cannot deny that they are always surprised at hearing of a good action and never of a bad one. [. . .] If you were in England, I dare say you would be able pick out more amusement from society[2] than I am able to do. To me it is all as dull as Louisville is to you. I am tired of theatres; almost all the parties I chance to fall into I know by heart; I know the different styles of talk in different places: what subjects will be started, and how it will proceed, like an acted play, from the first to the last act. If I go to Hunt's, I run my head into many-times heard puns and music; to Haydon's, worn out discourses of poetry and painting: to the Miss R's I am afraid to speak for fear of some sickly reiteration of phrase or sentiment; at Dilkes I fall foul of politics. 'Tis best to remain aloof from people and like their good parts without being eternally troubled with the dull processes of their everyday lives. When once a person has smoked[3] the vapidness of the routine of society, he must have either self-interest or the love of some sort of distinction to keep him in good humor with it. All I can say is that standing at Charing Cross and looking east, west, north and south I can see nothing but dullness.[4] I hope while I am young to live retired in the country; when I grow in years and have a right to be idle I shall enjoy cities more.

Your affectionate Brother,
John Keats.

[1]HBF 4.50–57; I use his text, the first wide publication of what HBF introduces as "a brilliant letter" to his "brilliant sister-in-law." *1848* has an abbreviated, heavily edited version; HBF edits, too. For the full text, see Rollins.

[2]Here and throughout K spells this, with a wry twist, as "Saciety" (see Rollins's edition 2:242–46); other wry spellings include "rediculous" (a favorite); the "hierogueglyphics" in an almanack of social doings; K's thought of "regreeting" GK instead of regretting (a usual emendation) his departure.

[3]seen through and found ridiculous.

[4]The reign of Dullness in Pope's *Dunciad* reappears in Shelley's satire, *Peter Bell the Third*, Part the Seventh; K may have read Hunt's ms (it was published in 1839).

Letter to Fanny Brawne, ? February 1820[1]

After a bad hemorrhage on 3 February, Keats reads his death warrant.

My dear Fanny,
[. . .] When I send this round I shall be in the front parlour watching to see you show yourself for a minute in the garden. How illness stands as a barrier betwixt me and you! Even if I was well—I must make myself as good a Philosopher as possible. Now I have had opportunities of passing nights anxious and awake I have found other thoughts intrude upon me. "If I should die," said I to myself, "I have left no immortal work behind me—nothing to make my friends proud of my memory—but I have lov'd the principle of beauty in all things, and if I had had time I would have made myself remember'd." Thoughts like these came very feebly whilst I was in health and every pulse beat for you—now you divide with this (may *I* say it?) "last infirmity of noble minds"[2] all my reflection.

God bless you, Love.

J. Keats.

from *1848*

TO FANNY.[1]

PHYSICIAN Nature! Let my spirit blood![2]
O ease my heart of verse and let me rest;
Throw me upon thy Tripod,[3] till the flood
Of stifling numbers[4] ebbs from my full breast.
A theme! a theme! great nature! give a theme;
  Let me begin my dream.

---

[1]HBF 4.158–59.
[2]Milton, *Lycidas*: a thirst for Fame is "That last infirmity of Noble mind" (70–71).

---

[1]Exact date of composition unknown; the congruity with the letter to Fanny suggests some time after 3 Feb. 1820, when K was confined indoors, next door. First published in *1848* 2.284–86.
[2]Common medical practice was to "bleed" (blood-let), thought to rid the body of toxins.
[3]the three-legged vessel at the oracle of Apollo in Delphi.
[4]poetic meters, with a pun on numbing agents.

I come—I see thee, as thou standest there,
Beckon me not into the wintry air.

Ah! dearest love, sweet home of all my fears,
And hopes, and joys, and panting miseries,—   10
To-night, if I may guess, thy beauty wears
      A smile of such delight,
      As brilliant and as bright,
As when with ravished, aching, vassal eyes,
      Lost in soft amaze,
         I gaze, I gaze!

Who now, with greedy looks, eats up my feast?
What stare outfaces now my silver moon!
Ah! keep that hand unravished at the least;
      Let, let, the amorous burn—   20
      But pr'ythee, do not turn
The current of your heart from me so soon.
      O! save, in charity,
      The quickest pulse for me.

Save it for me, sweet love! though music breathe
Voluptuous visions into the warm air;
Though swimming through the dance's dangerous wreath,[5]
      Be like an April day,
      Smiling and cold and gay,
A temperate lily, temperate as fair;   30
      Then, Heaven! there will be
      A warmer June for me.

Why, this—you'll say, my Fanny! is not true:
Put your soft hand upon your snowy side,
Where the heart beats: confess—'tis nothing new—
      Must not a woman be
      A feather on the sea,
Sway'd to and fro by every wind and tide?

---

[5]Dancing was regarded as hot flirtation. "Many will not allow man and woman to dance together, because it is a provocation to lust," writes Burton in a passage K marked in *Anatomy of Melancholy* (III.2.ii.4).

Of as uncertain speed
As blow-ball[6] from the mead?   40

I know it—and to know it is despair
To one who loves you as I love, sweet Fanny!
Whose heart goes fluttering for you every where,
     Nor, when away you roam,
     Dare keep its wretched home,
Love, love alone, his pains severe and many:
     Then, loveliest! keep me free,
     From torturing jealousy.

Ah! if you prize my subdued soul above
The poor, the fading, brief, pride of an hour;   50
Let none profane my Holy See of love,
     Or with a rude hand break
     The sacramental cake:
Let none else touch the just new-budded flower;
     If not—may my eyes close,
     Love! on their lost repose.

from *The Indicator,* 10 May 1820

The Indicator is Leigh Hunt's aesthetic (as opposed to political) periodical. The poem appeared in vol. 31, 246–48.

LA BELLE DAME SANS MERCY

Among the pieces printed at the end of Chaucer's works, and attributed to him, is a translation, under this title, of a poem of the celebrated Alain Chartier, Secretary to Charles the Sixth and Seventh.[1] It was the title which suggested to a friend the verses at the end of our present number. We wish Alain could have seen them.

---

[6] a dandelion's fuzzy seed-ball; *mead*: meadow.

---

[1] French court poet (1385–1433), best known for *La Belle Dame sans Merci*: "a gentleman finding no mercy at the hand of a gentlewoman dyeth for sorrow."

He would have found a Troubadour air for them, and sung them to La Belle Dame Agnes Sorel, who was however not Sans Mercy.[2] The union of the imaginative and the real is very striking throughout, particularly in the dream. The wild gentleness of the rest of the thoughts and of the music are alike old; and they are also alike young; for love and imagination are always young, let them bring with them what times and accompaniments they may. If we take real flesh and blood with us, we may throw ourselves, on the facile wings of our sympathy, into what age we please. It is only by trying to feel, as well as to fancy, through the medium of a costume, that writers become mere fleshless masks and cloaks,—things like the trophies of the ancients, when they hung up the empty armour of an enemy. A hopeless lover would still feel these verses, in spite of the introduction of something unearthly. Indeed any lover, truly touched, or any body capable of being so, will feel them; because love itself resembles a visitation; and the kindest looks, which bring with them an inevitable portion of happiness because they seem happy themselves, haunt us with a spell-like power, which makes us shudder to guess at the suffering of those who can be fascinated by unkind ones.

People however need not be much alarmed at the thought of such sufferings now-a-days; not at least in some countries. Since the time when ladies, and cavaliers, and poets, and the lovers of nature, felt that humanity was a high and not a mean thing, love in general has become either a grossness or a formality. The modern systems of morals would ostensibly divide women into two classes, those who have no charity, and those who have no restraint; while men, poorly conversant with the latter, and rendered indifferent to the former, acquire bad ideas of both. Instead of the worship of Love, we have the worship of Mammon; and all the difference we can see between the sufferings attending on either is, that the sufferings from the worship of Love exalt and humanize us, and those from the worship of Mammon debase and brutalize. Between the delights there is no comparison.—Still our uneasiness keeps our knowledge going on.

---

[2]Renowned for beauty, wit, and intelligence, Agnes Sorel (1422–50) met Charles VII when she was 20. Credited with curing him of a long depression, she became his publicly acknowledged mistress two years later. Treated as a virtual queen, showered with wealth, castles, lands, she earned powerful enemies and seems to have died from poisoning.

A word or two more of Alain Chartier's poem. "M. Aleyn," saith the argument, "secretary to the King of France, framed this dialogue between a gentleman and a gentlewoman, who finding no mercy at her hand, dieth for sorrow." [. . .]

LA BELLE DAME SANS MERCY.

Ah, what can ail thee, wretched wight,[3]
    Alone and palely loitering;
The sedge is wither'd from the lake,
    And no birds sing.

Ah, what can ail thee, wretched wight,
    So haggard and so woe-begone?
The squirrel's granary is full,
    And the harvest's done.

I see a lily on thy brow,
    With anguish moist and fever dew;   10
And on thy cheek a fading rose
    Fast withereth too.

I met a Lady in the meads
    Full beautiful, a fairy's child;
Her hair was long, her foot was light,
    And her eyes were wild.

I set her on my pacing steed,
    And nothing else saw all day long;
For sideways would she lean, and sing
    A fairy's song.   20

I made a garland for her head,
    And bracelets too, and fragrant zone;
She look'd at me as she did love,
    And made sweet moan.

---

[3]A half-pitying, half-derisive colloquialism for "fellow." Notes already supplied for the letter draft (p. 247) are not repeated here.

She found me roots of relish sweet,
  And honey wild, and manna dew;
And sure in language strange she said,
    I love thee true.

She took me to her elfin grot,
  And there she gaz'd and sighed deep,   30
And there I shut her wild sad eyes—
    So kiss'd to sleep.

And there we slumber'd on the moss,
  And there I dream'd, ah woe betide,
The latest dream I ever dream'd
    On the cold hill side

I saw pale kings, and princes too,
  Pale warriors, death-pale were they all;
Who cried "La belle Dame sans mercy
    Hath thee in thrall!"   40

I saw their starv'd lips in the gloom
  With horrid warning gaped wide,
And I awoke, and found me here
    On the cold hill side.

And this is why I sojourn here
  Alone and palely loitering,
Though the sedge is wither'd from the lake,
  And no birds sing.

CAVIARE.[4]

---

[4]The signature is keyed to Hamlet's praise of a Player's speech as "caviary to the general"—a delicacy too refined for playgoers with a taste for a jig or a tale of bawdry (2.2). K may have remembered this echo of *Hamlet* from the review of *Endymion* in the *Chester Guardian* (angry at the *Quarterly*'s put-down) (reported by D. Hewlett, *Adonais: A Life of John Keats* [1938] p. 186), and is wryly joking on the reception of his own spurned delicacies.

Letter to Fanny Brawne, before 12 August 1820[1]

I do not write this till the last that no eye may catch it.[2]

My dearest Girl,

I wish you could invent some means to make me at all happy without you. Every hour I am more and more concentrated in you; every thing else tastes like chaff in my Mouth. I feel it almost impossible to go to Italy – the fact is I cannot leave you, and shall never taste one minute's content until it pleases chance to let me live with you for good. But I will not go on at this rate. A person in health as you are can have no conception of the horrors that nerves and a temper like mine go through. [. . .] The last two years taste like brass upon my Palate.[3] *If I cannot live with you I will live alone. I do not think my health will improve much while I am separated from you. For all this I am averse to seeing you – I cannot bear flashes of light and return into my glooms again. I am not so unhappy now as I should be if I had seen you yesterday. To be happy with you seems such an impossibility! it requires a luckier Star than mine! it will never be. [. . .] If my health would bear it, I could write a Poem which I have in my head, which would be a consolation for people in such a situation as mine. I would show some one in Love as I am, with a person living in such Liberty as you do. Shakspeare always sums up matters in the most sovereign manner. Hamlet's heart was full of such Misery as mine is when he said to Ophelia "Go to a Nunnery, go, go!"*[4] *Indeed I should like to give up the matter at once – I should like to die. I am sickened at the brute world which you are smiling with. I hate men and women more. I see nothing but thorns for the future – wherever I may be next winter in Italy or nowhere Brown will be living near you with his indecencies*[5] – *I*

[1]ALS, Berg Collection, New York Public Library.

[2]After a bad attack on 22 June, K was too ill to live on his own (Brown had rented out his apartment for the summer), and he accepted Hunt's hospitality. Hunt's kindness notwithstanding, the noise and activity of the household and lack of privacy were so irksome that K left at night on 12 Aug. and moved in with the Brawnes, who cared for him until he left for Italy.

[3]Echoing Hyperion's sense of doom (*Hyperion* 1.188–89).

[4]*Hamlet* 3.1: a tirade against marriage, and more generally against the deceptions of womankind. This is K's last known letter to Fanny Brawne.

[5]Brown was bawdy, a flirt, and had fathered a child with his housekeeper-lover.

see no prospect of any rest. Suppose me in Rome – well, I should there
see you as in a magic glass going to and from town at all hours,
————I wish you could infuse a little confidence in human nature
into my heart. I cannot muster any – the world is too brutal for me –
I am glad there is such a thing as the grave– – I am sure I shall never
have any rest till I get there At any rate I will indulge myself by
never seeing any more Dilke or Brown or any of their Friends. I wish
I was either in your arms full of faith or that a Thunder bolt would
strike me.
God bless you—J. K—

§ Letter from Percy Bysshe Shelley, 27 July 1820[1]

Shelley sent this letter from Pisa in care of Leigh Hunt at The Examiner, *London.*

My dear Keats

     I hear with great pain the dangerous accident that you have undergone [. . .] . This consumption is a disease particularly fond of people who write such good verses as you have done, and with the assistance of an English winter it can often indulge its selection. I do not think that young and amiable poets are at all bound to gratify its taste; they have entered into no bond with the Muses to that effect. But seriously (for I am joking on what I am very anxious about) I think you would do well to pass the winter in Italy after so tremendous an accident, and (if you thinks it as necessary as I do[2]) so long as you continue to find Pisa or its neighbourhood agreeable to you, Mrs. Shelley unites with myself in urging the request, that you would take up your residence with us. You might come by sea to Leghorn, (France is not worth seeing, and the sea air is particularly good for weak lungs), which is within a few miles of us. You ought, at all events, to see Italy, and your health which I suggest as a motive, might be an excuse to you. I spare declamation about the statues, and paintings, and ruins, and what is a greater piece

[1]HBF 4.94–95.
[2]The ALS (at Harvard) shows the words from *if* to *do*, which HBF omits.

of forbearance, about the mountains and streams, the fields, the colours of the sky, and the sky itself.

I have lately read your *Endymion* again, and ever with a new sense of the treasures of poetry it contains, though treasures poured forth with indistinct profusion. This, people in general will not endure, and that is the cause of the comparatively few copies which have been sold. I feel persuaded that you are capable of the greatest things, so you but will. I always tell Ollier[3] to send you copies of my books. *Prometheus Unbound* I imagine you will receive nearly at the same time with this letter. *The Cenci* I hope you have already received—it was studiously composed in a different style

Below the *good* how far! but far above the *great*![4]

In poetry I have sought to avoid system and mannerism; I wish those who excel me in genius, would pursue the same plan.

Whether you remain in England, or journey to Italy, believe that you carry with you my anxious wishes for your health, happiness, and success, wherever you are or whatever you undertake, and that I am,

Yours sincerely,

P. B. Shelley

Letter to P. B. Shelley, 16 August 1820[1]

From Hampstead with the Brawnes, Keats sends his Lamia *volume with this very neatly written letter.*

My dear Shelley,

I am very much gratified that you, in a foreign country, and with a mind almost overoccupied, should write to me in the strain of the Letter beside me. If I do not take advantage of your

[3]Shelley's publisher, and the unhappy publisher, through his urging, of K's *Poems* (1817).

[4]The last lines of Gray's *The Progress of Poesy* (1757): "Yet shall he [the young spirit of Poesy] mount and keep his distant way / Beyond the limits of a vulgar fate, / Beneath the Good how far—but far above the Great" (121–23).

[1]ALS, Abinger Collection, Bodleian Library, Oxford.

invitation it will be prevented by a circumstance I have very much at
heart to prophesy – There is no doubt that an english winter would
put an end to me, and do so in a lingering hateful manner. Therefore
I must either voyage or journey to Italy as a soldier marches up to a
battery. My nerves at present are the worst part of me, yet they feel
soothed when I think that come what extreme may, I shall not be
destined to remain in one spot long enough to take a hatred of any
four particular bed-posts. I am glad you take any pleasure in my
poor Poems; – which I would willingly take the trouble to unwrite, if
possible, did I care so much as I have done about Reputation. I
received a copy of the Cenci,[2] as from yourself from Hunt. There is only
one part of it I am judge of; the Poetry, and dramatic effect, which by
many spirits now a days is considered the mammon. A modern work
it is said must have a purpose, which may be the God — <u>an artist</u>
must serve Mammon[3] – he must have "self concentration" selfishness
perhaps. You I am sure will forgive me for sincerely remarking that
you might curb your magnanimity and be more of an artist, and
'load every rift' of your subject with ore.[4] The thought of such discipline
must fall like cold chains upon you, who perhaps never sat with your
wings furl'd for six Months together. And is not this extraordinary
talk for the writer of Endymion? whose mind was like a pack of
scattered cards- I am pick'd up and sorted to a pip.[5] My Imagination
is a Monastry and I am its Monk — you must explain my metap[cs6]
to yourself I am in expectation of Prometheus every day. Could I
have my own wish for its interest effected you would have it still in
manuscript - or be but now putting an end to the second act. I

[2]According to Fanny Brawne, K carefully annotated the volume (since lost!). Shelley's drama of incest-rape, paternal tyranny, Church corruption, and parricide, set in Renaissance Italy, met with outraged reviews, and proved unstageable for decades.

[3]The false idol of worldly riches; "Ye cannot serve God and mammon," cautions Jesus (Matthew 6.24). By *magnanimity* (literally, great spirit), K may have in mind Shelley's dedication to Hunt, in mutual solidarity: "gentle, honourable, innocent and brave," in "patient and irreconcileable enmity with domestic and political tyranny and imposture" (iv–v).

[4]*FQ* II.vi.28: in the Cave of Mammon hang stalactites "Embost with massy gold of glorious gift, / And with rich metall loaded every rift, / That heavy ruine they did seeme to threat."

[5]in correct order; pips are marks on playing cards.

[6]shorthand for *metaphysics*.

*remember you advising me not to publish my first-blights, on
Hampstead heath[7] – I am returning advice upon your hands. Most
of the Poems in the volume I send you have been written above two
years, and would never have been publish'd but from a hope of gain;
so you see I am inclined enough to take your advice now. I must
express once more my deep sense of your Kindness, adding my
sincere thanks and respects for Mrs Shelley. In the hope of soon
seeing you [I] remain*

*most sincerely
John Keats*

§ from *The Indicator*, 20 September 1820

> *Leigh Hunt's Farewell to Keats; this was the last piece in the issue, pp.
> 398–400.*

RETURN OF AUTUMN

The autumn is now confirmed. The harvest is over; the summer
birds are gone or going; heavy rains have swept the air of its warmth,
and prepared the earth for the impression of winter.

And the author's season changes likewise. We can no longer
persuade ourselves that it is summer, by dint of resolving to think
so. We cannot warm ourselves at the look of the sunshine. Instead
of sitting at the window, "hindering" ourselves, as people say, with
enjoying the sight of Nature, we find our knees turned round to the
fire-place, our face opposite a pictured instead of a real landscape,
and our feet toasting upon a fender. [. . .]

Ah, dear friend, as valued a one as thou art a poet,—John
Keats,—we cannot, after all find it in our hearts to be glad, now

---

[7]In 1817, when they first met. By late summer 1820 *Endymion* finally won some
praise in *London Magazine* (April), and *Lamia & c* was praised by Lamb in *New
Times* (July, rpt. *Examiner*). And there were further periodical publications of odes
in *1820* across 1819–20, as well as other poetry, e.g., *La Belle Dame* and *On a
Dream* in the *Indicator*, May and June 1820.

thou art gone away with the swallows to seek a kindlier clime.[1] The rains began to fall heavily, the moment thou wast to go;—we do not say, poet-like, for thy departure. One tear in an honest eye is more precious to thy sight, than all the metaphorical weepings in the universe; and thou didst leave many starting to think how many months it would be till they saw thee again. And yet thou didst love metaphorical tears too, in their way; and couldst always liken every thing in nature to something great or small; and the rains that beat against thy cabin-window will set, we fear, thy over-working wits upon many comparisons that ought to be much more painful to others than thyself;—Heaven mend their envious and ignorant numskulls. But thou hast "a mighty soul in a little body";[2] and the kind cares of the former for all about thee shall no longer subject the latter to the chance of impressions which it scorns; and the soft skies of Italy shall breathe balm upon it; and thou shalt return with thy friend the nightingale, and make all thy other friends as happy with thy voice as they are sorrowful to miss it. The little cage thou didst sometime share with us, looks as deficient without thee, as thy present one may do without us; but—farewell for awhile: thy heart is in our fields: and thou wilt soon be back to rejoin it.

Letter to Charles Brown, 30 September 1820[1]

My dear Brown,

The time has not yet come for a pleasant Letter from me. I have delayed writing to you from time to time because I felt how impossible it was to enliven you with one heartening hope of my recovery [. . .] I wish to write on subject that will not agitate me much – there is one I must mention and have done with it. Even if my body would recover of itself, this would prevent it. The very thing

[1] A nod to the last line of *To Autumn*.

[2] "Their little bodies lodge a mighty soul" (Joseph Addison's translation of Virgil's *Fourth Georgic*, 97).

---

[1] ALS, Houghton Library, Harvard. K hoped Brown would go with him to Italy, but he was unreachable during his summer travels, returning just after K embarked on 17 Sept. Brown is now in Hampstead. Adverse weather made it impossible for K's ship to leave the channel until early October.

which I want to live most for will be a great occasion of my death. I cannot help it. Who can help it? Were I in health it would make me ill, and how can I bear it my state? I dare say you will be able to guess on which subject I am harping – you know what was my greatest pain during the first part of my illness at your house. I wish for death every day and night to deliver me from these pains, and then I wish death away, for death would destroy even those pains which are better than nothing. Land and Sea, weakness and decline are great seperators, but death is the great divorcer for ever [. . .] I seldom think of my Brother and Sister – in america. The thought of leaving Miss Brawne is beyond every thing horrible – the sense of darkness coming over me – I eternally see her figure eternally vanishing.[2] Some of the phrases she was in the habit of using at Wentworth-place ring in my ears– Is there another Life? Shall I awake and find all this a dream? There must be we cannot be created for this sort of suffering. [. . .] I shall endeavour to write to Miss Brawne if possible to day. A sudden stop to my life in the middle of one of these Letters would be no bad thing for it keeps one in a sort of fever awhile. Though fatigued with a Letter longer than any I have written for a long while it would be better to go on for ever than awake to a sense of contrary winds. [. . .] I feel as if I was closing my last letter to you. My dear Brown

your affectionate friend

John Keats

from *1848*

KEATS'S LAST SONNET[1]

Thus titled in 1848 and throughout the nineteenth century; now known as "Bright star"; first published in 1838. In the summer of 1818 Keats remarked that the scenery of the Lake country "refine[s] one's sensual vision into a sort of north star which can never cease to be open lidded and stedfast over the wonders of the great Power"; sometime before summer 1819 he drafted this sonnet, and in early autumn 1820 wrote it out again, with some variants, in the volume of

---

[2]After seeing her for the last time on 13 Sept., K could not bear to write to her or to read her letters to him.

---

[1]Sonnet XX (2.306), with this title.

Shakespeare's poems he took to Italy. The opening line of this Shake-
spearean sonnet chimes with Caesar's heroic declaration: "I am con-
stant as the Northern Star, / Of whose true-fixed and resting quality /
There is no fellow in the firmament" (Julius Caesar 3.1.58–62).

BRIGHT star, would I were steadfast as thou art—
    Not in lone splendour hung aloft the night,
And watching, with eternal lids apart,
    Like nature's patient sleepless Eremite,[2]
The moving waters at their priestlike task
    Of pure ablution[3] round earth's human shores,
Or gazing on the new soft fallen mask[4]
    Of snow upon the mountains and the moors—
No—yet still steadfast, still unchangeable,
    Pillow'd upon my fair love's ripening breast,
To feel for ever its soft fall and swell,[5]
    Awake for ever in a sweet unrest,
Still, still to hear her tender-taken breath,
And so live ever—or else swoon to death.*

* Another reading:—
Half-passionless, and so swoon on to death.[6]

Last Letters, to Charles Brown, November 1820

NAPLES,[1]
Nov. 1.

MY DEAR BROWN,

    Yesterday we were let out of quarantine, during which my
health suffered more from bad air and the stifled cabin than it had

[2]hermit, religious recluse.
[3]ritual washing.
[4]Punning on *masque*, the word in the 1820 version.
[5]ms] swell and fall
[6]Milnes's note (2.306), based on Brown's ms (which also supplies *mask*).

---

[1]*1848* 2.77–79 (first publication). Though the ship reached Naples on 21 Oct., it
was held in the harbor in quarantine, and K and Severn could not leave for Rome
until 7 Nov., arriving there midmonth.

done the whole voyage. The fresh air revived me a little, and I hope I am well enough this morning to write to you a short calm letter;—if that can be called one, in which I am afraid to speak of what I would fainest dwell upon. As I have gone thus far into it, I must go on a little;—perhaps it may relieve the load of *wretchedness*[2] which presses upon me. The persuasion that I shall see her no more will kill me. My dear Brown, I should have had her when I was in health, and I should have remained well. I can bear to die—I cannot bear to leave her. Oh, God! God! God! Everything I have in my trunks that reminds me of her goes through me like a spear. The silk lining she put in my travelling cap scalds my head. My imagination is horribly vivid about her—I see her—I hear her. There is nothing in the world of sufficient interest to divert me from her a moment. This was the case when I was in England; I cannot recollect, without shuddering, the time that I was a prisoner at Hunt's, and used to keep my eyes fixed on Hampstead all day. Then there was a good hope of seeing her again—Now!—O that I could be buried near where she lives! I am afraid to write to her——to receive a letter from her——to see her handwriting would break my heart—even to hear of her anyhow, to see her name written, would be more than I can bear. My dear Brown, what am I to do? Where can I look for consolation or ease? If I had any chance of recovery, this passion would kill me. Indeed, through the whole of my illness, both at your house and at Kentish Town,[3] this fever has never ceased wearing me out. When you write to me, which you will do immediately, write to Rome (*poste restante*)——if she is well and happy, put a mark thus +; if————

Remember me to all. I will endeavour to bear my miseries patiently. A person in my state of health should not have such miseries to bear. Write a short note to my sister, saying you have heard from me. Severn is very well. If I were in better health I would urge your coming to Rome. I fear there is no one can give me any comfort. Is there any news of George? O, that something fortunate had ever happened to me or my brothers!—then I might hope,—but despair is forced upon me as a habit. My dear Brown, for my sake, be her advocate for ever. I cannot say a word about Naples; I do not feel

---

[2]Brown reports that K put this word all in capitals (not underlined), a rare emphasis.
[3]K's residence, 4 May to 23 June.

at all concerned in the thousand novelties around me. I am afraid to write to her—I should like her to know that I do not forget her. Oh, Brown, I have coals of fire in my breast. It surprises me that the human heart is capable of containing and bearing so much misery. Was I born for this end? God bless her, and her mother, and my sister, and George, and his wife, and you, and all!

Your ever affectionate friend,

JOHN KEATS.

ROME,

30th November, 1820.[1]

MY DEAR BROWN,

'Tis the most difficult thing in the world to me to write a letter. My stomach continues so bad, that I feel it worse on opening any book,—yet I am much better than I was in quarantine. Then I am afraid to encounter the pro-ing and con-ing of anything interesting to me in England. I have an habitual feeling of my real life having passed, and that I am leading a posthumous existence. God knows how it would have been—but it appears to me—however, I will not speak of that subject. I must have been at Bedhampton nearly at the time you were writing to me from Chichester—how unfortunate—and to pass on the river too! There was my star predominant![2] I cannot answer anything in your letter, which followed me from Naples to Rome, because I am afraid to look it over again. I am so weak (in mind) that I cannot bear the sight of any handwriting of a friend I love so much as I do you. Yet I ride the little horse,[3] and, at my worst, even in quarantine, summoned up more puns, in a sort of desperation, in one week than in any year of my life. There is one thought enough to kill me; I have been well, healthy, alert, &c., walking with her, and now—the knowledge of contrast, feeling for light and shade, all that information (primitive sense) necessary for a poem, are great enemies to the recovery of

---

[1]*1848* 2.82–84; the first publication of K's last known letter. He had a bad setback on 10 Dec. and died late on 23 Feb. 1821, the news reaching London on 17 March.

[2]"Physic for 't there's none; / It is a bawdy planet, that will strike / Where 'tis predominant," rants Leontes, suspecting his wife of adultery (*Winter's Tale* 1.2.200–202; *physic:* cure).

[3]Dr. Clark prescribed the exercise; the hire of a horse was expensive.

the stomach. There, you rogue, I put you to the torture; but you must bring your philosophy to bear, as I do mine, really, or how should I be able to live? Dr. Clark is very attentive to me; he says, there is very little the matter with my lungs,[4] but my stomach, he says, is very bad. I am well disappointed in hearing good news from George,[5] for it runs in my head we shall all die young. I have not written to Reynolds yet, which he must think very neglectful; being anxious to send him a good account of my health, I have delayed it from week to week. If I recover, I will do all in my power to correct the mistakes made during sickness; and if I should not, all my faults will be forgiven. Severn is very well, though he leads so dull a life with me. Remember me to all friends, and tell Haslam I should not have left London without taking leave of him, but from being so low in body and mind. Write to George as soon as you receive this, and tell him how I am, as far as you can guess; and also a note to my sister—who walks about my imagination like a ghost—she is so like Tom. I can scarcely bid you good-bye, even in a letter. I always made an awkward bow.

God bless you!

JOHN KEATS.

---

[4]An astonishing misdiagnosis; there was almost nothing left of K's lungs when he died.

[5]K had just received a letter from GK, written 8 Nov., full of "bad news" about financial distresses, loneliness, hardship, and fatigue (though the marriage was a happy marriage).

Glossary of Mythological and Literary References

Keats owned and referred for mythology to "Edwin Baldwin" (William Godwin), *The Pantheon; or Ancient History of the Gods of Greece and Rome* (1806), and John Lemprière's *Classical Dictionary* (1788; 6th edition, 1806). Boldface indicates a cross-reference.

Adonis: Young hunter killed by a boar. *Proserpine* restored him to life, that he might be her lover in the underworld (where she is imprisoned). *Venus*, in love with Adonis, appealed to *Jove*, who decided that Venus could have him for half the year, in the upper world. An annual feast of Adonis celebrates his return to Venus.

Aeneas: Trojan prince and warrior who escaped the burning city, became the lover of **Dido** in north Africa, and eventually founded Rome (the subject of Virgil's epic *The Aeneid*).

Æolus: God of the winds. The **Æolian harp** or **lyre** was a familiar household object (its tuned strings swept into music by the wind)—and a famous metaphor for the soul in Coleridge's *The Eolian Harp* (*Sibylline Leaves*, 1817; the original title was simply "Effusion").

Apollo: In the Olympian generation of gods, the new god of the sun, and by extension all metaphorical light: learning, poetry, music, prophesy (with a famous oracle at **Delphi**), medicine.

Arcady, Arcadia: Beautiful pastoral district of ancient Greece frequented by the gods, especially *Pan*.

Ariadne: Daughter of Minos, king of Crete. When Minos imprisoned Greek Prince *Theseus* in his *labyrinth* prison, for certain death from its minotaur-monster, love-struck Ariadne helped Theseus escape, expecting him to keep his promise to marry her. He did, but soon ditched her on the Isle of Naxos, where *Bacchus* found and consoled her, giving her a tiara of stars.

Athena: The Greek counterpart of *Minerva* (goddess of wisdom, justice).

Aurora: Goddess of the dawn.

Bacchus: God of wine and revelry, attended by *satyrs*. He romanced *Ariadne* after she was jilted by *Theseus*.

caduceus, caducean: Magic wand of *Hermes*, given to him by *Apollo*, thus also the physician's emblem. It has two entwined snakes, with two wings at the top. With it, Hermes conducts the souls of the dead to the underworld; it can also lull mortals to sleep and raise the dead back to life.

car: Chariot (Bacchus's car, Apollo's car, etc.).

Ceres: Daughter of *Saturn*; harvest goddess, and mother (by *Jupiter*) of *Proserpine*.

Circe: Witch and enchantress, appears in *Endymion* Book III. In Homer's *Odyssey*, when Ulysses and his crew wind up on her island, all but Ulysses are changed into swine. *Mercury* helped reverse the spell.

Coelus: The sky god, spouse of *Tellus*, father of the 45 *Titan* gods.

Cupid: Boy-god of love (with a quiver of love-inducing darts), son of *Venus* and *Jupiter*, lover of *Psyche*.

Cynthia: *Diana*, the moon goddess.

Daedalus: Architect of the *labyrinth* in Crete; when he and his son *Icarus* were imprisoned there by King Minos, Daedalus fashioned wings of feathers and wax for a successful escape; **Daedalian** refers to any intricate, ingenious, freedom-promising artifice. Daedalus cautioned Icarus not to fly too high, lest the sun melt the wax. Enchanted by soaring, Icarus ignored him, and plunged to his death in the sea. The legend, from Ovid's *Metamorphoses* (Book VIII), is a fable of recklessly fatal youthful enthusiasm.

Delphi (delphic): The site of one of *Apollo's* oracles.

Diana: Daughter of *Jove*, twin of *Apollo*: in her reign on earth she is goddess of chastity and the hunt. Her name in Heaven is *Phoebe*, and in hell she is called *Hecate*.

Dido: Queen and founder of Carthage, the empire on the north coast of Africa. When her lover *Aeneas* deserted her, she burned herself to death on a pyre.

Dis: *Pluto*, god of the underworld.

dryad: Forest *nymph*.

Echo: Attendant of *Juno*; in punishment for her talkiness, Juno restrained her speech to echoes. Spurned by *Narcissus*, who had eyes only for himself, she turned to stone, which retained her voice (relaying echoes).

Elysium, Elysian fields: In the afterlife of classical religion, the underworld region of bliss for the heroes of the world.

Empyrean: In medieval cosmology, the highest region of the heavens.

Endymion: Mortal shepherd-prince, enamored of moon-goddess *Cynthia/Phoebe/Diana* after she caught a glimpse of him naked on Mount Latmos; bashful and modest, she visited him and made love to him nightly in his dreams.

ether: Pure airs of the upper atmosphere (*ethereal*); the anesthesia by that name was not known in Keats's day.

Eurydice: A nymph married to *Orpheus*, lost to him first by fatal snakebite, and again by his backward gaze as he led her out of the underworld.

faun (fawn): A *satyr*, half-man, half-goat, companion of *Pan*.

Flora: Roman goddess of flowers.

Hades: The underworld of classical mythology; unlike the Christian hell, it is not a place of punishment. Hades is also the name of the god of the underworld, Greek counterpart of the Roman god *Pluto*.

Hecate: The name by which *Diana* is known in the underworld, with powers of magic and enchantment.

Helicon: The mountain from which flows the *Hippocrene*.

Hera: Queen of the gods and spouse of Zeus in Greek mythology, counterpart of the Roman Juno.

Hermes: Greek counterpart of **Mercury**. The Greek name is derived from a verb that means "to interpret" or explain (whence *hermeneutic*).

Hesperus: The evening star; **Venus** as the evening star.

Hippocrene: Stream sacred to the *muses*, raised from the earth by the pawing of **Pegasus**.

Hybla: Mountain in Sicily famous for flowers, bees, and honey.

Hyperion: Sun God in the **Titan** order, brother of **Saturn** and **Oceanus**.

Icarus: Son of **Daedalus**, an icon of fatally reckless high-flying and the consequences of not heeding dad.

Jove/Jupiter: Son of **Saturn** and Ops, king of the gods in Roman mythology, counterpart of the Greek **Zeus**.

Juno: Daughter of **Saturn** and **Ops,** sister-wife of *Jove*, queen of the gods in Roman mythology, counterpart of the Greek **Hera**.

labyrinth: The prison designed by **Daedalus** for King Minos of Crete. Among the prisoners who managed to escape were Daedalus himself, his son **Icarus**, and Prince **Theseus** of Greece. Keats coins adjectives and verbs out of this eponym.

Lethe: When the new arrivals to the underworld crossed this river, they forgot everything about their mortal life.

Lucifer: *Venus* as the morning star; Satan's name in heaven, before he fell (light-bearer).

Mammon: False idol of riches, against whom Jesus cautions, "ye cannot serve God and mammon" (Matthew 6.24).

manna: The miraculous early-morning dew-like food that the wandering Israelites were able to gather in the desert (Exodus 16.14 ff).

May/Maia: Mother of **Mercury** by *Jove*, goddess of the month of May, and one of the Pleiades.

Mercury: The Roman name of **Hermes**. Lustful, wing-footed, wing-capped messenger of Jove, bearing a magic wand (*caduceus*). Son of *Jove* by **Maia**. God of speed and eloquence, magic and enchantment; also patron of merchants (like *Mercury*, *merchant* comes from *merces*), thieves, pickpockets, liars, and other shifty figures. *Mercenary* and *merci/mercy* (literally, an acknowledgment of obligation) derive from his name.

Minerva: Roman goddess of wisdom, daughter of *Jove*, from whose brain she sprung fully armed. *Athena* in Greek mythology.

Mnemosyne: *Titan* goddess, daughter of *Coelus*, mother of the *muses* by *Jove*. Her name means memory (whence *mnemonic*).

Moneta: A name sometimes given to *Juno* for her powers of warning; in Keats's refraction, a double of *Mnemosyne*.

Morpheus: God of sleep.

muses: The nine daughters of *Jove* and *Mnemosyne*, inspirers of various arts and learning.

naiad: *nymph* of inland waters (rivers, streams, wells, fountains).

Narcissus: This beautiful boy fell in love with his own image in a pool of water, and, thinking it a *nymph*, pined futilely after it. Drowning in desperation, he was transformed into the lakeside narcissus flower.

Neptune: Son of *Saturn*, *Olympian* god of the ocean, successor of the *Titan Oceanus*.

nereid: One of fifty sea *nymphs*.

nymph: Minor deity, indwelling spirit of nature.

Oceanus: *Titan* god, son of the sky god *Coelus* and earth mother *Tellus*; he was displaced by *Neptune*.

Olympians: The third generation of gods, ruled by *Jupiter*, and residing on Mount **Olympus** in Greece.

Ops: Harvest goddess in the Titan pantheon, and wife of Saturn. Jupiter is their son.

Oreids: Mountain *nymphs*, accompaniers of *Diana*.

Orpheus: This shepherd with powers of musical enchantment is the son of *muse* Calliope and music-god *Apollo*. Orpheus descended to *Hades* and with his music charmed *Pluto* into letting him reclaim his wife *Eurydice*. Pluto specified that he not look back at her during their ascent. He resisted the impulse almost to the end, then succumbed, and lost her forever.

Pallas: Pallas Athene, another name for *Athena*.

Pan: *Satyr* son of *Mercury*, god of shepherds, and resident of *Arcadia*. His name in Greek means "all" (still our prefix). Hot for the *nymph Syrinx*, he tried to ravish her; she fled, begging help from the gods, who in pity turned her into a reed, through which the wind blew with a plaintive sound. Not to be defeated, Pan used the hollow reed to make his pan-pipes.

Paolo and Francesca: The historically based tale of these adulterous lovers was famous from Canto V of Dante's *Inferno*, in which the pair are doomed to the second circle of hell, for voluptuaries (including Helen of Troy and Cleopatra). The Count of Ravenna, in order to make peace with his enemy, the Count of Rimini, engaged his daughter Francesca to Rimini's eldest son, Giovanni. Unhandsome (some say ugly) Giovanni thought it best to send his younger, handsome brother, Paolo, as proxy. When Paolo and Francesca fell in love, Ravenna's friends pleaded with him not to force the arranged marriage. But in 1275 the marriage to Giovanni took place. Giovanni hoped to allay Francesca's misery by engaging Paolo as her tutor. The two gave in to their passion, and Giovanni discovered and murdered them sometime between 1283 and 1286. The scandal was as much "incest" (relations with a brother-in-law) as adultery. Leigh Hunt based his *Story of Rimini* (1816) on the account in the *Inferno*.

Paphos: City in Cyprus, famous for its temple to *Venus*, who was born there, of ocean foam.

Pegasus: Winged horse, born of Medusa's blood, who lives on Mount *Helicon*. Striking the earth with his hoof, he raised the sacred *Hippocrene* fountain, and so was doted on by the *muses*. In this power, as well as his high soaring, he is a traditional emblem of, even name for, poetic imagination.

Philomel: A literary name for the nightingale. In a story in Ovid's *Metamorphoses*, Tereus, after raping his wife's sister Philomela, cut out her tongue to prevent her report. With her weaving she communicated the story to her sister, who was so enraged that she butchered her son and fed his flesh to his father. With Tereus on the verge of violent revenge, all three were turned into birds, Philomela into a nightingale; her name means "lover of honey, sweetness, song." In another myth, the nightingale is pierced through the heart by a thorn and sings in pain—an emblem of the lover's pain.

Phoebe: Sister of *Apollo*, counterpart to the Olympian *Diana*.

Phoebus: Another name for *Apollo*.

Pluto: Son of *Saturn* and *Ops*, god of the underworld, abductor of *Proserpine*; Roman counterpart of *Hades*.

Proserpine: Daughter of *Ceres*, abducted by *Pluto* from the fields of Enna in Sicily to be his wife, and allowed to return to the upper earth for only half the year. In her grief Ceres allows nature to die when her daughter leaves the earth, and to regenerate when she returns. This is a classical myth to explain the seasons.

Psyche: A *nymph* beloved of *Cupid*, harassed by Cupid's mother *Venus*. Cupid had to visit Psyche at night, in secret. She was eventually granted immortality by *Jupiter*, and thus became the latest addition to the *Olympian* order. The Greek word for *psyche* means both *butterfly* and *soul*, the former an emblem of the latter.

Pythia: Priestess of *Apollo* at *Delphi*.

Sappho: Lyric poet of ancient Greece (flourished around 600 BCE), famed for her poetry of passion. In Keats's day she was regarded as heterosexual, pining for boatman Phaon, and in despair, throwing her lyre into the sea, before hurling herself to her death.

Saturn: Son of *Coelus*; king of the *Titan* gods, overthrown by his sons, led by *Jupiter*. Keats suppresses the part of the lore in which Saturn eats his children, fearful of their rebellion against him.

satyr: A demigod, man from the waist up, goat below, with horned head, covered with hair. Attendants on *Bacchus*, satyrs are famed for orgies, lasciviousness, and general riot.

sirens: Sea *nymphs* whose singing lures sailors to shipwreck, or so enchants them that they forget everything else and starve to death.

Syrinx: A *nymph* pursued by *Pan*.

Tellus: The earth, mother of the *Titan* gods.

Tempe: A valley in Thessaly, Greece, renowed for its freshness and beauty.

Thalia: One of the three graces of classical mythology, the *muse* of festivals, comedy, and pastoral poetry.

Theseus: Serial rapist and Greek prince, imprisoned by King Minos in the Labyrinth of Crete, for certain death from the monster minotaur. Minos's daughter *Ariadne* showed him how to escape, on the promise of his marriage to her. He kept the promise briefly, but soon abandoned her on the Isle of Naxos.

Titans: The 45 giant gods, eventually overthrown by their children, the *Olympian* generation of gods. Among the Titans of most concern to Keats are *Saturn*, *Oceanus*, and especially *Hyperion*.

Venus: Sea-born goddess of beauty and love, mother of *Cupid* by her lover Mars. She fell in love with the moral *Adonis*, and when he was killed by a boar, she had him transported to an underworld bower, from which *Jupiter* allowed him to awaken every spring to join Venus for half the year. Also the morning and evening star, called *Hesperus* or Vesper in the evening.

Zephyrus: Son of *Aurora*, the sweet-breathed, generative west wind; **zephyrs** are light breezes. Enamored of the young man Hyacinthus, who preferred *Apollo*, in jealousy, Zephyrus blew a dart into Hyacinthus when he and Apollo were at play. Apollo changed his body into the flower that bears his name.

Zeus: King of the gods in Greek mythology, counterpart of the Roman *Jove/Jupiter*.

Contemporary References

Benjamin Bailey (1791–1853) began divinity studies at Oxford in October 1816 and through J. H. Reynolds met Keats the next spring. They became close friends; Keats wrote *Endymion* Book III while staying with him at Oxford in September 1817. Bailey championed him against negative reviews, but their friendship cooled in 1819 when Bailey, an ardent suitor of one of Reynolds's sisters, suddenly married the daughter of an important official in the Scots Episcopal Church. Keats's last letter to him was a strained congratulation.

Blackwood's Edinburgh Magazine and **Z.** This monthly was founded by William Blackwood in 1817, as a politically conservative antidote to the liberal *Edinburgh Review*. **Z** (John Gibson Lockhart) coined the term "Cockney School" to smear and ridicule new, reform-minded (politically and stylistically) writers, first tarring Hunt in 1817, then Keats in 1818, and soon Shelley. One year younger than Keats, Lockhart was loathed by his enemies and regarded a "scorpion" even by his colleagues.

Brawne family. Fanny (Frances) Brawne (1800–65) was the girl next door with whom Keats fell in love. When he and Brown toured in summer 1818, the family rented Brown's apartment at Wentworth Place. Keats met Fanny on his return, and they became engaged by year's end, planning to marry once Keats was financially capable. In April 1819 the Brawnes rented Dilke's half of Wentworth Place, with Keats and Brown as neighbors. Fanny and her mother cared for Keats in the summer of 1820, and he parted for Italy and from her on 13 September, so distraught that he could not bear a correspondence.

Her identity was not publicly known until after her death, in 1878, when H. B. Forman published Keats's letters to her.

Charles Brown (1787–1842), about eight years Keats's senior, an impetuous traveler and playwright (with a successful comic opera in 1814), met Keats in the summer of 1817; Keats toured the northern British Isles with him in summer 1818. He invited Keats to live with him at Wentworth Place after Tom died. They spent several weeks together in summer 1819 on the Isle of Wight, writing and vacationing. Brown adored Keats and cared for him after his hemorrhage, February 1820; but ever restless and independent, he left for his usual summer travel. Keats hoped he would go to Italy with him but was never to see him again. Keats's last known letter was to Brown.

George Gordon, Lord Byron (1788–1824). "Lord Byron cuts a figure," Keats wrote to George and Georgiana Keats in February 1819. He was the most famous, most scandalous poet of the day, and a permanent expatriot, having left England in April 1816 amidst the scandal of a broken marriage. Keats adored his early poetry of love and melancholy and began his career under the shadow of Byron's overnight success of 1812, *Childe Harold's Pilgrimage*, a retro-Spenserian romance with a modern aura of world-weary alienation and disenchantment. Keats did not like *Don Juan* ("Byron's latest flash poem") for its swings between sentiment and satire. Although they had a mutual friend in Leigh Hunt, Byron despised Keats for his attack on Pope and Augustan poetics in *Sleep and Poetry*. He managed some grudging praise of *Hyperion* but was quite sarcastic with his publisher John Murray about Keats's other poetry, and was incredulous at the fable of Keats's demise reported in Shelley's *Adonais*, coining a famously damning phrase: "snuff'd out by an article" (*Don Juan* XI; 1823).

Charles Cowden Clarke (1787–1877), about Brown's age, was the son of the headmaster of Enfield Academy, which the Keats brothers attended. Teacher and friend, Clarke helped shape Keats's taste in music and literature and introduced him to Leigh Hunt and Charles Lamb. Although the friendship drifted apart by early 1819 after Clarke moved to Ramsgate, he helped Milnes with *1848* and gave a vivid memoir of Keats in *Recollections of Writers* (1861).

Charles Wentworth Dilke (1789–1864), six years Keats's senior, was a civil servant and scholar, publishing a 6-volume *Old English Plays* (1814–16). He and Keats were friends by September 1817. With his schoolfellow Brown he built Wentworth Place, a double house in Hampstead, where the Keats brothers were frequent guests. Though his disapproval of the engagement to Fanny Brawne strained their friendship, Dilke helped the family after Keats's death, keeping in touch with George and supervising the financial affairs of Fanny Keats and Fanny Brawne.

Elgin Marbles. The British government's acquisition of these sculptural fragments from the Athenian Parthenon, rescued/stolen by Lord Elgin in 1803, was a hot controversy, the huge expense decried as an extravagance in a time of widespread social misery, the authenticity challenged by others, and the aesthetic value derided by others. Haydon was one of the champions and took Keats to view the marbles in March 1817.

William Gifford (1756–1826) became editor of the *Quarterly Review* in 1809 and was widely thought the author of its attack on Keats in 1818 (it was actually J. W. Croker). He was apprenticed to a shoemaker until a benefactor sponsored his education. Culturally and politically conservative, he edited *Antijacobin Review* in the late 1790s and contributed infamously satirical poetry. Hazlitt's caustic *Letter to William Gifford* (1819) delighted Keats; Hunt also had his say in *Ultra-Crepidarius; a Satire of William Gifford* (1823).

William Haslam (?1795/8–1851), schoolfellow and lifelong friend, lent Keats money and would have gone to Italy with him, had not family and business problems prevented him. He enlisted Severn and made the financial arrangements for the trip.

Benjamin Robert Haydon (1786–1846), champion of the Elgin Marbles, portraitist, and historical painter on an epic scale, fueled Keats's ambition for fame. *Christ's Entry into Jerusalem* has Keats, Wordsworth, Hazlitt, and other luminaries in the crowd. Keats met him in 1816 (at Hunt's) and frequently visited his studio; Haydon introduced him to Wordsworth and took him to see the Elgin Marbles. Their friendship cooled by summer 1819 as he kept borrowing money from a financially strapped Keats without repaying but still nagging him for more.

William Hazlitt (1788–1830), essayist, journalist, and lecturer. His views on art, literature, and various writers impressed Keats: the aesthetics of "gusto," the disdain of Wordsworth's "egotism," the praise of Shakespeare's intensity and lack of egotism, and admiration of Milton's diabolic aesthetics ("he does not scruple to give the devil his due"). Even more abused than Keats by *Blackwood's* Z, he gave as good as he got. Although he regretted Keats's poetical "effeminacy" (the languors and luxuries), he admired the beauties and originality of imagination.

Leigh Hunt (1784–1859), fearless editor of the radical-reformist weekly paper, *The Examiner*. In 1813 he and his brother were sentenced to two years in prison for libeling the Prince Regent as a libertine and spendthrift. Clarke introduced Keats and Hunt in 1816, and the same year Hunt published a number of Keats's poems and called them to Hazlitt's attention. Keats honored Hunt's political courage ("Libertas") and was influenced by his poetical principles, an allegiance that drew the fire of Tory critics. Even after Keats grew weary of Hunt, Hunt remained a generous, if overbearing, supporter. His essays on Keats in *Lord Byron and Some of His Contemporaries* (1828) and then in John Gorton's *General Biographical Dictionary* championed Keats against his detractors and kept his name and poetry in the public view.

Keats's family. **Fanny** (1803–89), the only sibling to live into old age, was kept away from her brothers by her guardian, Richard Abbey, after their grandmother died. The brothers lived together from 1816. **Tom** (b. 1799), whom everyone adored, contracted tuberculosis in 1817. Keats wrote him long letters from his tour in summer 1818 and then nursed him with care through the fall until his death, 1 December. **George** (1797–1841) married **Georgiana Wylie**, and the newlyweds left for a new life in America in June 1818. Keats wrote them long letters, filled with news, views, and poems. Always more adept at worldly matters, George returned to London in January 1820 to raise funds from Tom's estate. Unaware of Keats's own financial distress and his engagement to Fanny Brawne, George pressed his claims; Keats's letters to him ceased after this visit. When George prospered (after initial hardships), he repaid all of Keats's debts; he died of tuberculosis. Georgiana later married **John Jeffrey**, who in 1845 transcribed (imperfectly) many of Keats's letters to help Milnes with *Life, Letters, and Literary Remains.*

Richard Monckton Milnes, later **Lord Houghton** (1809–85), allied with Tennyson and other brilliant Cambridge undergraduates to sponsor the publication of Shelley's *Adonais* in England in 1829 (not all to the benefit of Keats's reputation). A member of Parliament from 1837 to 1863, and an admired poet himself, Milnes was buzzed as successor to Wordsworth as Poet Laureate, but he championed Tennyson as the better choice. Early in 1841 Brown gave him his memoir of Keats, and Milnes began gathering further material from Keats's friends. *Life, Letters, and Literary Remains, of John Keats* (1848), a turning point in Keats's reception, introduced a wealth of new poetry, and was the first publication of many letters. A new edition appeared in 1867, sans "Remains," because Milnes's edition of the poems had appeared in 1854 (republished throughout the nineteenth century). Milnes also introduced *Another Version of Hyperion* (i.e., *The Fall of Hyperion*) in 1856.

The Quarterly Review, founded and published by **John Murray** (1778–1843) and edited by William Gifford, was an influential periodical with a Tory, establishment orientation. Although its article on Keats's *Poems* and *Endymion* was not as nasty as *Blackwood's,* by force of its huge readership it had more impact, and was widely thought to have dealt Keats a fatal blow: it was this review that Shelley excoriated in his elegy for Keats, *Adonais.*

John Hamilton Reynolds (1794–1852), poet and reviewer, was of all Keats's friends his dearest, the one closest to his own age. He met Keats through Hunt in 1816 and introduced him to Bailey, Brown, Dilke, Rice, and publishers Taylor and Hessey. Reynolds's reviews vigorously defended Keats against the *Quarterly* and *Blackwood's.*

James Rice (1792–1832) met Keats in early 1817 through Reynolds (later Rice's law partner), and a warm friendship developed. They spent a month on the Isle of Wight in 1819. Witty and cheerful, Rice suffered from chronic ill health.

Joseph Severn (1793–1879), a friend of Hunt, Reynolds, and Brown, met Keats in 1815 or 1816. Though not close to Keats, he agreed to accompany him to Italy in 1820, for the sake of his art. When Keats's health collapsed, Severn cared for him with complete devotion (Keats died in his arms). His several portraits of Keats include a miniature that became a popular frontispiece in nineteenth-century editions of the poetry, some deathbed sketches, and one (posthumously imagined) of Keats reading by an open window. Severn returned to Rome, and at his own request he was later buried beside Keats in its Protestant Cemetery.

Percy Bysshe Shelley (1792–1821), controversial poet, friend of Hunt, and, after 1816, of Byron. He met Keats in 1817 through Hunt, and took a warm mentorial interest in Keats. Keats felt a little condescended to, and wrote the sensuous aesthetics of *Endymion* in reaction to the platonic dualism of Shelley's visionary death-romance, *Alastor* (1816). Hearing that Keats's health would not survive another English winter, Shelley invited him to Pisa. Keats never made it past Rome. *Adonais* (1821), Shelley's gorgeous elegy for Keats, launched the myth of a young poet hounded to death by cruel reviews; for the next quarter century at least, Keats was better known by this myth than by his own poetry.

John Taylor (1781–1864) and **James Hessey** (1785–1870), enterprising London publishers, with a list including Coleridge, Hazlitt, De Quincey, Clare, and Carlyle, took on Keats after he was dumped by the Ollier brothers. The firm published *Endymion* and *Lamia & c*, and the publishers were kind to Keats, with hospitality and introductions, defenses against hostile reviews, loans of books and money, and fundraising for the trip to Italy. Starting in 1821, Taylor edited *London Magazine*, which issued appreciative notices of Keats's poetry.

Richard Woodhouse (1788–1834), scholar, linguist, and lawyer (Taylor and Hessey's legal and literary adviser), adored Keats's poetry and Keats himself. He devoted himself to collecting and copying Keats's letters, manuscripts, and proof sheets; assembling anecdotes; and supporting Keats with loans of books and journals, advice about poetry, conversation about ideas, and introductions to the London literary world. He arranged the funds for the trip to Italy, and was one of the small band to see Keats off. After Keats's death, he collected Keatsiana and devoted himself to Keats's fame. He also died of tuberculosis.

William Wordsworth (1770–1850) met Keats in mid-December 1817, and encountered him again on a foggy morning on the 31st on Hampstead Heath. By 1817, Wordsworth was England's major poet, famous from *Lyrical Ballads* (1798–1805), *The Excursion* (1814), and big collections in 1807 and 1815. By the time he met Keats, he had become politically conservative, and he irritated reviewers such as Hazlitt and Francis Jeffrey with his "egotism" and didacticism. Though Keats, too, was irked by the "egotism," he saw a genius for the modern age, and was thrilled when Haydon sent Wordsworth a sonnet of his, and he himself sent him an inscribed copy of *Poems*. Despite the promptings of Hunt and Haydon, Wordsworth was never really interested in Keats (apparent from the pristine condition of Keats's gift-copy, which remained unread at Wordsworth's death).

Credits

ALS: Autograph letter, signed

John Keats letter to J. H. Reynolds, 24 August 1819. Berg Collection of English and American Literature, The New York Public Library, Astor, Lenox and Tilden Foundations.

John Keats letter to Fanny Brawne, August (before the 12th) 1820. Berg Collection of English and American Literature, The New York Public Library, Astor, Lenox and Tilden Foundations.

John Keats letter to P. B. Shelley, 16 August 1820. Oxford, Bodleian Library, [Abinger] s.n. The Bodleian Library, University of Oxford.

John Keats letter to Benjamin Robert Haydon, 23 January 1818. ADD 37538 f. 1. By permission of The British Library.

John Keats letter to Fanny Brawne, 13 October 1819. Transcribed from the photo-facsimile plate in A. E. Hancock, *John Keats* (Boston: Houghton Mifflin, 1908), after p. 188. Haverford College Library, Haverford, PA, Special Collections, Charles Roberts Autograph Letters Collection, No. 115.

John Keats letter to Benjamin Robert Haydon, 20 November 1816. ALS 1.3. By permission of the Houghton Library, Harvard University.

John Keats letter to Benjamin Robert Haydon, 21 November 1816. ALS 1.4. By permission of the Houghton Library, Harvard University.

John Keats letter to Benjamin Robert Haydon, 10–11 May 1817. ALS 1.7. By permission of the Houghton Library, Harvard University.

John Keats letter to John Taylor and James Augustus Hessey, 16 May 1817. ALS 1.8. By permission of the Houghton Library, Harvard University.

John Keats letter to Benjamin Bailey, 8 October 1817. ALS 1.13. By permission of the Houghton Library, Harvard University.

John Keats letter to Benjamin Bailey, 3 November 1817. ALS 1.15. By permission of the Houghton Library, Harvard University.

John Keats letter to Benjamin Bailey, 22 November 1817. ALS 1.16. By permission of the Houghton Library, Harvard University.

John Keats letter to Benjamin Bailey, 23 January 1818. ALS 1.20. By permission of the Houghton Library, Harvard University.

John Keats letter to Benjamin Bailey, 13 March 1818. ALS 1.23. By permission of the Houghton Library, Harvard University.

John Keats letter to Benjamin Robert Haydon, 8 April 1818. ALS 1.26. By permission of the Houghton Library, Harvard University.

John Keats letter to Benjamin Bailey, 21 and 25 May 1818. ALS 1.28. By permission of the Houghton Library, Harvard University.

John Keats letter to Benjamin Bailey, 10 June 1818. ALS 1.30. By permission of the Houghton Library, Harvard University.

John Keats letter to Benjamin Bailey, 18 and 22 July 1818. ALS 1.34. By permission of the Houghton Library, Harvard University.

John Keats letter to George and Georgiana Keats, 14–31 October 1818. ALS 1.39. By permission of the Houghton Library, Harvard University.

John Keats letter to Richard Woodhouse, 27 October 1818. ALS 1.38. By permission of the Houghton Library, Harvard University.

John Keats letter to George and Georgiana Keats, 14 February–3 May 1819. ALS 1.53. By permission of the Houghton Library, Harvard University.

John Keats letter to Benjamin Bailey, 14 August 1819. ALS 1.58. By permission of the Houghton Library, Harvard University.

John Keats ALS to John Taylor, 23 August 1819. By permission of the Houghton Library, Harvard University.

John Keats letter to Richard Woodhouse, 21–22 September 1819. ALS 1.64. By permission of the Houghton Library, Harvard University.

John Keats letter to Fanny Brawne, 19 October 1819. ALS 1.67. By permission of the Houghton Library, Harvard University.

John Keats letter to Charles Brown, 30 (dated by K 28) September 1820. ALS 1.87. By permission of the Houghton Library, Harvard University.

John Keats ms of "This living hand." Keats AMS 2.29.2. By permission of the Houghton Library, Harvard University.

Charles Brown's ms of the canceled first stanza of *Ode on Melancholy* 3.6, p. 7. By permission of the Houghton Library, Harvard University.

Various letters in Richard Woodhouse's Letter Book 3.3, pp. 13–14, 18–19, 28–30, 34–37, 43–48, 50–55, 58–60, 62–70, 74. Richard Woodhouse's transcript of K "Dear Reynolds," 25 March 1818. 3.2, f.65r. By permission of the Houghton Library, Harvard University.

John Keats letter to Leigh Hunt, 10 May 1817. Transcribed from T. J. Wise, *Ashley Library* 3 (1923), plate after p. 12; ALS is at Harvard: ALS 1.7. By permission of the Houghton Library, Harvard University.

Keats MS 1.64; MS Keats 2.2.f 165r; MS Keats 4.20.8. By permission of the Houghton Library, Harvard University.

John Keats holograph of the sonnet on reading *King Lear* in his facsimile reprint of Shakespeare's first folio. City of London, London Metropolitan Archives.

John Keats letter to C. W. Dilke, 20–21 September 1818. Transcribed from plates xix–xx in G. Williamson, *The Keats Letters, Papers, & c* (private printing, 1914). City of London, London Metropolitan Archives.

John Keats letter to C. W. Dilke, 22 September 1819. Transcribed from plates xxx–xxxiii, *ibid*. City of London, London Metropolitan Archives.

John Keats ALS to John Taylor, Esq., Friday, postmarked 30 January 1818. MA 213. The Pierpont Morgan Library, New York.

John Keats ALS, Hampstead, to John Taylor, Esq., 27 February 1818. MA 828. The Pierpont Morgan Library, New York.

John Keats, *Endymion*: [n.p.]: autograph manuscript [n.d.]. MA 208. The Pierpont Morgan Library, New York.

John Keats ALS, Teighmouth, to John Taylor, Esq., Friday, 27 April 1818. MA 791. The Pierpont Morgan Library, New York.

John Keats ALS, Dumfries, Scotland, to his sister Fanny M. Keats, 2, 3, and 5 July 1818. MA 975. The Pierpont Morgan Library, New York.

John Keats ALS, Winchester, to his brother George, Friday, 17–27 September 1819. MA 212. The Pierpont Morgan Library, New York.

John Keats ALS, Wentworth Place, to John Taylor, Esq., Wednesday, postmarked 17 November 1819. MA 210. The Pierpont Morgan Library, New York.

John Keats, sonnet: lines in autograph of Richard Woodhouse (14 lines) beginning, "The day is gone. . . ." MA 213. The Pierpont Morgan Library, New York.

Further Reading

CCJK: Wolfson, ed. *Cambridge Companion to John Keats*
P: Press / UP: University Press
KSJ: *Keats-Shelley Journal*

Editions

The Poems of John Keats, ed. Jack Stillinger. Harvard UP, 1978.
Scrupulously assembled; complete textual notes.
The Letters of John Keats, 1814–1821, ed. Hyder E. Rollins. Harvard UP, 1958. Keyed to this edition is David Pollard's *A KWIC Concordance to the Letters of John Keats* (1989).
The Letters of John Keats, ed. Robert Gittings, rev. John Mee. Oxford UP, 2002. A fine paperback selection, with some corrections of Rollins.

Facsimiles

Poems (1817); *Endymion* (1818); *Lamia, Isabella, The Eve of St. Agnes, and Other Poems* (1819); all from Woodstock P, 1989, 1990, and 1991, with introductions by Jonathan Wordsworth.
John Keats: Poetry Manuscripts at Harvard: A Facsimile Edition, ed. Jack Stillinger. Harvard UP, 1990. Photo-plates, transcriptions; an introduction by Helen Vendler.
Stillinger also edits a wealth of material across the 7 vols. of *The Manuscripts of the Younger Romantics: A Facsimile Edition, with Scholarly Introductions, Bibliographical Descriptions, and Annotations* (gen. ed. Donald H. Reiman), Garland P, 1985–89.

The Odes of Keats and Their Earliest Known Manuscripts in Facsimile, ed. Robert Gittings. Kent State UP, 1970. Some dispute about "earliest," but the photographs are worthy.

Chief Biographies (chronological)

Hunt, Leigh. "Mr. Keats." *Lord Byron and Some of His Contemporaries*. London, 1828.

Milnes, Richard M. *Life, Letters, and Literary Remains, of John Keats*. 2 vols. London: Edward Moxon, 1848 (rpt. one-volume Everyman, 1969).

Colvin, Sidney. *John Keats: His Life and Poetry, His Friends, Critics, and After-Fame*. Macmillan, 1917.

Lowell, Amy. *John Keats*. 2 vols. Houghton Mifflin, 1925.

Bate, Walter Jackson. *John Keats*. Harvard UP, 1963.

Hirst, Wolf Z. *John Keats*. Twayne, 1981.

Clark, Tom. *Junkets on a Sad Planet*. Black Sparrow P, 1994. A biography in poems.

Motion, Andrew. *Keats*. Farrar, Straus and Giroux, 1997.

Lifetime Reviews, Early Reception, Rise to Fame

Keats: The Critical Heritage, ed. G. M. Matthews. Barnes & Noble, 1971. Nineteenth-century reviews and comments track the evolving reputation.

The Romantics Reviewed: Contemporary Reviews of British Romantic Writers, ed. Donald Reiman. Part C: *Shelley, Keats, and London Radical Writers*. Garland P, 1972. Facsimiles.

Ford, George H. *Keats and the Victorians: . . . Influence and Rise to Fame 1821–1895*. Yale UP, 1944. Important reception history.

Marquess, William H. *Lives of the Poet: The First Century of Keats Biography*. Penn. State UP, 1985. Biases and strategies.

References and Bibliographies (chronological)

The Keats Circle, ed. Hyder E. Rollins. 2d edition; 2 vols. Harvard UP, 1965. Correspondence and memoranda.

The Romantics and Their Contemporaries, ed. Susan J. Wolfson and Peter J. Manning (vol. 2A of *The Longman Anthology of British Literature*, gen. ed. David Damrosch). Longman, 2006. A fine orientation to Keats's age, with a helpful bibliography.

Critical Studies

This list gives an orientation to Keats studies; for fuller resources and more specialized studies, see: Jack Stillinger, "John Keats," *The English Romantic Poets: A Review of Research and Criticism*, ed. Frank Jordan (Modern Language Assn., 1985, 4th edition); Greg Kucich, "John Keats," in *Literature of the Romantic Period: A Bibliographic Guide*, ed. Michael O'Neill (Clarendon P, 1998); Walter H. Evert and Jack W. Rhodes, *Approaches to Teaching Keats's Poetry* (Modern Language Assn., 1991; essays, bibliography, and other resources); and the bibliography in *CCJK*.

Books on Keats

Barnard, John. *John Keats*. Cambridge UP, 1987.

Bennett, Andrew. *Keats, Narrative and Audience: The Posthumous Life of Writing*. Cambridge UP, 1994.

Blades, John. *John Keats: The Poems*. "Analysing Texts" series. Palgrave, 2002.

Cox, Jeffrey. *Poetry and Politics in the Cockney School: Keats, Shelley, Hunt and Their Circle*. Cambridge UP, 1998.

Dickstein, Morris. *Keats and His Poetry: A Study in Development*. U Chicago P, 1971.

Ende, Stuart. *Keats and the Sublime*. Yale UP, 1976.

Jones, John. *John Keats's Dream of Truth*. Chatto and Windus, 1969.

Lau, Beth. *Keats's Reading of the Romantic Poets*. U Michigan P, 1991.

———. *Keats's Paradise Lost*. UP Florida, 1998.

Levinson, Marjorie. *Keats's Life of Allegory: The Origins of a Style*. Basil Blackwell, 1988.

Najarian, James. *Victorian Keats: Manliness, Sexuality, and Desire*. Palgrave, 2002.

Ricks, Christopher. *Keats and Embarrassment*. Oxford UP, 1976.

Robinson, Jeffrey. *Reception and Poetics in Keats*. St. Martin's P, 1998.

Roe, Nicholas. *John Keats and the Culture of Dissent*. Clarendon P, 1997.

Scott, Grant F. *The Sculpted Word: Keats, Ekphrasis, and the Visual Arts*. UP New Hampshire, 1994.

Sperry, Stuart M. *Keats the Poet*. Princeton UP, 1973.

Stillinger, Jack. *"The Hoodwinking of Madeline" and Other Essays on Keats's Poems*. U Illinois P, 1971. The once controversial title essay is now canonical; also very helpful: "Imagination and Reality in the Odes."

———. *Reading "The Eve of St. Agnes": The Multiples of Complex Literary Transaction*. Oxford UP, 1999.

Vendler, Helen. *The Odes of John Keats*. Harvard UP, 1983.

Waldoff, Leon. *Keats and the Silent Work of Imagination*. U Illinois P, 1985.

Walker, Carol Kyros. *Walking North with Keats*. Yale UP, 1992. The tour with Brown; beautiful photographs, letters rewardingly annotated, includes the poems composed.

Watkins, Daniel P. *Keats's Poetry and the Politics of the Imagination*. Farleigh Dickinson UP, 1989.

Wolfson, Susan J., ed. *The Cambridge Companion to John Keats*. Cambridge UP, 2001.

Articles, Essays, and Books with Chapters on Keats

Barnard, John. "Keats's Letters," in *CCJK*.

Bewell, Alan. "The Political Implication of Keats's Classicist Aesthetics," *Studies in Romanticism* 25 (1986): 221–30.

Bloom, Harold. "Keats and the Embarrassments of Poetic Tradition," in *The Ringers in the Tower*. U Chicago P, 1971.

Bostetter, Edward E. "Keats," in *The Romantic Ventriloquists*. 1963; U Washington P, 1975.

Bromwich, David. "Keats," in *Hazlitt: The Mind of a Critic*. Oxford UP, 1983.

———. "Keats's Radicalism," *Studies in Romanticism* 25 (1986): 197–210.

Brooks, Cleanth. "Keats's Sylvan Historian: History Without Footnotes" (1944), in *The Well Wrought Urn* (1947). Harcourt Brace Jovanovich, 1975. Exemplary close reading.

Cox, Jeffrey. *"Lamia, Isabella,* and *The Eve of St. Agnes,"* in *CCJK*.

Curran, Stuart. *Poetic Form and British Romanticism*. Oxford UP, 1986.

Dickstein, Morris. "Keats and Politics," *Studies in Romanticism* 25 (1986): 175–81.

Fry, Paul. "History, Existence, and 'To Autumn,'" *Studies in Romanticism* 25 (1986): 211–19.

Hartman, Geoffrey. "Poem and Ideology: . . . Keats's 'To Autumn'" (1973) and "Spectral Symbolism and Authorial Self in Keats's *Hyperion*" (1974), both in *The Fate of Reading*. U Chicago P, 1975.

Homans, Margaret. "Keats Reading Women, Women Reading Keats," *Studies in Romanticism* 29 (1990): 341–70.

Kandl, John. "Leigh Hunt's *Examiner* and the Construction of a Public 'John Keats,'" *KSJ* 44 (1995): 84–101.

———. "The Politics of Keats's Early Poetry," in *CCJK*.

Keach, William. "Byron Reads Keats," in *CCJK*.

———. "The Politics of Rhyme," in *Arbitrary Power*. Princeton UP, 2004. Keats's couplets, *ottava rima*.

Kelley, Theresa M. "Keats and 'Ekphrasis,'" in *CCJK*.

Kern, Robert. "Keats and the Problem of Romance," *Philological Quarterly* 58 (1979): 171–91.

Kucich, Greg. *Keats, Shelley, and Romantic Spenserianism*. Penn. State UP, 1991.

———. "Keats and English Poetry," in *CCJK*.

Levinson, Marjorie. "The Dependent Fragment: 'Hyperion' and 'The Fall of Hyperion,'" in *The Romantic Fragment Poem*. U North Carolina P, 1986.

Luke, David. "Keats's Letters: Fragments of an Aesthetic of Fragments," *Genre* 2 (1978): 209–26.

McGann, Jerome J. "Keats and the Historical Method in Literary Criticism" (1979), in *The Beauty of Inflections* (1985). Clarendon P, 1988.

Mellor, Anne. "Keats and the Vale of Soul-Making," in *English Romantic Irony*. Harvard UP, 1980.

———. "Keats and the Complexities of Gender," in *CCJK*.

Newey, Vincent. "*Hyperion*, *The Fall of Hyperion*, and Keats's Epic Ambitions," in *CCJK*.

Perkins, David. Chapters on Keats in *The Quest for Permanence: The Symbolism of Wordsworth, Shelley, and Keats*. Harvard UP, 1959.

Rajan, Tilottama. Chapters on the late romances and the *Hyperion* poems, in *Dark Interpreter: The Discourse of Romanticism*. Cornell UP, 1980.

Richardson, Alan. "Keats and Romantic Science," in *CCJK.*

Ricks, Christopher. "Keats's Sources, Keats's Allusions," in *CCJK.*

Rzepka, Charles J. "Keats: Watcher and Witness," *The Self as Mind: Vision and Identity in Wordsworth, Coleridge, Keats.* Harvard UP, 1986.

Sheats, Paul. "Stylistic Discipline in *The Fall of Hyperion*," *KSJ* 17 (1968): 75–88.

———. "Keats and the Ode," in *CCJK.*

Stewart, Garrett. "*Lamia* and the Language of Metamorphosis," *Studies in Romanticism* 15 (1976) 3–41.

———. "Keats and Language," in *CCJK.*

Stillinger, Jack. "The 'Story' of Keats," in *CCJK.*

Swann, Karen. "*Endymion*'s Beautiful Dreamers," in *CCJK.*

———. "Harassing the Muse," in *Romanticism and Feminism*, ed. Anne Mellor. Indiana UP, 1988. On *La Belle Dame.*

———. "The Strange Time of Reading," *European Romantic Review* 9 (1998): 275–82.

Vendler, Helen. "John Keats: Perfecting the Sonnet," in *Coming of Age as a Poet.* Harvard UP, 2003.

Vogler, Thomas. Chapter on the *Hyperion* poems, in *Preludes to Vision: The Epic Venture.* U California P, 1971.

Wolfson, Susan J. *Borderlines:* "Keats and Gender Acts," and "Gendering Keats," in *The Shiftings of Gender in British Romanticism.* Stanford UP, 2006.

———. "Keats Enters History: Autopsy, *Adonais*, and the Fame of Keats," in *Keats and History*, ed. Nicholas Roe. Cambridge UP, 1995.

———. "Keats the Letter-Writer: Epistolary Poetics," *Romanticism Past and Present* 6 (1982): 43–61.

———. "Keats's Late Lyrics," in *CCJK.*

———. Chapters on Keats in *The Questioning Presence.* Cornell UP, 1986.

Wu, Duncan. "Keats and the 'Cockney School,'" in *CCJK.*

Major Websites and Online Resources

Keyword searches of both poems and letters can be done at the subscription-service Chadwyck-Healey site: Literature on Line (LION).

http://www.englishhistory.net/keats
  Includes Charles Brown's biography, conveyed to R. M. Milnes,
  Sidney Colvin's 1917 biography, chronology, images, poems,
  ms images.

http://www.online-literature.com/keats
  Texts of poems and links to other sites.

http://www.keats-shelley-house.org
  The Keats-Shelley house in Rome.

http://www.rc.umd.edu/
  Professionally managed Romantic circles website, a hub for all
  kinds of information on Keats, his contemporaries, and the culture of Romanticism. Includes a set of essays: *Ode on a Grecian
  Urn: Hypercanonicity & Pedagogy*, ed. James O'Rourke.

Index

Not a comprehensive index, but a selective resource for locating Keats's poetry and miscellaneous writing, and references to people and subjects of interest to him (not indexed: Introduction, Table of Dates, Further Reading, the Glossaries, incidental mentions).

People, Publications, Writers of Interest to Keats

(addresees of letters, starting page only)